MODERN POLITICAL CONSTITUTIONS

By the same author:

THE STORY OF THE AMERICAN PEOPLE

DYNAMIC EUROPE

THE TWENTIETH CENTURY AND THE CONTEMPORARY WORLD

TEACHING FOR INTERNATIONAL UNDERSTANDING

HISTORY IN THE SECONDARY SCHOOL

MODERN POLITICAL CONSTITUTIONS

AN INTRODUCTION TO THE COMPARATIVE STUDY
OF THEIR HISTORY AND EXISTING FORM

BY

C. F. STRONG, O.B.E., M.A., Ph.D.

SIDGWICK & JACKSON LIMITED
LONDON

"Every creation of a new scheme of government is a precious addition to the political resources of mankind. It represents a survey and scrutiny of the constitutional experience of the past. It embodies an experiment full of instruction for the future."

LORD BRYCE.

First printed	1930
Second (Revised and Enlarged) Edition	1939
Third (Revised and Enlarged) Edition	1949
Second Impression	1950
Fourth (Revised) Edition	1952
Second Impression	1953
Third Impression	1955
Fifth (Revised) Edition	1958
Second Impression	1960

PREFACE

THIS book was written to meet a need felt by many setting out for the first time on the study of constitutional politics as a specialised branch of historical studies—the need of a suitable introductory text book. It was my business and pleasure, during several years, to help students to face without undue trepidation the difficulties of their first approach to Political Science. Here is one part at least of the fruit of my experience with them, and if I dedicated this book to any one it would be to those who, by their constant devotion in my classes and lectures, lightened the labour of preparing and presenting a difficult, though entrancing, subject.

My debt to the earlier giants of Political Science—Dicey, Maitland, Sidgwick, Lowell, Bryce, and the rest—will be apparent throughout to those who know anything of their superb writings. My book, however, is by no means a *réchauffé* of the books of those authors, but an attempt to present the subject, which, after all, is everybody's business, in an original, readable and easily comprehensible form. The book is designed to appeal not only to those who enjoy the advantage of a teacher but also to the private student and the general reader. In either case, I hope that the select readings, the list of books for further study, and the subjects for essays at the end of each chapter will encourage further inquiry and at the same time stimulate thought.

In the three decades of disaster through which we have lived since the book was first written, many changes have taken place both in the internal structure of constitutional states and in the machinery governing their relations with one another. These changes have made formidable the work of frequently revising the subject-matter and bringing it up to date. This recurrent task I could scarcely have contemplated, much less accomplished, but for the knowledge that many have found the book helpful in the past and my hope that others will find it equally useful in the future.

vi   *Preface*

The responsibility for any weaknesses and shortcomings in the book is wholly mine; yet I cannot refrain from recording my thanks to many friends and colleagues who have helped me in the preparation of the various editions, and especially to the late Professor F. C. J. Hearnshaw, the late Philip Guedalla, and the late Professor H. J. Laski, all of whom placed their unrivalled knowledge and experience ungrudgingly at my disposal when the book was first in the making; to Professor Herman Finer, who read and criticised the Introduction to the second edition; to Professor F. R. Beasley, Dean of the Faculty of Law in the University of Western Australia, who has given me unimpeachable guidance on the working of the Australian Constitution; to Mr. J. Hampden Jackson, who has put me expertly right on several points concerning Finland; to Mr. John G. Lexa, Lecturer on Comparative Law in the New York University Law School, who has prepared for my personal edification a detailed commentary on the text of several constitutions; to the High Commissioners of Commonwealth countries and the Cultural Attachés of various foreign Embassies in London, who have furnished me with documentary material otherwise difficult of access; to Mr. A. W. McClellan, Director of Public Libraries in Tottenham, for his generous help with books; to my publishers for their unfailing courtesy and encouragement; and finally, to my wife, always my acutest and most constructive critic.

C. F. STRONG.

LONDON,
June, 1958.

CONTENTS

PART I

THE SCIENTIFIC AND HISTORICAL APPROACH TO THE SUBJECT

CHAPTER I

CHAPTER II

PART II

COMPARATIVE CONSTITUTIONAL POLITICS

CHAPTER III

Contents

CHAPTER IV

CHAPTER V

CHAPTER VI

CHAPTER VII

CHAPTER VIII

CHAPTER IX

CHAPTER X

CHAPTER XI

CHAPTER XII

PART III
ADDITIONAL CONSIDERATIONS
CHAPTER XIII

CHAPTER XIV

CHAPTER XV

CHAPTER XVI

CHAPTER XVII

PART I

THE SCIENTIFIC AND HISTORICAL APPROACH TO
THE SUBJECT

CHAPTER I

THE MEANING OF POLITICAL CONSTITUTIONALISM

I. GENERAL

THE study of political constitutions is a branch of political science or the science of the state. Political science, being the science of the structure and government of political communities, is a study of society viewed from a special standpoint, and is, therefore, intimately related to the other social sciences, which may be classified as follows:

(1) Sociology, which is the study of all forms, civilised and uncivilised, of human association.

(2) Economics, which is the science of man's material well-being.

(3) Ethics, which is the science of what man's conduct ought to be, and why.

(4) Social Psychology, which is the science of the behaviour of the human animal in his social relationships.

Political science takes something from all these, for it is concerned with a particular type of human association, and is therefore partly sociological; with the material interests of the members of the state, and is therefore partly economic; with the moral cause and effect of state action, and is therefore partly ethical; and with the play of individual minds, whether of governors or governed, and is therefore partly psychological.

Nevertheless, it is a distinct science, with its own materials and data. These are found in the history of states and in their existing forms. The political scientist is concerned with the origin and development of the state, with its nature and organisation, with its purpose and functions, and with the theory of the state and its possible forms. Now, the student of political constitutions is concerned with all these facets of the subject in

I

a certain degree. He is interested chiefly in the institutions which the state builds up for its peace and progress, without which the state could not maintain itself, any more than society could maintain itself without the state. Our subject here, therefore, may be divided into the four parts of which we have just spoken as belonging to political science as a whole and which we may summarise as historical, descriptive, applied and theoretical.

It is our purpose here to take certain highly developed modern states and to examine their institutions, which, taken together in each case, are called the Constitution. Our mode of inquiry is what is usually called the comparative method. That is to say, we shall attempt to classify the constitutions we are to examine on the basis of certain likenesses and differences arising out of their history and existing form. But before doing this it will be necessary first to define the principal terms we must use, and secondly to trace in outline the general history of political constitutionalism.

II. SOCIETY

A study of any aspect of the state must begin with a definition of society, since a state is a society politically organised. A society may be defined as any association of human beings. Among such peoples as the British or the French, for example, there is a vast system of relationships among men and women dividing them socially into groups which by no means coincide with their political grouping. Sometimes, and more frequently, the group is very much smaller than the state, but often it passes right across the political frontier, and this is especially the case in commercial relationships.

The fundamental units of the association of the members of a community, considered socially and not politically, may be said to be three. The first is the family, the association into which men are born. The second is the type of association to which men are compelled to belong through some strong incentive, such as economic interest or social expediency, as, for example, a trade union or professional society. The third is what may be called the voluntary association, such as a club or (at any rate under modern conditions) a church. Now, while it is true that the state does not use its force, as a rule, actively to interfere with such associations as these, the fact remains that it could and is sometimes obliged to do so for reasons either of social health or of political expediency. While, on the one hand, such associations as we have mentioned play an important part in influencing and determining state action, on the other, many of them could not continue to exist without the conditions which the agency of the state alone can enforce, such as marriage laws, rights of property, laws of contract, and so on.

III. THE STATE

Yet the state is something more than a mere collection of families, or an agglomeration of occupational organisations, or a referee holding the ring between the conflicting interests of the voluntary associations which it permits to exist. In a properly organised political community the state exists for society and not society for the state; yet, however socially advanced a people may be, the society which it constitutes—made up of families, clubs, churches, trade unions, etc.—is not to be trusted to maintain itself without the ultimate arbitrament of force.

All associations make rules and regulations for their conduct, and when men are associated politically these rules and regulations are called laws, the power to make these being the prerogative of the state and of no other association. Thus, in the words of Professor Maciver, a "state is the fundamental association for the maintenance and development of social order, and to this end its central institution is endowed with the united power of the community." But this definition might conceivably cover a pastoral or nomadic society which, indeed, found a bond of union in the patriarch or head of the family who, in some sort, discharged the powers of government. Such a society, however, lacks territoriality, an indispensable condition of true political organisation, a condition emphasised by Professor Hetherington when he says: "The state is the institution or set of institutions which, in order to secure certain elementary common purposes and conditions of life, unites under a single authority the inhabitants of a clearly-marked territorial area." But what is this "united power of the community" in the first, this "single authority" in the second definition? It is the power or authority to make law. So we come to the definition given by Woodrow Wilson: "A state is a people organised for law within a definite territory."

IV. LAW AND CUSTOM

The essence of a state, then, as distinct from all other forms of association, is the obedience of its members to the law. The state being a territorial society divided into government and governed, we may quote a definition of law as "the general body of rules which are addressed by the rulers of a political society to the members of that society which are generally obeyed"; or, again, as "a command to do or abstain from doing a certain class of acts, issued by a determinate person or body of persons acting as a body, and involving the announcement, express or tacit, of a penalty to be inflicted on any persons who may disobey the command: it being assumed that the individual or body announcing the penalty has the power and purpose of inflicting it."

The force at the back of law has always been a social force. The social force by itself, however, is merely custom. Wherever a society, however rudimentary, exists, there will develop customary ways of carrying on social activities. A body of customs develops, forming a sort of unwritten code enforced by some pressure, such as parental or religious authority, or the opinion of the community concerned. Some of these customs may be found to have such a wide application for the general welfare that some stronger pressure than mere social authority or opinion is necessary to get them universally obeyed. These customs then cease to be social and become political—in fact, laws—being enforced by a constituted government.

That, then, is law, by whatever method established, which is enforced in courts properly constituted by the state. Its source may be (1) custom—*i.e.*, unwritten law become enforceable by perpetual usage; (2) the written decisions of earlier judges—*i.e.*, what is sometimes called case-law or judge-made law or common law; (3) statute—*i.e.*, by enactment of the legislature, or parliament, of the state.

V. SOVEREIGNTY

We have said that the peculiar attribute of the state as contrasted with all other units of association is the power to make

laws and enforce them by all the means of coercion it cares to
employ. This power is called sovereignty. This is a highly controversial term, and we shall have a good deal to say about it
later on. At this point it will suffice to define it in its double
aspect—internal and external. Internally it means the supremacy of a person or body of persons in the state over the individuals or associations of individuals within the area of its
jurisdiction. Externally, it means the absolute independence of
one state as a whole with reference to all other states. Etymolo-
gically the word sovereignty means merely superiority, but when
applied to the state it means superiority of a special kind, such
superiority, that is to say, as implies law-issuing power. In
seeking to find in any state where the sovereign power lies we
must distinguish three ways in which the term is used; thus it
may mean (1) the titular head of the state, *e.g.*, in the United
Kingdom the Queen, in France the President of the Republic;
(2) the legal sovereign—*i.e.*, the person or persons who, according
to the law of the land, legislate and administer the government
—*e.g.*, in the United Kingdom, the Queen in Parliament; (3) the
political or constitutional sovereign—*i.e.*, the body of persons
in whom power ultimately resides, sometimes called the collective
sovereign, and in the modern constitutional state found in the
electorate or voting public. Here we are chiefly concerned, for
the moment, with the second of these aspects of sovereignty,
though the third, as we shall see later, plays a tremendously
important part in the modern state.

Lord Bryce gives an excellent example of the process whereby
the true sovereign in any state may be discovered by taking the
case of an Englishman:

"A householder in a municipality," he says, "is asked to pay a
paving rate. He inquires why he should pay it, and is referred to
the resolution of the Town Council imposing it. He then asks what
authority the Council has to levy the rate, and is referred to a
section of the Act of Parliament whence the Council derives its
powers. If he pushes curiosity further, and inquires what right
Parliament has to confer these powers, the rate collector can only
answer that everybody knows that in England Parliament makes
the law, and that by the law no other authority can override or in
any wise interfere with any expression of the will of Parliament.
Parliament is supreme above all other authorities, or, in other
words, Parliament is Sovereign."

We shall see later that the sovereign power is not always so easily traced as in this case, but if we remember that that person or body of persons which is habitually obeyed in a state—and this implies the control of the armed forces of the state—is the sovereign power, we have all we need to proceed to the next definition.

VI. GOVERNMENT

In order to make and enforce laws the state must have a supreme authority. This is called the Government. Government is the state's machinery: without it the state could not exist, for "government is, in the last analysis, organised force." Government is, therefore, "that organisation in which is vested ... the right to exercise sovereign powers." Government, in the broad sense, is something bigger than a special body of ministers, a sense in which we colloquially use it to-day, when we refer to the Cabinet in our own country, for example, as the Government of the day. Government, in the broader sense, is charged with the maintenance of the peace and security of the state within and without. It must, therefore, have, first, military power, or the control of armed forces; secondly, legislative power, or the means of making laws; thirdly, financial power, or the ability to extract sufficient money from the community to defray the cost of defending the state and of enforcing the law it makes on the state's behalf. It must, in short, have legislative power, executive power and judicial power, which we may call the three departments of government.

VII. THE LEGISLATURE

The three departments of government just mentioned all play their part in the exercise of the sovereign power in a modern state. They are always intimately connected with one another, in some states more than in others, and yet they are everywhere distinct. The legislature is that department of government concerned with the making of laws, in so far as the law requires statutory force. Logically, law-making precedes its execution, and therefore the legislature is, at first sight, of greater importance than the executive which administers the law, or the judiciary which punishes its transgressors. But this is not always the case, since, as we shall see later, the powers of the legislature to control the other two departments vary. None the less, we may agree with the American authority who has described the legislative function as "the great and overruling power in every free government."

In modern constitutional states the legislative power is in the hands of a Parliament consisting, as a rule, of two Houses, one or both of which may be elected by the people. Closely associated, therefore, with the composition of the legislature in a modern state is the nature of the electorate, to which we have already referred as the political sovereign. The functions of the legislature increase with the growing complexity of modern society and with its consequent demands upon the law-making authority for the social good. In all states this pressure is brought indirectly to bear upon the action of the legislature by the very nature of society, in some more directly through a vital electoral system, and in others even more directly by the constitutional powers of the people to initiate legislation or to approve or disapprove it after its passage through parliament. The differences among modern legislatures, as we shall see later on, form a most important ground for the classification of existing states.

VIII. THE EXECUTIVE

The term executive is frequently used rather loosely, sometimes to designate merely the chief minister (as, for example, the President in the United States), sometimes to include the whole body of public servants, civil and military. In the latter sense a better term is administration. Here we use the word executive to mean the head of the government together with his ministers, generally called a Cabinet, or, in other words, that body in the state to which the Constitution gives authority to execute the law when it has received the sanction of the legislature. Though technically it is the legislature which initiates policy, in modern practice the executive formulates the bulk of it, and then presents it for approval to the legislature.

Such a body is bound to exist in any state, but particularly in the modern state, which corresponds to a large national community, and therefore requires that its chief ministers shall hold wide powers. The great distinction in composition between the legislature and the executive is a numerical one. The legislature is a large body, the executive (in the sense here indicated) is a small one, and necessarily so, since the legislature is a deliberative assembly whose business is to debate public matters, while the executive is a collection of ministerial heads of departments whose business is to act with decision and promptness. In some cases, as we shall see, the executive is controlled by the legislature, in others it exists apart from it, and this difference forms one of the chief grounds of our classification.

IX. THE JUDICIARY

The judiciary is the department concerned with the infliction of penalties upon those who infringe the law which may be either passed in the form of statutes by the legislature or permitted by it to exist. As one authority puts it, it is the business of the judiciary to "decide upon the application of the existing law in individual cases." Such judicial power is of the essence of government, which, as we have seen, is by its nature coercive. The judiciary always consists of a body of judges acting individually or in groups at the centre, or in outlying parts, of the state. The powers of judges greatly vary from one state to another. In some cases, as in the United Kingdom, the judges are bound to apply any law passed by the legislature, even though such a law should—and, indeed, precisely because it deliberately does —destroy all precedent decisions of the courts. In others, as in the United States, a supreme court of judges can frequently override the enactments of the legislature by refusing to apply the laws in particular cases on the ground that it is constitutionally beyond the power of the legislature to enact them.

In most states the judicial department of government is, to a greater or less degree, a creative force actually developing, in the course of its work, especially in Anglo-Saxon countries, an important element in the body of the law under which modern communities are governed. Law is everywhere the province of experts, and for this reason judges generally have a security of tenure and a freedom from interference by the other two departments of government which is one of their most valuable possessions, and, indeed, of the utmost importance to the community at large. At the same time, the executive always has certain judicial powers, chiefly connected with the granting of pardons and reprieves and the enforcement of discipline in the armed forces and the civil service generally, though such functions are, as a rule, ultimately subject to control by the legislature, through its power to grant or withhold supplies of money for the maintenance of these services.

X. THE CONSTITUTION

It is in the variation of the composition and relationship of these three departments of government that states differ. The modern constitutional state, which is the one with which we shall henceforth be concerned, is one which has developed a very definite set of rules and regulations for the working of these three functions of government. Lord Bryce defined a constitution as "a frame of political society, organised through and by law, that is to say, one in which law has established permanent institutions with recognised functions and definite rights." Again, a constitution may be said to be a collection of principles according to which the powers of the government, the rights of the governed, and the relations between the two are adjusted. The constitution may be a deliberate creation on paper; it may be found in one document which itself is altered or amended as time and growth demand; or it may be a bundle of separate laws given special authority as the laws of the constitution. Or, again, it may be that the bases of the constitution are fixed in one or two fundamental laws while the rest of it depends for its authority upon the force of custom.

It is true, of course, as Ivor Jennings says in *Cabinet Government*, that the distinction between laws and conventions is not really of fundamental importance, for, however fully written a constitution may be, the growth of custom and convention is bound in the course of years to modify it, apart from any positive measures taken to amend it. Moreover, as Jennings adds, a constitution necessarily rests on acquiescence, whether it is established by referendum or by tacit approval or even by force. If an organised public opinion regards it as noxious it will be overthrown. And if, as the author continues, a Louis Napoleon or a Mussolini or a Hitler considers that he can induce or compel acquiescence in a change, he will not hesitate to overthrow it because it is enacted as law. But whatever its form, a true constitution will have the following facts about it very clearly marked: first, how the various agencies are organised; secondly, what power is entrusted to those agencies; and thirdly, in what manner such power is to be exercised. Just as a human body is said to have a constitution consisting of organs which work harmoniously when the body is in health and unharmoniously otherwise, so a state, or body politic, is said to have a constitution when its organs and their functions are definitely arranged and are not subject, for example, to the whim of some despot. The objects of a constitution, in short, are to limit the arbitrary action of the government, to guarantee the rights of the governed, and to define the operation of the sovereign power.

XI. THE NATIONAL DEMOCRATIC STATE

These observations should help us to recognise the constitutional state. The roots of political constitutionalism lie deep in the history of the Western World, and in the evolution of the state, as we know it, constitutional principles appeared in some cases long before the emergence of nationalism as a conscious unifying force or of democracy as a militant political programme. Nevertheless, the modern constitutional state is necessarily nationalist in background and democratic in tendency. Nationality is of all political terms the most difficult to define, but we may safely say that in its modern form it is essentially a spirit of united action among a people with a common past and a desire to enjoy a common future struggling to embody itself in political forms. In the making of a constitutional state this sense of national unity may at first be concerned rather to establish the independence of the group than to achieve the liberty of its individual members, but ultimately it generates the driving power for the attainment of popular rights.

The term democracy, again, is variously used, sometimes to mean a form of government and sometimes to connote a condition of society. But in the contemporary world, just as nationalism has inevitably become the basis of political democracy, so democratic political organisation has become the instrument of social betterment. Here we are concerned with political democracy, which implies that government shall rest on the consent of the governed, that is to say, the consent or dissent of the people shall have real outlets for expression at elections, on the platform, in the Press, and so forth. By democracy in this sense we therefore mean a system of government in which the majority of the grown members of a political community participate through a method of representation which secures that the government is ultimately responsible for its actions to that majority. In other words, the contemporary constitutional state must be based on a system of democratic representation which guarantees the sovereignty of the people.

Our conclusion, then, is that, under modern conditions, the constitutional state is a national democratic state, and those states whose institutions it is our intention to examine in the following pages are of this type. To comprehend the nature of such a state it is first necessary to study the growth of political constitutionalism from its beginnings, and such an historical sketch we shall now attempt.

READING

FINER: *Modern Government*, Vol. I, Ch. i.
GETTELL: *Readings in Political Science*, pp. 16–24, 59–64, 127–145, 174–194, 282–6, 341–3, 363, 384–7, 501–5.
JENKS: *State and Nation*, Ch. i.
LASKI: *Grammar of Politics*, Pt. I, Ch. i.
LOWELL: *Government of England*, Vol. I, Ch. vii.
MACIVER: *Modern State*, pp. 3–22.
SIDGWICK: *Elements of Politics*, Chs. i, ii, xix.
WILSON: *State*, pp. 26–31, 69–92.

BOOKS FOR FURTHER STUDY

HETHERINGTON AND MUIRHEAD: *Social Purpose*.
MACIVER: (1) *Community*. (2) *Elements of Social Science*. (3) *The Web of Government*.
SEELEY: *Introduction to Political Science*.

SUBJECTS FOR ESSAYS

1. State the divisions of social science and explain the province of each.
2. How do you differentiate society and state?
3. Define the word "state" in its ancient and modern connotations.
4. Name the various types of law and show how they have developed in the modern state.
5. Explain the meaning and importance of the term "sovereignty."
6. To what extent is it right to describe government as the mechanism of the state?

7. "Government is, in the last analysis, organised force." Discuss this statement in reference to the modern state.

8. Name the three great departments of government and explain clearly the province of each.

9. What is a political constitution? Do you consider it necessary to the health of a body politic?

10. How far is it true to say that modern political constitutionalism has a nationalistic background and a democratic tendency?

CHAPTER II

THE ORIGIN AND GROWTH OF THE CONSTITUTIONAL STATE

I. INTRODUCTORY

THE rise of the constitutional state is essentially an historical process, and the student of the subject will find his chief materials in history. These materials are to be found not only in the history of institutions themselves but also in the history of the political ideas which have prompted their development or which have been stimulated by institutional growth; for to consider what was intended to be is often as important as to consider what actually was, and this is even more true of those institutions, such as we are studying now, which are still being moulded and remoulded in the very age in which we live. Not only in the past but also in the present, the discussion of the existing régime with a view to its improvement, or the analysis of the existing organisation with a view to definition, is what forms the basis of the bulk of political philosophy.

We have defined a constitution as a frame of political society organised through and by law, in which law has established permanent institutions with recognised functions and definite rights, and a constitutional state as one in which the powers of the government, the rights of the governed and the relations between the two are adjusted. Now this kind of state is at once very old and very new, as old as Greek antiquity and as new as the twentieth century. The oldest form of it of which we have any record is to be found in the Ancient World of the Greeks and Romans, but it was very different from ours. Modern constitutionalism, as we have said, has developed from the twofold basis of nationalism and representative democracy. But nationalism is of comparatively recent growth. The national constitutional state could not have grown in the soil of the Ancient World. Nationalism as a practical political programme

13

has developed within the mould of the state as it emerged in Europe in the fifteenth century. For the modern states-system of Europe began with that great era of change which we call the Renaissance. The significance of that series of revolutions in the spheres of letters, arts, science, maritime activity and politics, is best apprehended by studying what happened at that time to the state. The etymology of the word Renaissance does not help us much here, for if this period was marked by a rebirth of ancient ideals in learning, it was only very slightly so marked in politics. In a quite supreme sense it was, in this case, the death of something old and the birth of something new. What, in fact, emerged at that time was the principle of external sovereignty, and this marked a breach with the past, immediate and remote, of the profoundest political significance, as we shall now see.

II. GREEK CONSTITUTIONALISM

It is true that political separatism had been a marked characteristic of Greek life. Indeed, it was the almost religious devotion of the Greeks to the principle of autonomy, or the liberty of the group, which finally engulfed them. But they knew only the city-state, an area generally no larger than, say, an English county and with a population smaller than that of a large English town. The whole political outlook of the Greeks was determined by this fact; so that even the most brilliant political philosophers which Greece produced were incapable of looking beyond this conception of a state. Aristotle, indeed, in laying down what he conceived to be the physical limits of a true state, said that it should be large enough to be economically self-sufficing and small enough to permit of all the citizens meeting together in one place.

We may gather from this notion of the citizen how differently the second principle of our modern constitutionalism—democracy—was conceived by the Greeks. Whereas our nation-state, in developing its democracy, has necessarily introduced the principle of representation, such a principle was utterly unknown to the Greeks. A Greek citizen was actually and in person a soldier, a judge and a member of the governing assembly. Without a limitation of territory and of numbers, such as the Greek city-state implied, this personal discharge of a citizen's functions would have been impossible. This personal service, moreover, presupposed another institution, from which the conscience of modern civilisation recoils, namely, slavery. The ancient Greek was free to be an active citizen because the means of existence, generally speaking, were produced by slaves who were outside the pale of citizenship.

The state to the Greek was his whole scheme of association, a city wherein all his needs, material and spiritual, were satisfied. So that when Aristotle, for example, used the term state he comprehended within it all that we connote by the terms state, society, economic organisation and even religion. To him the state was a spiritual bond, not a mere piece of governmental machinery. The state exists, said Aristotle, not merely to make life possible but to make life good. To Greek philosophers like Plato and Aristotle there was no opposition between the individual and the state. The state, on the contrary, was the individual's only means of realising his own best ends, and a man could not be a good man unless he were also a good citizen.

The test of good citizenship, for such thinkers, was observance of the laws, or, in other words, the constitution. The law represented a fixed universal good which was a safeguard against individual caprice. In expounding their ideal constitutions both Plato and Aristotle emphasised the importance of political education, for only through an informed citizenship could the state be preserved from anarchy. In the view of both Plato and Aristotle anarchy had resulted from the unbridled development of democracy in Athens, and their criticism of the licence into which Athenian liberty had degenerated was the true occasion of those masterpieces of political philosophy, Plato's *Republic* and Aristotle's *Politics*. Plato's solution, as outlined in the *Republic*, lay in an aristocracy of political intellect, a body of "Guardians" qualified to rule through a rigid system of training which should lead up to the creation of his ideal state. Aristotle sought escape from the tyranny of the mob in what he called the "Polity," a type of middle-class government which should strike a mean between the unrealisable, or at least transitory, best and the intolerable worst.

But neither of these solutions was destined to realise itself, and so neither had a chance to show whether it was capable of saving the Greek city-state from extinction. The only possible way of perpetuating the liberty of Greece as a whole was one which never occurred to the Greek writers, though a practical attempt was made to adopt it, namely, by bringing about a wide political union. In attempting this, Athens first formed a league of equal states, called the Confederacy of Delos, but when she attempted to convert this into an Athenian Empire, in which she was in effect to hold the hegemony over the rest, she was set upon by a number of other states, headed by Sparta, because she thus threatened what was conceived as not only the very basis of the free state, but also the sole ground of true happiness. The Greeks never recovered from the wounds self-inflicted in the long civil war (the Peloponnesian War, 431-404 B.C.) which followed, and later fell an easy prey to the Macedonian invaders under Philip II and Alexander the Great.

What Greek political constitutionalism lacked was something which, as we shall see later, is vital to the continued existence of such a form of government, namely, an ability to move with the changing times and to meet new needs as they manifest themselves. But, although the political constitutionalism of the Greeks thus passed away, their political idealism remained, and it is difficult to see how our present political organisation could have become what it is without the inspiration afforded by this classical example.

III. THE ROMAN CONSTITUTION

Both Greece, as reconstituted after the Macedonian conquest, and the larger part of the empire founded by Alexander fell eventually within the bounds of the expanding Roman Empire, and it is therefore to Rome that we should next turn in tracing the history of political constitutionalism. Rome, too, was a city-state in its beginnings. But, circled and threatened as it was from its earliest years by hostile states, it was driven into a policy of expansion which did not cease until the Roman Empire came to be coterminous with the civilised world. The importance of Rome in the history of constitutionalism lies in the fact that its constitution played in the Ancient World a part comparable to that played by the British Constitution in the modern world. "Out of the Republic on the Tiber, a city with a rural territory round it no bigger than Surrey or Rhode Island," wrote Lord Bryce, "grew a World Empire, and the framework of that Empire retained till its fall traces of the institutions under which the little Republic . . . had risen. . . . In England a monarchy, first tribal and then feudal, developed from very small beginnings into a second World Empire of a wholly different type, while at the same time the ancient form of government, through a series of struggles and efforts, guided by an only half-conscious purpose, slowly developed itself into a system monarchical only in name." But, he went on, whereas Rome developed from a republic, partly aristocratic and partly democratic, to a despotism, the development of Britain has been exactly the reverse, from a strong monarchy to what is, in effect, a republic partly democratic and partly plutocratic.

The constitution of Rome was at first a quite determinate instrument of government, and yet nowhere could it be found stated in so many words. Like our own, it was made up of "a mass of precedents, carried in men's memories or recorded in writing, of dicta of lawyers or statesmen, of customs, usages, understandings and beliefs bearing upon the methods of government, together with a certain number of statutes." At first Rome was a monarchy, but later the kings were driven out and by about 500 B.C. the Republic began clearly to emerge. There followed a long struggle between the Orders (Patricians and Plebeians) which ended (about 300 B.C.) in the establishment of equal rights for the Plebs watched over by officers, specially selected for the purpose, called Tribunes. In this republican constitution there were three elements of government which were supposed to balance and check one another. First, the monarchical element (transferred from the original kings) manifested itself in the office of the Consuls, of whom there were two, elected annually, each with the right to veto the other. Secondly, the aristocratic element was embodied in the Senate, an assembly with, at one time, great legislative powers. Thirdly, the democratic element existed in the meetings of the people in three sorts of convention according to divisions of land or people (curies, centuries or tribes). The theory of this triple division of powers lasted till the fall of the Empire, but, as Rome expanded, it necessarily ceased to be a fact.

The Roman state lasted, in a certain sense, for twenty-two

centuries (from the traditional date of the foundation of the City, 753 B.C., to the capture of Constantinople, A.D. 1453), and during that time many changes took place in its constitution. The Roman Constitution, it must be remembered, was that of a city-state, and as Rome ceased to be a city-state and became (within the limits of contemporary civilisation) a world-state, the republican form became inconsistent with the facts. For here again, as in the case of Greece, we observe the absence of our two indispensable conditions or presuppositions of modern constitutionalism, namely, representative democracy and nationalism. The democracy of Rome, like that of the Greek city-states, was direct or primary democracy, and the idea of representation was foreign to the one as to the other. Manifestly, citizenship in this direct sense could not be maintained and at the same time include in its scope the peoples which Rome successively absorbed. Again, a nation could not be moulded out of the heterogeneous mass of peoples which came to compose the Roman world. The Roman method was to destroy nascent local feeling, to "divide and rule." It did not allow nations to exist, for it could not give its subject-peoples a share in the government without introducing the notion of representation, and this it never did.

Thus the old Republican Constitution fell into desuetude, and the conception of it as a nice balance of monarchical, aristocratic and democratic forces was no longer tenable after the great eastward expansion of the second century B.C., though as late as the middle of that century a Greek hostage in Rome, named Polybius, still attributed to this equipoise the stability of Roman government, a fact which had an important influence on later political theory and even to some extent on institutions. But, in reality, from this time what was called the Roman Republic was nothing more than the rule of the Senate. Yet always the theory remained that all powers were ultimately derived from the people. There had always been a provision for the establishment of a temporary dictatorship in times of crisis, and during the last century B.C., when civil war was rife in Italy, this expedient was often resorted to in order to cover with a constitutional cloak the despotic acts of some triumphant military commander, like Marius or Sulla. When at last Julius Cæsar crushed Pompey in 48 B.C., the Senate, recognising its own impotence, made him Dictator for life, and the Imperium, in fact if not in name, was born.

The theory of the Roman Imperial power we may clearly gather from the *Institutes* and *Digest* of the Emperor Justinian (A.D. 538–565), the great codifier of the Roman Law, who, though his actual rule, except for a brief period, was confined to the Roman Empire in the East, centred at Constantinople, still spoke of himself as the ruler of the world. The supreme legislative authority, according to this Code, still rested with the Roman people (though they had not exercised it for more than five centuries). The rights of the Emperor were the result of the people's delegation of them, a delegation, it is to be noted, not in perpetuity, but supposedly renewed with each new holder of office. The powers of the people were never formally abolished at any period in the history of the Empire, but fell gradually into oblivion. It was the peculiar flexibility of the Roman Constitution which made possible this fiction of delegation. The Emperors, from the first (Augustus, 31 B.C.–A.D. 14), were, according to this fiction, simply magistrates who concentrated in their hands the various offices of the old Republic. This is noteworthy, because the Roman magistrates (consuls, prætors, etc.) had a great power, constitutionally held, in the great days of the Republic. Once it was granted, therefore, that all their powers were concentrated in one person and that there was no time limit to his tenure, the office of Emperor appeared as nothing more than a unification of all the old republican magistracies, to which, however, had been surrendered the rights of the Roman democracy. The Senate, too, in continuing to meet gave the appearance of a retention of republican forms. But the Senate became totally enfeebled in the later days of the Empire and degenerated into a mere registry office of the Emperor's will.

Thus the Roman Constitution began as a happy blend of monarchical, aristocratic and democratic elements and ended as an irresponsible autocracy. Yet we cannot fail to see that this was an inevitable concomitant of the growth of the Empire, whose vast area, heterogeneous peoples and diverse interests demanded a swift and efficient instrument of action such as can be supplied only by an absolute sovereignty in the hands of one man. As we have suggested earlier, any other method must have

disintegrated the Roman World very much sooner than was
the case and antedated by many centuries the diversity of
states which we know to-day.

The absolute power of the Roman Emperor was not circumscribed even by such considerations as have limited the scope
of modern autocrats like the Tsars of Russia and the Prussian
Kings, for, after all, there was a certain homogeneity among
the peoples which the latter ruled. National feeling was entirely
absent in the Roman Empire. The subject-peoples knew nothing
of the rights enjoyed by the people of the Roman Republic
under a constitution which was always that of a city, and this
made the growth of autocracy all the easier. The fiction of the
maintenance of the Republic under the Empire had advantages
for Augustus and the earlier Emperors, who thereby avoided
the fate of Julius Cæsar, but it caused many a disputed succession to the Purple in later years, since the office of Emperor
had no constitutional foundations. But what was, at the time
of the change from Republicanism to Imperialism, the sovereign
power *in fact*—*i.e.*, the Emperor—came at last to be regarded
as the sovereign power *by right*, and the words of Justinian—
that what pleases the Prince has the force of law—were the
literal and accepted truth by his day, though the area of the
jurisdiction of that law was very much narrower than it had
been in the days before the break-up of the Empire in the West
in the fifth century A.D.

What, then, were the lasting influences of Roman constitutionalism? First, the Roman Law has had a great effect upon
the legal history of Continental Europe. The customs and laws
brought in by the Teutonic invaders of the Empire in the West
fused with and merged into the Roman Code which they found,
and this fusion has produced the legal systems which prevail
in Western Continental Europe to-day. Secondly, the Roman
love of order and unity was so strong that the men of the Middle
Ages were obsessed with the notion of the political unity of the
world in the face of the forces of disintegration. To the Roman
passion for unity and its continuity as an ideal in the Middle
Ages may be traced the prevailing dream of liberal minds in the
modern world that at last there may be established an international or supra-national authority for the prevention of war.
Thirdly, the double-sided conception of the Emperor's legal

sovereignty—on the one hand, that his pleasure had the force of law, and on the other, that his powers were ultimately derived from the people—persisted for many centuries and was responsible for two distinct mediæval views of the relations of government and governed. At the beginning of the Middle Ages it led to the blind acceptance of authority by the people and towards their close to the doctrine that the people, having originally delegated the sovereign power to the Emperor, might rightfully resume it. And this argument was the philosophical basis of the democracy with which the modern world began.

IV. CONSTITUTIONALISM IN THE MIDDLE AGES

With the inrush of the Barbarians into the western half of the Roman Empire in the fourth and fifth centuries the Roman political machine broke down. It continued, however, in the eastern half, where the Emperors maintained a precarious rule over an ever-diminishing area around Constantinople. This later Roman (or Byzantine) Empire became more and more a closely-knit and isolated state until, out of all touch with Western Europe, it finally fell a prey to the Turks, who captured its capital in 1453. In the West actual unity was impossible after the Barbarians had broken the universality of the Roman Law. But there always remained the legal theory of a world empire, and it was out of this theory that the Holy Roman Empire developed.

This Empire was founded by Charles the Great in the year A.D. 800, but it was a very different organisation from the original Roman Empire. It was the Roman Empire modified territorially, racially, socially, politically, and spiritually to such an extent that the old Roman constitutionalism entirely disappeared. The Teutonic elements were strong enough perceptibly to leaven the Roman lump, and the growth of the Catholic Church, which had begun to come into its own in the later days of the Western Roman Empire, encouraged it, amid the break-up of the old Roman centralism, to make such claims to universal power as to threaten the temporal arm. Before Charles the Great's Empire had time to develop a proper constitution, it first fell apart among his successors, according to the Frankish laws of inheritance, and then disintegrated in face of the Norse invasions of the ninth and tenth centuries. After this the Holy Roman Empire was never again what it had been under Charlemagne. It came to be confined to Germany with a vague and varying hold on the sovereignty of Italy.

All over Europe then rapidly developed the phenomenon of feudalism. This was a kind of mediæval constitutionalism, since it was to some extent systematised into a generally accepted form of social and political organisation. Its essential feature was a division of land into small units, the general principle of which was that "every man must have a lord." This added to the shadowy claims of the mediæval Empire without increasing their substance, for it was now possible to conceive of European society, without putting the conception to the test of fact, as a pyramid, at the apex of which stood the Emperor who was, in his turn, regarded as "God's vassal." The evil of feudalism lay in the inordinate power it gave to the great barons, and in proportion to their strength the day was delayed when a unified state could emerge. We therefore find that the strong kings of the Middle Ages were those who endeavoured to concentrate power in their own hands and so to systematise a central control necessarily detrimental to baronial supremacy.

In this way feudalism seems to have been an inevitable growth to bridge the gulf between the chaos of early mediæval times and the order of the modern state. It was on the western edge of Europe that these first great centralising moves were made. In England and France particularly, and to a less extent in Spain, the policy of the kings from the eleventh century onwards was to concentrate power in their hands, and to control and finally destroy the great feudal fiefs. And it is precisely to these countries that we may look for the first faint emergence of those two principles which we have described as the necessary conditions of the growth of modern constitutionalism, namely, nationalism and representative democracy. England was never within the limits of the Holy Roman Empire, nor was France after the break-up of Charlemagne's dominions. As to the Papal authority, both countries developed an independence sufficiently vigorous to establish what was, in effect, a national Church, and only in very abnormal times did the Pope hold any real sway within the confines of these two states. Moreover, it was in these two countries that assemblies containing representatives of estates less than the baronial first appeared. In England the first Parliament, which included Knights of the Shire and representatives of towns, was summoned in 1265, in France in 1302, the latter as a direct result of a Papal claim to the exemption of clergy from civil taxation. An added sense of nationalism was given to these states as a result of the Hundred Years' War (1337–1453), which emphasised the identity of interests of the subjects of each state respectively. The cry of Joan of Arc might well have been "France for the French," while the English were driven to concentrate upon the work of rectifying the disorders at home which the war had largely engendered.

The sense of nationalism in Spain grew out of a different set of circumstances. Here, in the eighth century, the Mohammedan Moors had conquered the greater part of the country. It fell to the tiny Christian communities left in the north to bind themselves together to expel the infidels. By the fourteenth century there were only two important states in the Peninsula apart from Portugal in the west and the remnant of Moorish territory (Granada) in the south-east corner. These were Aragon and Castile. Each of them had assemblies (or Cortes) containing representatives from rural and urban areas besides the barons and clergy. Towards the end of the fifteenth century the two states were united by marriage and became the Kingdom of Spain.

On the other hand, in Germany and Italy, where the conception of the Holy Roman Empire was much more generally accepted, feudal anarchy continued to a much later date than in the three more westerly states. The anarchical situation, moreover, was complicated by the perpetual conflicts between the Imperial and Papal authorities which grew in intensity from the middle of the eleventh century. After passing through the miseries of the Investiture Contest (1056–1125) and the degradation of the subsequent schisms caused by the rival claims of Cæsars and anti-Cæsars, Popes and anti-Popes, the two great mediæval institutions were so weakened by the end of the thirteenth century that they were never able to regain their former power. The only matter of constitutional interest which emerges from this long period of internecine struggle was the experiment generally known as the Conciliar Movement. This followed the scandal of the Great Schism (1378–1417) which divided Western Europe into two religious allegiances under different Popes. Failing the advent of a second Charlemagne, who might forcibly have ended this unseemly strife, an escape from anarchy was attempted in the revival of an earlier institution for the government of the Church, namely, the General Council, to which the Pope was to be forced to submit. The Council of Pisa (1409) was followed by the Council of Constance (1414–1418), to which were sent representatives of the Church, both clerical and lay, and which laid down the principle of permanent Conciliar control of the Pope. The constitution which it, in effect, drew up failed to work, however, in the next Council, the Council of Basel (1431–1449), and from that time the Conciliar system, as a method of Church government, disappeared.

But, though the Conciliar Movement itself was a failure, it has considerable significance in the history of constitutionalism in two ways. First, the organisation and procedure of the Councils acknowledged the national divisions into which Europe was now falling. At Constance, in fact, where the method of voting by nations was adopted, five such groups—viz., the Italian, French, German, English, and Spanish—were recognised; so that, while the spirit of mediæval unity was still sufficiently alive to convene such an œcumenical body as this, in doing so it emphasised the force that was destroying it. Secondly, the Conciliar Movement gave rise to much speculation as to the methods by which a General Council might be made to represent the views of the whole body of the Faithful, as distinct from those merely of Church dignitaries. The efforts to discover the means of thus establishing an effective organ of Church government produced in the fifteenth century a large volume of political philosophy—in the writings of such men as Marsiglio of Padua, William of Ockham, John Gerson, and Nicholas of Cues—which explored, in a pioneer fashion, a vast field of political problems, such as sovereignty, nationalism, representation and the limitation of monarchy, and thus foreshadowed the constitutional developments of the modern epoch.

Towards the end of the Middle Ages, then, in the whole of Western Europe, we find a fever of political speculation which arises out of the abuses of the Catholic Church and whose object is to give that Church a new constitution. But whereas, in this case, it never passed beyond the vague realm of theory and unsuccessful experiment, in the internal politics of the three more westerly countries, England, France and Spain, we find at this time the actual germs of the modern constitutional state. For in these states practical politics outstrode legal theories, and the ghost of the Holy Roman Empire was irrevocably laid. In Germany and Italy it continued to stalk for many years.

V. THE RENAISSANCE STATE

The process of the break-up of mediæval institutions which we have been tracing was given a tremendous impetus by the great revival of antique culture of the fifteenth century, which, with all its consequences, is generally called the Renaissance; for such political facts and ideas as the scholars of that epoch found in the work of the Greek writers fitted ill with the mediæval conceptions which were already becoming discredited by the facts. The general effect was at once one of atomisation and one of integration: it atomised the mediæval world but integrated individual states. In England, France and Spain it effected a more closely integrated state on national lines; in Germany and Italy the process of integration went on, but over much more confined areas, so that in those countries many little states arose. But in many respects the Renaissance undid the good work that had been going on in the three Western states.

The Renaissance state was not a truly constitutional, much less a democratic, state. Its essential quality, as we have noted earlier, was external sovereignty, which implied a strong central authority maintaining itself at any cost, chiefly with a view to strengthening the state against all its neighbours. The statesmen of the Renaissance, indeed, caught but little of the spirit of antique political philosophy, for, whereas Greek autonomy, as we have seen, was conceived as the only means of assuring the good life to the individual, Renaissance sovereignty was not at all concerned with the rights of the individual. In short, the Renaissance monarchs were concerned with politics and not in the least with ethics, that couple so closely wedded in the philosophy of the Ancient World. The truth of this is evident in the work of the only political theorist of any account which that age produced, namely, Machiavelli, himself a very child of the Renaissance. It was because Machiavelli's country, Italy, was not transformed at this time into a Renaissance sovereign state that he was concerned to appeal to somebody to do for her what had been done for the more westerly states. This is the burden of his book, *The Prince*, published in 1513, in which Machiavelli seeks a saviour of his country in this sense. The significance of this book is that it marks the epoch very clearly by recording and turning into a new philosophy the doctrine of "unmorality" as applied to the state—the doctrine, that is to say, which asserts that politics should not be circumscribed by any ethical considerations, for concern with such matters could only weaken the sovereignty of the state in a world where sovereignty counted for everything. The saviour of Italy was not found by Machiavelli, but it is worthy of notice that when that saviour, Cavour, at last emerged in the middle of the nineteenth century, he said of his own conduct in the crisis of the Italian unifying movement, "If we did for ourselves what we are doing for our country we should be great rascals."

The political effect of the religious Reformation of the sixteenth century was to give to the Renaissance state a divine sanction. The theological attitude of Luther, as first manifested in 1517, logically implied complete toleration of religious opinions. This was not feasible in a Catholic world in arms, against which Luther, in order to protect his position, sought the championship of a political prince. It was thus that the Elector of Saxony established a State Church. Such a Church was bound to become as exclusive and intolerant as the one it had superseded. Thus the political consequence of Luther's doctrinal onslaught upon the Papacy was to atomise the world still further, and to add to the prerogatives of the Renaissance sovereign the control of the religious practices of his subjects. The movement is most clearly seen in England, where the ecclesiastical supremacy of Henry VIII and Elizabeth was succeeded by the Erastianism of James I.

So Renaissance sovereignty flourished and effectively delayed the harvest of that constitutional seed which had been sown with such promise in Western Europe towards the end of the Middle Ages. It developed on the Continent into the type of monarchy known as Enlightened Despotism, which may be said to have lasted from 1660 to 1789. In France, in Prussia, in Austria the despotism became complete. In France the States-General, from the time of the Renaissance, met less and less frequently, and after 1614 they were not convened at all until the eve of the Revolution in 1789. The two great characteristics of this type of despotism were a professional army and a professional bureaucracy drawn generally from the middle class or bourgeoisie. Thus, as feudalism decayed, the only unifying force was the Crown which sought no aid from any representative body, and so the organs of a properly constituted body politic, instead of thriving by activity, atrophied through lack of use. That is the reason why, on the Continent, the full development of constitutionalism was delayed until the nineteenth century, and why, when it came at last, it took a series of revolutions to achieve it. In England alone Renaissance monarchy was not allowed to become an unchecked despotism, and it is therefore to the history of our own country that we must turn to trace the uninterrupted development of constitutionalism.

VI. CONSTITUTIONALISM IN ENGLAND

England, too, had its period of despotism in the Renaissance age, but peculiar circumstances prevented it from becoming strengthened and fixed as it did on the Continent. England could hardly escape the temporary establishment of the type of state which we have called the Renaissance State, for, besides suffering from the general phenomenon of the break-up of mediævalism, she had her own peculiar difficulties. The long war with France had exhausted her resources, and the civil war (the Wars of the Roses) which followed completed the process of disintegration. As we have seen, the first parliament including representatives of the counties and towns met in 1265. From 1295, the year of Edward I's "Model Parliament," parliaments met at irregular intervals, chiefly for the purpose of granting money to the king. But at the end of the fourteenth century it was given a new reason for existence, for in 1399, Richard II was deposed and a younger branch of the family of Edward III, the Lancastrians, usurped the throne. Having no true blood claim, Henry IV and his successors depended on

Parliament for their justification. The weakness of their position, however, grew with the failure against France and the incompetence of Henry VI, whose deposition was brought about by the Wars of the Roses. Edward IV, who now became king, had to continue the war, which was brought to a close by the defeat of his brother, Richard III, at the battle of Bosworth, by Henry Tudor in 1485. This was the occasion for the setting-up of the monarchy which is frequently referred to as the Tudor Despotism.

That, however, is a term which requires a good deal of qualification. The Tudor Despotism had three organs of government, only one of which can be compared to the highly-trained bureaucracy which, as we have observed, became a marked feature of despotic government on the Continent. This was the Council, which was the monarch's tool in the executive department. Its inordinate power was checked by the existence of the other two, namely, Parliament and the Justices of the Peace. It is true that Parliament sanctioned, generally without demur, the monarch's plans as drawn up with the aid of the Council, but the important point is that it continued to meet and to approve all legislative and taxative proposals. Undoubtedly, the Tudor parliaments were mostly subservient, but this was because, at any rate, three of the five Tudor monarchs voiced the will of the nation. When the monarch no longer embodied that will, Parliament, with all its machinery ready, revolted. The Justices of the Peace, who were the local administrators of the policy of the central government, were not, like the local administrators on the Continent, paid professional agents of the central authority, but unpaid workers drawn from the landed gentry.

The insularity of the country, which freed it from the constant need of armed defence against foreign aggression and cut it off from those forces which continued to strengthen the Continental autocracy, made it possible to blend the despotism of the monarch with the deeply-rooted principle of local and central self-government. The isolation of the state also strengthened its sense of nationalism, and this was enhanced by two great series of events in the Tudor period. The first was the Reformation, which transferred the headship of the Church from the Pope to the English monarch, and thus preserved it completely

from Papal interference. The second was the defeat of the
Spanish Armada. This victory exorcised for ever the dread of
that power which had filled the minds of Englishmen since its
emergence as an imperial force at the opening of the sixteenth
century. The defeat of the Armada at once freed Parliament
from the thraldom which had kept its mouth tightly shut on
matters of high policy, and when, in 1603, the Stuarts ascended
the throne in the person of James I, there began the long
struggle which was not to end until Parliament had triumphed
completely over the Crown.

A mere wrangle under James I, it became an armed conflict
under his son. The Civil War (1642–9) really destroyed whatever
chance there was of establishing in England the type of enlightened despotism which was developing apace on the Continent,
and though, after the period of the Commonwealth and with the
Restoration, the Stuart autocracy attempted, under Charles II
and James II, to raise its head once more, it was so utterly
overthrown by the Revolution of 1688–9 that any future
attempt to revive the royal power was bound to fail. We shall
examine the details of this change in a later section. Here it is
only necessary to emphasise two great facts connected with the
Revolution of 1688. The first is that the control of affairs was
effectively transferred from King to Parliament. The second is
that this change was placed upon a statutory basis. Before this
time there was, to all intents and purposes, no statutory law
of the Constitution, only customs and conventions; for Magna
Carta was hardly a statute, and, in any case, most of its provisions became obsolete with the passing of the feudal age which
produced it, though the Commons were glad enough to quote
it as a precedent. The Petition of Right of 1628, indeed, became
a statute when the king agreed to it, but its provisions were not
kept, and the whole question of the limitation of the Crown
passed into the melting-pot of the Puritan Revolution. Under
the Commonwealth and Protectorate fully written constitutions
were produced, but they passed away with the Restoration.
Certain financial provisions connected with the Restoration had
statutory force, but in any case they were included in the
general Revolutionary settlement.

The various statutes passed at the time of the Revolution
of 1688–9 placed the sovereignty of the British state irrevocably

in the hands of Parliament, for the Bill of Rights and the Mutiny Act gave Parliament the control of the Army, and by the simple device of annual supplies of money for its upkeep produced an effective preventive of tyranny. Yet this was only a general legislative supervision. The executive function Parliament was content to leave in the hands of the king and his ministers. Yet in the course of the eighteenth century, by a purely conventional growth, the cabinet system, founded upon party, grew up, and by the end of the century had become so firmly based that there was added to the powers of Parliament the control of the executive also.

Meanwhile, the legal history of the state had fixed the principle known as the "Rule of Law," which means the equality of all citizens of whatever rank before the law. Statutes like Habeas Corpus (1679) had secured, on the one hand, the immunity of the citizen from false imprisonment, and, on the other, the immunity of the judge from royal interference. Again, judicial decisions like that in connection with John Wilkes (1763) achieved simultaneously the security of the citizen from wrongful arrest and the subjection even of Ministers of the Crown to the ordinary processes of law. This Rule of Law was transferred to all the British Colonies and is hence the basis of the legal system to-day in all the Self-governing Dominions of the British Crown and of the United States of America.

Thus, by the second half of the eighteenth century Britain was a constitutional, though not a democratic, state. By conventional growth and by a series of statutes her three organs of government, legislative, executive and judicial, were properly constituted and related in such a manner as to ensure the absence of tyranny. The principle of representation was deeply rooted in this system, but no ideas of franchise extension had yet come to be accepted as practical politics. For this the country had to wait for the combined effects of the French and Industrial Revolutions, of which we shall speak later. Nevertheless, in the middle of the eighteenth century, Britain was the only constitutional state in the world. This is our justification for tracing it in this historical sketch at such length, for, as one authority says, "before the outbreak of the American and French Revolutions, the history of the British system (at home or in the daughter-lands) is in effect the history of self-government in the world." It was inevitable, therefore, that this system should become the model for the later constitutional development of other states.

The British Constitution was the result of a slow, conventional growth, not, like the others which we shall examine, the product of deliberate invention, resulting from a theory. Yet, though its development was not the result of a theory or theories, it was, nevertheless, made the starting-point of the political speculation which characterised the seventeenth and eighteenth centuries. If Britain was the only constitutional state in existence, and if men were seeking the means of circumventing the despotism under which the Continent lived, it was natural that they should attempt to examine and analyse this unique instrument of their age. But that instrument had grown up by an evolutionary process, and the question was how it could be applied to the revolutionary circumstances in which alone, it seemed, a change could now be brought about. The answer gives the key to understanding the essential difference between the British Constitution and those which could not but imitate it. The new constitutionalism whose emergence we must now examine was in the form of a document which attempted to sum up at a stroke the fruits of the experience of the state which had evolved its constitutionalism through several centuries. In this sense the various types of western constitutionalism met and merged, the older acting upon and being acted upon by the newer. But precisely because the British Constitution had developed so far, it was able to adapt itself to the new conditions and graft new elements produced by the later documentary constitutions on to the existing constitution without fundamentally changing it.

VII. THE CONSTITUTIONAL INFLUENCE OF THE AMERICAN AND FRENCH REVOLUTIONS

The political tyranny which the Renaissance had produced and the persistence of religious intolerance which the Reformation had done nothing to allay, gave rise to an explanation of the origin of the state which was to hold the field until the dawn of the nineteenth century. This was what is generally known as the Social Contract theory. In the modern world it was first upheld by the Huguenots in France and the Netherlanders under the Spanish yoke, who were the worst sufferers from the effects of these two phenomena. But it was by no means new. We find a champion of it in Plato's *Republic*, and it crops up again during the Middle Ages in the crisis of the struggle between the Emperors and Popes. Briefly stated, the Contract theory argues that the state is born in a compact among a number of men who come together to end an intolerable state of nature. By the compact men abandon certain of their natural rights, but only those necessary to the establishment of a civil condition of society. The object of political society is, therefore, to secure that the rights not so abandoned continue to be guaranteed to the citizens. If the establishment of government is contractual, it follows that when government becomes tyrannical it breaks the contract, and therefore the members of the state have the right to remove such a government. No doctrine could better suit those who, like the Huguenots and the Netherlanders, wanted to justify the destruction of despotism, and could thereby revolt with ultimate right on their side.

This theory went through many variations in the hands of several advocates. It is true that one of its earliest and most famous exponents, an Englishman, Thomas Hobbes, in his *Leviathan* (1651) used the argument to justify state absolutism, on the ground that the government thus set up was no party to the contract, and therefore could not break it. But, whereas most of its upholders were seeking to justify tyrannicide, Hobbes, writing immediately after the disorders of the English Civil War (1642–9), was looking for a philosophical escape from anarchy. Another Englishman, John Locke, who had a far-reaching influence on Continental thought in the eighteenth century, employed the theory in his *Treatises of Civil Government* (1690) as a justification of the English Revolution of 1688–9. This book was a Whig manifesto, championing the cause of that party which had dethroned James II and carried the Bill of Rights. The compact, according to Locke, was made between the subjects and the monarch to establish a common organ for the interpretation and execution of man's rights, as existing before the political condition was established. This general doctrine was easily applied by Locke to the special circumstances of 1688, and in fact had already been incorporated, in so many words, in the resolution of the Convention of 1689, which dethroned James II. This resolution asserted that the king "having endeavoured to subvert the constitution of the kingdom *by breaking the original contract between king and people* . . . has abdicated the government and the throne is thereby vacant." Thus, when James II, after three years of misgovernment, was dethroned, presumably a new contract was made to establish William of Orange and Mary on the English throne. Such was the Whig answer to the Stuart doctrine of the Divine Right of Kings.

But whereas Hobbes had reconciled liberty and authority by the convenient but illogical method of entirely destroying one of the parties to the reconciliation—that is, by sacrificing everything to vindicate the principle of absolutism—Locke had evaded the thorny problem of sovereignty by ignoring it. If revolution was justified, who or what was the authority which should decide that the time was ripe for its execution? Locke never answered this vital question, but contented himself with vaguely envisaging the "people" in the background as a superior embodiment of power. Yet it would be idle to pretend that the "people," as such, effected the Revolution which deposed James II and placed William and Mary on the throne of England in his stead. This, in fact, was the work of an oligarchy of Whig leaders whose opposition to James II issued in the Bill of Rights, a statute passed by an utterly unrepresentative Parliament whose basic constitution had not been materially reformed since its foundation in 1295. It was left to a Frenchman, Jean Jacques Rousseau, to attempt the difficult problem of reconciling sovereignty and democracy. In his *Social Contract* (1762), Rousseau made a brave attempt to build up a logical and even incontrovertible defence of democracy, developing Locke's theory by Hobbes' method. If man was born for freedom and yet was everywhere in chains, said Rousseau, the only means of rendering the slavery legitimate lay in the retention of the sovereign power in the hands of the people who had made the contract which turned a multitude of individuals into a society. The contract secured equality, since thereby each, in giving himself up to all, gave himself up to no one. This doctrine of popular sovereignty, as enunciated by Rousseau, was the trumpet blast to the gathering forces which were destined to overthrow the Old Régime in Europe, for if Rousseau's teaching came to be generally accepted, Enlightened Despotism would be unable at last to prevail against it.

Rousseau's *Social Contract* was probably the most epoch-marking book ever written, not so much in itself as in its influence upon the constitution-making which followed it. In his frantic efforts to find a philosophical justification for democracy, based upon his doctrine of the General Will, Rousseau landed himself into a logical morass, and the doctrine of the Social Contract as an acceptable theory of the state finally vanished in the transcendental mists generated by the idealistic philosophy of Rousseau's German successors, Kant, Fichte and Hegel. Rousseau himself derided the notion of representative democracy as a contradiction in terms, and his ideals of government, being founded on the classical notion of direct or primary democracy, were quite impracticable at the time in which he lived. But his disciples were not so uncompromising, and it may with truth be said that representative institutions, as developed since his time, have attempted, consciously or unconsciously, to give Rousseau's ultimate theory practical effect.

Rousseau's *Social Contract* was, in fact, only the literary forerunner of two great revolutions which occurred at the end of the eighteenth century, one in America, the other in France. The revolution in America was not confined to the War of Independence (1775–1783). It took the from also of a series of democratic changes in each of the Thirteen Colonies and the drafting of state constitutions which were collected and published in 1781. The collection was translated into French and had a considerable bearing on the constitution-making which marked the revolutionary period in France. But the influence of the War of American Independence itself and its consequences on the history of modern constitutionalism was even more striking. The war resulted from an economic régime which the American colonists regarded as tyrannical. Their slogan, "No taxation without representation," implied an ultimate revolt from the Mother Country, because, while some form of taxation had been rendered absolutely necessary to help to defray the cost of the Seven Years' War (1756–1763), fought largely in defence of the Colonies against the French, the representation of the American Colonies in Parliament at Westminster at that time was a manifest impossibility. So the American War of Independence broke out and ended in the establishment of a new political entity known as the United States of America, founded upon a constitution, promulgated in 1787, which came into operation in 1789.

This Constitution embodies the principles enunciated in the Declaration of Independence (1776) which states categorically:

that all men are created equal; that they are endowed by their Creator with certain unalienable rights . . . that to secure these rights, governments are instituted among men, deriving their just powers from the consent of the governed; that, whenever any form of government becomes destructive of these ends, it is the right of the people to alter or abolish it, and to institute a new government, laying its foundations on such principles, and organising its powers in such form, as to them shall seem most likely to effect their safety and happiness.

This is the true beginning of modern documentary constitutionalism. If the Social Contract theory, as an explanation of the origin of the state, has been found, under the searching lights of the Historical Method, to be baseless, no amount of research or argumentation can destroy the fact that the Americans did form a new body politic in 1789 and that they enshrined its rights in a document which, as the Constitution of the United States, remains the supreme authority in that country to this day. Moreover, the Americans, in working out a form of political organisation which should satisfy the various groups forming the new state, revived an older political method, namely, federalism, which was destined to have a tremendous influence on politics in later days. Of this we shall have much to say in a later chapter.

It would not, perhaps, be possible to assert that Rousseau's influence was directly felt by the Americans. It would be nearer the truth, probably, to say that the Fathers of the American Constitution were coevally informed by the same spirit as that which inspired Rousseau's political philosophy. But Rousseau was directly behind those who led the early movements of the French Revolution. Of this great series of events we need here only say that when the bankrupt government of France in 1789 resorted to the expedient of recalling into existence the States-General, which had not met since 1614, it carried into the forum all the idealistic dogmas of Rousseau and his followers, and thus brought them into practical conjunction with the promulgation of a political constitution. The National Assembly of 1789 thus drew up the "Declaration of the Rights of Man and of Citizen" before coming to its proper business of making a constitution. This document was saturated with the dogmas of the contractual origin of the state, of popular sovereignty and of individual rights, as shown by the following excerpts:

Men are born free and equal in rights. . . .

The aim of every political association is the preservation of the practical and imprescriptible rights of man. These rights are liberty, property, security and resistance to oppression. . . .

Liberty consists in the power to do anything that does not injure others; accordingly, the exercise of the natural rights of each man has for its only limits those that secure to the other members of society the enjoyment of these same rights. These limits can be determined by law. . . .

Law is the expression of the general will. . . .

Sovereignty resides exclusively in the nation. . . .

The nation has the imprescriptible right to change its constitution.

The Constitution, which followed in 1791, and to which this Declaration was prefixed, did not last, because the Legislative Assembly to which it gave birth was unable to deal with the state of anarchy within France and the state of war without. Nevertheless, this is the second great stage in the development of modern documentary constitutionalism, as the American Revolution is the first. Though the constitutionalism of the early years of the French Revolution had to give way, first to the anarchy of the Reign of Terror and then to the despotism of the Napoleonic régime which arose from its ashes, the Revolution had lighted a fire of political liberty which was never again to be permanently smothered. For, as one authority says, the French "ideal of self-government became—what it had never been in its British or even its American form—a challenge to every constituted government which did not recognise and embody the sovereignty of the people."

VIII. NATIONALISM AND LIBERAL REFORM

Paradoxically, the Napoleonic régime and its consequences in Europe did the rest, for now that the principle of democracy had been fairly launched on the Continent (and Napoleon himself, in spite of his militarism, was a disseminator of the revolutionary seed), all that was required to give effect to the spread of constitutionalism was a sufficiently vital sense of nationality among the various oppressed communities to which it was addressed. Napoleon's bizarre boundary-making, especially in Italy and Germany, outraged a nascent spirit not recognised as existing until it was thereby goaded into action, and Napoleon, aiming at the United States of Europe, merely succeeded in disuniting them to the point of his own destruction. The nationalism of which we spoke in connection with the Renaissance was a vague and largely unconscious development: the nationalism which followed the failure of the Napoleonic conquest of Europe was a mighty fire which first consumed the incendiary and then smouldered, to burst into flame again, from time to time, until it had burnt every remnant of the edifice of the Old Régime. Not for nothing was the Battle of Leipzig called the "Battle of the Nations," though the royal and aristocratic diplomatists who made the Treaties of 1814-15 failed to grasp the true purport of the movement which had engulfed the pretensions of Bonaparte.

Those Treaties restored, in most countries, the ancient despotisms which the Revolution had sought to overthrow, and revived, moreover, most of the pre-war frontiers. Where this was not done, they cut away odd areas and populations from their old allegiances and placed them under new ones without reference to the ideas disseminated by the Revolution, but according to the dictates of power, policy or the rights of the victor. The result was that the universal emergence of the national constitutional state was postponed, though it was no longer possible to abandon it altogether. Another result was that the zeal of the reformers was driven underground and burst out in occasional revolts. The evil of this was that it confused the issues of nationalism and liberal reform which should have been one. The diplomats who were supposed to have charge of the peace of Europe were concerned rather to crush this revolutionary spirit, wherever it appeared, but their hold weakened with time, and in the year 1830 there was a serious revolution in most Continental states. As usual, it began in France, where the restored Bourbon dynasty was overthrown and a still more limited monarchy was introduced under Louis Philippe. But this was the only movement which was attended by success at the time, with the exception of that in Belgium which led to the establishment of a new independent state under a constitutional monarchy. Another series of revolutions in 1848, much more serious than in 1830, showed once more the weakness of a mere liberalising movement not founded upon national unity. Of the constitutions promulgated at that time, only those of France, Sardinia, the Netherlands and Switzerland survived the reaction. Of these, the first was soon lost in the establishment of the Second Empire under Louis Napoleon in 1852, while the second persisted but feebly until it came to be associated with the unifying movement in Italy.

After the failures of 1848, therefore, a new turn was given to the aspirations of the Liberal reformers. Besides the obvious fact that the revolutionary method had failed, a new and very important factor was working towards the peaceful settlement of the political problem. This was the effect of that vast series of changes which we call the Industrial Revolution. Beginning in England in the second half of the eighteenth century as a succession of mechanical inventions which resulted in the application of power to the processes of industrial production, it progressed to the foundation of the factory system and modern capitalism, and ended in a complete recasting of social forces and a fundamental variation in the political equilibrium. When this economic revolution began to work itself out in England, it was inevitable that it should have a serious effect upon the political situation. It destroyed for ever the preponderant weight of the agricultural classes in the community and brought into being a new middle class, the capitalists, who year by year became more insistent in their demand for political recognition.

Emancipation was granted to this class by the Reform Act of 1832. This Act swept away many of the abuses which had accumulated through the centuries, redistributed parliamentary seats so as to destroy the representation of areas which had outlived their former political significance, and gave parlia-

mentary representation to the new urban areas which had
developed through the industrial changes. In doing this it
enfranchised the new capitalists, and though by no means
introducing a complete system of democracy, it was the first
step towards it, and in the right line of constitutional, as
opposed to revolutionary, progress, since it was found possible
to effect this reform without revolutionising the existing
methods of government. The enfranchisement of the middle
class, indeed, strengthened the cabinet system—*i.e.*, the control
of the executive by Parliament—already firmly founded during
the eighteenth century, by changing the centre of political
gravity from the Lords to the Commons and by bringing into
existence a new division of parties on which the maintenance
of a real cabinet system depends.

This great movement, arising from the Industrial Revolution,
inevitably spread to the Continent, and, as it did so, it brought
in its train consequences which strengthened the tendency to
changes on constitutional lines, for it effected an alliance
between existing governments and the new capitalists who
wanted, above all things, peace and order. Moreover, it gradually tended to intensify the existing sense of nationalism by
prompting a policy of economic protection, since the only way
that a country not yet industrialised could hope to compete
with those whose industrial changes allowed them to sell so
much more cheaply was to raise a tariff wall against the latter's
goods, and thus nurse those industries of which their resources
made them potentially the producers.

But these industrial changes also brought into existence vast
urban agglomerations of wage-earners who, in their turn,
demanded political rights. In England this led first to a work-
ing-class movement known as Chartism (1837–48), whose
purpose was to bring pressure to bear upon the government to
grant, among other things, franchise reform, and, when this
had worked itself out without success, to the two Reform Acts
of 1867 and 1884-5, the general effect of which was to enfranchise lodgers in the towns and agricultural labourers. But in
most countries, before the political machine could be so adjusted
as to grant such rights, revolutionary theories were already
being propounded whose object was to overthrow existing
governments and establish a new form of society. The chief of

these theories was that form of socialism associated with the
name of Karl Marx, whose teaching in his *Communist Manifesto*
(1848) and later writings, struck not only at the constitutional
development of parliamentary institutions but also at the
whole conception of nationality. The question now was, could
national constitutionalism stand sufficiently firm to maintain
successful battle against this revolutionary doctrine? The
history of the second half of the nineteenth century partially
answered this question.

IX. NATIONAL CONSTITUTIONALISM IN THE SECOND HALF OF THE NINETEENTH CENTURY

The second half of the nineteenth century was the heyday of
documentary constitutions. With the exception of those of
Great Britain and the United States, no existing constitution
is older than the nineteenth century, and most of those which
existed in the first half of that century have since either entirely
disappeared to be replaced by new ones or been so fundamentally amended and revised as to be in effect new.

This great surge of constitutionalism originated in the unifying movements in Italy and Germany, which were, in their
turn, largely responsible for the republican constitution promulgated in France after the war of 1870. In Italy, the Sardinian
Constitution, as we have said, was one of only three that
survived the catastrophe of 1848. Italy was still divided
into seven states, but not for long was it to be so. Between the
years 1859 and 1870 by a series of revolts and wars the various
states were amalgamated with Sardinia, and as each came into
the union the constitution of Sardinia was made to apply to
it, thus finally forming the kingdom of Italy. In Germany,
again, after the failure of 1848, the pre-existing system was
revived, but by means of three wars fought between 1864 and
1871, engineered and executed by the genius of Bismarck,
Denmark was defeated and lost the Duchies of Schleswig and
Holstein, Austria was expelled from the German Confederation,
and the Second Empire was overthrown in France. In this way
four new constitutional states emerged. In Denmark, in 1864,
the Crown was forced to accept a parliamentary system; in
Austria and Hungary new constitutions were drawn up in

1869, under a union of the Crowns; in Germany the German Empire was established in 1871; and in France the Third Republic was founded in 1875.

Each of these constitutions adopted parliamentary institutions which were copies, more or less revised, of the British model. Each of them contained democratic elements, but the powers of Parliament were not yet such as to satisfy all the demands of liberal reform. Moreover, nationalism had triumphed only up to a point. Italy had, outside her national boundaries, a body of Italians in Trieste and the Trentino still under Austrian sovereignty; Austria-Hungary, with her many dependents, could by no means be described as a national state. Germany, though much more solidly national than Austria-Hungary, still had a large number of Poles within her borders, and had snatched from France, as part of the price of her victory in 1871, the provinces of Alsace and Lorraine.

In the years that followed these events nationalism became the battle-cry of the Balkan peoples still oppressed under the heel of Turkey. In 1878, as a result of a war between Russia and Turkey and the interest taken by the Powers in the problem at the Congress of Berlin, three new states were established, namely, Serbia, Montenegro and Rumania. Greece had already secured her independence in 1832 and was governed under a constitution finally promulgated in 1864. There remained Bulgaria, only partially freed under the arrangements of the Treaty of Berlin, and Turkey herself. Abdul Hamid II had proclaimed a constitution for the whole Ottoman Empire as early as 1876, but it had been abrogated within two years. In 1908 the Young Turk party successfully revived this Constitution, deposed Abdul Hamid, and made Turkey a constitutional monarchy. Taking advantage of these Turkish disturbances, Bulgaria declared her complete national independence in the same year.

Thus, under the influence of Western Liberalism, the southeast corner of Europe, so long oppressed by the Oriental despotism of the Turks, had by the first decade of the twentieth century adopted at least the forms of political constitutionalism. In each case a new state was established on the basis of nationalism, a principle deliberately adopted as a means of emancipation. In no case, indeed, were national aspirations fully satisfied, and

2•

this fact led to the Balkan Wars of 1912 and 1913. Nevertheless, the whole history of the Balkan Peninsula in the second half of the nineteenth and the opening years of the twentieth century, shows how widespread was the hope that national democracy might prove to be the most satisfactory ground on which to build the progressive constitutional state.

X. CONSTITUTIONALISM AND THE FIRST WORLD WAR

By the eve of the First World War, in 1914, then, the national constitutional experiment was, in some form or another, being tried in every state in Europe, with the exception of Russia where attempts at constitutionalisation had gone no farther than the establishment of a partially elected assembly (the Duma) which, from its inception in 1906, became weaker rather than stronger. Nor was constitutionalism confined to Europe, the United States and the British Self-governing Dominions. It had spread also to many outlying parts of the earth, places as far afield as South America, Japan, and even China. The Europeanisation of the world, through the force of modern imperialism and the economic consequences of the Industrial Revolution, has had its counterpart in the dissemination of the Old World's political creeds and in the wider application of its political practices. And this constitutionalism was always moulded either on the British model or on the modified form of it adopted by the United States. That is to say, it established representative institutions and made the nation the basis of the state. Where a nation could not be said to exist, as in China, the constitutional trend nurtured the growth of nationalism and used it as a political platform.

Yet, far as it had gone in Europe, political constitutionalism had in most cases still farther to go in the matter of representative democracy and nationalism. France still had her lost provinces to recover; Italy her *Italia Irredenta*; Germany held some non-German elements, Danes in the north and Poles in the east; Austria-Hungary was aptly described as the "Ramshackle Empire," containing as it did Germans, Magyars, South Slavs, Bohemians, Poles and Rumanians; Russia, on her western border, was an agglomeration of Finns, Estonians, Letts, Lithuanians, Poles and Rumanians; the part of Turkey

still in Europe was regarded by the Balkan peoples as an outrage upon their nationality. If history proved, as it seemed,
that nationalism was the only firm foundation for constitutional
rights, the sole question was whether the so far unfulfilled
dreams of national unity could be realised by peaceful means
or whether it would require a catastrophe to bring the realisation about. At all events, whether the catastrophe was necessary
or not, it indubitably occurred when war broke out in 1914.
Moreover, there were some states in which, though they
possessed a constitution, the political organisation could not be
called democratic, especially in the lack of popular control
of the executive, which was particularly true of Germany.

It is not surprising, therefore, that a war fought, as Woodrow
Wilson said, to make the world safe for democracy, should have
had, as one of the most marked features of its aftermath, a rich
harvest of constitutionalism. The victors asserted that a lasting
peace could be founded only on the basis of the self-determination of peoples, which meant that the suppressed nationalities,
so far as this was practicable, should establish themselves as
independent bodies politic on a national basis. The application
of this principle involved the partial or complete break-up of
four great Empires—Germany, Austria, Russia, and Turkey—
which the war itself had already largely achieved. Under the
new arrangements Central and East-Central Europe became a
mass of small states where hitherto it had comprehended only
three. The peace treaties created new sovereign states like
Finland, Estonia, Latvia, Lithuania, Poland, and Czechoslovakia; dismembered others like Germany and Austria; and
enlarged yet others like Serbia (called Yugoslavia in its enlarged
form) and Rumania.

A new documentary constitution in each case resulted from
these changes, for in the new states no method of sovereign
government existed and in the old a revolution had taken place
involving the overthrow of the pre-war régime. Personal liberty,
popular sovereignty and nationality were the characteristics
of the constitutions of all these states, and they all, without
exception, adopted the British plan of parliamentary control
of the executive, with variations, though many of them went
farther in the matter of universal suffrage. So far as charters
could achieve it, democracy had certainly triumphed. With a

due regard to the exigencies of strategy and economic stability, nationality may be said to have triumphed also. True, there were non-national minorities as before, notably Austrian Germans in Italy and Magyars in the enlarged Rumania, but not at all to the same extent.

A yet further development of constitutionalism resulted from the First World War in the establishment of the League of Nations. The signing of the Covenant of the League was made inseparable from a signature to the Treaties. Here for the first time in history was an organisation of many states under a definitely constituted body of rules and set of organs. The League was at once empirical and experimental, founded, as far as the parallel could hold, on the constitutional practice of the states forming it, and permitting by its form expansion and amendment as experience might demand and circumstances allow. We call it a constitutional experiment, not because it was an independent body with sovereign powers (for that it certainly was not), but because it attempted to find a means for the peaceful settlement of conflicts between the sovereign bodies which were its members, and was, therefore, in line with that constitutional progress which had up to then been achieved in most Western states.

XI. THE FLIGHT FROM CONSTITUTIONALISM AND THE SECOND WORLD WAR

In the immediate post-war period, then, it seemed that nationalism and representative democracy had joined to achieve an almost universal victory for the rights of man and the Rule of Law, and that the lessons of political constitutionalism were to be at last successfully applied to the solution of the problem of world peace. Unfortunately it was soon to be forcibly demonstrated that political charters of themselves are not enough and that, if the will to make them work is not present among the people for whose benefit they are designed, unconstitutional practices will inevitably be adopted to nullify them. So it was that, in the years following the settlement of the First World War, an authoritarian reaction against democratic constitutionalism occurred in several states in eastern, southern and central Europe.

The Russians were the first to repudiate the political constitutionalism whose growth we have been tracing here. The Russian Revolution of 1917 passed through two phases: first, the political or liberal revolution in March, which destroyed the Tsarist autocracy and established a republican constitution with a parliament (Duma) and Cabinet modelled broadly on the French pattern; and secondly, the social, or Bolshevik, revolution in November, which overthrew the Duma and established the Workers' Republic. In the intervening period of eight months, the Soviets, or Workers' Councils, had existed side by side with the Duma, but before the new parliamentary experiment had time to justify itself, the Bolshevists, led by Lenin, declared Russia to be a Republic of Soviets. This Republic was at first confined to Russia proper, but similar revolutions followed in other parts of the old Russian Empire, both in Europe and in Asia, and in 1923 the various new states federated to form the Union of Soviet Socialist Republics (U.S.S.R.).

In 1918 Lenin had produced a constitution which was prefaced by a "Declaration of the Rights of the Labouring and Exploited Peoples," a phrase which clearly indicates the nature of the Russian breach with Western constitutionalism. As an application of the doctrines of Marx, the new régime in Russia was concerned to establish not the constitutional rule of the majority but the dictatorship of the proletariat, which Stalin, elaborating the original theses of Lenin, later called "substantially the dictatorship of the Communist Party as the force which guides the proletariat," although, as we shall see later, the new Constitution which Stalin was to promulgate in 1936 made some concessions to Western ideas. Moreover, the Revolution created a new social order in which the former owning classes were dispossessed, and all forms of wealth communalised. There were thus in the Soviet system, resulting from the Revolution of 1917, two elements which distinguished it from the constitutional state as we know it. First, a political dictatorship through the dominance of a single party to the exclusion of all others, and, secondly, a totalitarian system which used the political machine to control and direct every aspect of economic, social and religious life.

These features of dictatorship and totalitarianism also characterised Mussolini's régime in Italy and Hitler's Third Reich in Germany, which were established during the succeeding years, though the pre-existing conditions and the consequences of the Russian Revolution were very different from those of the Fascist outbreak and of the Nazi upheaval. For it must be recognised that Lenin and the Bolsheviks completed the destruction of an absolute autocracy and built on its ruins a new social and political order which enfranchised vast masses of the people formerly in a state of abject ignorance and subjection; whereas both the Fascists and the Nazis made a criminal attack on an established parliamentary system and replaced it by a black tyranny which deprived millions of their fellow-countrymen of the rights they had previously enjoyed.

In October, 1922, when the Fascist militia marched on Rome, the King, to avoid civil war, invited Mussolini to form a Cabinet. The Cabinet having been formed, the Chamber of Deputies, to save itself from immediate dissolution, granted Mussolini special powers. From that moment Mussolini, giving himself the high-sounding title of *Duce*, gradually undermined the constitutional system under which Italy had lived for more than half a century. The electoral law was modified so as to produce an artificial Fascist majority in Parliament and soon all other parties were suppressed and the Fascist Grand Council, which reflected the Duce's will, became the only effective organ of government. At the same time, Mussolini abolished all associations, whether social, political or cultural, which did not subscribe to the theory and practice of Fascism. Mussolini thus effectively destroyed the democratic structure and, by a series of measures, which we shall examine later, replaced it by the Corporate State, based on what he called National Syndicalism. In 1939, the Chamber of Deputies, emasculated as it was, finally disappeared and was replaced by an assembly known as the Chamber of Fascios and Corporations. At that moment nothing remained of the Italian Constitution, as it had evolved through nearly a century, from the Sardinian Statuto of 1848, except the Monarchy, which, deprived of all dignity and prestige, continued to exist only because it was satisfied to be tied to the chariot wheels of Fascism.

In Germany, Hitler and the National Socialists came into power in January, 1933. Here again the plot to overthrow the parliamentary system was at first covered with a constitutional cloak. Till then Germany had been governed under the Constitution of the Weimar Republic, founded in 1919, and Hitler accepted the Chancellorship—*i.e.*, the office of Prime Minister—at the hands of the President of the Republic. At no time did Hitler denounce that constitution, but, using the plenary powers granted to him by the *Reichstag*, and approved by the President, rapidly destroyed the foundations of the constitutional state. He forcibly dissolved all other parties but the National Socialists, though even as a purely Nazi assembly the *Reichstag* was reduced to nothing more than an occasional audience for the rhetorical outbursts of the *Führer*. In a decree of less than a hundred words, issued in January, 1934, Hitler demolished at a blow the federalism which had characterised the Reich for a thousand years, and a federal democracy was thus violently transformed into a centralised autocracy under the direct control of the *Führer*. In August of the same year, on the death of President Hindenburg, he announced his intention of assuming in his own person as *Führer* the two offices of President and Chancellor, a move for which, after the event, he received the overwhelming support of the people in a plebiscite. So gradually every constitutional protection secured by the Weimar Republic was torn away and finally the only political sanction that remained was the despot's whim.

Under Hitler's dictatorship all personal and social rights went the way of political safeguards. No individual or family was safe from the interference of the secret police (*Gestapo*) and every adolescent was forcibly enrolled in the Nazi Youth Movement (Hitler *Jugend*). None but Nazi organisations were allowed to exist. The many employers' associations and trade unions were dissolved and replaced by the so-called Labour Front. All independent opinion was suppressed and the Press became the tool of the Nazi Party. To justify the régime, the whole fabric of Hitlerite Germany was bolstered by a pseudo-philosophy of the state which argued that the Nazi Party was synonymous with the German nation and that Western democracy was an outworn creed. But, in truth, Nazism, as one of Hitler's renegade followers said, was nothing more than "a doctrineless nihilism."[1] And heavily indeed were Germany and the world to pay for their acquiescence in its excesses.

[1]Hermann Rauschning: *Germany's Revolution of Destruction*.

The success of the dictatorships in Italy and Germany had a disastrous effect on the political constitutionalism of neighbouring states. And this was especially true of Spain where in 1932, only a year before Hitler's assumption of power, a new constitution had been promulgated. Spain had been governed under the Constitution of 1876 until 1924, when the Constitution was suspended and for the next seven years King Alphonso XIII ruled through a Directory headed at first by General Primo de Rivera (Marqués de Estella) and later by General Berenguer. In 1931, however, municipal elections were held, and resulted in a heavy Republican majority, whereupon a Republican Provisional Government was formed and the King left the country. Elections then took place for a constituent assembly which produced the Republican Constitution of 1932. It was against this constitution that General Franco revolted in 1936 and for three years Spain was a prey to civil war. Covertly assisted by Hitler and Mussolini, Franco finally crushed the Republicans in the spring of 1939 and established his dictatorship.

In almost every continental state there were cells of Nazi propaganda, and it was only with the greatest difficulty that, in the few years of a precarious peace which remained, such states as Belgium and the Netherlands, Denmark and Czechoslovakia maintained their parliamentary institutions. Most of the others succumbed to Hitler's force or cajolery and allowed their constitutional safeguards to be whittled away by some form or other of dictatorship. Then Hitler began his series of open aggressions which in 1939 brought the Western democracies, awakened at last to the futility and danger of further appeasement, in arms against him, and the Second World War began.

The effect on political constitutionalism of the Second World War is much more complex and menacing than was that of the first. For the victory of the United Nations over the forces of tyranny and aggression has left three political creeds, each with its claim on the allegiance of the peoples. First, there is the traditional democracy of the West, championed mainly by the British and American Commonwealths, but gravely weakened in its prestige and appeal by the sufferings of the nations of Western Europe in the war and its aftermath. Secondly, there is the triumphant Soviet democracy of Russia, bestriding like a Colossus the whole of Eastern Europe and a large part of Asia, and profoundly influencing the political institutions of neighbouring communities in both regions. Thirdly, there are the discredited doctrines of Fascism and Nazism consumed by the fires of war but threatening to rise from their ashes with a claim to be the only power capable of lifting the people, crushed between the forces of what they call Pluto-Democracy, on the one hand, and Communism, on the other, out of their post-war malaise. In this situation political constitutionalism must show itself capable of survival, for without it there is no hope for the preservation of Western civilisation, of which the constitutional state is one of the corner stones.

And this is equally true of constitutionalism in the contact of one state with another. The attempt to apply constitutional methods to international relations after the First World War through the Covenant of the League of Nations failed to prevent a second total war. The end of the Second World War offered the nations a second chance to preserve world peace through the Charter of the United Nations Organisation. If the failure of the League proved costly, a like failure of the United Nations would be positively fatal, for civilised society would surely not survive a third holocaust under the conditions of the Atomic Age which it now confronts.

XII. SUMMARY

What, then, emerges from this historical sketch? First, that constitutional politics cannot possibly be understood without reference to their history. Every epoch that we have touched has supplied its quota to the existing whole. Greek constitutionalism gave political philosophy its inspiration and, during the Revival of Learning in the fifteenth century, opened men's minds to the finer purposes of political organisation. Roman constitutionalism gave the Western World the reality of Law and the ideal of Unity. Feudalism bridged the gulf between the chaos following the fall of the Roman Empire in the West and the emergence of the modern state. The progress of centralisation through the Crown in England, France and Spain during the Middle Ages was necessary to destroy the evils of feudalism and to lay the foundations of a national policy; while the growth of partially representative institutions in those countries marked in Western Europe the first faint beginnings of the democratic state. At the same time, the Conciliar Movement of the fifteenth century emphasised the nascent national divisions of Europe and inaugurated a wide discussion of representative methods of government.

The Renaissance carried forward the centralising process in the west of Europe and planted yet more securely the seed of nationalism there. The Reformation produced the ideal of religious toleration and at the same time enhanced the powers of the Prince through the development of a State Church, thus turning a religious discontent into a political revolt by causing men to believe that the way to religious liberty lay through political organisation. English constitutionalism supplied a continuity of life to liberal institutions through many centuries when elsewhere they were dead or had never lived, permitted the growth of its own institutions among those communities in all parts of the world of which England herself was the mother, and supplied the pattern of a constitution when the moment came for any newly-liberated community to found one. The iconoclastic theories of the eighteenth century laid the foundations of the modern doctrine of democracy. The American and the French Revolutions gave the modern world the first examples of documentary constitutions, thus finding an immediate way of reconciling liberty and authority, the rights of man, and established government. America, moreover, through the expedient of federalism, gave the world a lesson in political union which should not outrage local feeling, while the French Revolution, though itself overwhelmed, bequeathed to the nineteenth century the ideals of liberty, equality and fraternity, to be established upon a foundation more permanent than its original sponsors had been able to find. The Napoleonic conquest disseminated the ideals of the Revolution and, at the same time, brought to active life the dormant spirit of nationalism among the peoples whom Bonaparte conquered.

The nineteenth century saw the ideals of liberal reform and nationalism struggling for recognition, and their partial realisation in political forms. The Industrial Revolution enfranchised the middle class and built the ramparts of modern democracy by producing a new class of workers which more and more demanded an enjoyment of political rights. It also intensified both nationalism and constitutional reform, first by fostering the policy of economic protection and then by extensions of the franchise and the organisation of national parties. The First World War gave a tremendous incentive to constitutionalism by destroying the illiberal governments, by creating new states out of hitherto oppressed nationalities, by driving both these, thereby, to establish constitutions on the basis of nationalism and democracy, and finally by creating the will to international peace on constitutional lines through the establishment of the League of Nations. But in the succeeding years there was a violent reaction against political constitutionalism, and the Russian Revolution of 1917 was followed by the Fascist outbreak in Italy, the Nazi upheaval in Germany, and the victory of Franco over the Republicans in Spain, while the nations of Eastern Europe generally tended, under Nazi and Fascist influences, to sacrifice the constitutional safeguards they had so recently won. The dictatorships and totalitarian systems thus established led inevitably to external aggression which culminated in 1939 in the outbreak of the Second World War. The war left a complex and menacing situation for the national democratic constitutionalism of the West, which had to face the competing claims of Soviet Democracy, then dominating Eastern Europe and a large part of Asia, and the danger of a resurgent Nazism among the defeated nations. But the end of the war presented the nations with a second chance to apply constitutional methods to international relations through the Charter of the United Nations Organisation for the permanent establishment of world peace in the Atomic Age.

The second fact that should emerge from this sketch is that national democratic constitutionalism, ancient though its origins may be, is still in an experimental stage and that if it is to survive in competition with more revolutionary types of government, we must be prepared constantly to adapt it to the ever-changing conditions of modern society. The basic purpose of a political constitution is, after all, the same wherever it appears: the securing of social peace and progress, the safeguarding of individual rights, and the achievement of national well-being, and what we have to study here are the various

52   *Modern Political Constitutions*

means adopted to attain those ends. This involves a comparative survey of modern political constitutions and an examination of their likenesses and differences, which we shall now undertake.

READING

BARKER: *Essays on Government. Essay*, vii.
BRYCE: *History and Jurisprudence*, Vol. I, Essays i–iv. *Modern Democracies,* Vol. I, Ch. xvi.
BURNS: *Political Ideals*, Chs. ii, iii, v–viii, xi–xiii.
DICEY: *Law and Opinion*. Introduction and Lecture xii.
DICKINSON: *Greek View of Life*, Chs. ii and iii.
DUNNING: *History of Political Theories*, Vol. I, pp. 1–16, 106–113, Chs. v, ix–xi; Vol. II, pp. 1–7, 305–9, 335–340, Ch. vi; Vol. III, pp. 38–50, 166–184, 340–7, 371–6, 395–407, Chs. iii and vi–viii.
FINER: *Future of Government*, Chs. i, ii, iii.
GETTELL: *Readings in Political Science*, pp. 113–122, 167–9, 201–3.
HAYES: *History of Modern Europe*, Vol. II, Chs. xvii–xxx.
JENKS: *State and Nation*, Ch. x.
LASKI: *Grammar of Politics*, Pt. I, Ch. vi.
MACIVER: *Modern State*, Chs. i–iv.
MAITLAND: *Constitutional History of England*, pp. 165–329.
WILSON: *State*, pp. 9–11, Chs. vi, xxi–xxii.

BOOKS FOR FURTHER STUDY

BOWMAN: *The New World.*
BRYCE: *Holy Roman Empire.*
BUSSELL: *Roman Empire.*
COBBAN: *National Self-Determination.*
DUVERGER: *Political Parties.*
FOWLER: *City States of Greeks and Romans.*
FREEMAN: *Comparative Politics.*
FUSTEL DE COULANGES: *The Ancient City.*
GLOVER: *Ancient World.*
HAWGOOD: *Modern Constitutions since 1787.*
HAYES: *Essays on Nationalism.*
JENKS: *Law and Politics in the Middle Ages.*
KEIR: *Constitutional History of Britain.*
LICHTENBERGER: *Third Reich.*
MAITLAND: *Political Theories of the Middle Ages.*
MOORE: *The Roman Commonwealth.*
MUIR: (1) *Expansion of Europe.* (2) *National Self-Government.*
MURRAY: (1) *Political Consequences of the Reformation.* (2) *History of Political Science from Plato to To-day.*
OSTROGORSKI: *Democracy and the Organisation of Political Parties.*
POLLARD: (1) *Factors in American History.* (2) *Factors in Modern History.*
RITCHIE: (1) *Natural Rights.* (2) *Principles of State Interference.*
ROSE: *Nationality as a Factor in Modern History.*
SABINE: *History of Political Theory.*
SALVEMINI: *Fascist Dictatorship.*
SMITH: *Church and State in the Middle Ages.*
STRONG: *Dynamic Europe.*
WHEARE: *Modern Constitutions.*
ZIMMERN: *The Greek Commonwealth.*

SUBJECTS FOR ESSAYS

1. Account for the attachment of the Greeks to the idea of the City-State.

2. In what sense was the Roman Empire a world-state?

3. Discuss Feudalism as a transition between the fall of the Roman Empire in the West and the emergence of the modern state.

4. Show what constitutional progress had been made in Western Europe before the Renaissance, and give some account of the latter in its political aspects.

5. What were the political consequences of the Reformation?

6. Criticise the theory of the Social Contract as an explanation of the origin of the state.

7. Explain the importance of the American War of Independence and of the French Revolution in the history of constitutionalism.

8. Discuss the political aspects of the Industrial Revolution.

9. What effect had the First World War on constitutional development in Europe?

10. Describe the constitutional situation in Europe following the Second World War.

PART II

COMPARATIVE CONSTITUTIONAL POLITICS

CHAPTER III

CLASSIFICATION OF CONSTITUTIONS

I. THE OBSOLETE CLASSIFICATION OF ARISTOTLE AND OTHERS

A CLASSIFICATION of political constitutions or of states has often been undertaken in the past, but not in a way very satisfactory to the modern student. Among the earliest attempts to make such a classification we may note that of Aristotle who went much more fully into this matter than his master, Plato, who is very confusing on the subject, because he adopted one basis of classification in *The Republic* and quite a different one in another of his books, called *Politicus* or *The Statesman*. As to Aristotle, he first divided constitutions into two great classes, namely, good and bad, or true and perverted. His criterion here was the spirit informing the government. In each of the two great classes he found three types according to whether the government was in the hands of one, or few, or many.

Aristotle thought this classification exhaustive and exclusive because, having carried out a thorough investigation into no less than 158 constitutions, Greek and Barbarian, existing in his day (the treatise containing the details of this investigation is unfortunately lost), he came to the conclusion that all states went through a cycle of revolutions. Thus a state began with the finest possible type of government—the rule of one man who, from the point of view of political authority, was the supremely virtuous one. This was the Monarchy or Royalty. But after a time such a virtuous man could no longer be produced; yet the rule of one remained, and his power was maintained by force. This type of government Aristotle called the Tyranny or Despotism. But the tyrant would one day meet the opposition of a body of upright men who would overthrow him and rule in his stead. This was Aristocracy. Here, again, however, the spirit of the aristocracy would after a time begin to degenerate, and, though the rule of the Few would continue, it would cease

57

to stand on the basis of political virtue and maintain itself by
the use of force or corruption. This corrupt form of aristocracy
Aristotle called Oligarchy. Finally, against this hateful rule
there breaks out a popular uprising, and the Oligarchy is superseded by the Rule of the Many, or Democracy. In Aristotle's
view, democracy so easily becomes licence and anarchy that
he, like Plato, sees it as degenerate by nature; the rule of the
many cannot help being the rule of the mob (or, as he said, of
the poor), which is the very negation of rule. Out of the darkness, then, again arises the supremely virtuous man, some
Cæsar who alone can restore order and reason. The cycle is
completed and begins all over again.

Aristotle's problem was to discover a form of government
sufficiently stable to break this cycle, and he thought he had
found it in that type of middle-class government which he called
the Polity. It was his "golden mean" between the ideals of
Monarchy and Aristocracy, so difficult to attain and sustain,
and the perversions of Tyranny, Oligarchy, and Democracy,
which were undesirable. So essential to stability in government
did Aristotle consider the rule of the middle-class to be that the
term he used to describe it—the Polity—has now come to have
a general application.

Aristotle's classification of constitutions may be summarised
in tabular form as follows:

Type of Constitution	Good or true form	Bad or perverted form
Government of One	Monarchy or Royalty	Tyranny or Despotism
Government of the Few	Aristocracy	Oligarchy
Government of the Many	Polity	Democracy

It cannot be denied that we have much to learn from this
part of Aristotle's teaching. For example, he pointed out with
great emphasis that, since the object of all the citizens of a state
must necessarily be the safety of their association, everything
must be sacrificed to the maintenance of the constitution which
is the basis of that safety, and that any action on the part of
any citizen outside the bounds of the constitution (whether an
unconstitutional act carried out by the government of the day,

on the one hand, or what we have come to call "direct action" attempted by non-political associations, on the other) should not for a moment be tolerated—an argument which has even greater force in a modern democracy than it had in Aristotle's ancient polity. Again, it would be difficult to dispute the fact that the history of the world since his time has supplied many illustrations of a cycle of deteriorations and revolutions after the manner of Aristotle's analysis.

Nevertheless, we have to abandon Aristotle's classification of constitutions, since it is quite inapplicable to existing political conditions. It is no longer useful, for example, to employ the term Monarchy to describe a modern state, because it tells us nothing distinctive about it. Again, the term Democracy applies to so many modern states that it no longer helps us to a division of them. Nor are the classifications of some political philosophers more recent than Aristotle helpful in modern conditions. Montesquieu, for instance, in the middle of the eighteenth century, divided governments into three classes—republican, monarchical and despotic. Rousseau, again, a few years later, classified the forms of government into three—autocratic, aristocratic and democratic—but he held that there was only one form of state, namely, the Republic. Kant, a little later, saw three kinds of states corresponding to Rousseau's three forms of government, but only two forms of government— republican and despotic. But the term Republic in the modern world helps us no more than the term Monarchy to understand the form of the state to which we are referring. Take, for example, three existing republics—the United States of America, Switzerland and France—and three existing monarchies— Great Britain, Norway and The Netherlands. It is obviously fallacious to make this a basis of division and to say that the United States, Switzerland and France belong to one distinctive type of states, and Britain, Norway and The Netherlands to another. To do so would be to make ourselves the mere slaves of nomenclature. Coming to our own epoch, we find the modern German writer, Bluntschli, attempting to extend Aristotle's triple division by adding to it a fourth type of state which he called Ideocracy or Theocracy, in which the supreme ruler is conceived to be God or some super-human spirit or idea, as is seen, for example, in the original Jewish state and in Mohammedan countries. But this division carries us no farther in our endeavour to classify states according to real and existing likenesses and differences. We must clearly seek our ground elsewhere.

II. THE BASES OF A MODERN CLASSIFICATION

The truth is, it is impossible to divide states into classes by taking each state as a whole in turn, because the totality of powers of all states is the same; that is to say, every state is a sovereign body politic. If a community is not this, it is not a state. As an American writer, Willoughby, puts it, "the only manner in which states may be differentiated is according to the structural peculiarities of their governmental organisation." As soon as we begin to think about this in the light of that evolution of modern constitutionalism which we have sketched in the preceding chapter, a living classification begins to shape itself. We saw how all the communities of the Western World have been affected to a greater or less degree by the same influences, and likenesses among them are therefore bound to manifest themselves. On the other hand, nationalism has proved such a potent force for separatism that differences among them are equally strongly marked. In making our classification, therefore, we must find those attributes which are common to all modern constitutional states and divide the states according to the peculiarities of their organisation. In other words, we must examine each of the attributes in turn and divide our states into classes according to whether they conform to this or that variation of the attribute in question.

What those common attributes are we have already indicated in the opening chapter, where we saw that the government of every constitutional state has three separate departments, namely, the legislature, the executive and the judiciary. The basis of our classification must be found, therefore, under the five following heads: (1) the nature of the state to which the constitution applies; (2) the nature of the constitution itself; (3) the nature of the legislature; (4) the nature of the executive; (5) the nature of the judiciary.

The disadvantage of this classification is that it involves the necessity of dealing with each state several times, each time in respect of one attribute, for it by no means follows that because State A resembles State B in respect of the first attribute, it resembles it in respect of the second, or because State C differs from State D in respect of the third attribute, it differs from it in respect of the fourth. Indeed, it is this very truth which makes this sort of classification the only one in keeping with existing conditions, and that is an advantage which must be considered to override any disadvantages this method of classification may possess.

This classification, whose details we shall now examine, is based upon various suggestions made by three modern English political scientists, Lord Bryce, Edward Jenks and Sir J. A. R. Marriott, none of whom, however, worked them out according to the scheme adopted here. Our classification does not pretend to be exhaustive, because much of the subject-matter of comparative constitutional politics defies classification. But it does adequately cover sufficient ground to introduce the student to the subject. Some important matters which remain outside the scope of this classification will be dealt with in the third part of this book. Meanwhile, let us look more closely into our classification.

III. THE NATURE OF THE STATE TO WHICH THE CONSTITUTION APPLIES

Whether Unitary or Federal

Every modern constitutional state belongs to one of two great classes—unitary or federal—and this introduces a difference of the very first importance. A unitary state is one organised under a single central government; that is to say, whatever powers are possessed by the various districts within the area administered as a whole by the central government, are held at the discretion of that government, and the central power is supreme over the whole without any restrictions imposed by any law granting special powers to its parts. "Unitarianism" in the political sense has been well defined by the late Professor Dicey as "the habitual exercise of supreme legislative authority by one central power." Examples of unitary states are the United Kingdom, France and Belgium. In each of these cases there is no question of any limitation being placed upon the power of the central authority by any law-making body belonging to any smaller part of the state. Where, as in the case of the United Kingdom, local government is strong, there is still no restriction upon the central power, which can override the Local Authorities; for since, in modern times, the central authority has granted whatever powers are possessed by them, it can equally modify or withdraw those powers. Local Authorities in Britain are, in fact, not law-making but by-law-making bodies.

A federal state is one in which a number of co-ordinate states unite for certain common purposes. To quote again Professor Dicey, "a federal state is a political contrivance intended to reconcile national unity and power with the maintenance of 'state rights'." We have to distinguish clearly between local government in a unitary state and state government within a federal state. In a federal state the powers of the central or federal authority are limited by certain powers secured to the units which have united for common purposes. We note, therefore, in a federal state a distinction of powers between the federal authority and the authorities of the units forming the federation. This being the case, there must be some authority which determines this distribution. This authority is the Constitution itself. A federal constitution partakes of the character of a treaty. It is an arrangement made between certain bodies politic which wish to retain certain rights. Thus the constitution will state either the rights that are to be retained by the federating units or the rights that the federal authority takes over. In either case it stands to reason that neither the ordinary legislatures of the individual states nor the legislature of the union can have the power to alter the constitution without some special means being adopted for discovering the views of the constituent members. These means will in a true federal state be definitely stated in the constitution. There must further be some sort of authority to decide between the federal power and the state power if they should happen to come into conflict. This authority is generally a supreme court of judges.

Thus, completely developed federalism shows three clearly marked characteristics: first, the supremacy of the constitution, by means of which the federation is established; secondly, the distribution of powers between the federal state and the co-ordinate states forming it; and thirdly, some supreme authority to settle any dispute which may arise between the federal and state authorities. Not all states which we call federal states are exactly like this. Federalism is, in fact, of varying shades of completeness and exactitude. Those that do not exactly conform to the type of completely federalised state we may call quasi-federal states. These differences we shall examine more closely in a later chapter. Here we may note among existing federal states, the United States of America, Switzerland, Australia, Canada, and the U.S.S.R. Though these federations vary very much in detail, they all conform to the basic rule of a federal state, that each is constituted from a number of minor states which desire union but do not desire unity.

It will have been observed that, although we have spoken of a federal state, we have referred to the federating units themselves also as states. This is due solely to the paucity of language. As soon as a number of states have federated they become constituent parts of a federal state, and thereby cease to be states themselves in the full sense, for they have sacrificed some part of that essential quality of a state which we have emphasised earlier; namely, sovereignty. Thus the forty-eight states of the American Commonwealth are not true states. The union of the forty-eight states is the real state. Yet the states retain a wide legislative power, their legislatures being what we may describe as semi-sovereign law-making bodies. Again, none of the six states of the Australian Commonwealth is a real state. The Commonwealth is the state, and it is a state in spite of the fact that it is a part of the British Commonwealth of Nations, which has no federal element in its composition. We shall have a good deal more to say about this in a later chapter.

From all that has been said, it is clear that we have here a very sound basis for the classification of modern constitutional states. For, although, as we shall show, there are various kinds of unitary states and different kinds of federal states, no constitutional state of to-day can be entirely outside these two categories.

We might have added here a subsidiary basis of classification under this same head; namely, whether the state is centralised or localised; that is to say, whether there is a strong element of local government within the state or not. Great Britain, for example, is a localised state because local government plays a large part in the political life of the community. France, on the other hand, is a highly centralised state in which very little responsibility is thrown upon local authorities, and even when it is, it is jealousy watched and limited by an emissary of the central government known as the Prefect. But this question, although in many ways of great importance, must not detain us, since it would lead us too far from our main subject. We mention it here in order to emphasise the difference between local government and state government (within a federation), a difference clearly illustrated in the fact that, while France, a unitary state, is sluggish in local government, each of the states forming the United States, a federal state, has a very active local government of which it is extremely proud and jealous.

IV. THE NATURE OF THE CONSTITUTION ITSELF

(a) *Whether Unwritten or Written a False Distinction*

Constitutions are frequently divided into unwritten and written. But this is really a false distinction, because there is no constitution which is entirely unwritten and no constitution entirely written. A constitution generally called written is one in the form of a document which has special sanctity. A constitution generally called unwritten is one which has grown up on the basis of custom rather than of written law. But sometimes the so-called written constitution is a very complete instrument in which the framers of the constitution have attempted to arrange for every conceivable contingency in its operation. In other cases, the written constitution is found in a number of fundamental laws which the constitution-makers have either framed or adopted with a view to giving as wide a scope as possible to the process of ordinary legislation for the development of the constitution within the framework thus set.

The Constitution of Great Britain is said to be unwritten, but there are certain written laws or statutes which have very considerably modified the Constitution. For example, the Bill of Rights (1689) is a law of the Constitution as also are the various Franchise Acts of the nineteenth and twentieth centuries, and especially the Parliament Acts of 1911 and 1949, which curtailed the power of the Lords to amend or reject bills already passed by the Commons. On the other hand, the Constitution of the United States is the most completely written of all constitutions; yet certain unwritten conventions or customs have grown up in the very teeth of the will of the Fathers of the Constitution, without any verbal alteration, in this connection, in the Constitution itself. Note, for example, Article II, Section I, of the Constitution (together with the Twelfth Amendment), which says that for the election of the President, the people shall choose electors who shall meet and elect, by a majority, whomsoever they will. But this, as we shall show later, does not in practice happen at all.

We repeat, then, that a classification of constitutions on the basis of whether they are unwritten or written is illusory. It is, of course, sometimes necessary to distinguish between the so-called written and the so-called unwritten constitution, and, whenever we need to do so, we shall refer to the former as a documentary and to the latter as a non-documentary constitution.

(b) Whether Flexible or Rigid

The true ground of division, by virtue of the nature of the constitution itself, is whether it is flexible or rigid. It is a frequently-held but erroneous impression that this is the same as saying non-documentary or documentary. Now, while it is true that a non-documentary constitution cannot be other than flexible, it is quite possible for a documentary constitution not to be rigid. What, then, is it that makes a constitution flexible or rigid? The whole ground of difference here is whether the process of constitutional law-making is or is not identical with the process of ordinary law-making. The constitution which can be altered or amended without any special machinery is a flexible constitution. The constitution which requires special procedure for its alteration or amendment is a rigid constitution.

In the case of Great Britain, for example, exactly the same legislative procedure is followed whether the bill to be passed concerns, say, the placing of restrictions upon the methods of the trainers of performing animals or a radical alteration in the powers of the House of Lords. In the United Kingdom, in fact, there is no such thing as a distinctive constitutional law. The Constitution of the United Kingdom is, therefore, flexible. The

3

same was true of the former kingdom of Italy. Though Italy under the monarchy had a documentary constitution, no special procedure for altering it was laid down in the constitution. In fact, that constitution was the original Sardinian Constitution (*Statuto*) of 1848 adapted, by normal legislative procedure, to meet the requirements of an expanding state and a more progressive political society. So flexible was it, indeed, that Mussolini, in the earlier years of his dictatorship, was able profoundly to violate the spirit of the constitution without having to denounce it. All that is now changed in Italy, for the Republican Constitution of 1947, which we shall examine in detail later, is extremely rigid, containing as it does the most elaborate directions as to the ways in which it may be amended.

So we reach this rather curious paradox: that, although a constitution may be much written—that is to say, although it may consist of a large bundle of isolated statutes—it may still be flexible. Indeed, the very fact that it does consist of a large number of laws passed at various times will argue its flexibility, because, where special machinery has to be set in motion for constitutional amendment, the amendments are not likely to be so numerous. In further emphasis of the paradox, we may note that the Constitution of the Third French Republic, though a very slightly written instrument, was, none the less, rigid, simply because it required a special procedure to change its fundamental laws. The Constitution of the Fourth French Republic, promulgated in 1946, is equally, if not indeed even more, rigid, though it differs from that of the Third Republic in respect of its form, since it is a complete and comprehensive document. In the United States, again, the Constitution is rigid because it cannot be amended without special machinery being set in motion for the purpose. Indeed, in this case it is necessarily so, because the Constitution definitely states what powers the Federal Government possesses, and if the latter goes beyond these, it is not bending but breaking the Constitution. In short, then, we may say that the constitution which cannot be bent without being broken is a rigid constitution.

V. THE NATURE OF THE LEGISLATURE

The most important piece of machinery in the modern constitutional state is the legislature, or law-making body. Several ways of classifying states on this ground suggest themselves, but most of them are not very fruitful. For example, a division of modern legislatures into those made up of one House and those having two Chambers is not very real because it would put all the important states in one category, and all the less important states, as, for example, Finland and Turkey, in the other.[1] Again, to attempt to classify legislatures by methods of parliamentary procedure would not carry us far in our survey. What is far more vital is to observe the ways in which legislatures, and both the Lower and Upper Houses of the important ones, are brought into being, for this is where the citizen's contact comes. In this connection, modern legislatures are divisible into two types by virtue of two classes of facts. First, we may divide them on the ground of the nature of the electoral system by which members of the Lower House are chosen. Under this heading come the two questions of franchise and constituency. Secondly, we may divide them on the ground of the nature of the Second Chamber or Upper House.

(a) *As to the Electoral System*

(i) *Kind of Franchise.*—First, with regard to the electoral system, constitutional states fall broadly into two sorts, namely those which have manhood suffrage and those which have adult suffrage. By manhood suffrage is meant the possession of the right to vote by all males above a certain age without qualification, apart from the usual disfranchisement of paupers, criminals and lunatics. By adult suffrage is meant the same right enjoyed by both males and females.

In this division we have not gone quite far enough because some states with manhood suffrage may have some sort of qualification for voting for the Lower House, as, for example, in Japan before the Second World War, where the test was to write the name of the candidate on the voting-paper, which seems, looking at Japanese names with occidental eyes, a very formidable test; while, in some others, female suffrage may be less complete than male suffrage, which was the case in

---

[1] To the list of uni-cameral legislatures must now be added that of New Zealand, where the Upper House (the Legislative Council) was abolished on 1st January, 1951.

Britain from 1918 to 1928. We shall observe these details more closely later on. Here suffice it to note the four main kinds of suffrage in the modern constitutional state—*viz.*, manhood suffrage, qualified manhood suffrage, adult suffrage, and qualified adult suffrage.

(ii) *Kind of Constituency.*—The nature of the constituency provides a further basis of distinction, from the point of view of the electoral system, among existing constitutional states. This distinction is between those states in which the constituency returns one (or at most, two) and those in which it returns several members. The latter is generally associated with that innovation of democracy known as Proportional Representation, the object of which is to secure the representation of minorities which are otherwise voiceless in the elected assembly. But the multi-member constituency, as we may call it, does not necessarily involve the principle of Proportional Representation. In France, for example, the constituency was, between 1919 and 1927, merely a collection of adjacent and formerly separate constituencies. Whereas the French, before 1919, voted by *arrondissements*, after that for eight years they voted by *départements* (a system known as *scrutin de liste*). France has, in fact, since the establishment of the Third Republic, tried both methods by turns. In the last years of the Third Republic it reverted to the single-member constituency, only to revive a form of group-voting for the election of the Provisional Assembly, which drafted the Constitution of the Fourth Republic, and for the next General Election in 1951 introduced a highly complex system of party alliances, or *apparentements*. This method of enlarging the constituency was carried to an extreme in Italy under the dictatorship of Mussolini who transformed the whole country into one vast electoral college.

We shall deal with this question more fully in a later chapter. Here it is only necessary to observe that this question helps us to divide modern constitutional states into two great types. In some states, however, the single-member constituency is used for elections to the Lower House, and the multi-member one for those to the Upper. This, for instance, is the case in the Commonwealth of Australia. It is interesting for British voters to speculate on the possible advantages of a rearrangement of constituencies in this sense in the democracy of the future.

(b) Types of Second Chamber

The division as to types of Second Chamber forms the ground for a very interesting comparative study in modern constitutionalism. The main divisions under this head are two: the Second Chamber is either elective or non-elective. Lying between these two, however, there is a considerable indeterminate area filled by one or two well-known examples in which the Second Chamber is partly elective and partly non-elective, as it was in pre-Republican Spain, and in Japan until her defeat in the Second World War, and as it is in the Union of South Africa and in the Kingdom of Egypt. Still, the division forms a good method of approach to the study of the problem of the Second Chamber, to which we shall devote a chapter later.

Among the best known of the elected Upper Houses are the Senate in the United States, Australia, Eire, and Italy,[1] the Council of the Republic in France,[2] and the Council of States (*i.e.*, Cantons) in Switzerland. The most noteworthy instances of non-elective Second Chambers are the House of Lords in Great Britain and the Senate in Canada. Generally speaking, where the Second Chamber is elected, it is, as might be expected, a much greater force than where it is not. Thus, for example, whereas the Senate in the United States is much the more influential of the two Houses of Congress, in Great Britain the House of Lords has become almost powerless to affect the course of legislation.

VI. THE NATURE OF THE EXECUTIVE

Whether Parliamentary or Non-Parliamentary

Our fourth line of division concerns the nature of the executive. It is, as we have said earlier, the business of the executive to formulate policy and to execute or administer that policy when it has gained the sanction of law through the legislature. In all constitutional states there is a check or limitation upon the power of the executive. The executive, that is to say, is always responsible to somebody. There is an ultimate sense, of course, in which it is true to say that the executive, under

---

[1] *i.e.*, under the Constitution of the Republic (1947).
[2] *i.e.*, under the Constitution of the Fourth Republic (1946), the Council of the Republic having replaced the Senate of the Third Republic.

modern conditions, is always responsible to the people, but this, being universally true, will not help us in our classification. The question we wish rather to answer here is: where does the immediate responsibility lie? The answer to this question gives us a basis for dividing constitutional states into two great classes, for, in practice, the executive is either responsible to Parliament (*i.e.*, the legislature), which has the power to remove it should it lose the confidence of that body, or it is subject to some more remote check, as, for example, by means of a periodical presidential election. If it is immediately responsible to Parliament, it is said to be a Parliamentary Executive. But if it is immediately responsible at definitely arranged periods to some wider body and is not subject to removal by parliamentary action, it is said to be a Non-Parliamentary or a Fixed Executive.

This difference introduces one of the most important considerations in modern constitutional politics. It is here especially that we see the obsoleteness of a division based upon such terms as Monarchy and Republic. Taking as examples Great Britain and France, we should hereby be misled into supposing that the executive in the first case is the Queen; in the second, the President. Now neither of these things is true. On the contrary, the executive in both cases is the Cabinet, the Queen and the President being, politically considered, powerless against the decisions of their ministers. The last king of England who tried actually to interfere in the work of the executive was George III (1760–1820), and he quite failed to achieve his purpose. The last president in France who tried to interfere in the work of the executive was M. Millerand, and for so doing he was forced to resign.[1]

It is clear, therefore, that all states in which the executive is responsible to the elected assembly belong to a distinct category. This type of government is alternately known as Cabinet Government, since the executive in all such cases has been modelled more or less upon the type of ministry which was already emerging in England in the eighteenth century; or Responsible Government, a term most commonly confined to the Self-governing Dominions of the British Commonwealth,

[1]This is still true in the Fourth Republic, for, in spite of efforts to give the President real executive functions, the Constitution of 1946 left him with only nominal powers. This was one of the points at issue in the crisis of 1958.

where the establishment of Cabinet Government has been associated with the transference of ministerial responsibility from the British Government to the elected assembly in each of the Dominions.

The only considerable democratic state to-day where the executive is non-parliamentary or fixed is the American Commonwealth.[1] It was also fixed in the old German Empire, though in a quite different manner from America. In Imperial Germany the Emperor himself was the Executive in a very real sense, as he worked through an Imperial Chancellor whom he could appoint and dismiss at will, as was demonstrated, for example, in the famous "dropping the pilot" episode in 1890 when the Kaiser, Wilhelm II, removed Bismarck. But this is, of course, long past in Germany. Under the constitution of the Weimar Republic (1919) the executive was of the parliamentary type, and it is interesting to recall that the occasion of that great reform in Germany was President Wilson's demand for an assurance that, in his peace parleys with Germany in 1918, he was addressing a democratic government. Under Hitler's Dictatorship obviously the executive was not parliamentary, but that régime did not, in any case, belong to constitutional politics. And the same was true of the Fascist régime in Italy. The executive in the Turkish Republic is also to some extent fixed, but this is a peculiar case where the President holds a unique position, explained by the strange background of the revolution which created it.

In the United States the President and his Ministers form the executive, but far from the Ministers being subject to the will of Congress (Parliament), they are not allowed to speak or vote in either the House of Representatives or the Senate. The only personal contact between the Executive and the Legislature in this case lies through the President's message to Congress which is delivered once a year (or oftener, if unusual circumstances demand that he shall meet it in special session). The check upon the executive in this case lies in the election of the President which takes place every four years. But the President, once elected, may select or dismiss his ministers, subject to the approval of the Senate, and nothing can remove the President during the fixed term of his office, except actual misconduct for

[1]The executive system in Soviet Russia is outside this classification.

which he can be impeached—*i.e.*, tried by Congress—and at the end of his term, whether he stays or goes depends solely on the will of the people, as expressed in the election. Because the type of executive which we have called non-parliamentary or fixed is thus intimately associated with the American presidency, it is otherwise known as Presidential Government, in contradistinction to Cabinet Government.

VII. THE NATURE OF THE JUDICIARY

Whether subject to Rule of Law or under Administrative Law

Our last basis of classification concerns the third of the three great departments of government, the judiciary, and a consideration of it arises out of the subject which we have just been treating. As in the case of the legislature, there are several possible ways of classsifying judiciaries in constitutional states, but most of them would invade territory we have already occupied and shall later exploit. For example, we might divide them into those which can question and interpret the acts of the legislature, as in the United States, and those which are bound to apply such acts without question, as in the United Kingdom. But this is a distinction which we shall amplify in our more detailed discussions of the nature of the State and of the Constitution. The really vital distinction for us here is one that concerns the connection of the judiciary with the executive.

In most Continental states there is a special system of law to protect the servants of the state in the discharge of their official duties, if they should thereby be guilty of acts which, committed by unofficial persons, would be unlawful. This system was born in France, where it goes by the name of *Droit Administratif*. Most Continental states, which have been satisfied in other respects to model their executive systems upon the British pattern, have, in adopting an administrative law, departed utterly from the Anglo-Saxon spirit. For in Britain and those communities which have sprung directly from her, and have carried with them her legal, if not always her constitutional, system, a special system of administrative law for the protection of government officials is quite unknown. In the United Kingdom, in the Self-governing Dominions and Colonial Empire, in the United States, and in the Latin American Republics (mostly modelled upon the United States), the official is in precisely the same legal position as the private citizen, and the judiciary cannot take cognisance of the plea of state necessity in extenuation of acts on the part of state officials calculated to infringe the liberty of the subject. This non-immunity of the official is known as the Rule of Law.

The distinction here lies in the difference of legal systems. It is the Common Law of England, so different in its origins and growth from the legal codes of Continental states, that is the foundation of this Rule of Law, which leaves the government official thus unprotected; while on the Continent the more formal methods of legal codification have known how to protect the servant of the state by special administrative courts (acting outside the legal code) which give him a prerogative before the law over the private citizen.

We may summarise this distinction, then, by dividing states into two types, thus: (1) Common Law States, in which the executive, being subject to the operation of the Rule of Law, is unprotected; and (2) Prerogative States, in which the executive is protected by a special system of administrative law.

VIII. SUMMARY

The following table summarises our classification:

CLASSIFICATION OF MODERN CONSTITUTIONAL STATES

Ground of division	*First type*	*Second type*
1. The nature of the State to which the Constitution applies.	Unitary.	Federal or Quasi-Federal.
2. The nature of the Constitution itself.	Flexible (not necessarily unwritten).	Rigid (not necessarily fully written).
3. The nature of the Legislature.	i. (*a*) Manhood Suffrage. (*b*) Single-member Constituency. ii. Elective or partially elective Second Chamber.	Adult Suffrage. Multi-member Constituency. Non-elective Second Chamber.
4. The nature of the Executive.	Parliamentary.	Non-Parliamentary or Fixed.
5. The nature of the Judiciary.	In Common Law States (subject to the Rule of Law).	In Prerogative States (under Administrative Law).

3*

In examining the table the reader must again remind himself that any one state which he may select for examination does not necessarily conform to one type in all its characteristics. Each state must be judged on each ground of division separately. Let us take, for example, Britain and the United States. Britain conforms to the first type on the first ground; to the first type on the second ground; to the second type on the third ground (i, *a*); to the first type on the third ground (i, *b*); to the second type on the third ground (ii); to the first type on the fourth ground; and to the first type on the fifth ground. In short, Britain is a unitary state with a flexible constitution, a legislature elected on adult suffrage, with single-member constituencies, a non-elective Second Chamber, and a parliamentary executive subject to the Rule of Law. On the other hand, the American union of states, known as the United States, conforms to the second type on the first ground; to the second type on the second ground; to the second type on the third ground (i, *a*); to the first type on the third ground (i, *b*); to the first type on the third ground (ii); to the second type on the fourth ground; and to the first type on the fifth ground. In other words, the United States form a federal state, with a rigid constitution, a legislature elected on adult suffrage, with single-member constituencies and an elected Second Chamber, and a non-parliamentary executive subject to the Rule of Law.

We shall now proceed to a fuller discussion of each of these characteristics of constitutional states

READING

BRYCE: *History and Jurisprudence*, Vol. I, Essay iii. *Modern Democracies*, Vol. II, pp. 506–8.

DICEY: *Law of Constitution*, pp. lxxv–lxxx, 121–2, 134–140, 480–8.

DUNNING: *Political Theories*, Vol. I, pp. 33–7, 62–93.

FINER: *Modern Government*, Vol. I, Ch. vii.

GETTELL: *Readings in Political Science*, pp. 244–8, 252, 266–271, 284–6, 344–6, 391–3.

JENKS: *State and Nation*, pp. 259–275.

MARRIOTT: *English Political Institutions*, Ch. i. *Mechanism of the Modern State*, Vol. I, Ch. ii.

SIDGWICK: *Elements of Politics*, Ch. xxx.

WILSON: *State*, pp. 31–2.

SUBJECTS FOR ESSAYS

1. How did Aristotle classify the political constitutions of his day and in what respects must we regard his classification as obsolete?

2. Suggest a classification of constitutions in harmony with modern conditions.

3. Define the terms unitary and federal as applied to modern states.

4. What is the weakness of the division of modern constitutions into written and unwritten?

5. Explain what is meant by the terms flexible and rigid as applied to constitutions.

6. What is the importance of the electoral machinery in connection with the constitution of the legislature in the modern state?

7. Explain the terms franchise and constituency, and discuss the parts they play in the election of parliamentary representatives.

8. Detail the types of Second Chamber in the modern state, giving examples in each category.

9. How do you draw a distinction between the parliamentary and non-parliamentary, or fixed, executive?

10. What do you understand by the term Rule of Law? Show how the legal systems of states which enjoy this differ from those which do not.

CHAPTER IV

THE UNITARY STATE

I. SOVEREIGNTY, INTERNAL AND EXTERNAL

WE have said that a unitary state is one in which we find "the habitual exercise of supreme legislative authority by one central power," while a federal state is "a political contrivance intended to reconcile national unity and power with the maintenance of 'state rights'," one, in short, in which the legislative authority is divided between a central or federal power and smaller units, sometimes called states or cantons and sometimes provinces, according to the fullness of their power. To make this clearer, we must add something to our introductory remarks on the subject of sovereignty. The problem of sovereignty is one of the utmost difficulty. Its attempted elucidation has filled innumerable pages of the books of political philosophers and legal theorists, and it remains the cardinal question of the politics of our time. As we have seen earlier, sovereignty has two aspects, internal and external. We have defined internal sovereignty as the supremacy of a person or body of persons in the state over the individuals or associations of individuals within the area of its jurisdiction, and external sovereignty as the absolute independence of one state as a whole with reference to all other states.

As to internal sovereignty, the whole question revolves upon the meaning of the word state. Once grant that the state is nothing if it is not the whole association of individuals within it, organised politically, and you cannot fail to appreciate the logic of Rousseau's contention that sovereignty is popular, indivisible and inalienable. For, although the sovereignty is said to be vested in the rulers, ultimately it lies in the power of the governed. Even the most despotic government that ever existed is limited in its absoluteness by the truth that, as David Hume long ago pointed out, force is always on the side of the governed, who might, if driven far enough by outraged opinion, carry a revolution to overthrow the government. As we advance from despotic to constitutional states this limitation becomes more obvious. "If a legislature," wrote Leslie Stephen, "decided that all blue-eyed babies should be murdered, the preservation of blue-eyed babies would be illegal; but legislators must go mad before they could pass such a law, and subjects be idiotic before they could submit to it."

We have spoken of the distinction between the legal sovereign and the political sovereign, and have said that in Great Britain, for example, the legal sovereign is the "Queen in Parliament," and that the political sovereign is the electorate, which can, if it will, mould the legal sovereign to its desires. If you say that in practice it is hard to see that this happens you are not denying the reality of the political sovereignty of the people, but only pointing out that the medium for the expression of the popular will is not working well. At least it is fair to say that modern representative government does, as far as the world has yet been able to discover, bring the legal and political sovereigns as near to coincidence as it is possible to bring them. This representative government is established through usage and laws or through one finished document, either of which is called a constitution. The constitution is, from one point of view, an attempt to define the relationship between the government and the governed. Thus, while in theory the sovereignty of the legal sovereign remains illimitable and the sovereignty of the people inalienable, in practice the sovereignty of the one is very considerably limited and the sovereignty of the other to a great extent surrendered for the sake of social peace and political harmony.

The constitutional state, then, is the area of jurisdiction of a particular government whose functions are formulated in the constitution of that state. The constitution, therefore, defines the limits of the state both internally and externally, and the limits of the state become vital when we consider it in its external relations. External, like internal, sovereignty, is in theory unlimited, but in practice it is limited either positively by a desire for peace or some material advantage on the part of the community concerned, or negatively by a fear of the power of some neighbouring state to crush that community.

Either of these considerations may lead a state into an association with others more or less real according to its conditions. The simplest form of such an association is an alliance, which may be either defensive—*i.e.*, to give the association armed effect if any of its members are attacked—or offensive—*i.e.*, to arm the association even though one of its members is the aggressor. Now, this is not a formal limitation of sovereignty, since any member of such an association is free to withdraw from its conditions whenever it feels inclined, even though the conditions of the alliance may lay down limits of time. A good example of this was seen when Italy withdrew from the Triple Alliance with Germany and Austria at the outbreak of war in 1914, and in the following year allied herself with the enemies of her former allies, a *volte-face* which she repeated in 1943.

Or a state may pledge itself in association with others to perform or not to perform certain acts in certain eventualities. But this is not a real limitation of sovereignty either, as we saw in Germany's invasion of Belgium in 1914. A further step is taken when a personal union occurs, where two or more states are united only in the sense that the same monarch reigns over them. Such was the case, for example, between Britain and Hanover from 1714 to 1837. Two or more states so dynastically united may go farther and face the world as a diplomatic unit, as, for example, did Austria and Hungary from 1867 to 1918, and Norway and Sweden from 1815 to 1905. But the mere act of making an alliance, the mere act of crowning the same head more than once, the mere act of facing the world as a diplomatic unit—none of these acts makes one new state out of two or more pre-existing ones. For a state has sovereign power, internal and external, and only a formal limitation of that sovereignty can actually affect its statehood.

II. THE PROCESS OF STATE INTEGRATION

The nature of the state, then, is determined by its sovereignty. There is no state that we know to-day which has not been built into its existing form by a process of integration or knitting together. This is true whether we consider states with very ancient roots, such as Great Britain and France, or more recent political creations, like Czechoslovakia and Yugoslavia.

For the process of integration may be either slow or rapid according to the circumstances of its inception and growth. The particular process of integration may have been decided by war, where one local unit has conquered another and simply incorporated it. This was the case in the early history of Rome, of England and of France. Or the chances of war may have simultaneously liberated a number of neighbouring units which were by that hazard faced with the problem of founding some sort of union for their common advantage. This was the case with the American Colonies in 1783 and with the Serbs, Croats and Slovenes in 1918. Or, again, a number of isolated units may have come to realise the need for union through some danger not hitherto thought to exist, which was the case with Australia at the end of the nineteenth century.

But however it may be, when faced with this question of integration the communities concerned must decide whether they will integrate by federation or by mutual absorption. If they integrate by federation, then the sovereignty is, in practice at least, divided, the federating units retaining some share of it separately and surrendering a share to the central organ which they thereby establish. We are bound to admit that in the case of a federation there is, for all practical purposes, a division of sovereignty. It is true, as we have said, that theoretically sovereignty is indivisible, but there is no other logical way of facing the peculiar difficulty of a federal system than to say that the two authorities—of the federation and of the states—share the sovereignty which the federating states formerly possessed individually. This, be it observed, is something quite different from an alliance. The federating units abandon completely their external sovereignty to the common authority, and they therefore retain their internal sovereignty only in a truncated form, since there are certain powers that the government of each unit formerly exercised over its individual citizens which now only the federal government can exercise.

Ultimately, of course, the sovereignty is not divided. The legal sovereign in a federation is the constitution itself, which sets out the division of powers between the federal and state authorities. When a number of states integrate by federation they agree to submit to the conditions laid down in the constitution. The constitution is a treaty, but a treaty of very special sanctity which none of the contracting parties can infringe without following the procedure set forth in it. We may therefore rightly describe the states in a federal system as subsidiary sovereign bodies.

If, on the other hand, the integration takes the form of absorption, no powers are retained by the associating units. They appear separately as two or more sovereign powers, only to make a treaty whereby they are absorbed and melted into one. All powers are mutually abandoned to a common organ which is then not a federal but a central government. In that case the central government holds both the internal and external sovereignty absolutely and recognises no subsidiary sovereign bodies by virtue of this arrangement. Such is a unitary state.

III. THE ESSENTIAL QUALITY OF THE UNITARY STATE

We have said that, for practical purposes, we may usefully speak of a divided sovereignty in the case of a federal state. The essence of a unitary state is that the sovereignty is undivided, or, in other words, that the powers of the central government are unrestricted, for the constitution of a unitary state does not admit of any other law-making body than the central one. If the central power finds it convenient to delegate powers to minor bodies—whether they be local authorities or colonial authorities—it does so, be it remembered, from the plenitude of its own authority and not because the constitution says it must, or because the various parts of the state have a separate identity which they have to some extent retained on joining the larger body. It does not mean the absence of subsidiary law-making bodies, but it does mean that they exist and can be abolished at the discretion of the central authority. It does, therefore, mean that by no stretch of the meaning of words can those subsidiary bodies be called subsidiary sovereign bodies. And, finally, it means that there is no possibility of the central and local authorities coming into a conflict with which the central government has not the legal power to cope.

The two essential qualities of a unitary state may therefore be said to be (1) the supremacy of the central parliament and (2) the absence of subsidiary sovereign bodies.

(1) Wherever we find a unitary state we find the supremacy of the central parliament. Frequently, in a unitary state, as we shall see when we come to discuss the rigid constitution, there are certain sorts of acts which the constitution does not allow the ordinary central legislature to pass except under special conditions. But the central parliament in a federal state is checked in a more complete sense than this; for a federal constitution not only lays down the means of changing the constitution but indicates either what are the powers of the federal authorities or else what are those of the federating units. Hence in a federal state there are two kinds of legislature— the federal and the state—each with its own province, and neither universally supreme, whereas in a unitary state there is only one kind of legislature, which is always and absolutely supreme.

(2) The absence of subsidiary sovereign bodies is the second mark of a unitary state. The distinction which we have here drawn between subsidiary law-making bodies and subsidiary sovereign bodies is the distinction between the local authorities in a unitary state and the state authorities in a federal state. This distinction is realised as soon as we think of the state authority in a federation in relation to the federal authority rather than in relation to the constitution. The state authority has rights which the federal authority is incapable of enhancing or diminishing. The only power that can do that is the constitution itself when it undergoes amendment in that direction—a process which can be achieved only by consulting the desires of the various states forming the federation. Thus, in the case of the federation called the United States of America, the state of Virginia, say, has absolute powers in certain directions secured by the Constitution. Of these no act of the federal legislature (Congress) can deprive Virginia until the Constitution is changed (and this Congress alone has not the power to do) for that purpose. Compare this with the relation between a local authority and the central legislature of a unitary state. In the unitary state called the United Kingdom, the London County Council, say, has powers granted to it, not by the Constitution but by an act of the Parliament at Westminster. Of any or all of such powers the Parliament at Westminster could deprive the London County Council at any time by its own act. The

difference is that the Congress of the United States could in no conceivable circumstances abolish the state of Virginia, but the Parliament of the United Kingdom could abolish the London County Council without reference to any superior force.

In short, if a central authority has beneath it authorities with which it is powerless by the ordinary processes of legislation to interfere (otherwise than in the way laid down in the constitution), then that central authority is a federal authority, and the state over which it has this limited jurisdiction is a federal state; whereas, if a central authority has beneath it only those authorities which it can create or abolish at will, it is a supreme authority, and the state within the limits of which it has this unlimited jurisdiction is a unitary state. We shall now turn to a detailed study of some important unitary states of the modern world.

IV. HISTORICAL UNITARIANISM OF THE UNITED KINGDOM

The evolution of the United Kingdom provides an excellent illustration of the growth of a unitary state in which the process of integration has been through absorption and not through federation. This process of absorption may be watched from the very earliest times. Immediately after the first rush of Teutonic invasions we find in England as many petty kingdoms as there were marauding bands, and as many kings as there were leaders of them. As the invaders became settlers, the allegiance of the individual was transformed from a personal into a territorial one, and before the actual process of the conquest of Romano-Celtic Britain was completed, already we find the smaller kingdoms being absorbed by the larger. By 613, when, with the fall of Chester, we may consider the conquest to have been complete, there had already emerged out of the original welter, seven kingdoms (the Heptarchy), and the external struggle (with the Britons) immediately gave place to an internal conflict among the seven kingdoms of the invaders. Before long the heptarchy had become a triarchy. Then the Danish invasions supervened, but even this was not sufficient to stop the process of absorption. The Danes settled and were then incorporated, like the rest, into a united kingdom under the kings of the House of Wessex.

MORLEY HALL CRICKET CLUB

The following fixtures have so far been arranged :

Date	Opponents	Ground
Sunday June 7th	Pysar-Britex Sports Club	Hampstead Heath.
Sunday June 28th	E.A.Gill's XI	Wembley.
Sunday July 19th	E.A.Gill's XI	Clapham Common.
Sunday August 9th	Pysar-Britex Sports Club	Clapham Common.

P 34   line 26   "from" should be form

38   line 13   4 states mentioned
40 , " 20-1   Sardinia "one of 3"

63   48 States should be   50

66;69 5th Rep. in Fr. now ?
69   Kingdom of Egypt ?

The unitarianism of the Kingdom of England was only strengthened by the Norman Conquest, and the long process which finally resulted in the unification of England, Wales, Scotland and Ireland now began. Wales was conquered by Edward I, and the Statute of Wales (1283) definitely incorporated that country with its larger neighbour. In 1603, upon the extinction of the Tudor line and the accession of the Stuarts, directly descended from Henry VII, the whole island of Great Britain became united under one crown. But this made no unitary state. It was at best a personal union, exemplified solely in a common kingship. Then in 1707 the Act of Union turned the two states into an absolute unit. The two states made a treaty, but by the treaty each absorbed the other. Their separate identity as states disappeared from that moment. It was not so much a union of the Parliaments of England (which included Wales) and Scotland as the establishment of a new Parliament which included them both. The Act of Union was both a treaty and a statute. The moment it was agreed to by both parliaments the contracting parties existed no longer and therefore it ceased to be a treaty. It remained a valid Act upon the Statute Book of the Kingdom of Great Britain.

A similar absorption took place between the Kingdom of Great Britain and Ireland in 1800. Ireland had been a province under the English Crown, in theory since the days of Henry II in the twelfth century and in fact since the time of Henry VII at the end of the fifteenth. In 1782 Ireland was granted legislative independence, but the machine broke down, and in 1800 the second Act of Union was passed. Here again the two states came together for a moment to make a treaty and then to disappear as separate entities. Hence from 1800 there existed the United Kingdom of Great Britain and Ireland, and in the process of its development there was not the smallest element of federation. Not England nor Scotland nor Ireland retained even a modified sovereignty: that of each was melted in the general mass.

It is true that the special laws of Scotland and Ireland, which in each case existed before the Union, remained in force, but only in so far as they were compatible with the terms of the Union and only so long as they were not repealed—and this is the important point—by the Parliament of the United Kingdom. It is true, further, that some Acts passed by the united Parliament since that time may specially have excepted Scotland or Ireland from their scope, and others have applied only to each of those countries separately. But any desire that may have existed on the part of the framers of those two Acts of Union to make their provisions unalterable is proved under examination to have been quite illusory, and any attempt that may have been implied to bind future parliaments by these Acts has been proved a failure; for in both, Acts, chiefly with regard to religion, which were intended to be permanent, have been since repealed or amended. The only way, in fact, in which the untouchability of the Acts of Union by the united Parliament could have been secured would have been to maintain a special body for protecting or changing them, but in that case the sovereignty of the British Parliament would have become less than absolute, for then the United Kingdom would have ceased to be a unitary state and have become a federal state. The establishment of the Irish Free State in 1922 only truncated the area of the United Kingdom without fundamentally affecting its political nature, for what was left remained a unitary state under the title, the United Kingdom of Great Britain and Northern Ireland.

The principle of federalism is equally absent in the growth and political organisation of the British Empire and Commonwealth. It is impossible to speak of the Constitution of the British Empire. There is no such thing. There is a constitution of the United Kingdom and there is a constitution of each of the Self-governing Dominions. As to the Colonial Empire, some colonies have been granted partial self-governing institutions, but in this respect the Colonies are, *vis-à-vis* the government at Westminster, precisely in the position of local authorities in Britain. That is to say, every grant of partial self-government to a colony has been made by an Act of Parliament, just as certain local powers have been granted to a county or a borough within the Kingdom, and could be equally withdrawn by an annulling Act. That was also the traditional position of the Self-governing Dominions until quite recently, for their various constitutions were technically granted by the Acts of the British Parliament. But, in fact, these grants of Dominion Status were made in response to a growing sense of nationhood in the various Dominions, so that the Act granting the status in each case was more in the nature of a treaty than a statute.

What had been implicit in this respect in the earlier cases of Canada, Australia and South Africa was explicit in the case of the Irish Free State, whose Constitution was actually founded on a treaty which ended a state of civil war and was signed in 1922 between Great Britain and Southern Ireland (officially known, since the later Constitution of 1937, as Eire), and ratified by the British Parliament and an Irish Constituent Assembly. The preamble to the Constitution stated that:

"if any provision of the said Constitution or any amendment thereof or law made thereunder is in any respect repugnant to any of the provisions of the scheduled treaty, it shall, to the extent only of such repugnancy, be absolutely void and inoperative."

There were only two possible ways of satisfying the demands of this nationhood. One way was to make the whole Empire a federation in which all the component parts should be equal. The position categorically established in the Irish Constitution marked the climax to a controversy actually dating back to the loss of the American Colonies in 1783. The shock of that disruption of the old Empire gave rise at first to a sort of defeatist argument which came to be called the "Ripe Fruit Theory": that the Colonies, being to the Mother Country as fruit to a tree, when they ripened must, as in nature, fall away. This theory had recurred constantly afterwards in the minds of certain statesmen and thinkers at every Imperial crisis. By 1870 this way of solution had reached its climax, and it then gave place to a serious movement for federation which went on in some form or other till the close of the century. The other way was to do what has in fact been done. It was to form an alliance between the component parts of the Empire, which has been kept alive by Imperial Conferences. But this alliance by no means constitutes a diplomatic unit, for each of the Dominions has its own representatives abroad and separate membership of the United Nations Organisation.

After the Irish Treaty, events moved rapidly to a specific clarification of Dominion Status, and at the Imperial Conference of 1926 the rights of the Dominions were unequivocally stated in these words: "They (the Dominions) are autonomous communities within the British Empire, equal in status, in no way subordinate one to another in any aspect of their domestic or external affairs, though united by a common allegiance to the Crown, and freely associated as members of the British Commonwealth of Nations." Further, as a result of the Imperial Conference of 1926 the Governor-General had ceased to represent the British Government (conceived as the Cabinet) in a Dominion and it had become necessary to appoint a High Commissioner as, in effect, a liaison officer. This development of complete independence on the part of the Self-governing Dominions has been given Statutory force by the Statute of Westminster of 1931.[1]

The Statute is described as an "Act of the Imperial Parliament to give effect to certain Resolutions passed by Imperial Conferences held in the years 1926 and 1930." The Dominions concerned are named in the preamble to this Statute. They are the Dominion of Canada, the Commonwealth of Australia, the Dominion of New Zealand, the Union of South Africa, the Irish Free State[2] and Newfoundland[3]. The preamble states, *inter alia*, that "the Crown is the symbol of the free association of the members of the British Commonwealth of Nations," that "they are united by a common allegiance to the Crown," and that "it is in accord with the established constitutional position that no law hereafter made by the Parliament of the United Kingdom shall extend to any of the said Dominions as part of the law of that Dominion otherwise than at the request of and with the consent of that Dominion."

The second, third and fourth sections of the Statute are so vital and explicit as to be worth quoting verbatim:

"2. (1) The Colonial Laws Validity Act (1865) shall not apply to any law made after the commencement of this Act by the Parliament of a Dominion.

(2) No law and no provision of any law made after the commencement of this Act by the Parliament of a Dominion shall be void or inoperative on the ground that it is repugnant to the law of England, or to the

[1]For the effect of the decisions of the Imperial Conference of 1926 and the Statute of Westminster on the conception and practice of the Executive in the Self-governing Dominions see later, p. 225.

[2]As it then was, but the Constitution of 1937 only emphasised the independence thus recognised. See later, pp. 91–2.

[3]The Constitution of Newfoundland was in suspense from 1933 to 1948. For the developments of the latter year see Footnote p. 116.

provisions of any existing or future Act of Parliament of the United Kingdom, or to any order, rule or regulation made under such Act, and the Powers of the Parliament of a Dominion shall include the power to repeal or amend any such Act, order, rule or regulation, in so far as the same is part of the law of the Dominion.

"3.   It is hereby declared and enacted that the Parliament of a Dominion has full power to make laws having extra-territorial operation.

"4.   No Act of Parliament of the United Kingdom passed after the commencement of this Act shall extend, or be deemed to extend, to a Dominion as part of the law of that Dominion, unless it is expressly declared in that Act that that Dominion has requested, and consented to, the enactment thereof."

The penultimate section draws a clear distinction between a Dominion and a Colony in the statement that "the expression 'colony' shall not, in any Act of the Parliament of the United Kingdom passed after the commencement of this Act, include a Dominion or any Province or State forming part of that Dominion."

It will be clear from all this that the Crown remains as the sole unifying force and that the Governor-General of a Dominion directly represents the Queen, and is, *vis-à-vis* a Dominion Parliament, exactly in the position of the Queen *vis-à-vis* the Parliament of the United Kingdom; hence the official expression "Her Majesty's Government in the United Kingdom," "Her Majesty's Government in the Dominion of Canada," and so on.

It follows from what we have said, first, that we cannot discuss the Constitution of the Empire as a whole as that of either a unitary or a federal state, and secondly, that we must discuss each of the Dominions separately as either a unitary or a federal state. We will here take the cases of New Zealand and South Africa as examples of unitary states within the Commonwealth, and Eire (though no longer a Dominion), reserving for the next chapter the federal states of Canada and Australia.

V. EXAMPLES OF UNITARY STATES AMONG BRITISH SELF-GOVERNING DOMINIONS

(a) New Zealand

The history of New Zealand as a British possession begins in 1840, when it was formally annexed by Great Britain and a treaty was made with the Maoris guaranteeing them in the possession of their lands. A series of Maori wars about land-ownership ended in 1870, but since then the Maoris have lived in amity with the white people whose privileges they now share. The Maoris return four of their own number to the House of Representatives, and it has been customary in more recent years for at least one Maori to be a member of the Cabinet. Two Acts of the Imperial Parliament established first an elective Legislature (1853) and then a Ministry responsible to it (1856). These Acts did not legally disturb a practice which had been growing up for some years, namely, that a large share of the functions of government was discharged by Provincial Councils, one for each province, of which there were at first six, and later nine. And since the power of amending the Constitution rested entirely (with the normal reservation as to the powers of the Imperial Parliament) with the Legislature, it remained for the Dominion itself to decide whether it would retain the provincial system and develop into a federal state.

As it turned out, the Parliament established by the Act of 1853 and strengthened by the second Act three years later, proved such a centralising force that by 1876 the provincial system had entirely disappeared and New Zealand became definitely a unitary state, its central government recognising no subordinate sovereign bodies. The political destiny of New Zealand might have been different, for she was actually mentioned in the original Bill to establish the Commonwealth of Australia. In defining the word "states" as any Colonies for the time being parts of the Commonwealth, Section 6 of the Bill included New Zealand, "if it should be or become at any time part of the Commonwealth." But by that time New Zealand had so far developed her own institutions that, when it came to the point, she felt unable to sink her individuality in a wider federation.

(b) The Union of South Africa

The Union of South Africa offers a somewhat curious example of a unitary state, having in some respects the appearance of a federal form of political organisation. Yet in actuality it has so little of federalism about it that it would be quite wrong to describe it even as a quasi-federal state. The movements and

discussions in South Africa which culminated in the establishment of the Union in 1910 might have led one to suppose that a
federal system, after the model either of Canada or of Australia,
was about to be achieved. And such a federal system was
doubtless contemplated by some South African statesmen at
that time. But the governmental problems arising out of the
acuteness of the conflict between nationalities and races there
led the convention which drafted the Constitution to write it
with a view to strengthening as far as possible the central
government, which is, as must be clear by now, far more powerful under a unitary than under a federal system.

Hence the Union of South Africa, though made up of four
distinct entities which had, but a short time previously, been
in a state of armed strife, is in fact a unitary state with a central
government unrestricted by the existence of any subordinate
bodies. Each of the four original colonies—which by the Act
of Union became Provinces called the Cape of Good Hope,
Natal, the Transvaal, and the Orange Free State—has a Provincial Council whose powers are enumerated in the Constitution, but the enumeration is immediately followed by the
statement that

"any ordinance made by a provincial council shall have effect in
and for the province as long and as far only as it is not repugnant
to any Act of (the Union) Parliament."

Thus the South Africans followed, after all, not the precedent
of the Canadians or Australians, but that of the English and
Scots in 1707. The appearance of federalism is to some extent
maintained in the Senate where there are eight members from
each province, as well as eight for the whole Union nominated
by the Governor-General in Council, but they by no means
personify the province, as, for example, do the Senators the
state in the United States. The provinces in South Africa are,
in fact, for this purpose merely constituencies.

As a unitary state the South African Union has many complexities, unknown to European countries, which arise from
racial questions and doubts connected with the status of
surrounding territories under the British Crown. For example,
the principle of racial discrimination generally operates in the
Union, though not in Cape Province or in the native protectorates—Basutoland, Bechuanaland and Swaziland—within its

area, and this difference creates social and economic problems with important political bearings. Again, there was the question of the position of South-West Africa, the former German colony, for which the Union had been responsible since 1920 under the original League of Nations mandate. After the Second World War it became the policy of the Union Government to incorporate this mandated territory in the Union. In pursuit of this policy they submitted their case in 1946 to the International Court at The Hague, but failed to gain the Court's unqualified approval to the plan. Notwithstanding this judgment, while not formally incorporating South-West Africa, they nevertheless proceeded to bring it into the Parliamentary system of the Union by giving it six seats in the House of Assembly and two in the Senate, and in 1950 the new members of both Houses were accordingly elected.

The doubts about the future of the two Rhodesias created a further complication for the Union. It was hoped that Southern Rhodesia, which had become a self-governing Colony in 1924, would veer towards fusion with the Union. But, in fact, she gradually tended towards closer association with Northern Rhodesia, still in the hands of a Governor appointed by the Crown and assisted by a partly elected Legislative Council, and the Protectorate of Nyasaland. Shortly after the Second World War, despite the many disparities between the three regions, definite moves were started with the object of bringing about some kind of union among them.[1]

(c) *Eire*

Eire is an interesting example of a unitary state because, while Eire is a political unit, it is not coterminous with the geographical unit called Ireland. Through the many centuries of Ireland's association with (the Irish would, of course, say

[1] On this question a conference was held in London in March, 1951. It recommended that Southern Rhodesia, Northern Rhodesia, and Nyasaland should be joined in a federation to be known as British Central Africa. Three months later a conference was held at Victoria Falls, where all the local interests, white and native, were represented. The outcome of these discussions was that in 1953 there came into being, within the British Commonwealth, a new political entity called the Federation of Rhodesia and Nyasaland, and in February, 1954, the newly-appointed Governor-General opened the first Federal Parliament at Salisbury in Southern Rhodesia.

subjection to) Great Britain, she had always been thought of as an entity, and all the Bills and Acts of Parliament which had reference to her so regarded her. This, no doubt, was one of the causes of the failure to settle the Irish Question, for it was to fly in the face of the profoundest historical cause of dissension there. This dissension resulted from the basic differences in race, religion and ideals between Northern Ireland (or Ulster) and the rest. Every attempt made to surmount this perpetual obstacle to the internal peace of the British Isles, broke down in face of the antagonisms of these two parts of the smaller island. The earlier Home Rule Bills, connected with the administrations of Gladstone, never reached the Statute Book, and when at last one did (that of 1912, thanks to the disabling of the Lords by the Parliament Act) in 1914, it was a dead letter owing first to the opposition of Ulster and secondly to the supervention of the First World War.

Not until that war was over did we recognise the need for regarding Ireland not as one but as two entities, and then it was too late, for the unrest and rebellion of Southern Ireland during and after the war had made mere old-fashioned Home Rule quite unacceptable and manifestly obsolete. None the less, an Act was passed in 1920 which for the first time divided Ireland into two parts. Only Northern Ireland accepted this Act, and under its provisions that part of the country continues to be governed. The only solution that Southern Ireland would accept, after a devastating civil war, was that of Dominion Home Rule, and this was granted under the Act of 1922 following the treaty which ended the war and established the Irish Free State. The treaty upon which it was founded gave Northern Ireland the right to refuse to enter the Irish Free State and to continue to be governed under the Act of 1920. This, of course, she did. Thus Ireland presented the strange spectacle of a partition into two parts, one of which was as independent as Canada or Australia, the other enjoying, from its deliberate choice, a mere local autonomy and still sending members to the Imperial Parliament at Westminster.

A new constitution for the Irish Free State, renamed Eire, came into force on 29th December, 1937, after its acceptance by the people in a referendum in the previous July. The new Constitution abolished the office of Governor-General and

established in its place that of the President of Ireland (Eire),
though the King was implicity acknowledged as still King of
Ireland, so long as he should continue " to be recognised by the
associated Dominions as the symbol of their co-operation." To
that extent Eire might have been supposed to retain her connection with the British Commonwealth of Nations, though
when the testing-time came in the Second World War she
remained strictly, not to say sullenly, neutral. And the fact
remains that the language of the Constitution of 1937 was such
as to apply to an independent republic, for, as Mr. de Valera
said in the debates on it, "not a comma" of it would need to be
altered if the Republic of Ireland were to be declared. His
words proved to be prophetic, for in October, 1948, the Prime
Minister of Eire announced the intention of his Government
to break the last formal link with the British Commonwealth
by the simple process of repealing the External Relations Act,
a move which resulted in the establishment of the independent
Republic of Eire in 1949. The Constitution, moreover, was so
worded as to apply to the whole of Ireland as a unitary state,
in anticipation of the ultimate "re-integration of the national
territory."

VI. THE UNITARY STATE OF FRANCE

A unitary state is a type of political organisation deeply
rooted among the French, both in history and sentiment. From
the very earliest days of the French Monarchy, it was the policy
of the king, whose territorial power was at first very slight
compared with that of some of his barons who were his feudal
inferiors, to conquer and absorb the territories not actually
possessed by him; to undo, in fact, the work of feudalism. This
process went on until the baronage became politically quite
impotent and Louis XIV could, without much hyperbole, say,
"The State, it is I." All the political power being centred in the
Crown, we may judge of the cataclysmic effect of the Revolution which swept it away. There were no strong local bodies to
form the foundations of the new state. The sole corporation was
the nation. The Revolution left nothing but a tradition of
centralism and a philosophy which emphasised individual
rights and the sovereignty of the people. This tradition and this
philosophy have never been lost, and their prevalence accounts

for the fact that, as a French writer puts it, "all French political systems always gravitate automatically and rapidly towards unity and homogeneity of powers."

All these principles were inherent in the organisation of the Third Republic which lasted from 1875 to 1940. Though that Republic, with its emphasis on parliament, to some extent obscured the sovereignty of the people and discontinued the use of the plebiscite (or popular vote) for presidential election— a practice very common in revolutionary times—it did not decentralise the French state. It remained, in fact, the most perfect example of political unitarianism. All the powers of government resided in the legislative and executive organs at Paris. There were no subsidiary sovereign bodies. France was divided into *départements* and *communes, arrondissements* and cantons (the last two being merely electoral areas), but their form and extent depended entirely upon statute law. There was no local authority and no territorial division that the central government could not obliterate whenever it chose. The powers of all local officers were defined by national law and they were supervised in their actions by an envoy of the central government called a Prefect.

In the years between the two World Wars, there was a good deal of dubiety and discontent in France about the working of the political institutions of the Republic, and among those sentiments was a sense of the oppressiveness of the high centralism of the state. Consequently, among the various plans for reform was a movement called Regionalism, whose object was to break France up into local units and to give them a real measure of local autonomy in order to relieve the central government of some of its multifarious functions. But amid the welter of problems which pressed upon the governments of France after the First World War this movement had little opportunity to make any official headway. Nor does it appear to have been revived after the Second World War. It is true that the Constitution of the Fourth Republic, approved in the referendum held in October, 1946, makes rather more concession to the need for a certain amount of devolution than was admitted under the Third Republic. For Chapter X of the new Constitution states that, while the Republic is one and indivisible, it nevertheless recognises the existence of communes and departments

and territories overseas (*des collectivités territoriales*) and guarantees to them, by organic laws, an extension of the liberties
they formerly enjoyed. But, as far as can be judged at present
from a mere statement on paper, this seems to be nothing more
than an intention to vitalise French local government and to
secure greater co-ordination of functions between the state
departments and the units of local administration.

VII. THE KINGDOM AND THE REPUBLIC OF ITALY

The story of the struggle for an independent and united Italy
is, in one sense, as old as the reign of Theodoric the Ostrogoth
(493–526), in another, as new as the Second World War. Theodoric, the first to make a serious attempt at unification since the
break-up of the Roman Empire in the West, brought his policy
nearer to a successful issue than any was to reach until the days
of Cavour in the middle of the nineteenth century. And fourteen
centuries after Theodoric the struggle continued, as the Italian
people battled to free themselves simultaneously from the
darkness of the Fascist Dictatorship and the stranglehold of the
Nazi occupation. Italy gained neither her independence nor her
unity through all the years that intervened between the fall of
the Roman Empire in the West and the rise of the Italian
patriots of the nineteenth century—Mazzini, Cavour, Garibaldi,
and King Victor Emmanuel. She gained nothing from the fall
of Napoleon in 1815, and for some years after she was still called
by Metternich, her most notable oppressor, "a geographical
expression." In 1848 the rulers of seven of the eight states of
Italy were driven to grant constitutions to their people, but in
the bitter reaction against the Revolution which followed,
Sardinia alone precariously maintained hers, while all the others
were crushed out of existence beneath the iron heel of a recu-
perated Austria.

The survival of the Sardinian Constitution (the *Statuto*) of
1848 was crucial in the years of national resurrection (*Il
Risorgimento*) and of political integration which followed the
failures of the mid-century. In 1859 the Sardinians, allied with
France, drove the Austrians out of Lombardy, which was then
united to Sardinia. In the following year Tuscany and the
Duchies of the centre declared for union with the North and

were incorporated. Meanwhile, Garibaldi was liberating Sicily and Naples from the tyrannical Bourbon dynasty, and in 1861 the South united with the North, and the first Italian parliament was held. There still remained Venice and the Papal States outside the united kingdom. The former was secured as a result of the Austro-Prussian War of 1866, and the latter by the withdrawal of the French garrison from Rome under pressure of the Franco-Prussian War in 1870. Unification was then practically complete except for the two areas of Trieste and its environs and the Trentino which, called by the Italians *Italia Irredenta*, remained in Austrian hands until the end of the First World War, when they were added to the Kingdom of Italy.

Now, this gradual process of unification might very well have taken the form of federation, each area retaining certain rights and surrendering others for the common advantage to a federal authority. Indeed, many Italians, including Cavour, at one time contemplated the establishment of a federation, and some writers have since held that, in view of the great divergence of history and conditions among the various parts of Italy, the history of the state since its unification would, under such a system, have been much less chequered than has been the case. Instead of that, as the Kingdom of Sardinia expanded into the Kingdom of Italy, the *Statuto* was extended to the new territories. The Italians might have followed a procedure like that adopted by the United States and Canada in their westward expansions, adding new states to the federation as growth demanded. Instead, they followed the precedent of the Acts of Union in Britain, the various parts being absorbed into a unity rather than federated in a union.

Political unitarianism has remained an essential feature of the Italian state through the revolutionary changes of more recent times. Mussolini passionately maintained it as fundamental to the success of his dictatorship, and it again appears, though somewhat modified, in the latest Italian Constitution. In June, 1946, the Italian people, by a comparatively small majority in a referendum in which 90 per cent of the electorate, including women for the first time, went to the polls, evicted the House of Savoy after nine centuries of rule and at last adopted those republican principles for which Mazzini had struggled in vain in the days of the *Risorgimento*.   The consequent Republican Constitution of 1947, while it swept away together the foundations of the monarchy and every vestige of Mussolini's totalitarian system, nevertheless maintained the essential nature of the unitary state of Italy, for Article 5 of the Constitution states categorically that the Italian Republic is "one and indivisible."

The new Constitution[1] does, however, permit a measure of decentralisation unknown to the original constitution. In fact, Article 5, from which we have already quoted, adds that the Republic "recognises and promotes local autonomy," and there is a later group of Articles (114-133) which lay down the form and functions of a regional organisation. Nineteen regions are named, and of these, five, including Sicily and Sardinia, are given a special status. Each region must have a popularly elected Council, which elects an executive committee (*la giunta regionale*) and a President. The powers and functions of these regional bodies are stated in lists, but, generally, they are not wider than those of the larger Local Authorities (Counties and County Boroughs) in Britain, and, though the rights of the new Italian Regions are secured as part of the law of the constitution, they cannot be said to introduce a federal element into the frame of government. It is true to say, therefore, that the constitution of the new Republic, while it changes the titular headship of the state from an hereditary monarchy to an elective presidency, does not fundamentally disturb the eighty-year-old tradition of political unity in Italy.

READING

BRYCE: *History of Jurisprudence*, Vol. II, Essay x. *Modern Democracies* Vol. I, Ch. xviii; Vol. II, Ch. liii.
DICEY: *Law of the Constitution*, Ch. i.
FINER: *Modern Government*, Vol. I, pp. 243-4.
JENKS: *British Empire*, Ch. iii.
KEITH: *Constitution, Administration, and Laws of the Empire*, Pt. I, Chs. i–viii. *Responsible Government in Dominions*, Vol. II, Pt. VIII, Chs. ii and iii.
LASKI: *Grammar of Politics*, Pt. I, Ch. ii.
LOWELL: *Government of England*, Vol. II, Chs. liv, lv, lviii. *Governments and Parties in Continental Europe*, Vol. I, pp. 36-42, 146-150. *Greater European Governments*, pp. 84-6, 95-105, Chs. vi–viii.
MACIVER: *Modern State*, Chs. v–xi.
MARRIOTT: *Mechanism of Modern State*, Vol. I, Chs. vi–xii.

[1]This paragraph, as originally printed, was based on the Draft Constitution, which was materially amended by the Constituent Assembly. The paragraph is now revised to accord with the Constitution as it was promulgated.

NEWTON: *Federal and United Constitutions*, Introduction and pp. 56–66, 139–155, 359–407.
WILLIAMSON: *Short History of British Expansion*, pp. 537–573, 617–634.
WILSON: *State*, pp. 129–149, 256–8, 421–5.
CONSTITUTIONS OF ALL COUNTRIES: Vol. I. *The British Empire*, pp. 1–4, 5–18, 113–136, 140–188, 189–221.
ANNUAL REGISTER FOR 1946 AND 1947.
WHITAKER'S ALMANACK FOR 1946 AND 1947.

BOOKS FOR FURTHER STUDY

BOUTMY: *Studies in Constitutional Law.*
BROGAN: *Development of Modern France.*
FINER: *Governments of Greater European Powers.*
HALL: *British Commonwealth of Nations.*
KEITH: (1) *The Governments of the British Empire.* (2) *The Dominions as Sovereign States.*
LASKI: *Foundations of Sovereignty.*
PICKLES: *France: The Fourth Republic.*
STILLMAN: *Union of Italy.*
VILLARI: *Italy.*

SUBJECTS FOR ESSAYS

1. What do you understand by the term Sovereignty? Explain the difference between internal and external sovereignty.

2. Discuss the two processes of integration in the evolution of the modern state.

3. Define the term Supremacy of Parliament and show to what extent this supremacy exists in a unitary state.

4. Trace the growth of unitarianism in the history of Great Britain.

5. Demonstrate the truth of the statement that the Imperial growth of Britain has not destroyed the unitary character of the British state.

6. Examine the Union of South Africa as an example of a unitary state.

7. Explain the significance of the Statute of Westminster of 1931.

8. What justification is there for describing the French Republic as the most perfect example of a unitary state in the world to-day?

9. Trace the development of Italian unification and show how Italy might equally have become a federal state.

10. What concessions are made to decentralisation in the Constitutions of the French Fourth Republic and of the Italian Republic?

CHAPTER V

THE FEDERAL STATE

I. THE ESSENTIAL CHARACTER OF A FEDERAL STATE

THE importance of federalism to the student of political constitutionalism cannot be over-emphasised. Federalism, in some
form or other, has its roots in the remote past, for it was not
unknown among the City-States of Ancient Greece. We find
it again in the Middle Ages among some of the cities of Italy,
and, indeed, since the thirteenth century its history has been
continuous in the development of the Swiss Confederation,
which was born when the three Forest Cantons banded themselves together for protection in 1291. It is the basis of the
political organisation of several states to-day—states as divergent in situation and tradition as Yugoslavia and the United
States, Mexico and Australia—and, if the world is moving
towards the organisation of a universal state out of the international anarchy which we have hitherto known, it is pretty
certain that it is on federal lines that this will be achieved. A
political experiment with an influence so profound and widespread, certainly in the past and present, and possibly in the
future, cannot fail to claim the careful scrutiny of the serious
citizen or to repay the closest study.

Federalism varies in form from place to place, and from time
to time. In its loosest form it is a congeries of states which, in
fact, do not make a state at all. History is full of examples of
this type of loose league which, for the want of a better term,
we generally call a confederation. To go no farther back, we
may take the Germanic Confederation, established in 1815 on
the fall of Napoleon, as an example of this type of league. There
are two German words which in their compounding help us to
grasp the difference between a so-called confederation and a
true federation—*Staat*, meaning state, and *Bund*, meaning
league. The Germanic Confederation, as it existed from 1815 to

1866, was always spoken of by the Germans as the *Bund*, and the Diet at Frankfort, which was its only central organ, was, in effect, nothing more than an assembly of ambassadors of the various states of the league. Such a league of states the Germans called a *Staatenbund*, where the emphasis is laid on the plurality of states. In such a case there is little to distinguish the organisation from a close alliance. The internal sovereignty of each state remains quite unimpaired and its external sovereignty is limited only to a very small extent.

A *Staatenbund* has not, as a rule, proved for long satisfactory to its members, which have, in the course of time, either returned to their former isolation or knit themselves more closely together into a real union. This real union the German call a *Bundesstaat*, in which, it will be observed, the word *Staat* becomes singular. It is, in fact, not a federation of states (*Staatenbund*) but a federal state (*Bundesstaat*). Such an organisation is based upon, first, a treaty among the federating units, and then upon a federal constitution accepted directly or indirectly by their citizens. It differs essentially from a confederation in having a central (or federal) executive with real power over all the citizens within the area concerned. It is not a mere league of states (which does not make a state at all) but a union of people over whom the central power will have a certain amount of direct authority. It follows, therefore, that a true federal state requires for its formation two conditions, the absence of either of which would be sufficient to prevent the consummation of such a union. The first condition is a sense of nationality among the units federating. So true is this that we generally find that modern federal states have, prior to their federation, been either loosely connected in a confederation, as in the case of Germany, or subjected to a common sovereign, as in the case of the United States, Switzerland (where both phenomena existed), Australia and Canada. The second condition is that the federating units, though desiring union, do not desire unity, for if they desired the latter they would form not a federal but a unitary state.

It is obvious, therefore, that a federal constitution attempts to reconcile the apparently irreconcilable claims of national sovereignty and state sovereignty. And the main lines upon which this reconciliation shall take place are sufficiently clear, though, as we shall see, they vary very much in detail from one federal constitution to another. Whatever concerns the nation as a whole is placed in the care of the national or federal authority: whatever concerns the states individually, and is not of vital moment to the common interest, is placed under the control of the government of the states. This division of powers, however it may, in the various federations of the modern world, be carried out in detail, is the essential characteristic of the federal state.

II. VARIATIONS OF THE FEDERAL TYPE

The indispensable quality of the federal state being a distribution of the powers of government between the federal authority and the federating units, we note three ways in which federal states may vary one from another; first, as to the manner in which the powers are distributed between the federal and state authorities; secondly, as to the nature of the authority for preserving the supremacy of the constitution over the federal and state authorities if they should come into conflict with one another; and thirdly, as to the means of changing the constitution if such change should be desired.

The powers may be distributed in one of two ways. Either the constitution states what powers the federal authority shall have and leaves the remainder to the federating units, or it states what powers the federating units shall possess and leaves the remainder to the federal authority. This remainder is generally called the "reserve of powers." The object of stating the powers is to define and hence to limit them. Therefore, it may be taken for granted that where the federal constitution defines the powers of the federating units, as in the case of the Dominion of Canada, the aim is to strengthen the federal authority at the expense of the separate members of the federation. So true is this in the case of Canada that the federating units are called not states but provinces. Thus, where the "reserve of powers" is with the federal authority, the constitution approaches more to that of a unitary state than if it is with the states. In other words, such a state is less federal.

Where the constitution defines the powers of the federal authority, as in the case of the United States and the Commonwealth of Australia, the object is to check the power of the

federal authority as against the federating units. Such federating units wish to retain as much of their independence as is
consistent with the safety of the federation. They want a federal
state with a real power, through which they can express their
common nationality, but they want, at the same time, to maintain their individual character as states as far as possible. The
more they maintain that individual character, the more they
will wish to define the federal powers and the greater the
"reserve of powers" they will wish to keep for themselves.
Hence, the greater the "reserve of powers" with the states, the
more markedly federal is the state whose constitution permits
such reserve to them. In other words, the federal state whose
constitution defines the powers of the federal authority is less
centralised than the one whose constitution defines the powers
of the federating units.

The division of powers, by whichever of the two ways it is
carried into effect, implies that both the legislature of the federation and that of each of the federating units are limited in
their scope and that neither of them is supreme. There is something above them both, namely, the constitution, which is a
definite contract, a treaty in which the contracting parties
reduce the conditions of their union to writing. A federal constitution is, in fact, a charter of rights and duties of the federal
and state authorities. These rights and duties must be kept in
their proper proportions; the rights asserted by any one authority, and the duties required of one authority by another, must
not be beyond the schedule laid down in the constitution. In the
truly federal state the power to maintain this equilibrium is
granted to a supreme court of judges whose concern is to see
that the constitution is respected in so far as it distributes
governmental powers between the contracting parties and the
federal authority which by their contract they establish.

In the amount of authority given to such a court federal
states vary. In the completely federalised state, of which the
United States is the most perfect example, this court is absolutely supreme in its power to decide in cases of conflict between the federal authority and the state authorities. In other
cases the powers of the court are limited by rights in this respect granted to other authorities. Of such a limitation upon the
powers of the supreme judiciary in a federal state, Switzerland

affords the best example. For here not the Federal Court but the Federal Assembly is the final arbiter on all conflicts between state and federal authority, and the Federal Court cannot question the constitutionality of acts passed by the Federal Assembly. But in this case, as we shall show in a later chapter, such a power in the hands of the federal court would be superfluous, since the sovereign people has in Switzerland a very direct means of expressing its will.

Between these two extremes lie several examples of variation in the matter of deciding conflicts between federal and state authorities. Australia is nearest to the absolute case of the United States, the difference being that there are, in the Australian Constitution, certain clauses which may be altered by the Commonwealth Parliament without reference to any other authority, and in such cases, of course, there can be no question of infringing the rights of states. In the former Weimar Republic of Germany the Supreme Federal Court was called upon to settle disputes between state and federation, or between the states themselves, only in certain cases. In Canada questions of conflict occasionally arise, despite the fact that the powers of the Provinces are enumerated, and on such questions the Canadian Supreme Court may adjudicate.[1]

Thus in all federal states there prevails a certain legalism which is not present in most unitary states. And this fact gives rise to the question how the constitution is to be changed. We shall say more of this later. Here suffice it to observe that a federal constitution is necessarily documentary in form, for it is inconceivable that forces so nicely balanced could be left to mere convention and occasional legislation for their maintenance. Hence a federal constitution is rigid; that is to say, the conditions under which such a constitution may be changed are either explicit or implied. If they are explicit, that is, if the conditions of amendment are definitely laid down, then, clearly, it is rigid. If they are not expressed, then the rigidity of the constitution is implied, for either the constitution is unchangeable by legal means—*i.e.*, its alteration would involve a revolution—or else the only way to change it is for *all* the

---

[1] The powers of the Court were originally subject to the right of appeal to the Judicial Committee of the Privy Council in London, but this right was abrogated in 1951, when the old connection between these two tribunals ceased.

original contracting parties to agree to the change, in which case they, in effect, sign a new treaty and promulgate to that extent a new constitution.

As to the details of the methods of altering federal constitutions, we shall reserve this question for a later chapter on the rigid constitution. The remainder of this chapter will be occupied in examining the most important examples of federal states in the world of to-day.

III. THE FEDERAL SYSTEM IN THE UNITED STATES OF AMERICA

The Constitution of the United States is the most completely federal constitution in the world. By this is meant that it exemplifies in the most marked degree the three essential characteristics of federalism, namely, the supremacy of the constitution, the distribution of powers, and the authority of the federal judiciary. It reached this complete stage by two steps from a condition in which the original thirteen federating states bore, as colonies, a common allegiance to Britain. The first step was taken with the adoption of the Articles of Confederation in 1781, which constituted not a true federation, but a confederation, a loose league, "a rope of sand," as Woodrow Wilson called these Articles, "which could bindno one." The next step was taken in 1787 when a Convention at Philadelphia drew up the present Constitution, which was adopted by the Thirteen States and became effective in 1789. Now, this made a true federation because it established a central executive with very definite powers. And it made the state as a whole as federal as possible, that is to say, it made it as little unitary as it dared, having regard to the need of a strong federal government, as proved by the difficulties with which the Confederation had helplessly struggled for almost a decade.

As to the division of powers, the Constitution of the United States makes a double division; first it divides the three departments of government—*i.e.*, legislative, executive, judicial— and makes them quite distinct from one another. As to this we shall have something to say later on. Secondly, it divides the powers between the federal and state authorities in such a manner as to secure to the federating units all the powers not absolutely necessary to the federal authority for the common advantage. Thus the powers of the United States as a whole are strictly defined; the powers left to the states separately are undefined. In other words, the Constitution enumerates in a precise list what powers the federal authority is to exercise, adding a list of powers forbidden to the United States and a list of powers forbidden to the states. And so that there should be no loophole for abuse, the 10th Amendment (carried in 1791, so near to the original promulgation as to be, in effect, a part of it) states that "The powers not delegated to the United States by the Constitution, nor prohibited by it to the States, are reserved to the States respectively or to the people." The net result is that the Federal Government of the United States can claim no power not conferred upon it by the Constitution, while the states can exercise any power belonging to an independent sovereign state except those of which they have been directly or indirectly deprived by the Constitution.

As to the Legislative Department, the Constitution establishes a Congress of two Houses—the Senate and House of Representatives—in the upper of which it secures the equality of all states and makes this an immutable law. As to the Executive Department, it establishes a four-year Presidency and details the method of election to this office. It enumerates the President's powers and checks his diplomatic powers (treaty-making, appointment of ambassadors, etc.) by requiring for the exercise thereof the ratification of the Senate; so that the external sovereignty which the states have surrendered is still ultimately controlled by the House in which they are equally represented. As to the Judicial Department, the Constitution establishes federal courts whose jurisdiction extends to all cases arising out of the Constitution, including all those of an international character whether between the states of the United States or between the United States and any other state in the world. It also establishes a Supreme Court which is a final court of appeal for all the cases already mentioned. This makes it the ultimate interpreter of the Constitution, and places the Judicial Department above any legislature (within the limits of the Constitution) whether federal or state.

This Constitution, therefore, leaves a vast amount of power with the states which form the federation. Woodrow Wilson pointed out that of a dozen great legislative schemes carried through by the British Parliament in the nineteenth century only two would have come within the scope of federal legislation in America. He takes as examples Catholic emancipation, parliamentary reform, the abolition of slavery, the amendment of the Poor Law, municipal reform, the repeal of the Corn Laws, the admission of Jews to Parliament, the disestablishment of the Irish Church, the alteration of the Irish Land Laws, the establishment of national education, the introduction of the ballot, and the reform of the Criminal Law. Of these, he says, only the Corn Laws and Slavery would have been subjects for federal regulation, and even of these two the second was outside the scope of federal action until the amendment following the Civil War (1861–5) took it out of the hands of the states. These, surely, are very striking facts for the observer accustomed, as Englishmen are, to the supremacy of the central legislature. In America, indeed, the Federal Constitution is meaningless unless taken in conjunction with the State Constitutions, which are not merely useful additions thereto, but the indispensable complement of it.

A further illustration of the absolute power of the states concerning all the things not mentioned in the Constitution as belonging to the federal authority is seen in the fact that there is no appeal to the Supreme Court of the United States in any such matters. A modern example will prove the point. A few years ago a teacher in the state of Tennessee was indicted for teaching the theory of evolution in a state school, which was a breach of the state law. It was suggested at the time that, in this case, in which not merely local interests were concerned but the passions of the whole nation were ardently concentrated, an effort would be made to bring the case to the Supreme Court. But such an effort could not possibly be successful. There was no way of bringing such a case into the Federal Court (short of a constitutional amendment in that direction) for the excellent reason that education is not mentioned in the Constitution and is, therefore, a matter reserved completely to the state authority.

In spite of the security thus afforded to the states by the Constitution, it cannot be denied that since the foundation of the United States of America there has been a progressive strengthening of the Federal as against the State Government, not only through constitutional amendment but through the

4*

various judgments interpreting the Constitution in the Federal Supreme Court. Particularly it has been shown to be quite impossible for any state to secede from the federation. It took the most terrible—because the most fratricidal—war of modern times to demonstrate this fact beyond all controversy. The Civil War, or, as it is more strictly called, the War of Secession (1861-5), resulted from the attempt of seven Southern States (afterwards increased to eleven) to break away from the American Union and to establish a Confederacy of their own. So far as President Lincoln was concerned, the war was fought not primarily to abolish slavery—though the slavery question was the occasion of it, and the abolition of slavery was achieved by it—but to vindicate the principle of union. In doing this Abraham Lincoln appealed to the spirit of nationalism of the American people. Morally, he held that it was impossible for a nation to endure if it permitted within its borders at the same time the diametrically opposed principles of liberty and slavery. And, politically, he held that the Union was perpetual. "It is safe to assert," he said, "that no government proper ever had a provision in its organic law for its own termination."

The triumph of the North in the Civil War preserved and strengthened the Union. No single state in the United States to-day could possibly contemplate secession. How could one alone hope to succeed where eleven in combination formerly so signally failed? The War of Secession, in fact though not in appearance, modified in the profoundest manner the nature of the American Constitution. It did not, indeed, create a unitary state, but it proved that, in the last analysis, the American Union is as secure from disruption as any unitary state could be; if not, indeed, more so, for it is the peculiar achievement of the United States that they have perceived how to obtain all the advantages of common action among almost half-a-hundred states without denying to them all those powers fully necessary to their political and social well-being. In short, they have shown the world how to obtain peace through political organisation.

In recent years—and particularly during Franklin Roosevelt's first two Presidential Terms (1933–1941)—there has been an increasing sense among certain sections of opinion in the United States of the need to strengthen the Federal Government at the expense of the states, especially in order to cope with the growing complexities of American economic and social life, which seem to them to require a more powerful central control and direction than is permitted to the Federal Authority under the Constitution as it stands. For example, the inability of the Authorities to check the alarming spread of violent crime, racketeering and gangsterism in the United States was attributed to the existence of forty-eight different types of state criminal law and the ease with which the criminal might evade the grasp of the police of one state by escaping to another. To meet this menace American society was forced, from motives of sheer self-defence, to permit the use of a federal police force ("G" men) which had already existed, under strict federal law, for the enforcement of Prohibition. But when President Roosevelt attempted to use federal powers to attack the grave economic and social difficulties arising from the depression which had begun in 1929 and reached its crisis at the time of his inauguration, the whole constitutional machinery was put to the most searching test.

The constitutional position created by Roosevelt's proposals, compendiously described as the "New Deal," is worth noting as an illustration of the way the American Constitution works. The President's object was to use the resources of the whole American Commonwealth to relieve the distress in the separate states, which themselves were incapable of dealing with so grave a situation. He, therefore, persuaded Congress to pass Acts for the central control of money and credit, for the nation-wide regulation of agriculture, for national industrial recovery, federal emergency relief, including the promotion of public works and the opening of federal labour exchanges, and for the establishment of a general system of social security, including unemployment insurance and old age pensions. These measures aroused the bitter opposition of those who objected to the vast public expenditure involved and to what they regarded as unwarrantable infringements of personal and economic liberty, and violations of state rights. The Executive and the Legislature, on the other hand, held that the Constitution permitted the exercise of such powers because the Federal Authority was constitutionally responsible for the welfare of the nation and by virtue of the right of Congress to tax and regulate inter-state commerce.

Here was a conflict which the Supreme Court alone was competent to settle. Several cases arising from the New Deal legislation came before the Court in 1935 and 1936, and, while it upheld the financial policy of the Government, it declared invalid the whole of the Agricultural Adjustment Act on the grounds that it involved "an unwarrantable use of the taxing powers of the Federal Government" and that "the scheme violated the rights of individual states." When, in the next year, the Supreme Court finally declared the National Industrial Recovery Act unconstitutional, the President in a Message to Congress in February, 1937, boldly and categorically demanded a reorganisation of the entire Federal Judiciary. In a very significant, and possibly historic, conclusion, which sums up in a phrase the very essence of constitutionalism, the President said: "It matters not that Congress has enacted the law, that the Executive has signed it and that the Administrative machine is waiting to function . . . the Judiciary . . . is assuming an additional function and is coming more and more to constitute a scattered, loosely, organised and slowly operating Third House of the National Legislature."

As a way out of the *impasse*, the President proposed that, whenever a Federal Judge, having reached the age of 70, failed to retire within six months, the President might appoint an additional Judge. But he was charged with attempting to "pack the Supreme Court," and the bill was finally defeated in the Senate. So the New Deal legislation, passed by Congress, was largely nullified by the action of the Supreme Court, a constitutional situation which could not arise in a unitary state. Roosevelt continued his Presidency into a third and fourth term, but before the question could be further tested the United States was caught in the toils of the Second World War, which called for a national concentration of a more compelling kind. It cannot be doubted that Roosevelt's attempt to use the federal machinery as an instrument of social reform has left a lasting distrust in the minds of many Americans of anything remotely resembling collectivism. But whether the realisation of Jefferson's "American dream" of "life, liberty and the pursuit of happiness" is possible under modern conditions except by a progressive strengthening of the federal power remains a matter of great controversy in the United States.

IV. THE SWISS CONFEDERATION

In the Swiss Confederation we have the oldest of existing federal states. In spite of its name, it is now a true federation and not a confederation, if by the latter we mean a loose league of states without a strong central power. But it was not always so. Founded in the successful struggle of three districts—the Forest Cantons—against the overlordship of Austria in the thirteenth century, it expanded to thirteen states, the number existing in the Confederation when it was recognised as independent and sovereign by the Treaty of Westphalia in 1648. At that time it was a loose league of states with no strong central power, and so it remained as it continued its chequered career through the storms and confusions of the French Revolution and Napoleonic Europe. Even in the general settlement of 1815 it did not find its final basis of stability. It was still too loose, as was shown in a short civil war begun in 1847 by seven Roman Catholic cantons (the *Sonderbund*, as they were called) which, like the Southern Confederacy in the United States in 1861, attempted to secede from the general body. Revision of the Constitution immediately followed the defeat of the seceding cantons, and the Constitution of 1848 transformed the old Confederation (*Staatenbund*) into a federal state (*Bundesstaat*). The Constitution of 1848 was radically revised in 1874, and the Constitution of that year, subsequently amended in certain features, is the one under which Switzerland is governed to-day.

In some respects the Swiss Confederation affords an even more striking example than the United States of how conflicting state interests can be overcome, without annihilating state identity, by the political device called federalism. Switzerland mocks all attempts to define nationality, for, though the Swiss form a nation, with a solidarity which has resisted through the space of more than six centuries the multifarious attempts which have been made to undermine it, they have always lacked and still lack a common religion and a common language, while even their mountains do not form a ring which would make a natural boundary. Nearly two-thirds of the population speak German, most of the rest speak French, and the remainder Italian (or else a dialect called *Romanche*). These language differences are officially recognised in the Federal Legislature where a member may speak in German, French, or Italian. Not only this, but in their history the cantons showed an amazing diversity of political institutions, ranging from the most advanced democracy to the most reactionary aristocracy. While, now, these variations have been abolished and all the cantons of Switzerland conform to some type of democracy, the ardent patriotism which breathed life into the Confederation and maintains it in health and strength, has not destroyed that attachment to local self-government without which the federation, as it is to-day, would not exist. Indeed, the modern federal system has been built rather out of cantonal habit and experience than by the application of principles derived from constitutional theories or foreign examples.

Nevertheless, the resemblance in some broad aspects between the Swiss and American systems is due to conscious imitation on the part of the reformers of 1848 and 1874, though it was far from their purpose to Americanise their institutions, and the Swiss Confederation remains, in several particulars, distinctive. The Constitution, for example, speaks of the Swiss "nation," a word unknown to the American Constitution, but, at the same time, it divides the powers in such a way as to leave the "reserve" with the cantons. Yet it shows at some points both an incomplete nationalisation and an incomplete federation. For, on the one hand, Article 3 of the Constitution asserts that "the cantons are sovereign in so far as their sovereignty is not limited by the Federal Constitution, and, this being the case, exercise all rights not delegated to the federal power." In proportion as this article divides the sovereignty it decreases the national unity. On the other hand, Articles 5 and 6 make cantonal constitutions dependent upon a guarantee of the federal power, and so they are not so secure as are the state constitutions in the United States. In proportion as the cantonal constitutions depend upon the federal authority rather than upon the Constitution itself, interpreted by a Supreme Court of Judges, as in the United States of America, the state as a whole is less federalised.

But there is a security for rights, both national and state, in Switzerland, which does not exist at all for federal purposes in the United States; namely, the referendum. We shall speak of this more fully later on. Here it is only necessary to notice that, while Article 6 of the Swiss Constitution requires the guarantee of the federal authority for cantonal constitutions, it adds that this guarantee must be given if the people of the canton accept the constitution. Moreover, ratification of amendments cannot be withheld provided a majority of the people demand them. A further loosening of the unity of the states is manifested in the Upper House of the Confederation, called the Council of States (*Ständerat*). While, like the Senate of the United States, it has two members from each canton (forty-four members altogether), the Constitution, unlike the American, leaves every detail of their selection and period of service absolutely to the cantons, whereas in the United States (by an Amendment of 1913) the Constitution lays down a uniform method for the popular election of Senators.

The Federal Executive in Switzerland is of a special kind which we shall examine in a later chapter. As to the judiciary, members of a Supreme Court of judges are elected for six years by the two Houses of the legislature sitting together as one tribunal. But they may be, and often are, re-elected. This Supreme Court, however, has no powers of interpreting the Constitution comparable to those of the Supreme Court in the United States, for the Swiss Court cannot declare any federal law invalid as infringing some provision of the Federal Constitution. That power is expressly left to the legislature which passes the law. But the Supreme Court does decide in cases of conflict between cantons, and it is the court of final appeal in all cases.

To summarise, we may say that, in the Swiss Confederation, the powers are divided so that the "reserve of powers" is left with the cantons; the Constitution is supreme, but it is left open at every point to an absolute democratic check by the instruments of the referendum and the popular initiative; and finally the federal judiciary has no power of interpreting the Constitution.

V. THE COMMONWEALTH OF AUSTRALIA

In the Australian Constitution are present all the characteristic features of federalism—the distribution of powers among bodies of limited and co-ordinate authority, the supremacy of the Constitution, and the authority of the courts to interpret the Constitution. In all these essential features the Australian Commonwealth much more closely resembles the United States than does the Canadian Dominion, and for this resemblance in the one case and lack of it in the other there are historical causes of the profoundest significance. Australia supplies the only example in which a political constitution has been framed for a whole continent, and this is because it is the only case of a continent all of whose inhabitants are of one race. Consider the shortness of its life—the first settlement at Botany Bay was not made until 1788—and then ponder the rapidity with which it progressed to the position of one of the most advanced social democracies in the world, through an instrument of government fashioned less than half a century ago.

The peculiar circumstances in which the separate colonies were founded and their sense of national homogeneity made their common allegiance easy enough to observe, first to the Mother Country and then to the federal Constitution of 1900. But this Constitution was to apply to an area only slightly less than that of Europe and to provide for the political destinies of a population then smaller than that of London. Such physical facts—the vast area which the colonies covered and the awful distances which separated them in a land whose communications were as yet ill-developed—had tended inevitably to isolation and to the growth of local feeling which required the most delicate handling. This gives the key to the particular form of federalism which was adopted. The six colonies which federated would not have done so except under a common sense of danger from the imperialising tendencies of the Japanese, a peril not apparent until the closing years of the last century but one which was to become terribly real for the Australians in the Second World War. The concern of these colonies was, therefore, much less to found a strongly centralised state than to find the means of forming a union which should deprive the federating bodies of as little of their individual power as was consistent with the end in view.

At the same time, there was a general feeling that an authority with wider powers than any existing before the federation was necessary for industrial and social development, and that a supreme judicial authority ought to be established to avoid the expense and delay involved in carrying cases to the Privy Council in London; so that, in the result, the federation became something more than a league for common defence and has proved itself an efficient instrument for the furtherance of that social legislation in which the Australasians ardently believe.

The Constitution states the powers of the Commonwealth Government and leaves the rest to the states. The list of powers enumerated is a wide one, but it still leaves a large area of freedom to the states. The Constitution establishes a Federal Executive—nominally the Governor-General in Council, but actually responsible to the federal legislature which consists of two Houses, namely, the Senate and the House of Representatives. In the Senate the states are equally represented (ten from each), in the House on a population basis. The Constitution originally allowed the states to make what arrangements they liked for election to Parliament, but these provisions were among a number which the federal legislature might change without constitutional amendment; and the existing arrangement by federal law is that the House of Representatives shall be elected throughout the Commonwealth in one-member constituencies, while the Senators shall be elected in each state, the whole state being the electoral division, but both under a system of preferential voting, which will be explained later.

Further, the Constitution establishes a Federal Judiciary with a supreme court which has power to interpret the Constitution, as in the United States, and to deal with all cases of conflict between the states or between any of the states and the Federal Authority. The Supreme Court in Australia differs from that in the United States in that, while the United States Supreme Court cannot entertain appeals from states on pure state law, the Australian Supreme Court can and does.

The Australian Commonwealth being, as we have shown, a truly federal system, the states have a very real existence of their own. They are, as we have said, equally represented in the Senate, and they each have a Governor, not appointed by the Federal Authority, as in Canada, nor elected by the people, as in the United States, but appointed directly by the Crown, *i.e.*, in practice by the home Government with the concurrence of the existing Government of the state. The Constitution allows a state, if it wishes, to seek the aid of the Federal Parliament in

legislating for pure state matters. Further, in 1929, the Commonwealth took over all State debts, and became the sole borrowing
authority. Such provisions imply a closer connection between
federal and state authority than obtains in the United States.

Finally, the Constitution arranged for a federal district in
which eventually the Federal Government was to have its home,
independent of any state. The area, called Canberra and covering about 900 square miles, was ceded by New South Wales to
the Commonwealth. It is about equidistant from Sydney and
Melbourne, and the Federal Government was installed there in
1928.

In Australia in recent years there has been, as in America, a
good deal of controversy as to the respective spheres of the
federal authority and the states. In particular, the Federal
Government has found itself constitutionally unable to deal on
a Commonwealth basis with such vital questions of common
concern as public health, the conduct of trading companies,
industrial disputes, unemployment, agriculture and fisheries,
and control of aviation. In the House of Representatives on
22nd November, 1938, the Government announced its intention
of holding a Special Session early in 1939 to formulate amendments to the Constitution. Both sides of the House cheered this
announcement. The Leader of the Opposition had already said
that Australia was ruled not by a majority of electors but by a
majority of judges in the High Court "invalidating legislation
not on its merits but on the ground that it was *ultra vires* the
written constitution." Every national emergency, he said,
found Australia's hands tied by "constitutional manacles resulting in inaction and serious delay and bringing into ridicule the
parliamentary system." No sovereign unity could, he added,
be procured with seven sovereign Parliaments, each of practically equal status, embracing 13 Houses, with more than 600
members and 70 ministers, with separate overseas representatives and separate services.

In view of the unreadiness of the state legislatures to sacrifice any of their existing rights, it was decided that the only way
to settle the matter was to appeal to the people. But before the
question could be brought to the test of a referendum, the
Second World War supervened. In 1944 discussions were resumed at a Conference of Federal and State representatives,

but its plan for a radical surrender of State powers was defeated in the subsequent referendum. Yet in 1947 the people warmly endorsed a scheme to provide on a federal basis certain clearly-defined social services. In 1951, on the other hand, in a referendum on a proposal to authorise the Commonwealth Parliament to make such anti-Communist laws as it considered expedient, the Government was defeated. It would thus appear that the people are reluctant to approve any amendment which is not at the same time stated in specific terms and supported by the main political parties.

VI. THE MODIFIED FEDERALISM OF THE DOMINION OF CANADA

The Dominion of Canada is less federal than any of the three examples we have so far examined, for while in the case of the United States, of Switzerland, and of Australia, the "reserve of powers" is with the states, in Canada the reverse is the case. It is for this reason that we have spoken of Canada as a modified example of a federal state. In fact, the federated units of Canada are not states in any real sense. They are called provinces, though they are far more powerful than local authorities in England, or than the four provinces of the Union of South Africa. Though the Dominion of Canada is not a fully federalised state, it is something very different from a unitary state like Great Britain, France, or New Zealand. But there are most important differences between the federalism of Canada and that of the other states described in this chapter.

Though not the oldest of British Colonies—an honour which belongs to Newfoundland—Canada is the oldest of the British Self-governing Dominions, strictly so called, for she was the first to receive Dominion Status, that is to say, Responsible Self-government, and its general adoption in later years has been inspired by her successful use of it. We shall deal with this question of Responsible Government later. Here we have to note the federal system of Canada, which is quite distinct from the principle of Responsible Government. But here, again, Canada had a long lead of Australia, for her federal system was founded by the British North America Act of 1867. Consisting originally of four provinces—Ontario, Quebec, Nova Scotia, and New Brunswick—the federation soon extended to include seven, and now consists of ten.[1] The background of Canadian federation was different from the Australian. The urge was more internal than external, but there was both an internal and an external reason for the particular form which Canadian federation assumed. Unlike Australia but like South Africa, Canada was torn by a conflict of nationalities, French and British, the causes of which were of long standing.

A strong central government was an urgent need, and yet a unitary system had been tried and had failed after the Act of 1840. A further difficulty was that this Act had applied only to Quebec and Ontario, whereas now there was a desire on the part of two or even three others to come into a common scheme of government with the first two. A loose league—a mere confederation—between these provinces would have been worse than useless: it would have solved nothing. A unitary state, on the other hand, was not likely to prove workable. Neither the one nor the other fitted the situation, in view of the added fact that vast areas of Canada were as yet unopened. On the one hand, a loose confederation would inevitably have left free an avenue to later conflict. On the other, a unitary system—even if it could have been made to apply to the existing political units, which it could not—suited though it might be to fully developed bodies politic, might prove unfitted for those as yet unborn.

Why, then, did not Canada make a federation of the U.S.A. type? The answer is to be found in the date at which a federal union was being seriously discussed in Canada, viz. 1864–1867. The Civil War in America (1861–5) had caused many, especially the Canadians who were such close observers of it, to despair of federalism, as it had so far worked itself out in the United States. Federalism had apparently broken down. In the conviction that it had, the leading Canadian statesmen found a compromise between a true federal system, which had become discredited, and a unitary system, which was unsuited to

[1]Newfoundland might have joined the Dominion in its early days, but decided instead to work out her own destiny as a separate Dominion. In 1933, however, owing to financial difficulties, Newfoundland sought British aid, with the result that Responsible Self-government was suspended and the administration of affairs vested in a Special Commission until such time as the island should again become self-supporting. In 1948 a referendum was held on the issue whether Newfoundland should continue under the Commission, or resume Responsible Self-government, or join the Dominion of Canada, and resulted in a small majority for confederation with Canada. So in 1949 Newfoundland at long last became the tenth Province of the Dominion.

Canadian needs. This compromise was a federal union which should reduce to a minimum the likelihood of serious friction[1].

Thus the principle of the distribution of powers under the Canadian system is, in general, the antithesis of that employed in the United States. In Canada the powers of the provinces are enumerated, the "reserve of powers" is left with the Federal Authority; so that, though a list of the powers of the latter is actually given in the original Act of 1867, this is only for the sake of greater clarity and not to diminish the federal power. The grant of powers to the provinces is considerable, including such matters, unknown to ordinary local government, as the amendment of their own constitutions (except that it may not abolish the office of Lieutenant-Governor), direct taxation within the province, the administration of justice, criminal and civil, and the control of municipal government within the province.

Like Australia, Canada has a Governor-General, appointed nominally by the Crown but actually by the British Government with the concurrence of the Government of the Dominion. But, unlike Australia, the federating units have not each a governor appointed by the state government but a lieutenant-governor appointed by the Dominion Government. A further lack of individual identity in the provinces of Canada, as compared with the states of Australia, is to be observed in the Senate whose members are not elected but nominated for life, and not by the province, but by the Dominion Government as vacancies occur. Further, the Governor-General in Canada may, on the advice of the Dominion Government, veto an Act of a provincial parliament, a power not possessed as to Acts of state parliaments by the Governor-General in Australia.

Finally, as to the Judiciary, there is a Supreme Court in Canada, but it has hardly any power of interpreting the Constitution. Such a power has no reason for existence in Canada, because (1) the "reserve of powers" is with the Federal Authority, (2) the Federal Authority has, under the Constitution, the right to veto provincial legislation.

To summarise the differences between Australian and Canadian federalism: (1) the Australian Constitution defines the powers of the Federal Authority and leaves the "reserve of powers" to

[1] But on a possible redistribution of powers see footnote p. 153.

the states, while the Canadian Constitution states the powers of the provinces and leaves the rest to the federal power; (2) Australia leaves the state governors to be appointed apart from federal interference, whereas Canada gives the appointment of Lieutenant-Governors of the Provinces to the Government of the Dominion; (3) in Australia the Commonwealth Government has no right to interfere with state legislation, while in Canada the Dominion Government has a veto on provincial statutes; (4) Australia has a supreme court which may interpret the Constitution, whereas the supreme court in Canada has such power only in a very slight degree; (5) the Australian Senate is elected in equal numbers from the states, while members of the Canadian Senate are nominated for life by the Dominion Government. In general, then, the Commonwealth of Australia is far more federal than is the Dominion of Canada, or, to put it the other way, Canada approaches much nearer to the type of state called unitary than does Australia. Thus, in spite of the propinquity of Canada to the United States, and the vast distance which separates Australia therefrom, the federalism of Australia resembles that of the United States, in every particular, far more closely than that of Canada does.

VII. GERMAN FEDERALISM

Federalism has a very long history in Germany. After the death of Charles the Great in 814 his Empire fell to pieces, and when the German section of it was restored it was never again so centralised as it had formerly been. Feudalism wrought great havoc in Germany, and the history of the Holy Roman Empire is one long tale of attempts to conceal the facts of disintegration, or, at least, decentralisation, with the cloak of an elective Imperium. Within the confines of what appeared to be a federal empire there grew up, in fact, two great rival states: Austria and Prussia. Even after the fall of Napoleon, who only enhanced the atomisation of Central Europe, these two could not compose their differences and the compromise called the Germanic Confederation, set up at that time, proved but a prelude to the final conflict between them. In 1867, after his success in the Austro-Prussian War, Bismarck drove Austria out and established the North German Confederation, which was joined, during the Franco-Prussian War, by the South German States, and the war ended in the triumphal proclamation of the German Empire (1871) which was to last until the closing days of the First World War.

It is not proposed here to enter into the details of the constitution of either Bismarck's German Empire or the Weimar Republic (1919) which Hitler overthrew. But we should note some general points of likeness and difference. Under the Empire, as it was established in 1871, the federalism was of a unique kind. It appeared to come into being by the spontaneous desire of the federating units, though actually the desire was indirectly induced by the force of Bismarck. It cannot be said that the German bodies politic desired either unity or union. They did not *desire* anything, and thus submitted easily to Bismarck's domination and consequently to the hegemony of Prussia. Under the constitution of the Empire the hereditary German Emperor was also hereditary King of Prussia. This would not have mattered so much except that the power of the Emperor was not nominal but real, and while that was so, Prussia was supreme, not merely from the point of view of its numbers in the two Houses of the Imperial Legislature. Further, the House which was representative of the people, the *Reichstag*, had no real power. The real legislative power lay with the House in which sat the envoys of the states, the Bundesrat, and in this Prussia had a preponderant influence. Thus the old German Empire was neither truly federal nor truly democratic, for in no truly federal system do you find the preponderance of one state, and in no truly democratic state do you find legislation in the hands of an unrepresentative body of men. But the Empire was none the less a real union. The power of the federal authority was defined, that of the states undefined. But the stated powers of the federal authority were very wide, and the constitution could be changed by the ordinary process of legislation, so long as there were not fourteen negative votes. There was a supreme court which settled disputes between the federal power and the states or between one state and another. But this supreme court was nothing but the *Bundesrat* or the committee of the states, and, this being predominantly Prussian and the Emperor being the all but absolute monarch of Prussia, it is not difficult to realise how little of the air of real federalism was breathed in the German Empire before the First World War.

Now, the First World War destroyed not only the power of Prussia but the dynasties of all the states which had federated in the German Empire. The situation was, therefore, doubly propitious for recasting the whole basis of the German state. Since Prussia was no longer to be feared, there was a strong move to create a unitary state, but, after much discussion and drafting, it was decided to establish a new federation yet one with a strong federal authority and an elective presidency open to any German citizen. There was some territorial reorganisation and each of the new states (*Länder*) was obliged to formulate a democratic constitution.

In the Constitution of the Weimar Republic the powers of the Federal Government were enumerated, but in two lists. The first (Article 6) was a list of powers solely in federal hands. The second (Article 7) was a list of powers which the Federal Government shared with the states, and Article 12 asserted that "so long and in so far as the Federal Government does not make use of its legislative power, the States retain that power for themselves." This did not apply to the exclusive legislative powers of the Federal Government (*i.e.*, those enumerated in Article 6). Federal law overrode state law, and in the case of differences of opinion as to whether state law was compatible with federal law, an appeal had to be made to the supreme court for a more exact interpretation of the federal law. It is important to note that the supreme court was no longer the Upper House, but a court of justice.

The *Reichstag* became a real legislative body. The Upper House (*Reichsrat*) was still made up of envoys of the state governments, but its power was greatly diminished. It was quite unlike the Senate in the United States of America and Australia where, though the members are sent from the states, yet they are democratically elected, and where all states are equally represented. The Republican régime did not substantially affect the numerical preponderance of Prussia over the other states, since there was to be one member of the *Reichsrat* for every million inhabitants of any state. But, since its powers were strictly limited, and since the identity of Prussia and the Empire in the executive had disappeared, there was a very real difference between Prussia's power under the Weimar Republic and her power in the old Empire. The creation of a supreme court as partial interpreter of the Constitution introduced a true element of federalism. Beyond this the principle of the Referendum was freely introduced into the Constitution, and it could be invoked either by the government or the people themselves, and on questions of ordinary legislation as well as proposed amendments to the constitution.

Thus there were present in the Germany of the Weimar Republic the three essential characteristics of federalism— namely, the supremacy of the constitution, the distribution of powers, and a court to interpret it in case of conflict between the authorities dividing the power. But Germany still had unique features as a federal state. First, instead of an absolute division of powers in which either those of the federal authority or those of the federating units are stated, there was a triple division into those belonging exclusively to the federal authority, those it shared with the states, and those not mentioned (but even here federal law was to override state law). Secondly, the Upper House, representative of the states' interests as distinct from those of the people as a whole, instead of being, as in all other federal states of importance to-day, equally representative of all the states, was brought together on a population basis, which gave Prussia more than twice as many members as the next largest state (Bavaria) had. Thirdly, the President was popularly elected (in which respect Republican Germany was like the United States but unlike Switzerland) but acted through a ministry responsible to the legislature (in which respect Germany was like Canada and Australia, but unlike the United States).

We have spent some time on the federal aspects of the constitution of the Weimar Republic, because it was that constitution which Hitler overthrew, and inevitably it was used as a basis of discussion by the Occupying Powers after the Second World War in considering how best they might gradually restore to the Germans the political control of their country. The kind of unitary system which Hitler imposed, after he had abolished every vestige of federalism, was manifestly not the type of government which the Liberal elements in Germany would wish to restore or which the Occupying Powers would tolerate.

Indeed, in the course of the discussions at the Conference of Foreign Ministers at Moscow in the early months of 1947, it was clear that all four Powers (Britain, U.S.A., U.S.S.R. and France) favoured an ultimate federal solution, though the Western Powers suggested a rather looser federation than did the Russians, who feared that the lack of a strong federal government at the centre would leave the road open for the emergence of some future Bismarck or Hitler who would make national unity his rallying cry.

But in their desire to re-establish a German government without undue delay the three Western Democracies were soon driven to act independently of the U.S.S.R., and in September, 1948, the first draft of a Constitution for a Federation of German States, prepared by a Committee of Experts, was submitted to a German Constituent Assembly at Bonn. This federal plan, though so designed as to be ultimately applicable to the whole of Germany, was necessarily confined at first to the eleven Western States, which contained about three-quarters of the total German population. The new Republic, which was inaugurated in September, 1949, has a legislature of two Chambers—a Lower House, the Federal Diet (*Bundestag*), and an Upper House, the Federal Council (*Bundesrat*)—with a President elected by a Federal Convention of both Houses, to which he is responsible through a Cabinet of Ministers.

VIII. FEDERALISM IN SOVIET RUSSIA AND YUGOSLAVIA

Although, as we have seen in the historical chapter, Soviet Russia, in establishing her political institutions, repudiated the methods of Western constitutionalism, the U.S.S.R. is, none the less, a federal state, and the Stalin Constitution of 1936 in its federal aspects bears, on paper at least, a striking resemblance to some of those we have so far examined in this chapter. The same is true of the Constitution of the Federal People's Republic of Yugoslavia of 1946, which is broadly modelled on that of Soviet Russia. It is thus worth while to compare with the older federations these newer and more revolutionary models which have emerged from so different a background.

Lenin's original Soviet Constitution of 1918 applied only to the area of Russia proper in Europe, by then known as the Russian Soviet Federated Socialist Republic (R.S.F.S.R.). In

1923 the Union of Soviet Socialist Republics was established, at first by the voluntary federation with the R.S.F.S.R. of three other areas, including the Ukraine, which had carried out Soviet revolutions, and was gradually enlarged by the inclusion of further Soviet Republics which had been set up in various parts of the old Russian Empire in both Europe and Asia. In that constitution the powers of the federal authority were specifically stated and the residue left with the federating republics. Lenin's Constitution is now replaced by the one drafted by Stalin and adopted in 1936 by the All-Union Congress of Soviets at Moscow.

Chapter II of the 1936 Constitution covers the State Organisation. Article 13 states that the U.S.S.R. is a federal state formed on the basis of the voluntary association of eleven Soviet Socialist Republics (the Russian Soviet Federated Socialist Republic, the Ukraine, White Russia, Georgia, Armenia, etc.), some of which include, besides the main state, autonomous republics and autonomous regions. The powers belonging to the Federal Authority are stated categorically in Article 14; Article 15 states that "outside of these limits each Union republic exercises independently its state power"; while further Articles state that "every Union republic has its own constitution" (Article 16); "each Union Republic retains its rights freely to secede from the U.S.S.R." (Article 17); and that "the territory of the Union republics may not be changed without their consent" (Article 18).

Article 47 (as amended 1947) establishes a conciliation commission in the event of disagreement between the Chambers; if no agreement is reached by this course and there is still no agreement of the Chambers, then new elections are held.

The number of federated Soviet Republics is now sixteen, besides which there are twenty-two autonomous Republics. The sixteen Republics include the Republics of Estonia, Latvia and Lithuania, which were incorporated in 1940. These Baltic States had been established as independent political entities at the end of the First World War, but their existence was always precarious between their two powerful neighbours. Russian control of them was, however, recognised in the Russo-German Peace Pact of 1939, though they were, of course, overrun by the Germans in the early days of the war with Russia. In the

Russian westward drive later they came once more under Russian domination. But since the end of the War, the U.S.S.R. has shown no disposition to allow them to detach themselves from the Union. The significant fact is the federal elasticity of the Soviet Union, which can, presumably, absorb any neighbouring state without disturbing its federal character. Such, then, is the constitutional theory of the U.S.S.R., as distinct from its authoritarian practice.

Post-war Yugoslavia has maintained its freedom, but its new constitution reveals a marked Soviet influence. Yugoslavia was one of the new states established after the First World War by the incorporation with the original Kingdom of Serbia of certain surrounding areas, mostly former provinces of the old Austro-Hungarian Empire. That Kingdom was composed of the most heterogeneous population, most of whom were Serbs, Croats and Slovenes, but in the most divergent proportions. The Kingdom included the former kingdoms of Serbia and Montenegro, and the districts of Bosnia, Herzegovina, Croatia, Dalmatia, Slavonia which formerly belonged to Austria-Hungary, and a western strip of pre-war Bulgaria. Such a confusion of areas and peoples could hardly hope to form a strong united state, yet that is what was attempted. If ever a situation, preceding the establishment of a new state, cried out for the trial of a federal experiment, this one did. Yet a unitary system was decided on.

With the end of the Second World War the federal state, which the earlier circumstances seemed to demand, has now come into being. Towards the end of 1945 a Constituent Assembly decided to abolish the monarchy and to establish a Federal People's Republic. Article 1 of the Constitution, which came into force on 31st January, 1946, states that Yugoslavia is a federal people's state of republican form, a community of peoples who have expressed a will to live together in a federal state. Article 2 states that

The Federal People's Republic of Yugoslavia is composed of the People's Republic of Serbia, the People's Republic of Croatia, the People's Republic of Slovenia, the People's Republic of Bosnia-Herzegovina, the People's Republic of Macedonia, the People's Republic of Montenegro.

Thus all the Slavic peoples which, in the days before the First

World War, hoped for incorporation with Serbia now form with the Serbs a federation in which all the component states are equal. Article 44 gives, in a lengthy list, the powers belonging to the federal authority, which, besides the usual functions connected with defence and diplomacy, include basic legislation concerning labour, social insurance and co-operatives, education, health and social welfare. The reserve of powers is with the federating states. Yugoslavia, in fact, is, like Soviet Russia, a socialist state, but the federal character of its constitution makes it an interesting example of the way old methods can be adapted to new purposes in modern political organisation.

IX. FEDERAL CONSTITUTIONS IN LATIN AMERICA

Latin America is an area as yet only very partially opened up to the forces of civilisation, and what lessons it may have to teach us in the art of government belong rather to the future than to the present and past. Nobody would take the states of South America as examples of the beneficent working of democracy or of the advantages to be gained from documentary constitutions. Most observers, on the contrary, have used them as awful illustrations of the fate that awaits peoples who, without any experience in the art of self-government, break away from their ancient tutelage. And certainly the instability of political institutions in South America would seem to justify these dark warnings. Nevertheless, as Lord Bryce said, the vicissitudes and experiences of the states of South and Central America in the course of a century's development, since they threw off the yoke of Spain (and Portugal), shed a flood of light upon "certain phases of human nature in politics." For us their interest lies in the manner in which they show the influence of Western constitutionalism, and especially of that of the United States, even in areas which are not properly ripe for it. Once these states had declared their independence of their European masters, it is not easy to see what form of government would have been best for them. Political stabilisation is the urgent need in these areas, and certainly it cannot be said that federal constitutionalism has supplied it.

Of the twenty republics of Central and South America, three —namely, the Argentine, Brazil and Mexico—are interesting as examples of federal states. These three states declared their independence during the great period of revolt from Spain and Portugal (1810–1830). The Argentine in 1825 promulgated a Constitution based upon that of the United States and was otherwise known as the United Provinces of the Rio de la Plata. The states or provinces have a reserve of powers, but their rights have been generally abused by the political chicanery of dictators at the centre. And although the Argentine is now one of the most prosperous states in Latin America, the people are still under the heel of a dictator. Brazil declared its independence of Portugal in 1822, but continued to be governed down to 1889 by an Emperor, Dom Pedro II. On his abdication, two years before his death, Brazil was declared a federal republic, in which the state governments have a large "reserve of powers" which they are able to enjoy owing to the huge distances which separate the thickly populated areas. The Constitution at the centre, however, enjoys an authority which is largely theoretical. As to Mexico, it adopted a federal scheme of government, founded upon that of the United States, about a century ago, which, with one or two amendments, has since remained nominally in force. But there is no basis of self-government in the federating units of the United States of Mexico, and it cannot be said that the Constitution has ever been properly at work.

The only conclusion to be drawn from these observations is that federalism is an ideal which cannot be realised unless the desire for it is backed by the will to achieve it; which means, if necessary, the use of force to which the federating units subscribe in common. The force of opinion is a more obvious and immediate need for federalism than for any other constitutional form, and where political experience is lacking—and this is a mild way of putting the abysmal absence of any sort of education among the vast majority of Latin Americans—federalism can hardly succeed. Force, indeed, has not been absent in all Latin American states, but its use has been factious, partial and despotic. The moral is clear. "Do not," as Lord Bryce said, "give to a people institutions for which it is unripe in the simple faith that the tool will give skill to the workman's hand." Still, one or two of the more advanced states have begun to show real progress, and if this goes on, constitutionalism will yet achieve something. Federalism may yet be the line along which political stability will be maintained when it is seen that without that stability the vast economic resources of Latin America can never be fully exploited.

READING

BRYCE: *American Commonwealth*, Vol. I, Chs. ii, xxvii–xxx. *History and Jurisprudence*, Vol. I, Essay viii. *Modern Democracies*, Vol. I, pp. 367–385, Chs. xxxiii, xxxvi; Vol. II, Chs. xxxviii, xlvi.
DICEY: *Law of Constitution*, Chs. ii and iii, Appendix, Notes ii, viii and ix.
FINER: *Modern Government*, Vol. I, Chs. viii, ix, x.
KEITH: *Responsible Government in the Dominions*, Vol. I, pp. 505–560; Vol. II, pp. 597–621.
LOWELL: *Governments and Parties*, Vol. II, Chs. v–vii and pp. 180–192. *Greater European Governments*, Chs. ix, xi, pp. 270–283.
MARRIOTT: *Mechanism of Modern State*, Vol. II, Ch. xxxvii.
NEWTON: *Federal and Unified Constitutions*, pp. 66–100, 239–294, 324–358, 408–436.
REED: *Form and Functions of American Government*, Ch. iv.
SIDGWICK: *Elements of Politics*, Ch. xxvi.
STRONG: *Story of American People*, Chs. vi, xiv.
WILLIAMSON: *History of British Expansion*, pp. 484–536.
WILSON: *State*, pp. 249–254, 283–300, 387–392, 438–447.
ANNUAL REGISTER FOR 1936 (for Stalin Constitution).
CONSTITUTIONS OF ALL COUNTRIES: Vol. I, *British Empire*, pp. 19–56, 57–111.
  The text of the Constitution of the Federal People's Republic of Yugoslavia is given in a brochure issued in 1946 by the Yugoslav Government.

BOOKS FOR FURTHER STUDY

BROGAN: *Introduction to American Politics*.
BROOKS: *Government and Politics of Switzerland*.
FINER: *Governments of Greater European Powers*.
KRÜGER: *Government and Politics of the German Empire*.
MOORE: *Constitution of Commonwealth of Australia*.
PORRITT: *Evolution of the Dominion of Canada*.
WHEARE : *Federal Government*.

SUBJECTS FOR ESSAYS

1. Distinguish between a confederation and a federal state.
2. "A federal state is a political contrivance intended to reconcile national unity and power with the maintenance of 'state rights'." Discuss this definition.
3. In what sense is it true to say that in a truly federal state sovereignty resides in the Constitution?
4. What is meant by the term "Reserve of Powers"? Explain the ways in which the power in a federal state may be divided between the federal and the state authorities.
5. Explain the federal system in the United States of America.
6. Trace the history of federalism in Switzerland and compare its existing form with that of the United States.
7. State the likenesses and differences between the federal system of the Australian Commonwealth and that of the Dominion of Canada.
8. Trace the history of federalism in Germany. To what extent has the federal organisation of the Weimar Republic been restored in the Republic of Western Germany, set up after the Second World War ?
9. Compare the federal elements in the Constitution of the People's Republic of Yugoslavia under the Constitution of 1946 with those of the U.S.S.R. under the Constitution of 1936.
10. Account for the presence of federalism in some of the states of Latin America and show how far it has effected political stability in them.

CHAPTER VI

THE FLEXIBLE CONSTITUTION

I. GENERAL REMARKS

In the first chapter we gave, as the best definition of a constitution, that of the late Lord Bryce, who called it a "frame of political society organised through and by law, that is to say, one in which law has established permanent institutions with recognised functions and definite rights." When we consider that it is to the same author that we owe the terms "flexible" and "rigid," to denote a distinction between two great classes of constitutions, we have again emphasised for us the fact that the distinction sometimes drawn between written and unwritten, or, as we have called them, documentary and non-documentary constitutions, is a false one. For a constitution is none the less a constitution even though it be not set out in documentary form. To deny this is to fall into the error of de Tocqueville, the great French expositor of American Democracy, who, because he found no constitutional document in our country, asserted that the English Constitution did not exist.

The documentary constitution is a manifestation of an advanced political consciousness which is awakened to the inadequacy of existing methods of government. Paraphrasing Bryce, we may ascribe the urge to promulgate such a constitution to one or more of the four following motives:

(1) The desire of the citizens to secure their own rights when threatened, and to restrain the action of the ruler.

(2) The desire on the part either of the ruled, or of the ruler wishing to please his people, to set out the form of the existing system of government, hitherto in an indefinite form, in positive terms in order that in future there shall be no possibility of arbitrary action.

(3) The desire of those creating a new political community to secure the method of government in a form which shall have permanence and be comprehensible to the subjects.

(4) The desire to secure effective joint action by hitherto separate communities, which at the same time wish to retain certain rights and interests to themselves separately.

And again, following the same authority, we may say that documentary constitutions arise in one of four possible ways:

(1) "They may be granted by a monarch to his subjects to pledge himself and his successors to govern in a regular and constitutional manner, avoiding former abuses." Such was the case with the French Charter issued by Louis XVIII in France in 1814, and renewed with some differences in 1830 by Louis Philippe, the Constitution of Sardinia in 1848, and the Prussian Constitution of 1850.

(2) They may be brought into being by a nation throwing off its old form of government and creating an entirely new one, as was the case with the successive French Republics from 1790 and with the original thirteen states of the American Union.

(3) They may be created by a new community, not hitherto a national state, when it enters upon a formal existence as a self-governing entity. This was obviously the case with the states created in Europe after the First World War, such as Poland and Czechoslovakia.

(4) Finally, they may arise out of a tightening of the tie holding together loosely bound self-governing communities. By such a process a mere league of states becomes a federal state and the constitution on the basis of which such a change takes place is bound to be rigid. By such a process the loose confederation of North American States as it existed in 1783, at the moment of the official separation from Britain, became in 1789 the federal state we know to-day. The existing Swiss Republic is another example. So also was the modern German Empire which was created in 1871 by steps out of the Germanic Confederation of 1815.

Now, every existing constitution of importance is of this order except one, namely, the British. But more than one constitution is like the British in the sense that it can be altered by the ordinary method of legislation without following a special procedure for that purpose laid down in the constitution. Thus, the distinction drawn between unwritten and written constitutions is triply misleading. First, it misleads us by suggesting

5

that, while the force of custom and precedent is the sole ground of development in an unwritten constitution, the written constitution knows nothing of unwritten usage. But, as we have said, no constitutions are either written or unwritten in this absolute sense. If, when we used the term flexible constitution, we meant one in which no written laws existed for its perpetuation, we should be bound to admit that there does not exist in the world to-day a single instance of a flexible constitution. When we speak, for example, of the Constitution of the United Kingdom as being unwritten, we do not for one moment mean that there are no statutes in its composition, for, as we shall show, there are many. All we can say of the British Constitution in this connection is that it is more permeated by custom and convention than any other. And of all other constitutions we may say that not one of them is unaffected by custom and convention.

Secondly, the distinction between unwritten and written constitutions is misleading because it implies that there can be no laws of the constitution except those which are all brought together in one document called the constitution. If no such document exists, this argument seems to say, then there is no law of the constitution. This was the implication of de Tocqueville. He was writing in 1834, but he would probably say the same if he were writing in the twentieth century, for nothing has happened in the meantime to alter the argument: there is still no document called the British Constitution. Laws modifying the Constitution in this country have, it is true, been passed since de Tocqueville's time, but to say, as one recent writer says, that, since the passage of the Parliament Act of 1911, the British Constitution is a partially written one, is to ignore the great mass of laws which helped to mould the Constitution before that time. If it is now, since 1911, partially written, it was also partially written earlier.

Thirdly, this distinction is misleading because thereby we are persuaded to believe that law must necessarily be in a written form. This is certainly not true. Even if we could point to a constitution which had developed solely upon custom, we might still assert that it had law, for custom can have the force of law; and further than that, law may be written without passing through any process that we now know as legislation.

II. THE NATURE OF LAW

In our introductory chapter we spoke of three kinds of law. First, we have that bundle of social habits which we call custom, untouched by any formal legal procedure. Many of these remain in modern conditions as a sort of legacy from early times, but are, in highly civilised communities, like modern Western states, little more than rules of morals and manners. Secondly, we have a formal category of laws, not written out in statute form, but being fully enforced as law in properly constituted law-courts. This is case-law or judge-made law, and, in England, that great mass of law which we know as the Common Law. Thirdly, we have written laws called statutes, properly passed through a legislature or parliament.

These three branches of law all have the same ultimate sanction, which is society's desire for peace and progress; for the state, as we have emphasised earlier, is only society politically organised, and the more society becomes conscious of its political self, the more it will deliberately use instruments of government to protect and advance its purposes, and the more also it will check any abuse of power on the part of those instruments. A community organised for law (which, it will be remembered, was one of our definitions of the state) must move forward, but it is conscious that it must not do so too quickly. For society has two aspects, the static or still and the dynamic or moving, a fact emphasised in Auguste Comte's dictum that "progress is the development of order." And the cardinal problem of government is how to serve the one without outraging the other. Thus the three kinds of law interact upon one another. If, for example, custom seems to be developing too swiftly, judge-made law or statute law can stem its flow; if a decision of the judiciary is against the current of opinion, the legislature may be invoked to reverse that decision; if legislative enactment outrages the opinion of the community, that opinion can either force the hand of the legislature to alter or repeal it or make such a law a dead letter by merely refusing to obey it.

The same remarks apply to that branch of law which directly affects the constitution of a state, that law with which we are specially concerned here and which is generally called constitutional law. All states have this branch of law, and all three methods of law-making—the customs or conventions of the community, the decisions of judges, and enactments of the legislature—are employed, though in varying degree, in the creation of it. As to the first two kinds, constitutions differ only in degree, for there is no constitution without its conventions which have been founded on the basis of custom rather than of law, nor one in which the decisions of the courts have not played some part in constitutional development, from the few in the case of the United States or France to the many in the case of our own constitution. As to the third kind, *i.e.*, actual statute law, constitutions differ not only in degree but in kind. And here we must be careful to distinguish between two meanings of the term constitutional law. In its widest sense it means any statute-law or case-law which affects the constitution. In a narrower sense it means only that law contained in a document called the constitution, and laws passed to change or amend the constitution by some special process, the details of which are set out in the original constitution.

Now, it is clear that a non-documentary constitution, like our own, has no constitutional law in this narrower sense. It is also evident that a documentary constitution which lays down no special conditions as to its amendment—as was the case, for example, with the original Italian Constitution before Mussolini made it a dead letter—can have no amending constitutional law in this sense. The essential difference, then, is between the methods of bringing about changes in them. An observer would not expect a constitution whose roots are very old, like our own, to be in the form of a document, for the earliest forms of government are necessarily of a fluid and indeterminate type, the stream of custom being, so to speak, dammed from time to time by a wall of law. One would not here look for such a highly-polished instrument as a documentary constitution, forged by a society groping so blindly after its purposes. Such an instrument is a much later development, a manifestation, as we have said, of an advanced political consciousness, which finds occasion, through some upheaval, to express itself suddenly and completely. But, if a political society like our own has found no need for this sudden and complete expression at one time and in one document, that does not make its instrument of government any the less authoritative, and its constitutional changes, passed in the form of ordinary laws, are just as stable as if passed by a special process set out in a document.

The same is true of any constitution which, though in the form of a document, allows changes to be made in it by the ordinary process of legislation, and sets up no special machinery for such a purpose. Here, then, as we have shown, is a means of classifying constitutions according to the method by which the constitutional law is enacted. Certain constitutions state that this branch of law must be passed by a different method from that used in the ordinary business of legislation. Such are rigid constitutions. Others make no such distinction. Under such constitutions the body responsible for any legislation is responsible for all legislation, constitutional or otherwise. These are flexible constitutions, and the thing that characterises the state to which such a constitution applies is the unlimited authority of its Parliament.

III. THE TRUE CHARACTER OF A FLEXIBLE CONSTITUTION

The test of the flexible constitution, then, revolves upon the question of the method of amendment. If the method of passing constitutional laws is identical with the method of passing ordinary laws not of a constitutional character, then the constitution is flexible. Every modern constitutional state has, as we have said, a properly constituted legislature corresponding to the British Parliament, and the expression "unlimited authority of parliament" means that there is no power in the state which can either limit its scope or override its decisions. Not all parliaments have this unlimited authority, a fact we have already emphasised in the case of the federal state. But it is not only in federal states that we find restrictions of this sort placed upon the representative legislative assembly. In many unitary states the constitution is regarded as a document of special sanctity, not to be touched except by some special machinery much more cumbrous than the ordinary legislative process, or else as a law of superior obligation which imposes, for effecting changes in it, legal restraints upon the action of the legislature.

Broadly speaking, there are four methods of constitutional amendment in use among states with rigid constitutions: first, that by the legislature under special restrictions; secondly, that by the people through a referendum; thirdly, that method peculiar to federal states where all, or a proportion of, the federating units must agree to the change; and fourthly, that by a special convention for the purpose. We shall note these in greater detail in the next chapter. Here it is necessary to point out that in a state with a flexible constitution there is no restriction of this nature whatsoever. In the introductory note to his charming book, *The Government of England*, a great American, A. Lawrence Lowell, has observed that the difference between a flexible and a rigid constitution may be very slight, and that the distinction tends to get less clear with the passage of time. "From countries which can change their fundamental constitutions by the ordinary process of legislation," he says, "we pass by almost imperceptible degrees to those where the constitutional and law-making powers are in substantially different hands."

From this the author argues that the classification of constitutions into flexible and rigid is hardly a real one. Yet it is. If we care to regard the alteration of constitutions in the modern world as characterised by an ascending scale of difficulty, with the completely flexible constitution of the United Kingdom at one end and the highly rigid constitution of the United States at the other, is it possible safely to assert that we cannot find the dividing-line? Surely that line lies where the legislature begins to be hedged about with restrictions when it has to deal with constitutional law. On one side of this line are the states whose parliaments, even though established upon the basis of a documentary constitution, are unrestricted in this respect. On the other are those whose parliaments are not unlimited. The list of the latter begins with those, like Belgium and Rumania,[1] where a special quorum of members is required to be present when constitutional proposals are being considered, and a special majority is demanded for their passage into law. It rises to the case where the ordinary legislature is not allowed on its own initiative to pass constitutional acts at all, as in the United States.

[1] The Belgian Constitution, necessarily out of action during the German occupation in the Second World War, was restored to its normal working when the Germans were driven out. The Rumanian Constitution, having been undermined by the Nazis, was demolished by the Communists when in 1948, under the aegis of Russia, they founded the People's Republic of Rumania.

The true character of a flexible constitution is therefore clear. Flexibility and rigidity form a perfectly valid basis of classification, though, in fact, the rigid constitutions form the vast majority. Indeed, among modern states there are now only two in which no special procedure for constitutional purposes is known. These states are Great Britain and New Zealand. These two have, therefore, flexible constitutions. Their parliaments can do exactly as they like without legal hindrance. Where no documentary constitution exists, as in the United Kingdom, Parliament can repeal any or all of its separate laws, can legislate to end any merely conventional practice, and could, if it wished, introduce an entirely new and complete instrument of government. There are many serious reasons, of course, why it should not go to extremes in such matters, but there exists no technical prohibition against such action. Where there is a documentary constitution, as in the case of the other states now under consideration, either the statement as to amendment in the constitution categorically leaves the ordinary legislature a free hand to do as it likes, which is the case with New Zealand; or no conditions appear in the constitution as to what may be done to alter it, which was formerly the case in Italy.[1] Therefore, in New Zealand, as in Britain, the legislature is supreme in this regard. We will now proceed to a closer examination of the flexible constitutions of Britain and New Zealand, leaving for our next chapter a detailed study of some important rigid constitutions.

IV. GROWTH OF THE FLEXIBLE CONSTITUTION OF GREAT BRITAIN

The British Constitution is very old, but its age is sometimes exaggerated. There is left in Britain to-day, for example, little of the government which Alfred the Great knew, and if Magna Carta is the "Palladium of British liberty," very few of the current maxims of government in this country can be traced to that particular source. Indeed, to emphasise the venerability of the British Constitution is, perhaps, to put the emphasis in the wrong place, since the peculiar strength of that constitution lies not so much in its great age as in its flexibility, without which the ancient constitution would long since have

[1] i.e., from the time of the Unification of Italy until the later period of Mussolini's Dictatorship. See later, pp. 151-152.

disappeared in name as it has very largely in fact. The original prerogatives of the Crown of England have in the course of centuries been overlaid in practice so that they now remain only in a form of words. Thus nominally the United Kingdom remains a monarchy, and this nominalism is followed in the words of the very latest statutes, which, taken literally, are utterly meaningless and entirely out of accord with the facts of the moment. No more characteristic quality of the British Constitution, indeed, could be found than this lack of consistency between letter and spirit, for it has permitted change without great crisis and development without much violence, enabling the constitution to shape itself to the dynamic needs of our society without outraging that conservative sentiment which is the expression of its static self.

The story of the growth of the British Constitution is the story of a continual series of adaptations to changing needs, and this by two distinct sanctions—custom and law. These two elements have to be carefully distinguished, though they are frequently brought together under the heading of constitutional law. The first element is strictly not law at all, consisting as it does of maxims and practices which, although firmly fixed in our constitutional life, would not, if brought to the test, be recognised in a court of law. The second element is a body of true law which, whether written or unwritten, would be enforced by the courts. This body of law is made up of three elements, namely, (1) unwritten or common law; (2) statutes; (3) treaties. We have said something of this development in Chapter II. Here we may recapitulate and summarise the growth of this flexible constitution through five epochs, suggested by the great constitutional historian, Maitland, as follows: (i) from the earliest times to the death of Edward I (1307); (ii) to the death of Elizabeth I (1307–1603); (iii) to the death of William III (1603–1702); (iv) to the passage of Gladstone's Reform Acts (1884–5); (v) to the present day.

(i) Anglo-Saxon methods of government underwent considerable change after the Norman Conquest (1066) owing to the systematisation of feudalism (which already existed before that event) under William I and his successors. Many of the old institutions, however, remained, though with changed names, to suit the prevailing preponderance of Norman-French. The

most marked characteristic of this period was the centralisation
of government in the hands of the king, which proportionately
weakened the baronial tendency to disintegration. All through
the period from 1066 there was a struggle going on between the
King and the Barons whose opposition to the Crown on the
head of a weak king led to sheer chaos in the earlier part, as in
the reign of Stephen, but took a more regularised form in the
later, as is seen in the document called Magna Carta, under
John. The establishment of Parliament by Edward I in 1295,
following the example set by Simon de Montfort thirty years
earlier, marks a further stage in the conflict between the Crown
and the nobles, for this move introduced a leaven of commoners
into the counsels of the king, the effect of which was to counter-
balance the all-pervading influence of the Lords Spiritual and
Temporal in Parliament, though this was not the original
intention of the establishment of the Commons, which was to
obtain extra grants of money.

(ii) In the first part of the next period (1307-1603) the parliamentary experiment broke down. The Lancastrian Monarchy
(1399-1461), having no blood right, had to depend for its
perpetuation upon this institution, which became utterly discredited amid the manifold difficulties of the reign of Henry VI.
In this reign the baronage broke loose again and had its final
carnival of anarchy in the Wars of the Roses. Under the Tudors
(1485—1603) order was restored. Their monarchy was a despotism, but it was veiled in the cloak of constitutional forms. The
essential constitutional fact of the Tudor period is the more or
less continued existence of Parliament. It is not necessary to
ask what it did during this time, but to note the fact that it
existed. This marked the true beginning of the convention of
parliamentary government in England. Unconsciously, the
Tudors, by the use of Parliament, laid the foundations of the
conflict during the ensuing Stuart period between Crown and
Parliament. By the end of the Tudor period the need for a royal
despotism had passed and the fact that Parliament had had a
more or less unbroken existence in that epoch was all-important
in the next.

(iii) During the Stuart period the issue between Crown and
Parliament was fought out. After the quarrels of the reign of
James I and the Civil War under his son, the English state saw,
5*

for a short period (the Commonwealth 1649–1660), something that it had never seen before and was never to see again—a series of documentary constitutions. The Restoration brought the revival of the older parliamentary forms, but Parliament was now laying claims to power which it was to make good as a result of the Revolution of 1688–9. This Revolution, having dethroned James II, issued in the Bill of Rights which established in fact the supremacy of Parliament over the Monarch, though in form it left the sovereignty of the state in the hands of the King in Parliament. The Bill of Rights was the first of a long series of statutes which now form the mass of the written law of the constitution, and from that time it has been not only conventionally unconstitutional but statutorily illegal for any monarch to act as the Stuarts had acted. The Bill of Rights was soon followed by the Act of Settlement (1701), which emphasised the triumph of Parliament over the Crown.

(iv) The next period (1702–1885) was marked by the most extraordinary development of constitutional conventions. They are not to be found in written form during the period, yet they form the keystone of the arch of our government to-day. Here came the full establishment of the Cabinet System (of which we shall speak in a later chapter) and of modern parliamentary procedure. Some of this belongs to the conventions of the constitution, some to unwritten law, and some to statute law. Of statutes amending the law of the constitution, passed during the period, the most important were the Septennial Act of 1716 and the Reform Acts of the nineteenth century (1832, 1867, 1872, 1884, 1885) affecting the franchise, the ballot and the distribution of seats. Lastly, in this period there were some important examples of those statutes which we have called treaties, with Scotland, Ireland, and certain Colonies (with which we have already dealt in the chapter on the Unitary State).

(v) The last period belongs to our own times. The great constitutional act of this period is the Parliament Act of 1911 which arose out of a conflict between the two Houses of Parliament over the rejection by the Lords of Mr. Lloyd George's Budget of 1909. Nothing better illustrates the flexibility of our constitution and the unlimited authority of the British Parliament than the story of this conflict; and the subsequent statutes, by a simple Act of Parliament the relation between the two Houses was profoundly modified; the Lords agreed to a radical limitation of their power; and to achieve these ends the conventional procedure of legislation was gone through. Further than this, it illustrates the "dependence in the last resort of the conventions upon the law of the constitution." Before 1909 it had always been regarded as a convention of the constitution that the Lords would not amend or reject a Money Bill. When they did so, it required a statute to make the convention good against this threat. To this period also belongs the Parliament Act of 1949 which amended the Act of 1911 with the aid of the procedural machinery established by the original Act. The other great statutes of this period were the Representation of the People Act of 1918, which enfranchised a large number of women, and, finally, the Act of 1928 granting women the vote on the same terms as men, of which we shall speak in detail later.

V. THE BRITISH CONSTITUTION AT WORK

Out of this age-long development has emerged the constitution under which we are governed to-day. The Queen is still supreme in name, being nominally the law-giver, the judge, the commander-in-chief of the armed forces. But in fact the Crown is hedged about with so many limitations that as a political force it hardly exists any longer. The conventions, the unwritten laws and the statutes have so affected this original monarchy as to have transformed it into what is in practice, perhaps, the most real political democracy in the world. It is impossible to make a complete list of the conventions of the constitution, since by their nature they are constantly changing through the processes of growth and decay. But it is possible to distinguish them from the unwritten laws of the constitution by observing whether or no any court of law would take notice of their violation. The conventions are maxims and not laws, and, as Dicey observes, under a new and documentary constitution some of them would probably take the form of laws and others would disappear.

Among the principal conventions of the constitution are the following:

(i) "The Queen must assent to any bill passed by both Houses of Parliament."

It is fruitless to speculate on what would happen if the Queen refused her assent, because she never does. Presumably, if any monarch did refuse to sign a bill, a statute would be passed to correct the fault. While the convention is never violated, it is as good as a law in the Statute Book.

(ii) "Ministers must resign when they have ceased to command the confidence of the House of Commons."

This confidence need not be that of a majority held by one solid party, a fact illustrated during the Labour Administrations of Mr. Ramsay MacDonald in 1924 and 1929. If the confidence of the majority is lost there is no law to force the resignation of the Ministry. But if the defeated Ministry did not resign, supplies of money would be denied, government would be at a standstill, and at last anarchy would ensue.

(iii) A bill must be read three times in each House before being passed and receiving the royal assent.

This convention has been affected by the Parliament Act, as explained below.

To the unwritten laws of the Constitution belong the following:

(i) "The Queen can do no wrong."

This means that the Queen cannot be held responsible for any act performed in her name. Ultimately, this statement is to be taken quite literally, for if the Queen were to commit a crime (Dicey offers as an example the shooting of the Prime Minister) there is no process known to law by which she could be brought to trial. The statement also means that no one can plead the orders of the Crown in defence of any wrongful act. This is law, but it is not written.

(ii) "Some person is legally responsible for every act done by the Crown."

This responsibility of Ministers results from the facts that the Queen can do no wrong, that the Courts will not recognise any act as done by the Crown, and that the Minister affixing the Seal to any act is answerable for it.

Among the most important rules depending upon statute law are the following:

(i) "There is no power in the Crown to dispense with the obligation to obey a law."

This is definitely stated in the Bill of Rights. In practice it means that any government which refused to recognise the validity of a law existing in the Statute Book would be acting illegally.

(ii) A bill passed by the Commons in two successive sessions and each time rejected by the Lords (provided that one year has elapsed in the process, but irrespectively of the super-vention of a General Election within the period) goes straight to the Queen for signature. A money bill, passed once by the Commons and rejected by the Lords, becomes law after the passage of one month (the Speaker of the House of Commons deciding what is a money bill). The period of the Suspensive Veto is as laid down in the Parliament Act of 1949. This Act, as we have already noted, amended the Parliament Act of 1911 which had required three successive sessions and a minimum of two years. Under the procedure of the Act of 1911 the Welsh Church was disestablished in 1920 and under that of the Act of 1949 the Iron and Steel Industry was nationalised in 1951 by a statute which, however, was repealed two years later.

(iii) A parliament having been in existence for five years must be dissolved, as laid down in the Parliament Act of 1911.

From these remarks we see how flexible the British Constitution is. There is not one of these customs, not one of these unwritten laws, not one of these statutes which could not be abolished or repealed by an Act of Parliament. While customary developments are perpetually going on, the truth remains that Parliament is supreme and no judge or code of any sort can hold anything superior to its statutes. Nothing could be more eloquent of the supremacy of the British Parliament than the fact that on the very first occasion that it was called upon to dissolve under the Act of 1911—namely, in 1915, the last Parliament having been elected in 1910—it passed an Act to extend its life. The same thing happened in 1940. These exten-sions were, of course, due to the wars, but, in order to make them, Parliament sought no special powers, nor did it appeal to any tribunal beyond itself. A similar extension had taken place in the crisis of the Jacobite Rebellion which broke out in 1715. This was in 1716 when the Septennial Act was passed to extend the life of the then existing Parliament which had been elected under the provisions of the Triennial Act of 1694.

Yet the British Constitution, flexible though it is, has been taken as the model upon which many rigid constitutions have been founded. In Britain political institutions have grown upon an empirical basis, and the fact that experience rather than abstract principles has always informed their development is what gives them their peculiar stability. Only by a study of the institutions of those states which have founded theirs upon ours can we hope to answer the question whether it is possible to adapt with success that type of government which has been evolved through years of experience to the new-found needs of a community whose liberty, unexpectedly dawning, suddenly requires a fully developed political constitution.

VI. THE FLEXIBLE CONSTITUTION OF NEW ZEALAND

Of the Self-governing Dominions under the British Crown— to which the latest additions are Pakistan and Ceylon, established as Self-governing Dominions in 1947[1]—New Zealand is the only one with a flexible constitution. The principal remaining Self-governing Dominions—Canada, South Africa, and Australia—have constitutions of varying rigidity, and with these we shall deal in the next chapter. There is a sense, of course, in which until recently the constitutions of British Self-governing Dominions, without exception, were rigid. It was that, since the constitution in each of these cases was originally granted by an Act of the Imperial Parliament at Westminster—*i.e.*, the Parliament of the United Kingdom— no change in that constitution could be allowed without the sanction of that same body. But for some time before 1931[2] the veto had not in practice been effective, and, in any case, for New Zealand it was specifically removed in 1947 by the Constitution (Amendment) Act of that year.

We have already seen how the existing Constitution in New Zealand came into existence, and how, starting out upon a federal basis, the state became in 1876 definitely unitary by the abolition of the Provincial Governments. The Constitution of New Zealand, as a document, is found in the Act of 1852 which is entitled "An Act to grant a Representative Constitution to the Colony of New Zealand." Article 68 of this Act says :

"It shall be lawful for the said General Assembly (*i.e.*, the New Zealand Legislature established by the Act) by any Act or Acts to alter from time to time any provisions of this Act,"

[1] India and Pakistan have since become Republics. See later, pp. 302–303.
[2] The year of the Statute of Westminister.

and adds the proviso about "Her Majesty's pleasure" which, as we have seen, is no longer operative.

The original Act has been much changed, but merely by the ordinary process of legislation. Even the Act of 1876, which abolished the Provincial Governments and made New Zealand a unitary state, was an ordinary statute passed by the New Zealand Parliament to revise the constitution in this direction, as was also the Act which abolished the Second Chamber in 1951. The original Act has been since judged to have been a wise and liberal measure which not only granted independence in response to a sturdy demand of nationalism but allowed by its language amendment of the constitution by a method suited to the needs of a progressive community.

Thus the Constitution of New Zealand is unique among flexible constitutions. While the Constitution of the United Kingdom is, as we have seen, a non-documentary one which may thus be revised or amended without special procedure, the Constitution of New Zealand is a document containing a statement as to the means of amendment, which, however, categorically leaves the normal legislature supreme in this regard. It is the only case in which such supremacy is stated in so many words. Again, among Self-governing Dominions, New Zealand, from the constitutional point of view, stands alone. Like South Africa and Eire, but unlike Canada and Australia, New Zealand is a unitary state. Of these five the constitutions of all except Canada detail the method of revision. Canada's does not do so beyond reference to an appeal to the Privy Council in London. Yet Canada's is a rigid constitution, owing to the federal character of the state. Of those which state the method of amendment New Zealand alone permits the ordinary legislature to revise the constitution without restriction. The other three make definite conditions in this respect, and we shall therefore deal with them, together with the Constitution of Canada, in the next chapter on Rigid Constitutions.

READING

BAGEHOT: *English Constitution*, Ch. ix, pp. 241–258.
BRYCE: *History and Jurisprudence*, Vol. I, Essay iii. *Modern Democracies*, Vol. II, Ch. lvi.
DICEY: *Law of Constitution*, pp. xlviii–lix, 1–34, 106–123, Chs. xiv–xv. Appendix, Notes vii, xiii.
FINER: *Modern Government*, Vol.I, pp. 181–5.

GETTELL: *Readings in Political Science*, Ch. x.
JENKS: *Government of British Empire*, Chs. i and ii.
JENNINGS: *Cabinet Government*, Ch. i. *Law and Constitution*, Chs. i–iv.
LOWELL: *Government of England*, Vol. II, Chs. liv, lv, lviii. *Governments and Parties*, Vol. I, 150–152.
MACIVER: *Modern State*, Ch. xii.
WILSON: *State*, pp. 178–189, 213–215, 424–425.

BOOKS FOR FURTHER STUDY

AMERY: *Thoughts on the Constitution.*
ANSON: *Law and Custom.*
GREAVES: *British Constitution.*
ILBERT: *Parliament.*
KEITH: *Constitution of England.*
LOW: *Governance of England.*
POLLARD: *Evolution of Parliament.*

SUBJECT FOR ESSAYS

1. Explain precisely what is meant by a documentary constitution, and state the motives which lead a people to create one and the ways in which it may be brought into existence.

2. Criticise de Tocqueville's dictum that "the British Constitution has no existence."

3. Show how law develops in a community and compare its force with that of custom.

4. Define the term "constitutional law" and show how it differs from other sorts of law.

5. Name the essential characteristics of a flexible constitution, and show how they are exhibited in the case of any one such constitution in the modern world.

6. Trace the growth of the British Constitution and show from its history to what extent we are justified in describing it as flexible.

7. "By the passage of the Parliament Act in 1911 the British Constitution has become a partially written one." Criticise this statement.

8. Distinguish between the conventions and the laws of the existing Constitution of the United Kingdom.

9. "The fact that experience rather than abstract principles has informed their development is what gives them their peculiar stability." Demonstrate the truth of this statement as applied to British political institutions.

CHAPTER VII

THE RIGID CONSTITUTION

I. SPECIAL MACHINERY FOR CONSTITUTIONAL LEGISLATION

WHILE the outstanding characteristic of the flexible constitution is the unlimited authority of the parliament of the state to which it applies, that of the rigid constitution is the limitation of the power of the legislature by something outside itself. If there are some sorts of laws which the legislature is not permitted by the normal method to enact, it is manifest that that particular legislature is not supreme. There is, in such a case, a greater law than the law of the ordinary legislature, and that is the law of the constitution which is, as we have said, a law of superior obligation unknown to a flexible constitution. The simplest way to grasp the distinction between these two kinds of law is to consider how rigid constitutions have, most commonly, come into existence. In most cases they have been born of the deliberations of a special body called a constituent assembly. The business of such a body is not to enact ordinary legislation but to devise an instrument of government within the limits of which the ordinary legislature shall function.

The constituent assembly, knowing that it will disperse and leave the actual business of legislation to another body, attempts to bring into the constitution that it promulgates as many guides to future action as possible. If it wishes, as it generally does, to take out of the hands of the ordinary legislature the power to alter the constitution by its own act, and since it cannot possibly foresee all eventualities, it must arrange for some method of amendment. In short, it attempts to arrange for the re-creation of a constituent assembly whenever such matters are in future to be considered, even though that assembly be nothing more than the ordinary legislature acting under certain restrictions. At the same time, there may be some elements of the constitution which the constituent assembly wants to remain unalterable by the action of any authority whatsoever. These elements are to be distinguished from the rest, and we may call them fundamental law. Thus, for example, the American Constitution, the oldest of existing rigid constitutions, asserts that by no process of amendment shall any state, without its own consent, "be deprived of its equal suffrage in the Senate," and the two most recent rigid constitutions —that of the Fourth French Republic (1946) and that of the Italian Republic (1947)—both contain a clause stating that the republican form of government cannot be the subject of an amending proposal.

We have seen how the term rigid constitution is to be distinguished from the term documentary constitution. It does not follow, let us repeat, that because a constitution is documentary it is therefore rigid. The sole criterion of a rigid constitution is whether the constituent assembly which drew up the constitution left any special directions as to how it was to be changed. If in the constitution there are no such directions, or if the directions explicitly leave the legislature a free hand, then the constitution is flexible. If there are restrictions, no matter how slight, then the constitution is rigid. We have already indicated in summary the main methods of modern constitutional amendment, which are:

(1) by the ordinary legislature, but under certain restrictions;
(2) by the people through a referendum;
(3) by a majority of all the units of a federal state;
(4) by a special convention.

Before enlarging on these it is necessary to observe, first that they are arranged in order of increasing rigidity as to the method, and secondly that in some cases the system of amendment is a combination of two or more of these methods.

(1) There are three possible ways in which the legislature may be allowed to amend the constitution, apart from the case where it may do so in the ordinary course of legislation. The simplest restriction is that which requires a fixed quorum of members for the consideration of proposed amendments and a special majority for their passage. This latter condition operated in the now defunct constitution of Rumania. A second sort of restriction is that which requires a dissolution and a general election on the particular issue, so that the new legislature,

being returned with a mandate for the proposal, is, in essence, a constituent assembly so far as that proposal is concerned. This additional check is applied in Belgium, Norway and Sweden. It might be said to hold also, up to a point, in the case of the United Kingdom, for it is unlikely that a modern administration would propose a radical change in the constitution without a previous appeal to the people, an appeal which, for example, took place twice in 1910 before the passage of the Parliament Bill. But certainly we cannot say that British constitutional law or even the conventions of the constitution require it. In 1928, for instance, Parliament passed a new Franchise Act and discussed the Reform of the House of Lords, though neither of these questions was an issue at the election of 1924 which returned that Parliament. Again, more recently, in 1948, the Bill to curtail the period of the suspensive veto of the House of Lords from two years to one was passed by a House of Commons which, whatever the merits of the case, had certainly received no specific mandate to this end at the General Election held three years earlier.

A third method of constitutional change by the legislature is that which requires a majority of the two Houses in joint session, that is to say, sitting together as one House, as is the case, for example, in South Africa.

(2) The second plan is that which demands a popular vote or referendum or plebiscite. This devise was employed in France during the Revolution and again by Louis Napoleon, and in Germany by Hitler. It has never been used in Great Britain, though it was suggested as a way out of the *impasse* reached during the two-year controversy over the Parliament Bill which finally became law in 1911. This system prevails in Switzerland, Australia, Eire, and, in certain circumstances, in France under the Fourth Republic and in Italy under the new Republican Constitution.

(3) This method is peculiar to federations. There is no federation, of course, whose constitution does not require, in some form or other, the agreement of either a majority or all of the federating units. The voting on the proposed measure may be either popular or by the legislatures of the states concerned. In Switzerland and Australia the referendum is in use; in the United States any proposed amendment requires ratification

by the legislatures, or special conventions [referred to in (4) below], of three-fourths of the several states.

(4) Lastly, there is the method in which a special body is created *ad hoc* for the purpose of constitutional revision. As we have said, in a certain sense this is the case where the legislature may revise the constitution under special restrictions, and more obviously where the two Houses hold a joint session. But in some cases the convention is quite distinct from any other body. In some of the states of the American Union, for example, this method is in use, in connection, of course, with the constitution of the state concerned, and such a method is allowed for—if the Federal Congress so proposes—in the Constitution of the Union as a whole. It also appears in the original constitution of Bulgaria and of certain states of Latin America.

Broadly speaking, then, there are two methods of constitutional amendment most in use among states with rigid constitutions: first, that by the legislature under special restrictions; secondly, that by the people in a special reference. Of the other two methods, one is peculiar to federal states, but even so is not universal, and the other is generally only permissive. Geographically, the legislative method of revision is characteristic of Europe (with the important exception of Switzerland), while the larger legal restraints are confined principally to the United States and some of the Self-governing Dominions of the British Crown. We will now analyse in greater detail the method of constitutional amendment in some of the more important states with rigid constitutions.

II. THE RIGID CONSTITUTION OF THE FRENCH REPUBLIC

The Constitution of the Fourth French Republic, which was approved by a small popular majority in a referendum held in 1946, is a complete document. In this respect the new constitution is like its many predecessors, with the important exception of that of the Third Republic which was rather fragmentary. The French, in the course of the eighty years preceding the establishment of the Third Republic in 1875, had experimented amazingly in constitution-making, a branch of practical politics in which the world had come to look upon Frenchmen as pre-eminent craftsmen, who, to quote one of their own authorities, were accustomed to conceive of a constitution as a philosophical work in which everything is deduced from a principle; as a work of art of which the order and symmetry must be perfect; as a scientific machine of which the plan is so exact, the steel so fine and firm, that the very smallest hitch is impossible. In the exercise of this political ingenuity the French had contrived to devise no fewer than a dozen constitutions in the space of less than a century. But the circumstances in which the Third Republic was constituted after the French disaster in the Franco-German War were such as to drive French statesmen away from this tradition of the complete document and to found the new régime on three separate laws passed in July, 1875.

The real hope of the constitution-makers at that time was that the new constitution would not last, since the majority of them were not Republicans at all, but Royalists. The Republic, though not definitely organised until 1875, was actually born in September 1870, immediately after the capture of Napoleon III and his army at Sedan. After five months of desperate resistance to the Germans, Paris fell, an armistice was arranged, and in February, 1871, a National Assembly was elected by universal manhood suffrage to decide whether the war should be resumed. But it went far beyond this, and, having made peace, it governed France for the next four years and, before dissolving, carried the Republican Constitution. This body became a constituent assembly because in it the Monarchists of various kinds completely outnumbered the Republicans, and they feared a loss of power if another election was held. But, as Thiers, the dominant figure in the Assembly, who was destined to be the first President of the Republic, said, there was only one throne and three claimants for a seat on it. The supporters of these three (*i.e.*, the descendants of the Bourbon and Orleanist monarchies and the discredited Bonaparte family) failing to fuse, sank their differences in a compromise and acquiesced in the establishment of a "conservative republic," which, they hoped, would leave the future completely untrammelled. The more advanced Republicans agreed to this Republic because they hoped to change it in a radical direction. The Monarchists agreed to a Presidency, called a Republic, because they hoped to turn the President later into a King or an Emperor.

The general effect of the three laws of 1875, which were the bases of the constitution, was to establish a legislature of two Houses, that is, the Senate and the Chamber of Deputies, and the method of amendment was by means of a joint session of the two Chambers, called, when so joined, the National Assembly. Such a joint session could be convened if either Chamber, by an absolute majority, decided upon it. When so constituted the National Assembly had full power to amend the constitution as it might decide, except that, by a law of 1884, the abolition of the Republic could not be the subject of a proposal for revision. In fact, however, the National Assembly under the Third Republic made very few changes in the constitution during the sixty-five years of its existence.

The situation in which the French constituted the Fourth Republic was very different from that which saw the birth of the Third. It is true that both were conceived in the aftermath of invasion and enemy occupation, but the French people faced in 1946 the effects of a war, or rather of two wars, far more universal and devastating than that of 1870–1871. At all events, in 1946 nobody questioned that a republic was the only acceptable form of government. The point at issue, as we shall show later,[1] concerned rather the nature of the executive and the limitation of the powers of the President. Here we should note that in 1946, as there were no monarchists with whom to compromise, the French went back to the earlier tradition of the fully documentary constitution, and the new constitution is consequently far more rigid than the old. Most of the institutions of the Third Republic are revived, though under other names. Thus the new constitution speaks of Parliament (*le Parlement*) and says that it is composed of the National Assembly (former Chamber of Deputies and not, as before, the two Chambers in joint session) and the Council of the Republic (the former Senate).

The method of amendment is set out in a lengthy chapter containing six Articles (90–95). The initiative in this matter lies with the National Assembly, but any proposal for revision has to be examined by a small standing constitutional committee made up of the President and elected members of each Chamber. Any such law which in the opinion of the Committee implies an amendment of the Constitution is re-submitted

[1] See pp. 225–230.

to the Assembly, and must then follow the special amending procedure. If a proposed amendment is passed, on second reading, by a two-thirds majority in the National Assembly or by a three-fifths majority in each of the Chambers, then, within eight days of its adoption by Parliament, it must be promulgated by the President of the Republic. But if it is adopted only by an absolute majority in each Chamber (that is to say, less than the proportions mentioned above) it must be submitted to a referendum and then requires for its adoption the favourable vote of a majority of the people voting.

Beyond these limitations there are certain other restrictions. For example, any proposed amendment touching the existence of the Council of the Republic cannot be accomplished without the consent of the Council itself or by recourse to a referendum. And the last Article of the section of the Constitution dealing with revision states categorically that the republican form of government cannot be the subject of a proposal of revision. Such is the rigidity of the constitution of the Fourth Republic of France and all students of politics will watch with interest its operation in practice.

III. THE RIGID CONSTITUTION OF THE ITALIAN REPUBLIC

The Constitution of the Italian Republic promulgated in 1947 is like that of the former Kingdom in being in the form of a document but quite unlike its predecessor in its rigidity. There appears to be no doubt that the original *Statuto* of Sardinia of 1848 was intended by its framers to be final and for that reason contained no reference to methods of amending it. But, obviously, as it came to be applied to the whole of Italy and to operate through a period of rapid growth and change, some means had to be found to adapt it to new circumstances. This was achieved by the simple expedient of regarding the silence of the original constitution-makers in the matter of amendment as an indication that changes could be made by means of ordinary legislation. This was the view of responsible Italian statesmen in the last quarter of the nineteenth century. The Liberal Prime Minister, Crispi, for example, refused to admit the "intangibility of the *Statuto*," and said, in 1881, that the Parliament of Italy is "always constituent." "In Italy to-day," wrote another authority towards the end of the century, "the theory of parliamentary omnipotence is scarcely less firmly entrenched than it is in Great Britain."

In other words, in pre-Fascist Italy there was no distinction, any more than there is in Britain, between ordinary and constitutional legislation. Modifications of the actual text of the constitution were frequently debated but never effected. What happened was that successive Parliaments contented themselves with passing statutes making effective constitutional changes without altering its text or even adding clauses to it. Examples of such legislation were the law regulating the organisation of the Judiciary, the law of Papal Guarantees, and the several laws modifying from time to time the franchise and the nature and size of constituencies. Indeed, so flexible was the former constitution of Italy that Mussolini, in the earlier years of his dictatorship, was able to bend it to his will without breaking it, though he certainly hammered it out of all recognition later on when he finally constituted the Corporate State.[1]

The Constitution of the new Italian Republic, on the other hand, lays down in precise terms the way in which it may be amended, and, though the section of the Constitution dealing with revision is not so full as that in the Constitution of the Fourth French Republic, the Italian method of amendment is very similar to the French. The procedure for constitutional revision (set out in Article 138) may involve the electorate as well as Parliament (the Chamber of Deputies and the Senate). The law of constitutional revision must be carried in each Chamber in two readings, with an interval of not less than three months between them, and requires at the second reading an absolute majority of members of each House. The law must be submitted to a referendum if, within three months of its publication, a demand is made to that effect by one-fifth of the members of either Chamber, or by 500,000 voters, or by five Regional Councils, but this condition does not hold if the law is approved at the second reading by a majority of two-thirds of the members of each Chamber.

IV. RIGID CONSTITUTIONS UNDER THE BRITISH CROWN

The three Dominions with which we are here concerned have constitutions of varying degrees of rigidity. Taking them in

[1]See later, pp. 318—322.

increasing order of rigidity, we may say that the rigidity of the Constitution of the Dominion of Canada depends mainly on its federal character. The Union of South Africa is a unitary state, and this aspect of rigidity, therefore, does not arise. The rigidity of the Constitution of the Commonwealth of Australia depends only to some extent upon its federal character. With these constitutions we may conveniently examine that of Eire, although it is no longer a Dominion.

(i) *The Dominion of Canada.*—The Dominion of Canada was established, as we have said, by an Act of the British Parliament of 1867, entitled the British North America Act. This Act made a federation of four Provinces, the number of Provinces in the Dominion having now increased to Ten. The Constitution states the powers of government granted to the Provinces and leaves the rest to the Dominion Government (though it enumerates the chief of these also). Hence the only distinction in Canada between ordinary legislation and constitutional law is that the former concerns all matters not specially stated as within the ambit of provincial legislation, while the latter concerns any fundamental change in this division of rights. Obviously, then, the restriction upon the Dominion Parliament in the matter of constitutional amendment is measured by the powers expressly granted to the Provinces which the Federal Authority cannot touch without their consent.

It is true that the Act of 1867 states expressly what is only implied in the Acts conferring Dominion Status upon the other Colonies—that changes can only be carried with the consent of the Imperial Parliament—but this is due to the much greater age of the Canadian Act, passed at a time when the attitude of the Mother Country to the Colonies was utterly different from the spirit which prompted the British Parliament to pass the Statute of Westminster of 1931.[1] The material point to observe is that if once the Provinces of Canada agreed to some change in their relations to the Dominion Authority, no further machinery would have to be used to make such a change law than is

[1] The Act of 1867 says that the Constitution can be changed only through an Address by both Houses of the Dominion Parliament to the Monarch in Britain, but in 1949 the power to pass such legislation without reference to Westminister was finally transferred to the Parliament at Ottawa, and in 1950 discussions began there between the Federal and Provincial Governments concerning a possible re-distribution of powers among them, a procedure necessarily to be followed whenever Provincial rights are involved.

employed for ordinary legislation. Thus the Constitution of the Dominion of Canada is the least rigid in the British Commonwealth. Because of its federal elements it is clearly not a flexible constitution. But, granted the consent of the Provinces to any diminution of their rights as bestowed by the Dominion Constitution, any change can be carried by the normal act of the Dominion Parliament.

(ii) *The Union of South Africa.*—The Constitution of the Union of South Africa is slightly more rigid than that of Canada, and less so than that of Eire and the Australian Commonwealth. The Union of South Africa consists of four Provinces, two British and two Dutch. The solution of the problems arising out of Anglo-Dutch antagonism, revealed in the two South African Wars at the end of the last century, and the mutual bitterness which followed them in the early years of this, was found in the establishment of the Union by the Act of 1909. This, as we have shown earlier, is a federation only in appearance, not at all in fact, for, although the powers of the Provinces are indeed stated, they are hardly distinguishable from what we understand in this country as those of Local Authorities, and the Provinces do not hold these powers as of right, but only subject to the will of the Union Parliament. It is not here, therefore, that the rigidity of the South African Constitution lies.

The process of amendment is definitely laid down in Section 152 of the South Africa Act. It states that the Union Parliament may repeal or alter any provisions of the Act except (*a*) one which concerns the rights of the natives within the Union; (*b*) another establishing the equality of the Dutch and English languages; and (*c*) those laid down in a Schedule attached to the said section, which concerns the administration of native territories (Basutoland, Bechuanaland and Swaziland) which are Protectorates under the High Commissioner appointed by the Crown. (*a*) and (*b*) but not (*c*) may be changed by a bill passed by both Houses of the Union Parliament sitting together and at the third reading agreed to by not less than two-thirds of the total number of members of both Houses. Such is the rigidity of the Constitution of the Union of South Africa.

(iii) *The Commonwealth of Australia.*—The Constitution of the Commonwealth of Australia is, as we have already seen, that of a fully federalised state. It was established by an Act of Parliament of 1900 and came into force in 1901. The Commonwealth is composed of six states (the five divisions of the island of Australia, and Tasmania) all of which have a very lively individual existence. Their rights are very securely safeguarded, for the Constitution enumerates the powers of the Federal Authority, which consists of a legislature of two Chambers and an executive responsible to it, nominally under a Governor-General appointed by the Crown, and leaves the residue to the states, each of which is nominally under a Governor appointed, not by the Commonwealth Government, but by the Crown.

The means of amendment are contained in the final chapter (VIII) of the Constitution. Any law proposing an amendment passed by both Houses must be submitted to the electors of the House of Representatives in each state to vote upon it. Or, if any such law is passed by one House and rejected by the other, and is passed again by the same House after the passage of three months or in the next session, the Governor-General may submit it, with or without amendment by the House which objects to it, to a referendum. If then it is accepted by a majority of the electors in a majority of states and by a majority of all the electors voting, it becomes law. But if the amendment proposes an alteration of the limits of any state or a diminution of its proportion of members of each House or a change of any sort in its separate rights under the Constitution, then, besides the conditions already mentioned to be fulfilled, a majority of electors voting in that particular state must approve the proposed amendment.

As we have seen, recent attempts radically to enlarge the powers of the Federal Authority at the expense of the States have failed. But even if they should succeed in the future, there seems no reason to suppose that the amending machinery will be altered, and the Commonwealth of Australia is likely to remain the most rigid constitution in the British Commonwealth, for not only is it confined within the limitations of a federal state but amendment is safeguarded by a most elaborate process of referendum.

(iv) *Eire.*—Eire, as Southern Ireland has been called since 1937, was founded, under the name of the Irish Free State, as the result of a treaty signed between Great Britain and the part of Ireland concerned, following the devastation caused by repression and civil war, in 1922. The treaty granted to Southern Ireland the status of a Self-governing Dominion, establishing a legislature of two Houses (Dail Eireann and Senate) and an executive responsible to it, nominally in the hands of a Governor-General appointed by the Crown, though, as stated earlier, the Constitution of 1937 abolished the office of Governor-General, while a later Act of 1948 made Eire an independent Republic. The method of amendment was clearly stated in Article 50 of the original constitution, but added that the arrangements outlined were not to come into force until after the passage of eight years from the date of promulgation. The method of amendment there indicated is substantially the same in the Constitution of 1937 and is now, of course, operative. Article 46 (2) of the new Constitution states: "Every proposal for an amendment of this Constitution shall be initiated in *Dail Eireann* as a bill, and shall, upon having been passed or deemed to have been passed by both Houses of the *Oireachtas* (Parliament), be submitted by referendum to the decision of the people in accordance with the law for the time being in force relating to the referendum." And Article 47 (1) states that every proposal so submitted to the people shall be held to have been approved by the people if the majority of the votes cast at the referendum are given in favour of the proposal.

V. THE RIGIDITY OF THE SWISS CONSTITUTION

The present Constitution of Switzerland, as we have said, came into existence in 1874. Its federal character we have already discussed. Here we have only to note the method of revising it. The Swiss Confederation is composed of twenty-two cantons (*i.e.*, states) of which three are each divided into two for political purposes, making twenty-five. The federal legislature, called the Federal Assembly, consists of two Houses— the National Council and the Council of States. The powers of the Federal Authority are stated in the Constitution; the rest remain with the cantons. The methods of revision are precisely stated, in Chapter III of the Constitution, and they introduce not only the Referendum but the Popular Initiative, whereby the people themselves may propose amendments. (*a*) If one House does not accept a proposal made by the other for total revision, then it must be submitted to the people and if it is approved by a numerical majority of the citizens voting and of the cantons, elections are held. (*b*) If 50,000 citizens decide that a certain amendment is desirable, they may send it up as a specific amendment or ask the Assembly to prepare it for them. If the Assembly agrees, it prepares and submits the amendment to popular vote. If not, it may issue an alternative draft or recommend rejection. But if the popular request is for total revision and the Assembly disagrees, it must first submit to popular vote the question whether such an amendment should be prepared, and if the answer is in the affirmative (by the two majorities stated), then the Assembly prepares the amendment and submits it again for final approval by the people.

Thus the Constitution of the Swiss Confederation admits of both the legislative and popular methods of amendment, but makes in every case the final sanction of the people an indispensable condition for the adoption of a proposed amendment and its incorporation into the Constitution.

VI. THE RIGID CONSTITUTION OF THE UNITED STATES OF AMERICA

In the case of the United States we find the most rigid Constitution in the world. Its rigidity is due mostly to its federal character, a question with which we have already dealt in Chapter V. What we have to note here is the manner in which the Constitution may be changed. The history of the Constitution since its inception sufficiently illustrates the difficulty of amending it. The Constitution having come into force in 1789, the first ten amendments to it were adopted in 1791, the eleventh and twelfth in 1798 and 1804 respectively. After that, sixty-one years elapsed before the adoption of three amendments connected with the liberation of the Negroes, in 1865, 1868 and 1870 respectively. Only seven amendments have been carried since that time, the first in 1913 and the last in 1951 (Amendment xxii: limiting the President to two terms). Thus in 160 years only twenty-two constitutional amendments were carried, and even one of these (the twenty-first, 1933) actually repealed an earlier amendment (the eighteenth, 1918) which had established Prohibition. These facts prove that this oldest of existing documentary constitutions has, for all its rigidity, shown remarkable elasticity, and this has been due mainly to the decisions of the Supreme Court which is the interpreter of the Constitution. Also, during so long a period there has naturally been a certain amount of change in practice by conventional growth, so far as that has been possible without directly conflicting with the letter of the Constitution. The point we wish to emphasise here is that the legislature (Congress) of the United States has no power of its own motion to carry constitutional amendments: it can only propose them, as one of the ways of setting in motion the machinery of amendment which is laid down in the Constitution.

The history of the foundation of the Constitution accounts for this extreme rigidity. Up to the year 1775 the eastern seaboard of what is now the United States was occupied by a number of separate British colonies, the oldest of which had not been in existence for more than 170 years. They all had a greater or less tendency in their political institutions to break away from the Mother Country who, however, held them in what they at last came to regard as an intolerable economic bondage. The Thirteen Colonies had no common political interests, but had developed their own institutions in isolation, though there had been vague movements towards economic union. What, therefore, urged them to an alliance in arms against Great Britain was no positive stimulus to union, but a negative incentive to get rid of an unbearable external dominion. This is very clearly shown in the Declaration of Independence in the year following the outbreak of war. "These united colonies," it declares, "are, and of right ought to be, free and independent states." There is no word here concerning a form of common government. And when the war was virtually over in 1781 there began a long internal battle as to what form the Constitution of the Union should take, a battle which continued after the peace of 1783 had officially given the Americans their independence and their sovereignty.

The Articles of Confederation of 1781, under which the United States continued to be governed for the next eight years, were in effect "scarcely more than an international convention," the central authority having no effective will of its own. The passionate attachment of the states to their individual independence made them afraid to grant to any central authority an executive power which might ultimately deprive them of all their rights. At last a Convention met in Philadelphia in May, 1787, and drew up a Constitution which was "a work of selection rather than of creation." This is sufficiently clear in the Preamble, which says:

"We, the people of the United States, in order to form a more perfect union, establish justice, insure domestic tranquillity, provide for the common defence, promote the general welfare and secure the blessing of liberty to ourselves and our posterity, do ordain and establish this Constitution for the United States of America."

Its primary object being to secure the rights of the states while at the same time gaining the advantages of common action, this Constitution, which came into force in 1789, carefully enumerates what the common organ—*i.e.*, the Federal Authority—may do, the powers not so mentioned remaining with the States. It established the three great organs of government thus:

(i) The executive—a President elected for four years under rules definitely laid down.

(ii) The legislature—a Congress made up of two Chambers, the Senate and the House of Representatives.

(iii) The judiciary—a Supreme Court of judges given power to interpret this instrument of government.

It was a compromise which won acceptance by guaranteeing to all the states, irrespectively of their size and population, equal representation in the Senate—namely, two for each state —while the House of Representatives was to be composed of members from the various states in proportion to their population. The great power which the states had sacrificed was the right to make peace and war; in short, diplomatic power. But, while Congress as a whole must approve a declaration of war, making treaties requires the ratification of the Senate—*i.e.*, the House in which all the states are equally represented. Having stated categorically what powers Congress has, the Constitution goes no further into detail. It is concerned with what they may do, not *how* they shall do it. The Constitution furnishes only the great foundations of the system, but in that direction it is absolutely complete, and secure from abuse, for it lays down definitely and categorically the means of amending the Constitution.

Amendments may be proposed in one of two ways. Either
(*a*) two-thirds of all members (not members present) of each
house of Congress may agree that certain amendments are
necessary; or (*b*) Congress shall call a special convention to
consider amendments when petitioned to do so by the legislatures of two-thirds of the states. These conditions, be it observed, only concern proposals for amendments. When amendments
have been thus proposed they have to be agreed to by three-
fourths of the states. When this ratification has been secured the
amendment becomes part of the Constitution.

Here, then, is a very definite demarcation between statute
law and constitutional law in the American Union. This special
machinery for constitutional law is very cumbersome, hard to
set in motion and harder still to work to a successful conclusion.
The number of states has grown from the original thirteen to
the existing forty-eight.[1] The passage of time, therefore, and the
startling growth of the United States have only made amendment more difficult, since no amendment can now be adopted
without the concurrence of thirty-six states. But the Americans,
as we have seen, have in their separate states, each of which has
its own constitution, other outlets for their political activity
besides those laid down in the hard lines of the Federal Constitution.

VII. THE RIGIDITY OF GERMAN CONSTITUTIONS

In view of the restoration of constitutional government in
Western Germany, in 1949, it may be of interest, by way of
concluding this chapter, to indicate the rigid character of the
earlier constitutions. The Constitution of the Weimar Republic,
as we have seen, was promulgated in 1919. Apart from the
abolition of monarchy throughout Germany, the Republican
Constitution differed in many particulars from that of the
German Empire which the First World War overthrew. In the
German Empire, which was founded in 1871 at the conclusion
of the Franco-Prussian War, the quasi-federal character of the
constitution was most apparent in the Upper House, or *Bundesrat*. This latter, as we have said, was really a body of ambassadors from the various states, which were unequally represented
in that assembly. Seventeen minor states had in it one member

[1]Forty-nine when Alaska becomes a state, as agreed by Congress in 1958.

each. Any proposed constitutional amendment could be defeated in the *Bundesrat* by fourteen votes. Thus the representatives (or, rather, envoys) of the minor states could, by combining, prevent any change which might be detrimental to their status in the Empire. Or, again, Prussia, which had seventeen seats of its own, could prevent any such change.

In Germany after the First World War the situation was quite different, because the *Reichstag.*, *i.e.*, the Lower House, had a real existence and force which it had not formerly possessed, for under the old Imperial Constitution no constitutional amendment could have been even discussed by the *Reichstag*. The following was (according to Article 76 of the Weimar Constitution) the method of amendment. The constitution, it stated, might be altered by legislation, but only when the amendment was passed by a two-thirds majority of a quorum (two-thirds) of the *Reichstag* and by a two-thirds majority of the votes cast in the *Reichsrat* (formerly the *Bundesrat*). Moreover, if one-tenth of the voting population itself proposed an amendment to be submitted to the people, it had to be so submitted and a majority of the voters on the register could decide for or against. If the necessary majority in the *Reichsrat* was not reached and within two weeks it demanded a submission of the amendment to the people, it had to be so submitted for their approval in the manner stated.

Thus, in Germany under the Weimar Constitution, an amendment might be carried without a referendum by ordinary legislative methods under certain restrictions as to majorities in the Chambers, but either the Upper House or the people might bring the machinery of the referendum into operation under restrictions of time and percentage of numbers respectively.

The Bonn Constitution, technically known as the Basic Law, under which Western Germany has been governed since 1949, is equally rigid from the Parliamentary point of view, since it requires for its amendment a two-thirds majority in both Houses, although there is no reference in it to the use of the referendum. The Constitution may be amended only by a law which expressly alters or adds to the text of the Basic Law, but it does not admit of any amendment which would affect the organisation of the Federation into *Länder*, the basic co-operation of the *Länder* in legislation, or the basic principles
6

laid down in the Constitution concerning human rights and the democratic, social and federal character of the Republic. For so long, however, as the Occupation Statute might remain in force, a further restriction was imposed by Article 5 of that Statute which provided that any amendment to the Basic Law required the express consent of the Occupying Powers. In 1955 Western Germany regained full sovereign rights.

READING

BRYCE: *American Commonwealth*, Vol. I, Chs. iii–iv and xxxi–xxxv. *History and Jurisprudence*, Vol. I, Essay vi. *Modern Democracies*, Vol. I, pp. 249–252, 382–390. Vol. II, pp. 191–6, Ch. xxxix.
DICEY: *Law of Constitution*, pp. 123–164, 524–5, 533–5, Appendix Note i.
FINER: *Modern Government*, Vol. I, pp. 181–5.
GETTELL: *Readings in Political Science*, Ch. xv.
KEITH: *Responsible Government in Dominions*, Vol. I, Pt. iii, Chs. i–iv. Vol. II, pp. 741–2.
LASKI: *Grammar of Politics*, pp. 303–9.
LOWELL: *Governments and Parties*, Vol. I, pp. 2–13. Vol. II, Chs. viii–x. *Greater European Governments*, pp. 284–5.
MARRIOTT: *Mechanism of Modern State*, Vol. I, Chs. v and xvi.
REED: *Form and Functions of American Government*, Chs. i–iii.
SAIT: *Government and Politics of France*, Ch. i.
WILSON: *State*, pp. 146–151, 248–262, 354–5, 412.

BOOKS FOR FURTHER STUDY

BROGAN: (1) *Development of Modern France*. (2) *The American Political System*. (3) *Introduction to American Politics*.
BROOKS: *Government and Politics of Switzerland*.
DAWSON: *Government of Canada*.
TAYLOR: *Fourth French Republic*.
VILLARI: *Italy*.

SUBJECTS FOR ESSAYS

1. What do you understand by the term constitutional amendment?
2. How would you recognise a rigid constitution? How is it to be distinguished from a flexible constitution?
3. Detail the methods now in use of amending rigid constitutions.
4. Recount the circumstances in which the present Constitution of France was born and explain how far it is a rigid constitution.
5. In what sense are the Constitutions of the Dominion of Canada and the Commonwealth of Australia rigid?
6. Compare the method of constitutional amendment in South Africa with that detailed in the Constitution of Eire.
7. What peculiar features of amendment are present in the Constitution of the Swiss Confederation?
8. Distinguish between the procedure in use for proposing, and that for carrying, constitutional amendments in the United States.
9. In what ways is the Constitution of the United States more rigid than that of the Commonwealth of Australia?
10. Describe the procedure for constitutional amendment as it was set out in the Constitution of the former Weimar Republic.

CHAPTER VIII

THE LEGISLATURE

(1) SUFFRAGE AND CONSTITUENCIES

I. INTRODUCTORY

WE have observed in the first chapter that the functions of government are to be divided into three, namely legislative, executive and judicial; that is to say, the departments concerned respectively with the making of laws, the execution of laws, and the enforcement of the laws when made. In modern government the importance of the legislative function has greatly increased in proportion to the rising tide of democracy. Legislation, as we understand it to-day, in fact, is a comparatively recent development. In earlier political society there was no distinction between legislative and executive business. The government declared what laws were necessary and carried them into effect. And in the very earliest days of Parliament in England, for instance, the elected element of it, namely, the Commons, sought to evade the duty of legislation, wishing to leave it, in effect, to the body—the King and his Council—which had always performed it. The earliest business of the Commons, as we showed, was to make not laws but grants of money. But the modern conception of legislation, which results from the growing political consciousness of the mass of the people in whose collective interest most laws are now passed, has given the legislative organ an entirely new significance and at the same time raised questions as to the best means of making it do its work with the active consent of the citizens. A discussion of modern legislatures, therefore, involves a study of the democratic methods by which they are elected, and an inquiry how far the Upper House or Second Chamber is subject to a democratic check. The second point we shall defer to the next chapter. In this we shall confine ourselves to an analysis of modern electoral systems, from two points of view: first from the standpoint of the suffrage or franchise, and secondly from the standpoint of the electoral area or constituency.

II. THE GROWTH OF POLITICAL DEMOCRACY

By democracy we mean "that form of government in which the ruling power of a state is legally vested, not in any particular class or classes, but in the members of a community as a whole." It is necessary to emphasise this at the outset of a discussion of electoral questions, because democracy is sometimes taken to denote the rule of the "masses," as opposed to the "classes." Indeed, the Greek word *demos*, from which it is derived, was often used by the Greeks to describe the many, as distinct from the few, rather than the people as a whole; and Aristotle, as we have observed earlier, defined democracy as the rule of the Poor, simply because they always formed necessarily the more numerous class. But we use the term democracy here in the sense of the rule of the majority of the community as a whole, including "classes" and "masses" (if such a distinction has still any meaning), since that is the only method yet discovered for determining what is deemed to be the will of a body politic which is not unanimous. This will is expressed through the election of representatives. The evolution of this democratic method in modern times has been set within the limitations of the nation-state which has required a representative system. The advance of democracy, that is to say, has been by way of an ever-increasing extension of the franchise and by way of experiments in the manipulation of the size, form and distribution of constituencies in the hope of securing a legislature most truly representative of the views of the electorate.

This development is entirely modern, for, although the Ancient World had its democracies, notably in Greece and, to some extent, in the Roman Republic, the forces which have determined the democratic trend of modern times were absent then. Those forces may be summed up as religious ideas, abstract theory, social and political conditions favouring equality, and discontent with misgovernment. In so far as any of these forces were operative at all in the Ancient World, they arose out of causes quite different from those of the modern epoch. The Middle Ages in this respect may be said to have been one long period of complete eclipse of all interest in democratic politics, except for some obscure strivings after equality in some of the mediæval cities of Italy, until the Renaissance ushered in the modern era. For democracy, be it observed, is not to be confused with republican fervour, as we find it, for example, in the earlier days of the Swiss Confederation, or with the introduction of an element of Commons to assist the King's purse, as in the case of England in the fourteenth and fifteenth centuries, for such phenomena can easily co-exist with an oligarchical and even an autocratic régime.

It was not until after the Reformation that religious ideas began to play a part in the assertion of political rights which came to be conceived as the only means of gaining religious liberty. This is best illustrated in the conflict with the Crown under the Stuarts in England. It was the search after the enjoyment of religious rights which led to the establishment of the New England Colonies, and the Civil War in the reign of Charles I was as much a war of religious as it was of political principles. Abstract theory played an important part in the history of the eighteenth century, a truth which can be demonstrated by an appeal to the documents of the American and French Revolutions. When the authors of the Declaration of Independence and of the Declaration of the Rights of Man postulated that men were born free and equal, they were trying to lay the foundations of an edifice of practical politics, and not merely, as in the case of the early Christian Fathers, making an assertion of the equality of all men in the eyes of God. The influence of the theory of equality upon the franchise has been tremendous because the most obvious application of it was in the attempt to realise the idea of "one man one vote."

In the nineteenth century, with the improvement in material conditions and the advance of popular education, the general situation was favourable to extensions of the franchise. Western Liberalism assumed the existence of a "theoretically perfect body of citizens between whom there could be no discrimination at the polls." Moreover, the parliamentary system itself worked towards a widening of the electorate, since politicians sought the championship of an ever-increasing body of supporters. There was no great popular outcry, for example, in favour of such a measure as Disraeli's Reform Bill of 1867, which was described by his own party as a "leap in the dark," but the political situation and the social atmosphere made it opportune to establish what was called the "lodger vote." Lastly, discontent with misgovernment has always been a fruitful cause of franchise extension. Its realisation, it is true, has not always brought into existence the desiderata of its advocates, but, granted the forum of Parliament upon which grievances could be aired, political reformers (as distinct from revolutionaries) have unfailingly looked to electoral reform as a means of improving the conditions of the society to which they belonged. So it was with the Chartists in England from 1837 to 1848, with the Italians before the Unification, with the Liberals in Tsarist Russia, and with the oppressed minorities of the Austro-Hungarian Empire in the days before the First World War.

A very broad franchise is therefore characteristic of all existing constitutional states. The older states have carried out electoral reforms which have led to either adult or manhood suffrage, while the newly established states almost invariably wrote into their constitutions a clause bestowing universal suffrage irrespective of sex. And with this advance after the First World War emerged problems connected with electoral areas. Besides the question of the redistribution of seats arising from industrial progress and from the enfranchisement of sections of the community concentrated in areas hitherto unrepresented, a new problem has been born of the emergence of new minority groups which these changes have brought into existence. These groups have clamoured for such reform as would assure them a voice in the elected assembly or assemblies. The acuteness of this question may be gathered from a perusal of any election returns in a state not so reformed, showing the comparative figures for votes and seats. The realisation of its urgency has led in many states to constituency reform; in others, so far, only to an exploration of possible ways of removing what is on all hands admitted to be a weakness of the representative system.

III. THE SUFFRAGE AND ATTENDANT QUESTIONS

From the point of view of the franchise, then, we may say that states are divisible into two classes—viz., those with manhood suffrage and those with adult suffrage irrespective of sex—though it is sometimes necessary to qualify this absolute

demarcation. In some states there were till lately certain qualifications even for men voters, while in others, which had granted
an unrestricted franchise to men, the vote had been bestowed
upon only those women who complied with certain conditions.
In yet others, women were permitted to vote in municipal but
not in national elections. Broadly speaking, until recently manhood suffrage was characteristic of Latin Europe where there
still lingered a religious prejudice against the political emancipation of women. Thus until after the Second World War women
were still voteless in France and Italy, but the new Republican
constitutions in both those countries have enfranchised them.
In Spain, again, women had not the vote until it was granted
to them by the Republican Constitution of 1932, though that
constitution has, of course, been superseded by Franco's
dictatorship. On the other hand, of the states newly created
after the First World War, Yugoslavia alone failed to give
women the vote, though this is no longer true since the establishment of the Federal People's Republic in 1946. Woman
suffrage was even introduced in Turkey in 1934, and in the
following year no fewer than seventeen women were elected to
the Grand National Assembly. Women also voted for the first
time in Japan in the elections held, under American ægis, in
1947. To-day the only democratic state in Europe in which
women are voteless is Switzerland, where, as late as 1958,
their enfranchisement was still under discussion.

In tracing the history of political enfranchisement on the
Continent, we cannot fail to be struck by the influence of
France, which was the original home of the abstract theory of
political equality. The constitutions arising out of the French
Revolution, themselves largely modelled on the British Constitution, have been the pattern for many paper constitutions
in Continental states. And yet France lagged far behind most
of those who copied her constitution in granting women the
right to vote. There was, it is true, no great public outcry by
women for the vote in the countries mentioned, such as marked
the first years of the present century in some other countries,
especially Britain and the United States. There seems to be no
reasonable argument against the grant of the franchise to
females, once it is admitted that it is a right that all adult males
ought to enjoy. Female suffrage is, in fact, in the logic of

democracy, and this the French have accepted in the Constitution of the Fourth Republic. In short, it is difficult to distinguish between the "rights of man" and the rights of mankind. Outside Europe there are fewer constitutional states with only manhood suffrage than those with adult suffrage. In all British Self-governing Dominions women have the vote.

The voting age varies greatly from one state to another. In Russia, Turkey, Yugoslavia and the Argentine the age is eighteen; in Switzerland and France (under Fourth Republic) it is twenty; in the United States, Britain, Italy (for election of Deputies) and Western Germany twenty-one; in Norway twenty-three, as it is also in Denmark. Some states make voting compulsory. In Mexico, for example, an Act of 1917 denied the vote, for what it might be worth in that country, to those who would not exercise it. In Australia, again, by an Act of 1924, a fine is imposed on voters who do not record their votes for both the House of Representatives and the Senate. Compulsory voting is also the law in Belgium and Switzerland, and was imposed in Czechoslovakia under the constitution suspended during the German occupation, though this restriction does not appear in the new Constitution of 1948. A similar coercion exists in the Argentine, where the pressure is, in practice, probably of a more violent nature. As to secret voting, this is, in theory at least, common to most states. In Great Britain up to 1948, when University seats were abolished, the vote recorded by a university graduate required the signature of the voter and of a witness. In some states the ballot-box is hardly as secret as it might be. In the United States, for instance, the system of "voting by ticket" (*i.e.*, where all the candidates for various kinds of elective office in each constituency are placed in long lists under party labels) makes it difficult always to maintain the principle of secret voting.

Among states with adult suffrage, Britain, between 1918 and 1928, stood in a middle position. A series of electoral reforms, carried out in 1832, 1867 and 1884–5, had introduced a system of manhood suffrage, but with a diversity of qualifications which were mostly removed by the Representation of the People Act in 1918. This Act extended the Parliamentary franchise to all males of twenty-one, not subject to legal incapacity, who had resided in a constituency for six months or who occupied land or premises of not less than £10 annual value. By this Act also the principle of female suffrage received wide, but not complete, recognition. Women of over thirty were given the Parliamentary vote if Local Government electors, as occupiers of £5 annual value, or as wives of electors. In other words, this Act, while admitting the principle of the "lodger vote" in their case, denied to women, even if over thirty, a mere residential qualification.

The Act of 1918 also abolished plural voting except in the case of men who, besides a residential qualification, occupied other premises or land, as owners or tenants, of not less than £10 annual value, and in the case of university graduates (men and women). Both these classes were allowed a second vote, but nobody could have more than two votes. The general effect of the Act was to raise the number of male voters from 8,357,000 to 10,449,820 and to add 7,831,583 women to the register. If women, it was felt, were enfranchised on precisely the same terms as men, the female electorate would greatly outnumber the male, and this was presumably why the continued demand for equalisation of rights was for a long time denied satisfaction. Yet few people could fear any longer what had been feared before the First World War when the Woman Suffrage campaign was at its height—that the parliamentary system would suffer a revolution if this reform were carried out—for it could not be said that experience had shown that the partial enfranchisement of women had greatly affected the balance of political forces. Faced with this insistent demand, and the difficulty of logically answering it, the British Government in 1927 began seriously to explore the possibilities of extending the Act of 1918, and it was the general impression that a compromise would be reached by instituting equal qualification for men and women and finding a voting age for both somewhere between the existing two—say, twenty-five years. But in 1928 a Bill was introduced to enfranchise women on exactly the same conditions as those already existing for men, and this became the law for the General Election of 1929. The suggestion at the time of the Bill, to make the voting age of all new voters, male and female, twenty-five, merely took the form of a proposed amendment which was easily defeated. As a result of this Act, the total electorate in the United Kingdom was 26,750,000, *i.e.*, 12,250,000 men and 14,500,000 women.

6*

Examining the growth of franchise extension in this country from the first measure of reform to the last, we find that before the Reform Act of 1832 the electorate numbered 435,391, and that that measure added 217,386 voters to the register. The Act of 1867 added 938,427 voters to the existing electorate of 1,056,659. The Act of 1884 added a further 1,762,087 names, and in 1918 13,000,000 new voters were registered. Under the Act of 1928 5,240,000 women were newly enfranchised. It is now safe to say that the process of mere franchise extension, as distinct from less traditional methods of electoral reform, has gone about as far as it can go in Britain. There are other possible lines of democratic reform which we shall discuss later.

As in Britain, female suffrage was granted universally in the United States after a long agitation on the part of women. In the United States the Federal franchise has become very important in elections for three distinct kinds of office, namely, Representative, Senator and President. The original Constitution laid down no precise rules about these elections. As to Representatives, it merely said that they were to be "chosen every second year by the people of the several States, and the electors in each State shall have the qualifications requisite for the most numerous branch of the State legislature." As to the Senate, it was to "be composed of two senators from each State chosen by the Legislature thereof." As to the President, each State was to appoint the necessary number of electors "in such manner as the Legislature thereof may direct." In each of these cases, then, the detailed method of choice was left to the states individually. But since the Constitution was originally promulgated, some profound modifications affecting the vote have been introduced. In the first place, the vote became a vital part of the Presidential Election as soon as the practice grew up of electing Electors not because of their suitability for that office, but because they were pledged to the support of a particular candidate; when, that is to say, the Presidential Election became, in effect, a popular affair. Secondly, by the Seventeenth Constitutional Amendment (1913), the popular election of Senators was made obligatory on all states, the Amendment adding that "the electors in each State shall have the qualifications requisite for electors of the most numerous branch of the State Legislatures."

The position at the end of 1913 in the United States, therefore, was that whoever had the vote for the election of the Lower House in any state had also the vote for the election of members of both Houses of Congress and also for the election of Presidential Electors (*i.e.*, of the President). And since no details were laid down on the matter in the Constitution, it was always within the power of any state to grant women the vote for either or both Houses of its own Legislature. But if women in any state had the vote for elections to the state Lower House (*i.e.*, the more numerous branch of the State Legislature) they, by the Constitution, had the vote also for Federal Representatives, and, from 1913 onwards, for Federal Senators, and by practice also for Presidential Electors. Some twenty-nine states had already bestowed the franchise on women when during the First World War an agitation began for a constitutional amendment to grant nation-wide suffrage to women. In 1919 the proposal was passed by Congress, after a close fight in the Senate, and submitted to the states for the necessary ratification on the part of thirty-six out of the forty-eight states. By the end of 1919, only twenty-two states had ratified the Amendment, but, thanks to a campaign cleverly organised by the National Woman Suffrage Association, the thirty-sixth state was won over in time for the Presidential Election of 1920.

The position in the United States now is, to quote the words of the Nineteenth Amendment, that

"(1) The right of citizens of the United States to vote shall not be denied or abridged by the United States or by any State on account of sex. (2) Congress shall have power to enforce the provisions of this article by appropriate legislation."

This means, in practice, complete and unqualified adult suffrage throughout the American Commonwealth.

IV. THE SINGLE-MEMBER CONSTITUENCY

From the point of view of electoral problems, states are again divisible into two classes according to the type of electoral area or constituency that they possess. The constituency in a modern constitutional state is arranged so that it returns either one or several members. Generally speaking, when representative democracy was in its infancy, the normal constituency arrangement was the division of a country into a number of electoral areas, urban and rural, each returning a single member. But this territorial division was a mere convenience, and with a rapidly fluctuating relationship of population to district, constant redistribution of seats was necessary. In an expanding industrial epoch, however, it was not possible in most cases thereby to keep pace with the never-ceasing increases and variations of the population. Nor was this the only objection to this flat system of territorial division into single-member constituencies. A second, and even more urgent, problem was that of securing a system of voting which should result in the elected representatives forming an assembly that should adequately reflect the balance of opinion in the electorate.

The system of single-member constituencies is the one in force in Great Britain and the United States. In all constituencies, except one or two, in Great Britain one member is returned and in no constituency are more than two returned. All redistribution Acts have perpetuated this system. The House of Commons at the election of December, 1910, for example, was elected in 643 constituencies, of which only twenty-seven (including three of the University constituencies) returned two members. The Representation of the People Acts of 1918, 1928 and 1944, did nothing fundamentally to change this situation, though the number of seats fluctuated and the Representation of the People Act of 1948 abolished the University seats and all other remnants of plural voting. In the United States all constituencies for both Senate and House of Representatives are single-member constituencies. It is in these two countries, therefore, that constituency reform has been most urgently advocated, for it cannot be said that in either case the electoral system has achieved the end of the adequate representation of the views of the electorate.

It has, on the contrary, led to the most glaring anomalies, at any rate in Britain, for thereby it is not even assured that the majority party in the country will gain a majority in the House of Commons, while a very large minority may be quite inadequately represented there. At the General Election of 1922, for example, the Conservatives won 296 seats with 5,381,433 votes, the Labour Party 138 seats with 4,237,490 votes, and the Liberals 53 seats with 2,621,168 votes. This means that the Conservatives polled only 18,180 votes per seat, the Labour

Party 30,706 votes per seat, and the Liberals as many as 48,540 votes per seat. Again, at the General Election of 1924, the Unionists won 382 seats with 7,450,990 votes, or 19,505 votes per seat; the Labour Party secured 142 seats with 5,483,088 votes, or 38,613 votes a seat; and the Liberals obtained 34 seats with 3,008,097 votes, or 88,473 votes per seat. At the same election, in seven counties of Southern England the Unionists secured 84 seats with 1,456,702 votes, the Liberals one seat with 445,726, and the Labour Party no seats, though actually polling more votes than the Liberals, viz., 483,873. In Scotland at this election the Unionists (36 seats) secured ten more seats than the Labour Party (26 seats) while actually polling 8,755 votes less than the Labour Party (Unionists, 688,298; Labour, 697,053). Further to illustrate the chaos of electoral chances under the existing system, we may add that, while at the election of 1923 in Manchester the Unionists secured one seat with 104,027 votes, at the election of 1924 they obtained six seats with 136,195 votes, and the Liberals, having in 1923 won five seats with 71,141 votes, secured not a single seat in 1924 with 50,350 votes.

In the General Election of 1935 in the United Kingdom, the Government supporters polled 11,570,179 votes against a total opposition vote of 9,930,460, and yet the number of seats secured by the Government was 428, while those secured by the Opposition numbered only 184. In other words, though the Opposition polled over 80 per cent of the number of votes polled by the Government, they secured only 30 per cent of the seats. The result of the election was that the Government had one member for every 27,000 votes cast for them, the Labour Party one for every 53,000 votes, while the Liberal Party had only one member for every 85,000 votes. In the election of 1945 the Liberals obtained only eleven seats with $2\frac{1}{4}$ million votes, while the Liberal Nationals won thirteen seats with only 750,000 votes. Labour gained 392 seats with 12 million votes and the Conservatives gained 189 seats with $8\frac{1}{2}$ million votes. In other words, the Conservative vote was more than two-thirds of Labour's, yet they gained less than half the number of seats gained by Labour. Later elections tell the same story.

From the United States come similar illustrations of the shortcomings of the one-member constituency system. For example, at the Congressional Election of 1924 the Republicans in the State of Pennsylvania secured the whole of the 36 seats with a total poll of 1,322,070, while the Democratic Party with 481,400 votes secured no representation whatever in the House of Representatives. In the eight New England States, again, the Republican Party secured 28 Congressional seats with 1,330,585 votes, whereas the Democrats obtained only four seats with 804,473 votes. At the same election eleven Southern States (the "Solid South") returned 76 Democratic Congressmen with 1,144,007 votes, while not a single Republican was returned, though that party's total vote reached 336,076.

In the elections of 1938 in the United States for the Seventy-Sixth Congress the Democrats secured 262 seats and the Republicans 170 seats in a House of Representatives with a total of 435 seats. Thus over the whole Union, the Republicans secured only 39 per cent of the seats. Yet in 24 (mostly Northern) of the 48 States they scored 51 per cent of the total votes cast. Again at the Congressional Election of 1944 the Democrats secured 243 seats with slightly less than 23 million votes and the Republicans only 190 seats with slightly more than 21 million votes. So, with almost 50 per cent. of the votes, the Republicans secured only 43 per cent. of the seats. Similar inconsistencies have marked more recent elections.

All the parties in both countries are alive to the injustices of this system, but how they are to be overcome is a moot question. A Royal Commission on Electoral Reform sat in England in 1909–10, but the only positive recommendation for change that it made was not adopted. Later, in 1916–17, a Speaker's Conference was held, but again its recommendations were shelved. In the United States, a large and influential society has worked for the removal of the anomalies, but their efforts have never received official support or recognition. Generally speaking, the line of reform suggested is what is usually referred to as Proportional Representation, and it is, therefore, necessary to deal with this question in some detail.

V. THE MULTI-MEMBER CONSTITUENCY

Many states have now either incorporated into their existing political systems, or made an integral part of a new constitution, the electoral system called Proportional Representation.

But this term means very little, taken by itself, since there are many variations of it—almost as many, in fact, as there are states which have adopted it, and many more in theory. But all the variations have at least one common factor, which is, indeed, indispensable to this method of voting; it is that no system of Proportional Representation can possibly be worked on the basis of a single-member constituency. In any constituency under a system of P.R. (the abbreviation by which it is generally known and which we shall employ henceforth) the object of a candidate is not to gain a majority, as it is ordinarily understood, but to reach what is called a *quota*, *i.e.*, in its simplest form, a number of votes equal to the total of votes cast divided by the number of seats to be filled. The simplest form of the system is what the French call *Scrutin de Liste* or "general ticket" (not to be confused with the "voting by ticket" system in single-member constituencies, which, as we have seen, obtains in the United States). By a new electoral law of 1919 in France the *Département* became the constituency where formerly the electoral area had been the *Arrondissement*. The latter was a single-member constituency. All that happened under the new law was that all the electors of a *Département* voted for as many Deputies as there were seats (*i.e.*, a number equal to that of the *Arrondissements*) in the *Département*. Candidates might offer themselves singly or in combination in a list or ticket up to a number equal to the number of seats to be filled, and it was in such lists that most candidates offered themselves for election. Any candidate receiving a majority was elected, and in practice, since the average voter gave his vote to the whole list *en bloc*, this meant that the strongest party generally made a clean sweep of the whole *Département*. So far, then, the French system achieved nothing for the representation of minorities.

But the law of 1919 provided also that, if an absolute majority was not obtained, the seats were to be distributed among those candidates who reached the *quota* (*i.e.*, the number of votes divided by the number of seats). The share of each list was determined by the number of times the "average" (*i.e.*, the aggregate vote of all its candidates divided by the number of its candidates) contained the *quota*. For example, suppose that a *Département* had a population of 450,000 and a register of

100,000 voters, that 78,000 of these actually voted, and that the constituency returned six members. Then the *quota* was 78,000 divided by six—*i.e.*, 13,000—and each party received a number of seats according to the quotient. Thus a party scoring, say, 40,000 would have three seats, that scoring 30,000 would have two seats, and so on, any seat left over going to the party with the highest average.

The system of 1919 did not work well, and in July, 1927, the French reverted to *Scrutin d'Arrondissement* (single-member constituency). However, in the elections for the Constituent Assembly which prepared the Constitution submitted to a referendum in 1946, a form of *Scrutin de Liste* was revived, for the people had to vote for their candidate in groups under an arrangement devised to secure the proportional representation of the three main parties (Socialists, Communists and M.R.P.).

For the General Election held in June, 1951, an even more complicated system was devised, with the deliberate intention of excluding from power both the extreme Left and the extreme Right. Except in the Paris area, where a straight system of P.R. operated, the new law permitted the affiliation (*apparentement*) of parties and groups to form a *bloc* which came into being if no single party in the multi-member constituency obtained 51 per cent of the votes. In that case, if the *bloc* had a majority they took all the seats to the exclusion of the rest, and the seats were divided proportionately among the parties forming the *bloc*. If neither a party nor a *bloc* gained a majority, then the seats were allocated by simple P.R.[1]

The system more usually associated with the term P.R. is one that involves what is called the "single transferable vote," often called the Hare System because it was first suggested by an Englishman named Thomas Hare in a pamphlet entitled, "The Machinery of Representation" (1857), and expanded in his later treatise, "The Election of Representatives" (1859). Warmly endorsed by John Stuart Mill in his *Representative Government* (1861), it has been taken up and modified by later reformers. The idea in itself is very simple, once the prin-

---

[1] This political prestidigitation justified itself in the election, for it furnished the Centre parties with the combined power to form a government and, given the will, to maintain it, while it left the Gaullists and the Communists with rather more or less than a hundred seats each in an Assembly of 627 seats.

ciple of the multi-member constituency is grasped. Suppose you group four existing single-member constituencies into one constituency: then, instead of having to gain an absolute majority, the candidate needs only to reach the *quota*, *i.e.*, the number of votes cast divided by the number of seats to be filled. The voter indicates his preferences in their order. He has only one effective vote, but he may place a number against the names of other candidates besides the one he most desires to see elected, in order to indicate the candidate he would next choose, up to the number to be returned for the constituency. Thus, if there are ten candidates and four seats to be filled, the voter may place beside four of the names the numbers 1, 2, 3, 4 to express his preferences. Then, if all the seats are not filled owing to the fact that not a sufficient number of candidates reaches the *quota*, the other seats are filled by taking the second preference of the voters who have voted for the already successful candidate or candidates who therefore do not require these votes, then the third and so on until all the seats are filled. But the vote may be transferred in another way. If a sufficient number of candidates cannot be brought up to the *quota* by transferring the surplus votes of the successful candidate or candidates to others, then the candidate with the lowest number (or more than one if necessary) is eliminated and his or their votes are added to others according to the preference expressed. So a voter may help to get his second or third or fourth choice in, though the candidate of his first choice fails to be elected.

P.R., in some form or other, has been widely adopted in recent years. Thomas Hare himself would have turned the whole of any country into one vast constituency. But this, in the course of working out the scheme, has been abandoned as impracticable, though in a certain sense it was the principle involved in Mussolini's electoral laws in Italy, the effect of which, however, was intended by its authors to be something very different from a proportional representation of parties. In the elections in English-speaking countries which have adopted the system, the single transferable vote is, generally speaking, in use. In most Continental states, some form of vote by ticket has been adopted, so that in these the candidates submit themselves in lists with various types of safeguard against mere majority election. In Great Britain the single transferable vote was used for the election of Members of Parliament for certain Universities from 1918 until the abolition of University seats effected by the Representation of the People Act of 1948; for the National Assembly of the Church of England, for the House of Laity since 1919 and the House of Clergy since 1921; for Education Authorities in Scotland since 1918; and in Northern Ireland for both Houses of Parliament since 1920. As to the British Dominions, in South Africa P.R. is in use for local council elections in certain municipalities; in Canada for some municipal elections; in Tasmania for the House of Assembly; in Malta for a part of the Senate and for the House of Assembly. In Eire it is used for all elections. In India it was introduced, under the Act of 1935, for those members of the Federal Assembly elected by Provincial Legislative Councils of certain provinces. In the United States the adoption of P.R. has never gone beyond one or two cities, including New York, Cleveland (Ohio) and Cincinnati, which have thus used their wide powers of self-government.

On the Continent of Europe several states had adopted P.R. for some or all of their representative assemblies long before the First World War. For example, in Denmark it was first partially used for the Upper House of Parliament (*Landsting*) as long ago as 1855; in Switzerland for some Cantonal Councils in 1891; in Belgium for local government elections in 1895, and for the Chamber of Deputies and Senate in 1899; in Sweden for all elections in 1907. Denmark applied it to all elections in 1915, Holland in 1917, Switzerland in 1918, and Norway in 1919. Finally, all the constitutions promulgated by European states, including Germany, after the First World War included some form of P.R. It is also in use in Republican Italy.

One other principle should be mentioned in this connection, namely, what is called the Second Ballot. This is a device for securing an absolute majority. As elections come to be more keenly contested, there is a tendency for the number of political groups contesting it to increase, so that, instead of the old-fashioned duel, we often find, in a single-member constituency, a three-, four-, five-, or even six-cornered fight. If, as a result of this, no one is elected by an absolute majority, a second election is in some states held, generally between the two candidates with the highest number of votes in the first. Whenever

France, for example, has reverted to the single-member constituency she has adopted the principle of the Second Ballot. But there is, indeed, nothing in the Second Ballot which cannot be secured by the transferable vote, and, in fact, there are electoral systems which secure the objects of the Second Ballot without the inconvenience of holding it. This is by means of what is generally called preferential voting. Under this system the voter states on the paper a second preference which is brought into effect if, on the first count, no candidate gains an absolute majority and if the voter's first choice is not one of the two at the top of the poll. This system obtains, for example, in Australia for Commonwealth elections and for those of some of the separate states.

In Great Britain there have been two brave attempts to concentrate the efforts of the advocates of P.R. in official commissions. The first—the Royal Commission of 1909–10—made a sole recommendation of a positive nature. It was that an alternative vote should be given on the voting-paper, not for the purpose served by the transferable vote, but to secure the objects of a Second Ballot—to wit, an absolute majority—as in the case of Australia, explained above. Yet even this ewe lamb proved to be stillborn. The second—the Speaker's Conference of 1916–17—recommended the adoption of the principle of the transferable vote, as a sort of partial "try-out," for one-third of the seats of the House of Commons. This, too, Parliament rejected, and the only semblance of P.R. in Britain at the moment (since the abolition of University seats by the Act of 1948) is, as we have seen, the presence of the principle of the transferable vote in elections for the National Assembly of the Church of England, for Education Authorities in Scotland, and for the Parliament of Northern Ireland.

VI. PROPORTIONAL REPRESENTATION IN THEORY AND PRACTICE

There is much to be said for and against the principle of P.R. In theory it has everything in its favour; in practice not so much. There is no question that in both theory and practice a real system of P.R. does do what it sets out to do. It does undoubtedly secure the representation of minorities and it does overcome the objections which we have noted to normal majority representation. And for this reason the principle has received growing support in many constitutional states in recent years. But too often those who have adopted it merely pay lip-service to it, particularly in the case of France where it has often been a mere compromise to shut the mouths of its advocates, and in some states, where, at the end of the First World War, it was introduced only (it is feared) to comply with those clauses of the Treaties designed to safeguard the rights of non-national minorities.

The practical objections are many, some of little importance, some quite grave. While it secures minority representation, P.R. is calculated to encourage what somebody has called "minority thinking" and freak candidatures, which may be positively inimical to social health; if, for example, possibly sinister interests, like betting and the anti-social forms of money lending, should gain representation through a sufficient number of interested parties getting together by the enlargement of the constituency. The enlargement of the electoral area is itself a danger, first, because it inevitably destroys personal contact between candidate or member and constituent, and secondly, because it may multiply the number of candidates to the point where the elector is embarrassed as to his preferences. (In Belgium, for example, the largest constituency before the Second World War returned no fewer than twenty-two members.) Thirdly, the principle of the transferable vote may be puzzling to voters, and so complicated in the process of counting votes as to place the elector at the mercy of the counting authority; but this, at any rate in countries which enjoy fairly good political health, is a mechanical objection which is removed if the authority can be absolutely trusted by the voter; and the compensating advantage is that the exercise of the single transferable vote is itself a political education, since it is impossible for the elector to state his preferences without serious reflection, whereas, faced with a choice between two candidates, he hardly needs to think at all.

The old theoretical argument in favour of P.R.—that it would destroy the party "Caucuses"—is found in practice to be quite without foundation. The party machine is even stronger under such a system. The more the constituency expands the more effective becomes the impersonal "pulling of wires." This truth was very clearly seen in Italy under Mussolini's electoral laws.

The gravest objection of all is that P.R. is said to lead to government instability by tending to bring to the legislature a number of small groups, rather than two massed parties in opposition, thus necessitating fragile coalition governments which fall whenever one section of opinion in them is outraged. In Belgium between the wars, for instance, P.R. was operated with such mathematical nicety that statesmen had the utmost difficulty in forming a Cabinet, owing to the multifarious interests involved and the difficulty of finding a line of common action among them.

On the other hand, it may not be a bad thing that various representative sentiments should have to be consulted in forming a ministry, and such coalition Cabinets have in some cases shown remarkable powers of survival, notably in Sweden where, between the wars, one ministry maintained itself in power during a period of two or three years. This effect of P.R. has again shown the system to be well adapted to states passing through a difficult stage of transition, though the hope that the German ship of state under the Weimar Republic might thereby be steered to safety on an even keel was certainly not justified in the event.

Whether it is a good or bad thing that it should be so, it seems that P.R. must have, as its unavoidable concomitants, parliamentary groups with a consequent coalition Cabinet, rather than great parties and a homogeneous Cabinet. And this is undoubtedly the reason why it has not been adopted in Great Britain, in which the party system is so deeply rooted and which, consequently, as Disraeli once said, "hates Coalitions." It is not without significance that the two great states in the world which have not yet tried P.R., namely, the United Kingdom and the United States, are the only two where the tradition of two great parties in opposition has always been very strong, while those which have adopted it are either states like Germany which in its constitutional days had always had a group-system in parliament, or entirely new states like Czechoslovakia (after the First World War)[1] without any such political tradition to change. It is, perhaps, the fear that the full adoption of P.R. would involve for Great Britain and the United States, not merely a change in the electoral system, but

[1]There is no reference to P.R. in the new Czechoslovak Constitution of 1948.

a violent breach with the Party tradition that has caused the legislatures of those states so long to hesitate to introduce it.

VII. PROBLEMS CONNECTED WITH THE REPRESENTATIVE SYSTEM

The problems arising out of the development of the representative principle are many. The first is that of making the number of enfranchised citizens correspond to a real embodiment of the national will. But does it necessarily follow that representative government is unreal because the principle of universal suffrage without restriction is not put into practice? Many enlightened people have held and hold that popular government does not consist in a simple counting of heads.[1] "Equal voting," wrote John Stuart Mill in 1861, "is in principle wrong. . . . It is not useful, but hurtful, that the constitution of the country should declare ignorance to be entitled to as much political power as knowledge." Every elector, he contended, should be able to read, write and "perform a sum in the rule of three." Universal education, he further urged, should precede universal enfranchisement; all electors should be payers of direct taxes, however small; and, finally, voting should not be secret, because secret voting violates the spirit of the suffrage, according to which the voter is a trustee for the public whose acts should be publicly known.

As we have shown in this chapter, the reforms in general since Mill's day have not at all followed the restricting lines that he laid down. On the contrary, the tendency has been all the other way: to make the franchise direct, equal and universal, to reduce or remove property qualifications, to make the ballot secret, and to simplify registration. It may be admitted that in the more progressive states, such as Britain, the British Dominions, the United States, and the Scandinavian countries, Mill's educational conditions have been largely fulfilled, but a great number of European countries have instituted manhood or adult suffrage, in spite of a vast proportion of illiterates among their populations, and this is true not only of Balkan and East European countries, but of such Western states as Italy and Spain. Democracy, however, is not only a method of govern-

[1] In this connection it is interesting to note a novel form of voting introduced under the Constitution of 1933 in Portugal where the unit is not the individual, but the head of the family, whether man or woman.

ment but a condition of society. It is a question of emphasis. Those who regard it merely as the first, think of the representative principle as of its very being. To those who think more of the spirit than the mechanism of it, the system of government is not of primary importance, provided that it does not hinder the free play of a democratic spirit. But can that spirit be assured free play without the machinery of full representative government? In some modern states, of which we have spoken, if the people had to wait for the proper conditions of culture and stability before instituting a system of universal and equal suffrage, it is certain, they feel, that they would get neither the preliminary advantages of the one nor the ultimate benefits of the other.

Another problem that goes with the question of suffrage is that of getting candidates to stand for the office of representative who are both competent and incorruptible. Unless some means can be discovered for finding really capable persons for such work, no system of franchise, whether founded among a people largely illiterate or developed in a highly cultured nation, can be of any avail. The representative system demands from the representative or deputy a freedom to devote himself to the public service which is necessarily lacking to the ordinary citizen. In other words, the parliamentary candidate must necessarily be a professional politician whether he is paid for his services or not. Therefore, he may as well be paid, and almost every constitutional state to-day has adopted a scheme for the payment of its legislators. This has very considerably widened the area of choice of potential representatives, though it cannot be said to have decreased the evil influence of the party caucus which makes the existence of the best type of independent deputy very difficult. The party machine, indeed, appears to be an inevitable concomitant of the growth of political democracy. Nor, as we have said, is its power diminished under a system of P.R.

It must not be forgotten that the *raison d'être* of a legislature is not only to reflect the opinion of the country but to maintain good government. Schemes of electoral reform, whose object is to produce the best possible type of legislature, may therefore have to sacrifice something of the ideal electorate. The reflection of the opinions of the electorate in the legislature is only partially feasible and not always desirable. Any conceivable system of election is at best an arbitrary attempt to approximate to a correspondence between the electors and the elected body. Government must, after all, be relative to the conditions of the society it governs, and account must always be taken of the peculiarities of the people to which it in each case applies. Nevertheless, a certain scepticism concerning the adequacy of the representative system by itself has manifested itself in some states, and this distrust of it has led to the trial of certain direct democratic checks upon its action, like the Referendum, the Initiative, and the Recall, of which we shall have more to say in Part III.

READING

BAGEHOT: *English Constitution*, Essay v.
BARKER: *Essays on Government*, Essay iii.
BASSETT: *Essentials of Parliamentary Democracy*, Part II.
BRYCE: *American Commonwealth*, Vol. I, Chs. iii–xvii. *Modern Democracies*, Vol. I, Chs. iii–viii; Vol. II, Chs. xli, lxxiv–lxxv.
BUELL: *Democratic Governments in Europe*, Sections I and II.
BURNS: *Political Ideals*, Ch. xii.
DICEY: *Law and Opinion*, Lecture iii, pp. 248–258. *Law of Constitution*, pp. lxii–lxv.
FINER: *Modern Government*, Vol. I, Chs. xi–xiii, xvi; Vol. II, Chs. xviii–xxi.
GETTELL: *Readings in Political Science*, Ch. xvi.
JENKS: *State and Nation*, pp. 288–294.
JENNINGS: *Parliament*, Chs. ii–x.
KEITH: *Responsible Government in Dominions*, Vol. I, pp. 560–9; Vol. II, pp. 623–661, 712–714.
LASKI: *Grammar of Politics*, Pt. I, Chs. iii and iv, pp. 311–327.
LOWELL: *Government of England*, Vol. Chs. ix–xvi; Vol. II, Chis. xxxi–xxxvii. *Governments and Parties*, Vol. I, pp. 14–18, 156–7, Ch. v.; Vol. II, pp. 211–214, 232–4, Ch xiii. *Greater European Governments*, Chs. ii, iii, vii, pp. 292–300.
MACIVER: *Modern State*, Ch. xiii.
MARRIOTT: *English Political Institutions*, Chs. viii-x. *Mechanism of Modern State*, Vol. I, Ch. xix.
REED: *Form and Functions of American Government*, Chs. xxi–xxii.
SAIT: *Government and Politics of France*, Ch. vi.
SIDGWICK: *Elements of Politics*, Chs. iii, xx, xxvii, xxix.
WILSON: *State*, pp. 35–40, 209–210.
Encyclopædia Britannica: (i) In the 11th Edition, Articles on Election (Vol. 9), Representation (Vol. 23), Woman Suffrage (Additional Vol. 32). (ii) In the 13th Edition, Article on Electoral Laws, Changes in (New Vol. 1).

BOOKS FOR FURTHER STUDY

BROGAN: *Introduction to American Politics*.
DANIELS: *The Case for Electoral Reform*.
DUVERGER: *Political Parties*.
FINER: *The Case against P.R.*

HUMPHREYS: (1) *Proportional Representation:* (2) *Practical Aspects of Electoral Reform.*
LASKI: (1) *Rise of European Liberalism.* (2) *The American Democracy.*
LIDDERDALE: *Parliament of France.*
MCKENZIE: *British Political Parties.*
MILL: *Representative Government.*
PICKLES: *France: The Fourth Republic.*
RUSSELL: *Freedom and Organisation.*
THOMSON: *Democracy in France.*
WILLIAMS: *Reform of Political Representation.*
WOODWARD: *French Revolutions.*
Journal of the Proportional Representation Society.

SUBJECTS FOR ESSAYS

1. Trace the growth of political democracy in modern times.
2. "Manhood suffrage was until recently characteristic of Latin Europe." Discuss this statement.
3. Outline the history of political enfranchisement in Britain and show the position at the moment.
4. Explain the importance of the Nineteenth Amendment to the Constitution of the United States.
5. Define the term constituency and show how it varies in form in modern states.
6. How did the idea of Proportional Representation originate? Explain its essential features.
7. Explain the working of P.R. in any European state which uses the system.
8. What are the main arguments for and against P.R.?
9. "Equal voting is in principle wrong." Discuss this dictum of John Stuart Mill's.
10. Suggest lines of reform in the British electoral system.

CHAPTER IX

THE LEGISLATURE

(2) SECOND CHAMBERS

I. GENERAL REMARKS ON BI-CAMERAL CONSTITUTIONALISM

ANY discussion of legislatures in modern constitutional states which failed to treat of the nature of the Second Chamber or Upper House would be incomplete. It is everywhere a vital question, and in some states it is an urgent and unsolved problem. For no lesson of political history has been more deeply imbibed than that which teaches the uses of a Second Chamber. Uni-cameral constitutionalism is a comparatively rare, and almost always temporary, phenomenon in the history of great states; while bi-cameral constitutionalism is the method characteristic of all important states to-day. The existing exceptions are all small states, such as Portugal, Finland, Turkey, and Czechoslovakia (under the new Constitution of 1948), although to these must now be added New Zealand which abolished its Second Chamber, by a simple Act of Parliament, in 1951. Experiments in the uni-cameral method have generally been tried during periods of revolutionary reconstruction, only to be ended, in the succeeding period of reaction or even while the revolutionary régime persisted, by the re-establishment of the Second Chamber, as was the case in England, for example, under Cromwell.

In France, again, the constitutions of the First and Second Republics, at the end of the eighteenth and the middle of the nineteenth centuries, were based on the uni-cameral principle. But in the former case this was largely due to the course of the Revolution itself which very early manifested the effeteness of the system of the Three Estates of Clergy, Nobility and Commons. Not that the French Revolution was without its theoretical arguments against more than one House. The Abbé Siéyès, the most prolific constitution-monger of the period, who had a very great influence on the form of the constitutional experiments connected with the first Revolution, argued that if a Second Chamber is in agreement with the first, it is superfluous, and if it is not in agreement with it, it is pernicious. Broadly speaking, this is still the contention of those who nowadays oppose the bi-cameral principle. Such opponents, however, are very rarely found among responsible statesmen. The verdict of later times is that Siéyès propounded a false dilemma, since all the great constitutions promulgated since his age have included a Second Chamber in the legislature they have established. Yet, in so far as Siéyès' criticism applies to an ancient institution which has not been remoulded to conform with the changing times, it seems to be a fair one. It should not be beyond the power of the political architect to create a Second Chamber which shall act as a court of legislative revision, provided that it is given a co-ordinate authority with the Lower House. But if the selection of the members of the Upper House is beyond democratic control, then inevitably, as the claims of the electorate become more insistent, the power of such a Second Chamber will tend to decline, the co-ordinate authority will cease to exist, and abolition or reform will be demanded, for, as Goldwin Smith said, "to suppose that power will allow itself on important matters to be controlled by impotence is vain."

The arguments used in favour of Second Chambers must, therefore, be considered in conjunction with the way in which the Upper House is constituted. Those arguments are: that the existence of a Second Chamber prevents the passage of precipitate and ill-considered legislation by a single House; that the sense of unchecked power on the part of a single Assembly, conscious of having only itself to consult, leads to abuse of power and tyranny; that there should be a centre of resistance to the predominate power in the state at any given moment, whether it be the people as a whole or a political party supported by a majority of voters. In the case of a federal state there is a special argument in favour of a Second Chamber which is so arranged as to embody the federal principle or to enshrine the popular will of each of the states, as distinct from that of the federation as a whole.

In the analysis which follows, in the remaining sections of this chapter, of the different existing types of Second Chambers, we shall note that they are variously named—in Britain the House of Lords; in Switzerland the Council of States (*Ständerat*); in France, under the Fourth Republic, the Council of the Republic; in Italy, under the new Republic, the Chamber of Senators; in Germany, under the Bonn Constitution, the Federal Council (*Bundesrat*), and in most of the others the Senate. It is not, however, on the basis of nomenclature that we classify them, but rather on that of their true nature—whether they are non-elective (hereditary or nominated) or elective (partially or wholly). But this will not carry us far unless we also seek to discover, first, how far the Upper House whose selection is outside all popular control retains any real powers; secondly, to what extent the elected element in a partially elected House leavens the lump and gives it vitality; thirdly, in what manner deadlocks between the two Houses are resolved if the power of the Upper House is sufficiently real to impede the free action of the Lower; and fourthly, how the elected Second Chamber is given a dignity which does not attach to the Lower House. Our classification into two types—non-elective and elective—is, as we have said, not exhaustive, because these two types are again divisible into two. We shall therefore examine the composition and function of the Second Chambers which we have selected in the following order: Hereditary, Nominated, Partially Elected, and Fully Elected, concluding with the special cases of Switzerland, Germany, the U.S.S.R., and Yugoslavia.

II. THE HOUSE OF LORDS: PAST AND PRESENT

The hereditary Upper House was formerly much more common than it is now. The hereditary Second Chamber was in most states a survival of the mediæval system of government by Estates, of which there were generally three—Clergy, Nobility, and Commons—to which, however, a fourth, the Merchants, was in some cases added. In the course of time the Estates in most cases were gathered together in two Houses, the Upper being composed of the Lords and Higher Clergy. Several states whose legislatures were thus made up of two Houses had, under various constitutional revisions, by the end of the nineteenth century adopted either a modified form of hereditary chamber; for example, by the addition of certain members nominated for life, as was the case in Portugal from 1896 up to the Revolution of 1911 (when it became fully elective);¹ or a fully elective Upper House, as happened in the Kingdom of the Netherlands when its constitution was revised in 1848. There still remained certain hereditary Second Chambers, like the Austrian *Herrenhaus* and the Hungarian Table of Magnates, but these were swept away after the First World War.² And now the only hereditary Upper House of any importance left is the British House of Lords.

The true origin of the House of Lords is to be found in that body of chief Barons and high Church dignitaries which met the Norman kings in council three times a year. This was known as the Great or Common Council, the latter being the name under which it is referred to, for example, in Magna Carta. In the Model Parliament of 1295 Edward I grafted on to this body two knights from every shire and elected representatives from certain cities, towns and boroughs. For a time they all sat together, but they were essentially two Houses, and what distinguished them, apart from social and official differences, was the method by which they were summoned. The Lords and Church officials were called individually (*sigillatim*, as the old records have it), whereas the Commons were convoked through the Sheriffs. This last is the origin of the existing office of Returning Officer. Under Edward III they definitely took to meeting in separate Chambers. The Lords and Higher Clergy formed the House of Lords, the representatives of rural and urban areas the House of Commons, while the lower clergy, who had at first been represented in the general assembly, dropped the practice of attending altogether, and devoted themselves to their own assembly, called Convocation.

¹A new constitution in Portugal in 1933 created a Single-Chamber legislature (the National Assembly), though it established at the same time an advisory body, called the Corporative Chamber, composed of representatives of local authorities and commercial and industrial organisations, including trade unions. The Corporative Chamber has to be consulted on bills introduced in the National Assembly. But all this is little more than a façade behind which works the dictatorship of Salazar. (See later, pp. 322–323.)

²Under the constitution of 1920 Austria became a federal republic with an elective Second Chamber (*Bundesrat*) representing the provinces forming the federation, but this, of course, disappeared with all her other institutions when Austria was annexed to Germany by Hitler's so-called *Anschluss* in 1938. When the Republic was restored in 1945 it re-established a bi-cameral legislature. Hungary, having established a Single Chamber legislature by the constitution of 1920, reintroduced in 1926 an Upper House which in its composition somewhat resembled the Table of Magnates but this, of course, has not been restored in post-war Hungary, whose institutions remain under powerful Soviet influences.

Since the reign of Edward I, only for one brief period in her history has England had a legislature without an Upper House. This was during the Commonwealth, immediately following the execution of Charles I in 1649. A uni-cameral experiment almost belonged to the logic of that revolution which destroyed at a blow the Crown, the House of Lords and the Episcopate. But already before Cromwell's Protectorate ended he had been persuaded to restore the House of Lords, and from that time its existence has been continuous.

Its composition has changed from time to time, as circumstances have demanded an increase or decrease in its membership. We need not stop to raise again the highly controversial, and indeed unanswerable, question, What originally gave a baron the right to sit in the House of Lords? It is sufficient to remark that in later days the conferment of a baronage necessarily bestowed the right to a seat in the Upper Chamber, and that this is still the case. Only one member of a noble family may sit in the Lords, though his sons may bear the title of barons, unless, of course, any of those sons is made a baron in his own right. And since they cannot sit in the Lords they may stand as candidates for the Commons.[1] On the passage of the Act of Union of 1707 sixteen Scottish peers were added to the House of Lords. It was arranged that at each new Parliament the whole body of Scottish Peers should meet and elect sixteen of their number for the duration of that Parliament. But it was further enacted by this law that no Scotsman should henceforth be created a Scottish peer, but should receive a peerage of the United Kingdom which would automatically give him his seat in the House. As any Scottish peer was liable to be elected by his fellows for any new Parliament, it was also laid down that he could not, in any circumstances, be elected to the Commons. By the Act of Union of 1800, twenty-seven Irish lay peers, as well as four Bishops, were added. The former were to be elected by the Peers of Ireland, but in this case for life. Hence an Irish peer who had not been elected to the Lords, unlike his Scottish counterpart, was permitted to be elected to the Commons. Such

[1] A good illustration is supplied by the family of the late Marquis of Salisbury. Only the Marquis at first sat in the Lords, while two of his brothers, Lord Hugh Cecil and Lord Robert Cecil, were elected to the Commons. Later both these brothers entered the Lords on being created peers in their own right for their services to the state, Lord Robert as Lord Cecil of Chelwood and Lord Hugh as Lord Quickswood.

a one was Lord Palmerston. These last arrangements, of course, were undone by the establishment of the Irish Free State in 1922, but they still apply, in a modified form, to Northern Ireland. The Scottish arrangements also stand.

Besides these hereditary and elective Peers, the two Archbishops (of Canterbury and York) and twenty-four of the Bishops sit in the House of Lords by virtue of their office. Further, there is a certain number of Law Lords, or more strictly, Lords of Appeal in Ordinary, who sit as life-peers only, unless they are, beyond this ex-officio ennoblement, created peers in the usual way, in which case, of course, the title becomes hereditary. There is no limit to the number of hereditary peers. They can be created at will, nominally by the Crown, actually by the Ministry of the day. The normal method of creating peers is to make an announcement in an Honours List, but occasionally it is done entirely outside such customary times when special circumstances demand it. On one famous occasion in our history peers were actually created for the purpose of passing a law through the Lords. This was when the Lords refused to ratify the Treaty of Utrecht in 1713. A Tory majority passed it in the Commons, but there was a Whig majority in the Lords. To redress the balance, the Tory Ministry persuaded Queen Anne to create twelve peers and the Treaty was ratified. At two other critical moments a similar procedure was threatened—to pass the Reform Bill of 1832 and the Parliament Bill of 1911—but on both these occasions the threat was enough, and each Bill was passed by the Lords, whom the brandishing of this weapon had brought to see the futility of resistance.

The powers of the House of Lords up to 1911 were theoretically co-equal with those of the Commons. At one time it was truly so. As late as 1784, for example, the Younger Pitt was the only member of the Ministry, of which he was Prime Minister, in the Commons. But even before that time the focus of power had been steadily moving away from the Lords and towards the Commons, and during the nineteenth century the bulk of the Ministry came to be drawn from the Lower House. With this development came a decline in the real powers of the Lords in legislation, though in theory they remained what they had always been. We have shown in Chapter VI how the convention that recognised the inability of the Lords either to amend or reject a money bill was rudely broken in 1909, and how, as a result, their actual inferiority was given statutory recognition by the Parliament Act of 1911, since which time, despite the further Parliament Act of 1949, no real attempt has been made to tackle the problem of reform.

This is not the place to attempt even to suggest the bases of such a reform. But there emerge from this brief outline of the history, composition and powers of the House of Lords, certain points which should be borne in mind when approaching it. First the powers of the Lords, as left by the Parliament Acts, may still, in certain circumstances, prove very real. The suspensive veto, which gives the Lords the right to hold up the passage of a non-money bill for one year,[1] might easily prevent the measure passing altogether, for many changes in the Commons can occur in that time. A general election during such an interval might change the whole balance of parties in the Commons so that the measure in question would not be resubmitted to the Lords. Secondly, the House of Lords remains the final court of appeal in this country. But here, one must remember, it is, in fact, a small body of seven or eight legal specialists (generally peers only for life) who form this court, and even if an ordinary peer took upon himself to sit in such a court, he would probably be quite unable to follow the abstractions put forward in a forensic atmosphere so refined, and he is, in any case, prohibited from giving judgment. Even if the House of Lords were abolished, a final court of appeal would still be necessary. Thirdly, it might be urged that, though many hereditary peers are lacking in a sense of public duty and in legislative ability, this criticism does not apply to those Commoners who are created peers as a reward for public services. As to this, two points should be remembered. First, though one who is created a peer is doubtless generally a man of great ability in some walk of life, it by no means follows that his *métier* is legislating. Secondly, a son may lack the ability and public spirit of his father. Meanwhile, the truth remains that the Parliament Acts have shorn the House of Lords of the substance of its power and left its composition untouched,

---

[1] *i.e.*, as under the Act of 1949 which reduced the period from two years, as laid down in the Act of 1911.

although a slight modification will be introduced with the implementation of the Act (1958) to create a certain number of life-peerages for both men and women.

From 1893, when the Lords rejected Gladstone's second Home Rule Bill, the reform of the House of Lords became a firm plank in the Liberal platform, but the Parliament Act of 1911, resulting from their intransigence over a Money Bill, was not regarded as anything more than a provisional step in the right direction. Meanwhile, more absorbing political considerations have tended to push the matter into the background. It is true that in 1948 the problem of reform was mooted again as a means of resolving the conflict between the Houses over the Parliament Bill of 1947. But nothing came of it, and the proposal merely to reduce the period of the suspensive veto from two years to one was allowed to take its constitutional course in isolation from the larger question. Yet in the years ahead this question is almost bound to come to the front again, for the present position satisfies no one. On the one hand, the vast majority of the more than 700 members of the House of Lords never attend its sittings except on ceremonial occasions, and political realism demands that this state of things should not continue. On the other hand, the standard of debate among those who do attend is very high indeed, and it is wrong that such contributions to the nation's political life should be largely powerless to affect the course of affairs. How can the dead wood be cut away and the vitality that remains be used to the national advantage? Perhaps an examination of some other existing Second Chambers will help us to see the shape that a reformed Upper House in Britain might take.

III. THE NOMINATED SECOND CHAMBER IN CANADA

The next type of Second Chamber which we must examine is that which is made up of nominated members. What most obviously distinguishes this from the hereditary type is the fact that, while the office of hereditary peer is handed down from father to son and cannot be resigned, that of nominated senator is terminable with death, or earlier if the holder of the office so desires or if the Constitution lays down some defined period of tenure. The most important fully nominated Second Chambers are those whose members hold office for life. Of this type of Second Chamber that of Canada is the most interesting.

The Senate in Canada is nominated by the Crown, through the Governor-General; in practice, on the advice of the Ministry of the day. It is limited in numbers, and, since it applies to a quasi-federal and not a unitary state, there are certain territorial restrictions as to appointment of Senators based upon a ratio between numbers and Provinces. This nominated Senate has appeared as an element of the legislature in all the successive constitutional acts which have applied to Canada—Pitt's Act of 1791, the Canada Act of 1840, and the North America Act of 1867, under which Canada is governed to-day. By the last of these three Acts a Senate of seventy-two members was constituted—twenty-four from each of the three original provinces (the two Maritime Provinces for this purpose being reckoned as one). But this principle of equality has not been maintained with the expansion of the Dominion and the addition of new Provinces. The Act said that when Prince Edward Island should join the federation it should be represented by four Senators, and then the other two Maritime Provinces should have their number changed to ten each. This has happened.

Further, by an Act of 1871, the Canadian Parliament was authorised to add Senators for any new Province created and added to the Dominion. Beyond this, the sole power granted to the Governor-General (*i.e.*, the Ministry) is the right to add from three to six members apportioned equally to the three original provinces. In other words, six additional members may be nominated, but no more, and presumably they may be kept up to that number. The net result of these arrangements is that the Canadian Senate to-day consists of one hundred and two members, but the numbers representative of the various Provinces range from twenty-four to four. The Senator is nominated for life, but under certain conditions. He must be at least thirty years of age, resident in the Province for which he is appointed, a British subject, and possessed of property worth at least 4,000 dollars. He may resign whenever he likes, and must vacate his seat if he is absent for two consecutive sessions, changes his allegiance, becomes bankrupt, is convicted of felony, or ceases to be qualified.

The Senate in Canada attempts the impossible. The constitution tried to model the Senate on the House of Lords,

adopting the plan of nomination for life in place of the hereditary principle. At the same time, it wished to do what it could
not do consistently with the system of choice by the central
power, namely, to maintain the federal idea. This can only be
done on the basis of equality among the states forming the
federation, each choosing its own senators. All that the constitution achieves is that the three original Provinces shall not
have their membership of twenty-four each increased or decreased. But the original third Province now consists of three,
namely, New Brunswick, Nova Scotia, and Prince Edward
Island, two of which have each ten Senators and the third four,
while the remaining Provinces, including Newfoundland, have
six each. These cross-purposes have had their effect on the
prestige of the Senate in Canada, which has neither the power
attaching to an elective Second Chamber nor the usefulness of
an Upper House which enshrines the federal idea. What that
sort of Upper House should be, we shall see in a later Section.

IV. THE PARTIALLY ELECTED UPPER HOUSE

(a) *The Senate in South Africa*

An interesting example of a partially elected Senate is that
of South Africa. By the Act of 1909, which brought the present
Constitution into existence in 1910, temporary arrangements
were made for the first ten years, after which, unless the South
African Parliament should pass an Act to alter its constitution,
the Senate was to consist of forty members. Eight were to be
nominated by the Governor-General in Council, and eight to be
elected by each Provincial Council sitting together with the
members of the House of Assembly for the Province. The Senate
was enlarged by the addition, at various times, of two nominated members, four representatives of native interests, and
two from South-West Africa, so that by 1950 there were
forty-eight members. From that time on, the racial question in
South Africa had widening constitutional repercussions, and in
1955 the Senate Act made radical changes in the structure and
election of the Senate. The number of seats was thereby
increased from forty-eight to eighty-nine, nineteen of them
nominated. Provincial representation, instead of being equal,
was to be related to the number of voters in each Province,
and Senators were to be elected, not in proportion to party

power in the various Provincial Councils, but by the direct vote of the majority party. The object of this Act, according to a Government statement, was to "place the sovereignty of Parliament beyond doubt and to provide for separate representation of the Coloured people".

The term of the Senate has now been reduced from ten to five years. But one of the ways, set forth in the Constitution, for ending a deadlock between the two Houses (after the passage of the first ten years) is for the Governor-General to dissolve, before the end of their statutory term, both the House of Assembly and the Senate. But this does not affect the nominated Senators who hold office for five years in any case. The Senate is a considerable force in South African politics, owing partly to the way it is convened, and partly to the fact that Ministers speak in it even if members of the Lower House. The unitary character of the state is thus maintained.

(b) *The Senate in Eire*

The Senate in Eire under the Constitution of 1937 is the same in size as that set up by the Constitution of the Irish Free State (1922) but there is an important difference in the way it is formed, for, whereas the earlier Senate was fully elected, the present Senate is partially nominated. Also the Senate of Eire allows for the representation of functional interests which under the original Constitution were intended to be concentrated in *ad hoc* Councils representing various branches of the social and economic life of the nation, a plan now, apparently, abandoned.

The Senate of the Irish Free State (*Seanad Eireann*) was composed of sixty members, holding office for twelve years, a fourth of them retiring every three years. They were directly elected, on the principle of proportional representation, the whole state forming one electoral area. But the nomination of candidates was placed under certain very stringent conditions. The Constitution laid down that only those citizens were eligible who, having reached the age of thirty-five, had done honour to the nation or, by virtue of special qualifications or attainments, represented important aspects of the nation's life. Before each election a panel of nominees was formed consisting of three times as many qualified persons as members to be elected. Two-thirds of these were nominated by *Dail Eireann* (House of

Representatives) and a third by the Senate voting by proportional representation. To this panel was added any former or retiring member of the Senate who notified in writing to the Prime Minister his desire to stand.

The plan for the Senate under the Constitution of 1922 seemed at the time a little too academic. Its powers, too, were strictly limited, since it had no function in financial legislation, and in non-money bills only a suspensive veto, rather like that of the House of Lords in Great Britain. The most interesting changes in the new constitution are principally contained in two Articles. Under Article 18, of the sixty members of the Senate eleven are nominated (by the Prime Minister) and forty-nine elected. Any citizen who is eligible for election to the House of Representatives (*Dail Eireann*) is eligible for election to the Senate, *i.e.*, any man or woman of twenty-one years. Of the forty-nine elected members, six are elected by the two Universities and the remaining forty-three from panels of candidates constituted under certain rules. Before each election five panels are formed from the names of those eminent in culture, literature, art and education; agriculture and allied interests; labour, industry and commerce, including banking, architecture and engineering; public administration and social services. Not more than eleven and not less than five members shall be elected from one panel. A general election for the Senate must take place not later than ninety days after a dissolution of the Dail, and every member, unless he previously dies, resigns, or becomes disqualified, shall hold office until the day before polling day of the general election of the Dail.

Article 19 allows for a variation of the basis of election as set out above, in order to admit of functional representation. The Article reads as follows:

"Provision may be made by law for the direct election by any functional or vocational group or association or council of so many members of *Seanad Eireann* as may be fixed by such law in substitution for an equal number of the members to be elected from the corresponding panels of candidates constituted under Article 18 of this Constitution."

(c) *The Former Spanish Senate*

The Spanish Republican Constitution of 1932, which Franco overthrew, introduced a single-chamber legislature in place of the bi-cameral system under the Constitution of 1876. The Second Chamber under the original constitution was a Senate, which might well be revived if ever the present dictatorship is replaced by a restored monarchy. Whether that is to happen or not, a study of the former Spanish Senate is of interest to us, because its composition, it has been suggested, is such as might possibly form a model for a reformed House of Lords in Britain. The original Spanish Senate consisted of 360 members, half of whom were Senators in their own right (Princes, Grandees with a certain income, etc.), ex-officio members (Archbishops, the President of the Supreme Court, etc.), and members nominated by the Crown (*i.e.*, by the Ministry) for life. The total number under these heads was never to exceed 180, and the nominated members had to be drawn only from certain specified categories, as also were the remaining 180 who were to be elected. The elected Senators were chosen as follows: (1) one by the clergy of each of the nine Archbishoprics; (2) one by each of the six Royal Academies; (3) one by each of the ten Universities; (4) five by certain Economic Societies; (5) the remaining 150 by Electoral Colleges in each province of Spain made up of representatives chosen from municipal councillors and the largest taxpayers in urban and municipal districts. The elected portion was, of course, dissolved with the Lower House whether it had run its statutory term or not. Ministers might speak in both Houses of the Spanish legislature, which gave the Senate, in normal times, a somewhat greater prestige than it would otherwise have had.

V. THE ELECTED SECOND CHAMBER IN A UNITARY STATE

A study of the composition and powers of the fully elected Second Chamber in a unitary state should be of special interest to Britons, since Britain is a unitary state. The two examples we select here are France and Italy, as they were reconstituted after the Second World War.

(a) *The Council of the Republic in France*

Under the Constitution of the Fourth French Republic, as promulgated in 1946, Parliament is composed of two Chambers, the National Assembly, formerly the Chamber of Deputies, and the Council of the Republic, formerly the Senate, which, as before, meet in joint session for the election of the President. The new constitution, however, institutes a third assembly unknown to the Third Republic. This is called the French Union (*L'Union Française*), and is concerned with the affairs of France and her Empire as a whole. The Union has two Houses: the High Council (*Haut Conseil*) and the Assembly (*l'Assemblée*), and is composed of representatives of Metropolitan France, the Departments and Overseas territories (formerly represented in the Senate). The President of the Republic is the President also of the Union, whose function it is to advise Parliament on all matters of imperial interest. For France this is an entirely new constitutional device, which would seem to have something of the purpose of the Imperial Conferences of the British Commonwealth, though its composition and mechanism are far more closely defined. In fact, the long chapter (VIII) of the Constitution, with its twenty-three Articles concerned with this new institution, is a very good illustration of that French precision in constitution-making which we have already observed,[1] and affords a good example of the difference between the British and French attitude and approach to constitutional questions. But whether, for all the exactitude with which it is designed, it will serve the purpose intended, only time and experience will tell. There is established, besides, an Economic Council which we shall examine in a later chapter.[2]

It is the Council of the Republic with which we are here specially concerned. This is different in some ways from the Senate of the Third Republic. The Senate consisted of three hundred members with a term of nine years, one third of the membership being renewed every three years. Whereas the Chamber of Deputies was popularly and directly elected, the Senate was indirectly elected, by means of electoral colleges constituted for the purpose in the several Departments and Colonies. The powers of the Senate were constitutionally equal to those of the Chamber of Deputies in all matters except finance. The Senate frequently forced the resignation of a Ministry and no dissolution of the Chamber of Deputies could take place before the expiration of its statutory term without the consent of the Senate, though in practice such a dissolution did not occur after the first few years of the Third Republic's existence.

[1]See pp. 148–149.   [2]See pp. 314–316.

The Constitution of the Fourth Republic leaves the questions of the size and life of the Chambers to ordinary legislative process, but maintains the earlier rule that both Chambers are elected on a territorial basis and that, while the National Assembly is elected by universal direct suffrage (now including women), the Council of the Republic is elected indirectly by Communes and Departments.[1] But whereas the Senate was renewable by thirds, the Council of the Republic is renewable by halves. At the same time, the National Assembly may itself elect not more than a sixth of the Council, and the membership of the Council may not be less than a third or more than a half of that of the National Assembly.

As to the powers of the Council of the Republic, first it cannot initiate money bills but it can, under certain restrictions of time, propose amendments to bills passed by the National Assembly. Secondly, non-money bills are transmitted by the National Assembly to the Council of the Republic, which must take no longer in reaching a decision on them than the time taken by the Assembly. If the Council approves the Bill or if it has not reached a decision within the time limit, the Bill becomes law. If the Council proposes amendments they can finally be overruled by a two-thirds majority of the total membership of the National Assembly.

(b) *The Senate as Reformed in the Italian Republic*

The Second Chamber of the Italian Parliament in the new Republic is radically different from that under the original constitution, for, whereas the Italian Senate was formerly nominated, it is now elected. Under the Monarchy the Senate consisted exclusively of Princes of the Blood Royal and members nominated for life by the King only from certain classes. They included Church dignitaries, deputies who had served in the Lower Chamber for a certain number of years, persons of fame in science and literature, and those who had rendered distinguished service to the state. There was no limit to the number

[1]By a law passed in the autumn of 1946, it was enacted that the Council of the Republic should consist of 315 members distributed as follows: (1) 200 members elected by delegates of Metropolitan France. (2) 50 members elected by the National Assembly. (3) 14 members elected by Algerian areas. (4) 51 members elected by the General Councils and territorial Assemblies of Departments and territories of France overseas. It was further enacted that candidates for the Council must be not less than 35 years of age.

of Senators, and since their appointment was actually in the hands of the Ministry of the day, the power was sometimes used to force laws through the Senate. For example, in 1890 as many as seventy-five Senators were appointed at one time. For this reason, Mussolini had no need to revolutionise the nature of the Senate, as he did that of the Chamber of Deputies, in his creation of the Corporate State, for, as H. Finer says,[1] the King obligingly swamped the Senate with Fascists. And, although the powers of the Senate in monarchical Italy were technically co-ordinate with those of the Chamber of Deputies, in practice the method of appointment could force the assent of the Upper House to any measures passed by the Lower, and, in fact, the Senate had, even before the coming of the Fascist Dictatorship, lost its equality with the Chamber of Deputies.

The new Republican Constitution establishes a Parliament comprising the Chamber of Deputies and the Senate, which meet in joint session for certain purposes, as, for example, to elect the President (when they are joined by representatives of the Regional Councils), to receive the President's Oath on taking office, and, if necessary, to impeach him. The Senate is elected on a regional basis.[2] To each Region is allotted one Senator for every 200,000 inhabitants (or a fraction above 100,000). No Region (except La Valle d'Aosta, a very small one) has fewer than six Senators. The Senate is elected by universal and direct suffrage of all citizens who have reached the age of twenty-five years.

The Draft Constitution contained a list of categories of persons eligible for election to the Chamber of Senators (the name which appeared in the Draft but which was afterwards dropped in favour of the former usage, Senate). The list included, among others, ex-Presidents, ex-Ministers, ex-Secretaries of State, those decorated for valour in the War of Liberation (1943–1945), and commanders of divisions in that war. Little remained of this restrictive design in the constitution as finally approved. The final constitution states that an ex-President of the Republic is a Senator for life and that the President may nominate as life-senators five citizens who have done specially meritorious service in science, art or literature.

[1] In *Mussolini's Italy*, p. 257, footnote.

[2] For the Regional organisation of Republican Italy, see earlier, p. 96.

7*

For the rest, the Constitution lays down that no citizen who has not reached the age of forty may stand as a candidate for election to the Senate.

The normal life of the Senate is six years, whereas that of the Chamber of Deputies is five. But the Senate may, like the Chamber, be dissolved before the end of its full term. In 1958, for example, the two Houses were dissolved simultaneously, and a general election was held for both. Senators, like Deputies, receive a salary, which is fixed from time to time by law. The two Chambers have equal powers to initiate bills, as, indeed, have also the people on the principle of the Initiative.[1] But a bill must first be submitted to a Commission for examination before coming to the Chamber of Deputies or Senate for detailed debate. Moreover, the Italian Senate has the right to move a vote of censure or no-confidence against the Government. As this right is denied to the French Council of the Republic,[2] it is evident that the equality of the Chambers is more real in Republican Italy than it is in France under the Fourth Republic.

VI. THE ELECTED SENATE IN A FEDERAL STATE

The Senates in the two fully federalised states which we have noted earlier, namely, the United States and Australia, manifest three marked characteristics. First, the Senate in both cases is composed of members equally representative of the states forming the federal whole. This equality is an essential feature of it, since in a true federation the sovereignty which the federating units have abandoned should not be surrendered into the hands of a body outside their control or one in which the strength of any one of them is overweening. Secondly, in both cases, the Senators are elected from and in the states individually and without interference from the Federal Authority, in a manner which combines the advantages of popular election and of state identity. And thirdly, the term of office of the Senator is so determined as to ensure a continuity of life to the Senate. Such continuity is completely achieved in the United States, but not quite so completely, for reasons which we shall see in a moment, in Australia. This method of retirement of only a portion of the Senate at one time is what dis-

[1] See later, Chapter XIII.   [2] See earlier, pp. 229–231.

tinguishes the Upper from the Lower House in such states and gives the former the dignity attaching to venerability without removing it from popular contact and control.

(a) *The United States*

In the United States, as we have had occasion to mention before, the Senate consists of ninety-six members (two from each of the forty-eight states). The senatorial term is six years, a third of the Senate retiring every two years. Thus, in every period of six years, any one state has two senatorial elections, *i.e.*, at the end of each period of two years, and then misses one. For example, if the State of New York elected a Senator in 1946 (for the Congress opening in 1947), he will not retire until 1953. Hence, if the same state also elected a Senator in 1948 (for 1949), then in 1950 (for 1951) there will be no senatorial election in the State of New York. This was secured in the original Constitution by dividing the original Senate by ballot into three equal groups, the first retiring after two years, the second after four. Thus, the Senate in the United States has never been renewed at any one time to the extent of more than a third of its membership since the year 1789. It is this fact which has always given it its peculiar dignity, as it is the more recent method of popular election which gives it its great power and vitality. At first the Senators were chosen by the legislature in each state, but, as we have said, by the Seventeenth Amendment (1913) popular election was enforced throughout the Union. The Senator was never at any time, and certainly is not now, in any sense the delegate of the government of his state, but the representative of the people of the state organised as a corporate body politic. Moreover, each Senator represents his state, not in partnership, but singly, and he is expected to vote according to his own individual opinion. And this must be so, since it may easily happen that the two Senators from any state, having been elected at different times, are drawn from opposing parties.

The qualifications for the office of Senator in the United States are very few and simple. The candidate must have been a citizen of the United States for at least nine years, he must have reached the age of thirty, and he must be at the time of his election a resident in the state which he is chosen to represent.

The powers of the Senate are very great. Probably no Second Chamber in the world to-day has an influence so real and direct, not only in the most obviously national concerns, such as foreign affairs, but down to the very minutest business of federal legislation, including finance. So powerful is the Senate, indeed, that it is regarded by some as the *sole* effective Federal Chamber in the United States. Certainly nothing that either the Executive or the House of Representatives is legally empowered to do can modify the rights which the Senate not only constitutionally possesses but actually enjoys. Through the standing committees into which it divides itself, it is able to cope with the multifarious questions which come before it, and to keep in touch with the executive department which, as we shall show later, works in isolation from the legislature. The most powerful of all the committees of the Senate is the Committee of Foreign Affairs, for in this department the Senate alone ultimately controls the actions of the President. Treaties are ratified not by Congress as a whole, but by the Senate,[1] and this is perfectly logical, for in the House of Representatives the states are represented in the most diverse proportions. At no time was the diplomatic power of the American Senate more clearly manifested than at the end of the First World War, when the work of President Wilson, who had personally signed the Treaties and the Covenant of the League of Nations on behalf of the United States, was entirely undone by the action of the Senate, which refused to honour the President's signature to any one of the instruments of peace.

(b) *Australia*

Like the American, the Australian Senate represents the federal idea, as may be judged from the fact that, when the Constitution was in process of being drawn up, the alternative titles suggested for the Second Chamber were the *House of the States* and the *States Assembly*. In spite of the protests of the more important states at that time, equality was secured, and so the Australian Senate is composed of ten members from each of the six states of the Commonwealth, making a total of sixty Senators. Moreover, it is provided in the Constitution that, though Parliament may increase or diminish the number of

[1] A declaration of war has to be approved by the whole Congress.

Senators for each state, the equal representation of the states may not, by its action, be destroyed.[1] The electorate for the Senate is precisely that for the House of Representatives, but the constituency is different, the whole state being the electoral area for senatorial elections and each voter having as many votes as there are places to be filled. The senatorial term of office is six years, half the Senate retiring every three years. But this partial retirement does not necessarily secure in Australia, as it does in the United States, a continuity of life to the Senate, because there is another stipulation in the Constitution that, in the event of a deadlock between the two Houses, the Governor-General may dissolve them both, in which case, of course, a wholly new Senate, as well as a wholly new House of Representatives, is elected. But, actually, this has happened on only two occasions so far in the history of the Commonwealth of Australia, as the result of acute differences between the Houses; the first in 1914, the second in 1951.

The functions of the Senate in Australia are, unlike those in America, purely legislative, and it has "equal power with the House of Representatives in respect of all proposed laws," with the exception of finance bills which must originate in the Lower House and cannot be amended, though they may be rejected, by the Senate. The Senate was deliberately constituted by the Founders as a "States' House," but in practice it has always divided on the same political lines as the Lower House, and considers all measures from a party, not a state, point of view. Consequently, the party that wins two successive General Elections controls most of the Senatorial seats.

VII. THE SECOND CHAMBER IN SWITZERLAND AND WEIMAR GERMANY

The Council of the States (*Ständerat*) of the Swiss Confederation offers some striking contrasts with the Senate in America and Australia, and is worthy of close study as the Second Chamber of a federal state. Again, it is useful to examine the form and function of the Council of the Empire (*Reichsrat*) in Germany, as it existed under the Weimar Republic and before Hitler destroyed the federal character of the German state,

---

[1] The original number of Senators for each State was six. It was increased to ten by an Act of 1948.

since it has been used to some extent as a model for the Federal
Council (*Bundesrat*) of the Federal Republic of Germany under
the Bonn Constitution, which, as we have seen, came into force
in Western Germany in 1949 under the aegis of the Western
Occupying Powers.

(a) *The Swiss Confederation*

In one respect the Swiss Council of States is like the Senate
in the United States and the Commonwealth of Australia, for
in it the cantons (*i.e.*, states) are equally represented. It consists of forty-four members; that is to say, two members from
each of the nineteen cantons and one member from each of the
half-cantons into which the remaining three cantons are divided.
But in no other particular does it resemble the other two. The
Constitution leaves every detail of the election and term of
service of the member to the cantons themselves. Thus from
some cantons members are sent for one year, from others for
two years, from others for three, and from yet others for four.
In most of the cantons the members are now popularly elected,
but in seven they are chosen by the legislative body of the
canton. But the Swiss Council of States is not strictly either a
federal chamber or a second chamber as ordinarily understood.
For if it were a truly federal chamber, part of its business would
be to safeguard state interests in the hands of the authority
to which they have sacrificed their sovereignty, and if it were
a normal Second Chamber it would have certain defined
functions of legislative revision or veto.

In fact, however, the two Houses in Switzerland are co-
ordinate in all respects. The initiation of legislative proposals
is shared between them by arrangement made between their
respective Presidents at the beginning of each parliamentary
session. The Ministers, as we shall show later, are responsible
to, and may vote in, neither House, but must answer questions
put to them equally in both. Finally, for certain (not abnormal)
purposes the two Houses sit together and vote as one Chamber.
Thus the Swiss Legislature, like the Swiss Executive, is unique;
it is the only legislature in the world the functions of whose
Upper House are in no way differentiated from those of the
Lower. Anything that comes within the competence of the
Federal Legislature requires the concurrence of both Houses,

but both the federal organs of government—executive and legislative—may be reduced to an equality of subordination to the national will through the instrument of the referendum, a matter we shall discuss more fully in a later chapter.

(b) *The German Republic*

The German Constitution of 1919 categorically stated in its Sixtieth Article that "a *Reichsrat* is formed in order to represent the German States in the legislation and administration of the Reich." The states, it further said, were represented in the *Reichsrat* by members of their governments. This was a survival of the system obtaining under the old Empire; but whereas in those days the *Bundersrat*, or Council of the *Bund*, was the real organ of legislation, the situation was entirely reversed, and the *Reichsrat* under the Weimar was overshadowed by the *Reichstag*. The *Reichsrat* had no power to initiate legislation. That was the function alone of the Executive and the *Reichstag*. Nor was the consent of the *Reichsrat* required for the passage of legislation, though its consent was necessary for the introduction of any Bill in the *Reichstag* by the Government. Nevertheless, the *Reichsrat* had an important and peculiar veto. If it objected to any Bill passed by the *Reichstag*, it had to lodge an objection with the Government within two weeks of the final vote in the Lower Chamber. If then the Houses could not agree, the President might order a referendum on the bill in question. If he did not do this within three months, and if the *Reichstag* voted again in favour of the Bill by a two-thirds majority (of the whole House), the President either had to promulgate the law or order an appeal to the people.

Thus, while the German *Reichsrat* was definitely representative of the point of view of the individual states, it lacked the power it formerly had of giving the individual state an effective voice. And, while it failed to embody the safeguarding principle of federalism—that the states should be equally represented in the Upper House—it was yet disarmed from acting to the detriment either of the smaller states through the preponderating influence of the larger ones, or of the Reich as a whole, by virtue of a strength superior to that of the House which was popularly elected. At the same time, by the power which was given it to force either the consent of a vast, and often unobtainable, majority of the popular Chamber to a Bill to which it objected, or else an appeal to the people themselves, it at once assumed the dignity proper to a Second Chamber and vouchsafed to the sovereign people the ultimate control of their own representatives.

Under the Bonn Constitution of 1949 the Federal Council, or *Bundesrat*, is, like its predecessors, composed of representatives of the governments of the various *Länder* forming the federation, and, as under the Weimar Republic, the number of representatives varies according to the population of the *Land*. Thus those *Länder* with a population of more than six millions have five members, those with less than six but more than two millions have four members, and those with less than two millions have three members. How vital a part the *Bundesrat* is destined to play in the Federal Republic of Germany depends upon political developments whose course it would be difficult at the present juncture to forecast.

VIII. THE SPECIAL CASES OF THE U.S.S.R. AND THE FEDERAL PEOPLE'S REPUBLIC OF YUGOSLAVIA

Though the U.S.S.R. and the Federal People's Republic of Yugoslavia are not generally constituted on Western models, as federal states they nevertheless owe something to Western influences, and it is interesting and significant to compare the form and functions of the second federal Chamber in each case with those belonging to constitutional organisation as normally understood, which we have already examined.

In the Stalin Constitution of the U.S.S.R. (1936), Chapter III refers to the Supreme Organs of State Power in the Union. The principal organ is the Supreme Soviet which replaces the old Congress of Soviets of the Union. The Supreme Soviet consists of two Chambers, namely, the Soviet of the Union and the Soviet of Nationalities, the first elected by the citizens of the U.S.S.R. on the basis of one deputy for 300,000 of the population and consisting of 600 members, the second consisting of deputies elected, in relative numbers,[1] by the citizens

---

[1] I.e. (as amended 1947) 25 Deputies from each Union Republic, 11 Deputies from each Autonomous Republic, and 5 Deputies from each Autonomous Region.

voting by Union Republics. Each of the Chambers is elected for four years. They have equal legislative power and a simple majority in each is enough to give approval to a law. Sessions are convened by the Presidium of the Supreme Soviet twice a year (normally), and extraordinary sessions may be called for special purposes.

In the Constitution of the Federal People's Republic of Yugoslavia of 1946, Chapter VII, a long section containing twenty-eight Articles, is concerned with the Supreme Federal Organs of State Authority. The Federal Parliament is called the People's Assembly of the Republic and consists of two Houses, the Federal Council (the lower) and the Council of Nationalities (the Upper). The Federal Council is elected on the basis of one deputy for each 50,000 inhabitants. The Council of Nationalities is elected by the citizens of the several Republics (30 deputies each), Autonomous Provinces (20 deputies each) and Regions (15 deputies each). The two Chambers are elected for a term of four years and are equal in their rights. They normally sit separately, but meet in joint session on special occasions laid down in the Constitution, such as for the election of the Executive, which is a Presidium of the Soviet type, and for the proclamation of any amendment to the Constitution. Decisions at a joint session require a majority vote, but can be reached only if a majority of the members of each House are present. A Bill may be introduced in either House and, on being passed, is sent to the other. If the other House does not pass the Bill it goes to a co-ordinating committee, composed of an equal number of members of each House. If agreement cannot be reached on the co-ordinating committee's report, then both Chambers are dissolved and new elections take place.

It is evident from this brief survey of the Second Chamber in Soviet Russia and Republican Yugoslavia that, even in those federal states which have been established under extremely revolutionary conditions in the contemporary world, the Second Chamber is regarded as having an important function to perform. It may be, of course, that political practice in these two states is not altogether in harmony with the high constitutional intentions expressed on paper. But it is perhaps not without significance for the future that at least the intentions are there.

IX. CONCLUSIONS

This somewhat exhaustive, and perhaps exhausting, analysis has none the less been of a very summary character, for many points of interest have been necessarily omitted. The object has been to direct the attention of the student to those outstanding matters which emphasise the constitutional functions of those Second Chambers which are worthy of examination. The conclusions which seem to emerge from such an analysis are: first, that no great state to-day is satisfied with a unicameral legislature; secondly, that the more the choosing of the Second Chamber is out of popular control, the more it tends to become detached from the realities of politics and thus to lose vitality; thirdly, that when this is the case, there is a consciousness, not that the Second Chamber should be allowed to fall into desuetude, but that it should be made alive again by reform; and fourthly, that a Second Chamber with real powers is vital to the successful working of a federal system; although, in view of some latter-day developments, this statement, particularly in relation to Australian federalism, can be made only with certain reservations. These questions are surely of great interest to any student of comparative politics; and they should be of special concern to the British citizen in considering the possible pattern of a reformed House of Lords.

READING

BAGEHOT: *English Constitution*, Essay x.
BRYCE: *American Commonwealth*, Vol. I, Chs. x–xii and xviii. *Modern Democracies*, Vol. I, Ch. xix and pp. 385–393, 514–518; Vol. II, pp. 63–6, 203–6, Chs. lvi, lxiv.
FINER: *Modern Government*, Vol. I, Ch. xvii.
GETTELL: *Readings in Political Science*, Ch. xviii, Sect. ii.
JENKS: *Government of British Empire*, Chs. vi–vii.
JENNINGS: *Parliament*, Ch. xi and Appendix v.
KEITH: *Responsible Government in Dominions*, Vol. I, Pt. iii, Chs. vii–viii.
LASKI: *Grammar of Politics*, pp. 328–355.
LOWELL: *Government of England*, Vol. I, Chs. xxi–xxii. *Governments and Parties*, Vol. I, pp. 19–26, 154–5, Ch. ii; Vol. II, pp. 208–210.
MARRIOTT: *English Political Institutions*, Chs. vi–vii. *Mechanism of Modern State*, Vol. I, Chs. xiv–xv.
PORRITT: *Evolution of Dominion of Canada*, Ch. xi.
REED: *Form and Functions of American Government*, Chs. v–vii.
SAIT: *Government and Politics of France*, Ch. v.
SIDGWICK: *Elements of Politics*, Ch. xxiii.
WILSON: *State*, pp 153–4, 212–6, 251–260, 325–6, 351–361, 410–412, 433–4, 448–455.

BOOKS FOR FURTHER STUDY

BROGAN: *Introduction to American Politics.*
FINER: *Governments of Greater European Powers.*
LEES-SMITH: *Second Chambers in Theory and Practice.*
LIDDERDALE: *Parliament of France.*
MARRIOTT: *Second Chambers.*
PICKLES: *France: The Fourth Republic.*
SLOAN: *How the Soviet State is Run.*
TEMPERLEY: *Senates and Second Chambers.*
WEBB: *Soviet Communism.*
ZINK: *Government and Politics in the United States.*
Annual Register for 1936.

SUBJECTS FOR ESSAYS

1. What is the importance of the bi-cameral legislative system in the modern world?

2. "To suppose that power will allow itself on important matters to be controlled by impotence is vain." Do you consider that the modern history of Second Chambers justifies this conclusion of Goldwin Smith?

3. Trace the history of the British House of Lords and explain its existing powers.

4. Show how the nominated Senate in Canada is constituted.

5. Of what value to an Englishman is the study of the composition of the original Senate in Spain under the Constitution of 1876?

6. What is the significance of the presence of nineteen nominated senators in the South African legislature?

7. What justification is there for the statement that the Senate in the United States is the most powerful Second Chamber in the world?

8. Compare and contrast the composition and powers of the Senate in Australia with those of the Senate in Eire.

9. Explain the changes that have been made in the Second Chamber (a) in France under the Constitution of the Fourth Republic as compared with that of the Third; (b) in Italy under the Republic as compared with that under the Monarchy.

10. How is the Soviet of Nationalities constituted in the U.S.S.R. under the Constitution of 1936, as amended in 1947; and how is the Council of Nationalities constituted in Yugoslavia under the Constitution of 1946 ? Compare their form and functions with those of (i) the Council of States in Switzerland; (ii) the *Bundesrat* in the new Federal Republic of Germany.

CHAPTER X

THE PARLIAMENTARY EXECUTIVE

I. THE EXECUTIVE: APPARENT AND REAL

IN spite of the vast importance of the legislative function in modern government, it tends to be overshadowed by the executive; first, because modern executive business is concerned not only with executing laws, but also, in many cases, with initiating policy to be sanctioned by the legislature; and secondly, because the mass of collectivist legislation, of which we spoke before, is so great that, though the legislature may control the passage of the laws, it is bound to leave a wide discretionary power in the hands of those who execute them. Thus the growth of democracy has produced in modern constitutional states this paradox—that the greater the volume of legislation passed by the legislature elected by the people whose needs require it, the greater the area of uncontrolled executive power in the prosecution of the laws so made.

The executive, then, is in many respects the most important department of government in the modern constitutional state; and while constitutionalism, in seeking to limit the powers of government and protect the rights of the governed, has defined the executive branch, and confined it within proper limits, on the other hand, the growth of democracy has greatly multiplied executive duties and the number of officers and departments to discharge them. The powers of the executive in the normal constitutional state to-day may be summarised as follows:

(i) Diplomatic power—relating to the conduct of foreign affairs.

(ii) Administrative power—relating to the execution of the laws and the administration of the government.

(iii) Military power—relating to the organisation of the armed forces and the conduct of war.

(iv) Judicial power—relating to the granting of pardons, reprieves, etc., to those convicted of crime.

(v) Legislative power—relating to the drafting of bills and directing their passage into law.

As we have pointed out earlier, the term executive is used in two senses. In the first, the broader sense, it means the whole body of Ministers, of the civil service, of the police, and even of the armed forces. In the second, and narrower sense, it signifies the supreme head of the executive department. It is with the executive in this latter sense that this and the next chapter will be concerned. We must be careful here not to be misled by mere nomenclature, by virtue of which executives are often divided into two classes, hereditary and elected, on the basis of which classification states are divided into monarchies and republics. For this, as we have said in Chapter III, may tell us nothing. We must go farther and ask: is the hereditary executive and the elected executive real or only nominal? Now, before the First World War there were still certain European states—Germany, Austria-Hungary and Russia, for example—which had real hereditary executives of varying degrees of absoluteness. But all these hereditary executives were swept away as a result of the war, and it is true to say that in the Western World to-day, though there remain nominal hereditary executives, nowhere do we find a real hereditary executive.

But there is a further fact to observe, namely, that even the elected executives may hide their true nature beneath an outward form, and just as in all Western monarchies to-day the monarch is nowhere the real executive, so also in some republics the president is not the real but only the nominal executive. In existing constitutional states there are only two possible sorts of executive, using the term in its narrower sense, as referring to the supreme head of the executive department. One is the sort that is controlled by parliament, the parliamentary executive; the other is the type that is outside parliamentary control, the non-parliamentary or fixed executive. It is necessary that the student should not allow himself to be misled by the mere *form* of the executive, judged by the tradition or name of the state, but should look more deeply into the actual working of the executive to discover to which of these two types it in reality belongs.

II. THE THEORY OF THE SEPARATION OF POWERS

The existence of the three departments of government—legislative, executive and judicial—is due to a normal process of specialisation of function, a phenomenon to be observed in all branches of thought and action as civilisation advances, as its field of activity increases and as its organs grow more and more complex. Originally the king was the lawgiver, the executor of the law and the judge. But inevitably there grew a tendency to delegate these powers of monarchy, and the tripartite division resulted. This process does not involve a division of the sovereign power: it is merely a convenient means of coping with the increasing business of the state. The specialisation of function was a simple need, and the consequent delegation was a simple fact. But as the king's power came to be checked and constitutional ideas came into prominence, this simple fact became a theory, a theory that the basis of liberty lay in not only the convenient specialisation of these functions but their absolute distinction in different hands. It is this accident of reading into a normal piece of governmental evolution a theory of liberty and rights which has given a strange twist to certain constitutions and made the modern difference between parliamentary and non-parliamentary executives.

The strangest thing about the emergence of this theory of the separation of powers is that it was first propounded as being the peculiar virtue in the stability of the British Constitution, of which it is absolutely untrue and to which it does not in the least apply. It appeared first in Montesquieu's *Esprit des Lois*, published in 1748, in which the author attempted to abstract, so to speak, the quintessence of the British Constitution. His conclusion was that "when the legislative and executive powers are united in the same person or body of persons there can be no liberty, because of the danger that the same monarch or senate should enact tyrannical laws and execute them in a tyrannical manner." Nor was this peculiar view of the English Constitution confined to this French thinker, for nearly twenty years later, the English jurist, Blackstone, in his *Commentaries on the Laws of England* (1765) expressed himself on the same point in almost identical terms. "Wherever," he says, "the right of making and enforcing the law is vested in the same man or one and the same body of men, there can be no public liberty."

This view became a definite part of the political philosophy of the later eighteenth century, and was incorporated in the French constitutions of the Revolutionary epoch. The doctrine of Montesquieu and Blackstone was also adopted and put into practice by the Fathers of the American Constitution, since they naturally believed, at this time, that they were imitating a sound feature of the British Constitution. The system of the existing executive in England had not developed fully at that time, and has now passed beyond the possibility of such an interpretation of its secret strength. But it was none the less a misconception of the spirit which was informing its evolution even then. Yet such was the hold that this theory gained that it was not until 1867, when Walter Bagehot's great book, *The English Constitution*, appeared, that it was finally consigned to limbo.

Now, in no constitutional state is it true that the legislative and executive functions are in precisely the same hands, for, as we have said earlier, the executive must always be a smaller body than the legislature. But it is not to this distinction that the theory of the separation of powers points. The application of the theory means not only that the executive shall not be the same body as the legislature, but that these two bodies shall be utterly isolated from each other, so that the one shall have no control over the other. Any state which has adopted and maintained this doctrine in practice in its full force has an executive entirely beyond the control of the legislature. Such an executive we call non-parliamentary or fixed. This type of executive still exists in the United States, whose Constitution has not been altered in this particular since its inception. But France, which, as we have said, applied the doctrine in its first constitutions born of the Revolution, later adopted the British executive system, and this feature appears in the Constitution of the Fourth Republic as it did in that of the Third. The system is one in which a cabinet of ministers is dependent for its existence on the legislature of which it is a part, the members of the executive being also members of the legislature.

This system, generally known as the Cabinet system, has

been, in its broad features, adopted by most European states, and it matters not at all whether they are called monarchies or republics. It has also been adopted in the Self-governing Dominions of the British Crown. The non-parliamentary system, on the other hand, is peculiar to the United States and those Latin American Republics which have founded their constitutions upon that of their great neighbour. In this and the next chapter it is proposed to examine some of the foremost states of the modern world from the point of view of their executive systems. Our purpose is to discover whether the system in any given case is parliamentary or non-parliamentary, though there are one or two indeterminate examples which we shall also observe.

III. THE HISTORY AND PRESENT FORM OF THE CABINET SYSTEM IN BRITAIN

The history of the growth of the Cabinet system in Britain is one of the most instructive studies in the whole realm of the science of government. This system, which has been adopted and incorporated in the documentary constitutions of the British Self-governing Dominions and of the principal states of Europe, was, until 1937, utterly unknown to English law, for until then it was not to be found in any legal document, statutory or otherwise. But in that year was passed the Ministers of the Crown Act, which increased and stabilised ministerial salaries, and for the first time placed on the Statute Book the terms Cabinet and Cabinet Minister and gave to the Prime Minister, as such, legal status. The Act, in fact, fixed the Prime Minister's salary at £10,000 a year, whereas hitherto he had had no salary at all as Prime Minister, the salary of £5,000 a year which he had drawn up to that time having been by virtue of the sinecure of the First Lordship of the Treasury or some other office which he might hold. The Act also officially established the position of Leader of the Opposition with a salary of £2,000 a year. But the very fact that the constitutional position of the Cabinet and the Prime Minister was not given statutory force until after more than three centuries of evolution only emphasises the strength of that customary or conventional element in the British Constitution which we have already observed. To know something of the history of this political phenomenon, whose influence has been so universal, is, therefore, of great importance to the student of comparative politics.

The emergence of the modern British Cabinet is generally associated with the ascendancy of the Whigs under Walpole (1721–42), but, though it is true that it assumed at that time the definite features which have since, with very slight intermissions, characterised it, we have to look farther back than that period for its true origin. We pointed out in the last section that in early political society the king was the law-giver, the executor of the law, and the judge; in other words, that in his office he combined all three departments of state: legislative, executive and judicial. Under William I, in England, the Great Council was organised to assist the King in this triple duty. This body of barons was the basis of our modern institutions, for from it has sprung, by almost imperceptible stages of modification and growth, the whole effective organisation of the present government of Britain: Parliament, Cabinet and Law Courts. But the Great Council normally met only three times a year, and naturally there evolved from it a special group in constant session, made up of certain high officers of state, such as the Archbishops of Canterbury and York, the Justiciar, Treasurer, and Chancellor, and called the Permanent Council. But this, in its turn, became too unwieldy for the purpose of intimate relations with the King, and in the reign of Henry VI (1422–1461) it was virtually superseded by yet another inner circle of councillors, called the Privy Council, which then became the chief executive body of the realm.

Under the Tudors, the Council was remoulded and assumed vast arbitrary powers, and its exercise of them became even more tyrannical as its effective strength passed to yet another inner circle of itself with the increasing size of the Privy Council. This special "interior council," as Macaulay called it, met the King not in the usual council chamber, but in a "cabinet" or smaller room set apart for the purpose. It had reached this point by the reign of Charles I (1625–1649). If now we can show that the prerogatives of the Crown passed at last into the hands of Parliament, we shall also show how it was that the Executive in England ultimately became a parliamentary one. This tremendous transition was effected, broadly speaking, in three stages. The first was the Great Rebellion under Charles I, which broke out in 1642. To prove how the question of the responsibility of Ministers to Parliament was involved in this struggle, we have only to quote a passage from a document presented to the King in the preceding year, namely, the Grand Remonstrance, one of the many attempts to stave off an armed conflict. It begged that:

"Your Majesty will vouchsafe to employ such persons in your great and public affairs, and to take such to be near you in places of trust, as *your Parliament may have cause to confide in.*"

Though Parliament won and the King was executed, the Restoration of the Monarchy under his son Charles II saw a reversion to some of the old abuses, and the second stage in the development of the existing executive system was reached in the Revolution of 1688. By the reigns of William III (1689-1702) and Anne (1702-1714), the Cabinet, though still unknown to law, had, in fact, become "the sole supreme consultative council and executive authority in the state." But the monarch was still the chairman of this body. It required but one more turn of the wheels of chance to place it beyond the King's power altogether and to put at its head a minister, the Prime Minister. This was effected by the accident of the Hanoverian succession on the death of Anne. Sacrificing nationality to religion, the English people preferred a German Protestant to an English Catholic (the son of James II). George I and George II were unable to speak English, and therefore dropped altogether the practice of attending Cabinet Councils, whose chairmanship then passed to the chief minister.

To trace the development of the Cabinet, therefore, is not the same thing as to trace the growth of the office of Prime Minister. Under Walpole, however, the two developments coincided. Under him those characteristics which mark the Cabinet to-day definitely emerged, and after a period of vagueness following his fall in 1742 and the consequent weakening of the Whig power, of which George III took advantage to attempt the restoration of the royal prerogative, the Cabinet towards the close of the eighteenth century took that shape again permanently. H. D. Traill has summarised the political conception of the Cabinet as a body necessarily consisting:

"(*a*) of members of the Legislature,

"(*b*) of the same political views, and chosen from the party possessing a majority in the House of Commons,

"(*c*) prosecuting a concerted policy,

"(*d*) under a common responsibility to be signified by collective resignation in the event of parliamentary censure; and

"(*e*) acknowledging a common subordination to one chief minister."

These characteristics may be further summarised as homogeneity, solidarity, and common loyalty to a chief.

The essence of this executive system is that, in the last analysis, the Cabinet is a committee of Parliament, tending to be, with the advance of democracy, a committee of the House of Commons. The historical development of the sway of Parliament over the executive has been associated with the growth of the party system. And neither of these growths had until recently anything to do with the law of the Constitution. As we have said, the Cabinet, as such, was before 1937 nowhere mentioned in the laws of this land, and no man can be a member of the Cabinet without being a member of the Privy Council, out of which, as we have shown, the Cabinet evolved. The abuse of the Privy Council by the King was the real cause of the growth of a Cabinet of Ministers responsible to Parliament. Far from liberty being achieved, as Montesquieu and Blackstone had asserted, by the utter separateness of the legislative and executive functions, our history has shown that liberty is secured rather by their intimate association. For a brief period in our history the statute law went against the whole spirit of this customary development of our Constitution. A clause in the Act of Settlement of 1701 stated that no office-holders should sit in the House of Commons. Six years later this clause was repealed, but neither at the time that this was incorporated into the law nor when it was repealed could statesmen have realised its full bearing on the future of the mechanism of government. The Cabinet emerged while still the royal prerogative had not been wholly demolished, and the purpose of the clause in the Act of Settlement was to restore executive functions to the larger body, the Privy Council. It was supposed that by withdrawing members of the Council from the Commons the king's power of intrigue through a corrupt parliamentary system would be reduced.

As it was, the repealing Act—the Place Act of 1707—saved the Constitution from this unrealised peril, but left the clause operative in two directions. First, part of what remained of the clause secures that no office-holder shall be in a position to hold government contracts, so that a Cabinet Minister must resign all active interest in any company concerned in such contracts. Secondly, the clause still applies to the permanent Civil Service, no member of which can sit in Parliament. The Privy Council remains in law, but it has now no political force whatever. As we have said, a member of the Cabinet must be sworn of the Privy Council on taking up office, but once a member of the latter, always a member; so that the Privy Council consists not only of existing ministers but of all ex-Ministers, among others, and is therefore a very large body of men, and, nowadays, occasionally women, each with the title Right Honourable.

The Cabinet in Britain is, therefore, dependent upon the good opinion of Parliament, which, under modern conditions, means the confidence of the House of Commons. This implies that the ultimate control is in the hands of the electorate. As Walter Bagehot acutely pointed out, the Cabinet is a creature, but, unlike all other creatures, it has the power of destroying its creator, *i.e.*, the House of Commons. For if the Cabinet is defeated in the Commons it can, instead of resigning, advise the Queen to dissolve the assembly upon which it depends. Then the electorate decides whether the party from which the appealing Cabinet is drawn shall return with a majority or not.[1] From this it is seen how vitally the stability of Cabinet government depends upon the party system. At those times in our history when the Government has had to depend upon the help of other sections of the House outside its own party, its tenure has always been insecure, as was proved, for example, in the case of the Labour Government in 1924, and again in the period 1929–1931.[2]

[1]But see L. S. Amery: *Thoughts on the Constitution* (1947), in which the author denies that "political power is a delegation from the citizen through the legislature to an executive dependent on that legislature," and maintains that our system is a "Union of Crown and Nation," the first, represented in the Cabinet and Ministry, governing and initiating; the other, represented in Parliament, criticising and consenting.

[2]In the latter year the Prime Minister, Ramsay MacDonald, saved his office only by dropping the vast majority of his own followers and forming a National Government by a coalition mainly with the Conservatives.

If it is the party system which gives the Cabinet its homogeneity, it is the position of the Prime Minister which gives it solidarity. Indeed, in essence, the Cabinet in England is much more the rule of one man than that of a committee. He must face the House with a united Cabinet. But that united front depends upon him. The Ministers come into and go out of office together. But if there is dissension in the Cabinet the Prime Minister has it in his power either to force the resignation of the dissentients individually or himself to resign with the whole body of Ministers. It is in this way that the party system is inextricably interwoven with the Cabinet system in England. In those states where the Cabinet system has been adopted without a strong party system from which it draws its strength —namely, a solid majority to back it in the elected assembly— the Government is never so stable, and what is called a Cabinet crisis is much more frequent than in England, as is notably the case in France.

To summarise, the noteworthy aspects of the British executive system are that it is dependent for its existence upon the support of the majority in the elected Chamber, that it is drawn from one party (except occasionally at times of national crisis), that the position of the Prime Minister gives it solidarity, that neither the Cabinet nor the office of Premier was known to the law until the passage of the Ministers of the Crown Act in 1937, that the body always known to the law, namely, the Privy Council, to which all Cabinet Ministers past and present belong, has no longer any real political significance. This development has destroyed absolutely the ancient prerogatives of the Crown, which have passed, together with the whole of the executive power, into the control of the legislature. This system has been transplanted to soils which had not been prepared so long to receive and mature it, and it is interesting to note one or two examples of states where this has been carried out, as we shall do in the succeeding sections of this chapter.

IV. RESPONSIBLE GOVERNMENT IN THE BRITISH SELF-GOVERNING DOMINIONS

A Self-governing Dominion is one which has responsible government, and what is called responsible government is in practice nothing more nor less than the application of the

Cabinet system to colonies where the executive function was formerly in the hands of the Imperial Government. For responsible government means not only that the Dominion to which it applies shall enjoy a liberty of legislation where its own interests are concerned, but that its executive shall be controlled directly and absolutely by the chosen representatives of the people. Thus, what has happened in each Self-governing Dominion is exactly what happened in Britain itself, except that the development took place over a much shorter space of time. Under the earlier dispensation—generally referred to as the Old Colonial System—the Governor-General of the colony represented the Crown, *i.e.*, the Home Government. But just as the King's actual political power at home was at first checked and finally destroyed by the growth of a Cabinet of Ministers responsible to Parliament, so in the Colonies the power of the Governor-General was destroyed by his being forced to choose his counsellors from the majority party in the elected assembly. When this was achieved, the executive power passed, *ipso facto*, out of the hands of the British Government into those of the Dominion itself.

This way of solving the thorny problem of a continued connection between Britain and her Colonies has gone very much farther than its inventors intended. Its inception followed the rebellions of 1837 in Canada, after which Lord Durham was sent there as Governor-General with the special duty of reporting on the state of the country and making proposals for its future government. His Report of 1839 is a great landmark in British Imperial history, for it did nothing less than make the movement towards responsible government possible. But Durham had attempted to distinguish between local and imperial questions with regard to the executive function, and he earmarked certain matters which should be permanently reserved to the Government at Westminster. Later history has justified the doubts of many worthy people in England at that time as to whether the maintenance of this distinction was possible, and their conviction that a time would come when all powers should pass to the Dominion. But far from being a reason, as those critics would have had it, for shelving Durham's report, it has justified its adoption abundantly; for responsible government, once conceived as practical politics, made possible all those developments of unfettered power on the part of the Dominions without which the Commonwealth could not have remained intact.

The Canada Act of 1840 did not establish the Cabinet system in Canada, but it made possible its growth through the statesmanship of the successors of Durham in the office of Governor-General, especially Lord Sydenham and Lord Elgin. It gradually became the practice of these officers to choose the Executive Council from members of the legislature who were the political party in the majority in the Lower Chamber. And so successful was this policy, in spite of the efforts of the Home Government to retard its development by appointing reactionary Governors-General, that, by 1849, Lord John Russell, then British Prime Minister, was able to say in the House of Commons:

"If the present Ministry in Canada are sustained by popular opinion and by the assembly, they will remain in office. If, on the contrary, the opinion of the province is adverse to them, the governor-general will take other advisers, and will act strictly in accordance with the rule that has been adopted here."

This attitude was endorsed by majorities in both Commons and Lords, and from that time there has never been any question as to the right of Canada to control her executive by her legislature. The Act of 1867 establishing the Dominion of Canada assumed the existence of the Cabinet system when it stated in its eleventh article that "There shall be a Council to aid and advise in the Government of Canada to be styled the Queen's Privy Council of Canada," which is, in practice, the Cabinet.

Meanwhile, the principle of responsible government had been granted in 1850 to New South Wales, Tasmania, New Zealand, and Cape Colony. Then, as each other colony reached the stage at which it could be safely entrusted with its own affairs, it was granted responsible government, the latest case being that of Ceylon in 1948. Thus, when the time came for the establishment of the Commonwealth of Australia and the Union of South Africa, Cabinet Government, having been already adopted in the previously separate units, became an essential part of the executive arrangements under the new Act in each case. The Commonwealth Act says, in Article 64:

"After the first general election no Minister of State shall hold office for a longer period than three months, unless he is or becomes a Senator or a member of the House of Representatives."

Similarly, the South African Act states, in Article 14:

"After the first general election of members of the House of Assembly, no minister shall hold office for a longer period than three months unless he is or becomes a member of either House of Parliament."

Again, Article 51 of the Irish Free State Constitution Act (1922) well illustrates the meaning of Cabinet government in the Dominions, and though the Constitution of 1922 has now been superseded by that of 1937, the original article is worth quoting. It reads as follows:

"The Executive Authority of the Irish Free State is hereby declared to be vested in the King, and shall be exercisable, in accordance with the law, practice and constitutional usage governing the exercise of the Executive Authority in the case of the Dominion of Canada, by the Representative of the Crown. There shall be a council to aid and advise in the government of the Irish Free State to be styled the Executive Council. The Executive Council shall be responsible to the Dail Eireann (Chamber of Deputies), and shall consist of not more than seven and not less than five Ministers appointed by the Representative of the Crown on the nomination of the President of the Executive Council."

The new constitution makes no mention of the King and contains no Oath of Allegiance. Nevertheless, in the previous December, an Act had been passed by the Parliament of the Irish Free State, which then still existed, in common with other Dominions, recognising the successor of Edward VIII on his abdication "for the purposes of the appointment of diplomatic and consular representatives and the conclusion of international agreements so long as the King continues to be recognised by the associated Dominions as the symbol of their co-operation."

The President is elected by direct vote of the people and holds office for seven years. His executive power is normally operated through a Cabinet with a Prime Minister (*Taöiseach*) responsible to a Parliament of two Houses (*Dail Eireann*) and Senate, the lower elected by adult universal suffrage, the upper partly nominated and partly elected from panels prepared under special provisions. But besides this the President has certain powers exercised with the aid of a Council of State, a consultative and advisory body, made up of seven *ex officio* members (including the Prime Minister) and others nominated by the President. There is a Supreme Court of Judges to which the President may refer any bill before he signs it for a decision whether any of its provisions are repugnant to the Constitution, and he is not obliged to consent to the Bill until the decision of the Supreme Court is announced. There are also provisions giving the President the right to address a message to the nation at any time and allowing for the use of the referendum in the case of bills which may, under certain conditions, be referred to the people for their decision.

As a result of the Imperial Conference of 1926 and the Statute of Westminster of 1931, the Governor-General in a Dominion has ceased to represent the British Government (as we have seen earlier) and become, in effect, the Queen's deputy. This change left the Home Government without even a channel of communication in any of the Self-governing Dominions and has necessitated the appointment of an official in each case who acts as a liaison officer between the Government at home and that of the Dominion to which he is appointed. In Canada, for example, this official is known as "High Commissioner in Canada for Her Majesty's Government in Great Britain." Thus has the British Government been deprived of even the semblance of executive control in the Dominions, and responsible government been made complete. It is difficult to conceive what other executive system was possible in the case of the Colonies consistently with the independence of the Dominions and the perpetuation of the moral bond with Britain simultaneously. For, if the real executive were outside instead of within the control of parliament in a Dominion, then either the Governor-General would be the supreme executive, in which case there would be no independence, or there would be no Governor-General, in which case the moral bond with Britain would be completely severed.

V. THE CABINET IN THE FRENCH REPUBLIC

If the student fails to grasp the significance of Cabinet government in France he misses the whole meaning of the Republic in that country. "There is," wrote Sir Henry Maine, speaking in the early days of the Third Republic, "no living functionary who occupies a more pitiable position than a French

8

President. The old kings of France reigned and governed. The constitutional king, according to M. Thiers, reigns, but does not govern. The President of the United States governs, but he does not reign. It has been reserved for the President of the French Republic neither to reign nor yet to govern." This statement, if a little over-emphatic in its language, described with broad truth the position of the President of the Third Republic, as it was in its earlier years and as it essentially remained to the end. Nor has the Constitution of the Fourth Republic (1946) substantially changed the real powers of the President. It is still true, in fact, that the President is only the nominal and not the real executive in France. The real executive is a Cabinet of Ministers (*le Conseil des Ministres*) with a Prime Minister (*le Président du Conseil des Ministres*) at their head, responsible to Parliament, though, whereas under the Third Republic the Cabinet was responsible to both Chambers, it is, under the Fourth Republic, responsible only to the National Assembly (formerly the Chamber of Deputies), the original power of the Senate (now the Council of the Republic) in this respect being specifically abrogated in the new Constitution.

Here, then, in the Fourth Republic, as in the Third, is a President elected for seven years, not by the people but by the two Houses of the French Parliament in joint session. He cannot act in any executive matter except through his Ministers, who must, by the Constitution, countersign his every decree. In spite of a large array of powers with which the Constitution of 1946 accredits the President, it states categorically (as did the Constitution of 1875) that he is "responsible" only in the case of High Treason (Article 42). There is, as we have said, a Council of Ministers of which the President is nominally head, but as this Council is responsible to the Assembly it becomes a Cabinet of which the Prime Minister is head. The Constitution states that the President shall communicate with Parliament by messages addressed to the National Assembly, but this only emphasises the responsibility of the Cabinet, since such a message corresponds to our own Queen's Speech, which at the beginning of each parliamentary session outlines the policy of the Government of the day. Thus, as a great French writer has said, the President is "the prisoner of the Ministry and of Parliament." He is exactly in the position of a constitutional king. "He is a titular executive, nominally endowed with large powers and really restrained from employing them by the action of a responsible parliamentary cabinet." He is, in short, "a constitutional king for seven years."

The Cabinet in France is, in several respects, different from the Cabinet in Britain. The law does not say that ministers shall be members of either House, but in practice they are, because they have, in any case, the right and, indeed, the need, to speak in either House, and in forming his Cabinet the Premier has to consider the value of the political weight of his colleagues. Secondly, the new Constitution provides, as did the old, that ministers shall be collectively responsible to the National Assembly for the general policy of the Government and individually for their personal acts. This would appear to open an avenue to divided counsels, but, in practice, the Cabinet works as a body and comes as a whole to the rescue of a minister individually attacked in the Chambers. Thirdly, the position of the Premier in France is somewhat different from that of his counterpart in Britain. He can appoint and dismiss ministers, but, in fact, he must go warily because of the peculiar group-system in France. There is no party strong enough to form a majority in the Chambers. It is therefore dependent for its continuance upon the support of a coalition of parliamentary groups. The Prime Minister gets their support while he does not outrage the opinions of any section of them. He is therefore in perpetual dread lest he should overstep the narrow area thus marked out for him; and this is the reason why a change of ministry is much more frequent in France than in this country.

This question of Cabinet crises requires a little elucidation. In Britain and the Dominions a Cabinet crisis is generally associated with a dissolution, for a Cabinet defeated in the Commons either resigns or advises the Queen to dissolve the House of Commons. If it resigns, then the new Cabinet generally fails to gain sufficient support from the existing House of Commons, and is then forced to dissolve. The decision then rests with the electorate. Very seldom in Britain does a Parliament last out its statutory term.[1] For, in time, an administration begins to lose hold, bye-elections go against it, and it dissolves

[1] Except, of course, in wartime. In both World Wars the life of the House of Commons was extended by special legislation.

228 Modern Political Constitutions

Parliament before things get worse. Now, in France they order things quite differently. Under the Third Republic the statutory life of a Parliament in France was four years, and the Constitution allowed for an earlier dissolution by the President with the consent of the Senate. But only once in the history of the Third Republic was the expedient of earlier dissolution resorted to, in 1877 under the Presidency of McMahon. This was regarded as an anti-Republican trick, an intrigue between Senate and President to get behind Parliament; in other words, to undermine the Republic, as constituted two years earlier, and to establish a plebiscitary system. So discredited was this device in the eyes of good republicans that it was never again employed during the existence of the Third Republic.

All that happened in France under the Third Republic when a ministry resigned was that a re-grouping took place in order to obtain the support of a majority in the Chamber, and a politician who held a portfolio in the Cabinet just resigned would often take up another in the new one. If France had been involved in the turmoils of a General Election every time a French Cabinet fell to pieces owing to the alienation of one of the parliamentary groups represented in it, democracy there could not possibly have survived. But the fragile group-system, on which Cabinet government in France was based, led to many abuses and did more than anything else to discredit the system of parliamentary executive in France. Not having been founded firmly, as in England, its original home, upon a true party system, the Cabinet was formed, and maintained, in France by the distribution of government favours, and the Prime Minister was constantly preoccupied with recruiting friends, to save himself from the crisis which hovered over him like the boulder in Virgil's Hades. The strongest criticism perhaps that can be brought against the French Cabinet system is the alarming fact that the average life of a Cabinet under the Third Republic was only ten months.

The framers of the Constitution of the Fourth Republic showed their consciousness of the danger of constant Cabinet crises to the safety of parliamentary institutions in France, and endeavoured to take precautions against it. Four articles of the Constitution elaborate the methods and consequences of votes of confidence in, or censure of, the Cabinet. Such questions can only be put and discussed in the National Assembly, since the Council of the Republic cannot take any part, as could the old Senate, in matters involving the period of life of the Cabinet or the Assembly. Under the rules laid down in the new Constitution, if after the first eighteen months of the life of a Parliament two Cabinet crises arise in any period of eighteen months, the Ministry can, after consultation with the President of the Assembly, decide to dissolve the Assembly, and if it does so decide, the President of the Republic must issue a decree of dissolution and order a general election, which must take place within a month of the dissolution. Despite these precautions, the average Cabinet life during the first decade of the Fourth Republic actually fell to six months.

In the early days of the Fourth Republic, the Ministry was formed by a coalition of the three main groups in the Assembly: the Socialists, the Communists and the Christian Democrats (M.R.P.),[1] but before long it had to give way to other groupings. And, in any case, there are many Frenchmen who doubt the virtue of a parliamentary executive, however broadly based. They object in principle to a President elected by Parliament and with only nominal functions, on the ground that such a system weakens the hold of the government at home and its prestige abroad, and seem to prefer the American system,[2] under which the President is popularly elected and has real powers unfettered by the legislature. This attachment to the conception of the non-parliamentary, or plebiscitary, executive is of long standing in France and derives from the Napoleonic tradition which made possible the election of Louis Napoleon as President of the Second Republic in 1848, his *coup d'état* in 1851, and his successful establishment of the Second Empire in 1852. The same political feeling was behind the movement of General Boulanger who precipitated a grave crisis in 1886 through his attempt to re-establish the plebiscitary executive. The Boulanger plot was heavily crushed by the forces of the Republic, but that the hope of restoring a popularly elected Executive free from parliamentary shackles is not dead in France would seem to be proved by the strength of the backing which General de Gaulle received when, in 1947, he

---

[1] *Mouvement Républicain Populaire.*   [2] Described in the next chapter.

initiated the movement known as the "Rally of the French People" (*Rassemblement du Peuple Français*).[1]

VI. THE CABINET SYSTEM IN THE NEW ITALIAN REPUBLIC

Under the Constitution of the new Italian Republic the principle of Cabinet responsibility is revived. For that principle was inherent in the Sardinian *Statuto* in 1848 and developed strongly under the successive governments of the Italian Kingdom until it was overborne and superseded by the Fascist Dictatorship. Article 65 of the original Constitution said that the King appointed and dismissed Ministers, but Article 67 stated that the Ministers were responsible to Parliament and that no laws or governmental acts could take effect until they had received the signature of a Minister. Article 66 said that Ministers should have no vote in either the Chamber of Deputies or the Senate unless they were members of one of them, but that they had the right of entrance to both Houses and might be heard on request. That clause was normally interpreted as placing the Prime Minister under the obligation either of appointing a Minister without a seat to one in the Senate or of causing him to stand for a seat in the Chamber at the first vacancy. There, then, was an example of the working of the Cabinet system under a constitutional monarchy, as we know it in Britain.

When, therefore, we consider that the Italians, up to the advent of Fascism, had more than fifty years of such constitutional practice behind them, we are not surprised to find that they should wish, in their reaction against dictatorship and all its miserable consequences, to restore the principle of the parliamentary executive. In the new Republic the President is elected for seven years by the vote of Parliament (*i.e.*, the two Chambers in joint session) with the participation of three delegates from each Regional Council so elected as to ensure the representation of the minority. But the President has no direct political powers. Two articles of the Constitution (viz., 89 and 90) state that none of his acts is valid without the confirmation of the Prime Minister or an appropriate Minister,

[1]The mere backing of the R.P.F., however, was not enough, and De Gaulle withdrew from active politics. When, in the fateful crisis of 1958, the President recalled him as Premier, he was granted wide emergency powers by parliamentary majorities. But the ultimate effect on the French parliamentary executive of these desperate measures remains to be seen.

who takes responsibility, and that he has no responsibility except for acts of treason or in violation of the constitution, in which case he can be impeached by Parliament.

Five Articles of Chapter Three of the Constitution of the new Republic deal with the status, form, and functions of the Cabinet or Council of Ministers. They state that the President nominates the Prime Minister who proposes the Ministers, and that the Cabinet so constituted must gain the confidence of both the Chamber of Deputies and the Senate within ten days of its formation. The two Chambers have equal competence to move a vote of censure of or no-confidence in the government. But the Cabinet is not obliged to resign as the result of an adverse vote in either Chamber, a safeguard calculated to reduce the chances of government instability. The Ministers are collectively responsible for the acts of the Cabinet and each is responsible for the acts of his department. It is clear, then, that the President of the new Italian Republic is only the nominal executive and that the real executive is the Prime Minister and Cabinet who are responsible to Parliament. In other words, the Italian Republic has a parliamentary executive and its constitution is in this respect similar to that of the original constitutional kingdom of Italy, to that of Great Britain, and to those of the Third and Fourth French Republics.

VII. THE CABINET SYSTEM AS ADOPTED IN GERMANY AND OTHER STATES AFTER THE FIRST WORLD WAR

The Cabinet system, which had become characteristic of most constitutional states in Europe before the First World War, was generally adopted by those states newly formed or enlarged by the war, as well as by Germany under the constitution of the Weimar Republic. Whether we consider the more important states then created, such as Austria, Poland, Yugoslavia and Czechoslovakia, or the comparatively small and unimportant ones, such as Finland, Estonia, Latvia and Lithuania, this same phenomenon was to be observed. Most of them were republics, and, in fact, only the Balkan States retained their hereditary monarchies, but each of them instituted a parliamentary executive. Many of the constitutional arrangements under the influence of the political optimism which characterised the immediate post-war period were gravely disturbed in the years that followed, not only in Germany but in most of the surrounding states affected by the same growing social and political unrest. And in the Second World War they suffered the common agony of Nazi occupation. With their release from that thraldom and their struggle for constitutional rehabilitation in face of Soviet Russia's domination of the eastern half of Europe, it is worth while briefly to recall the character of the parliamentary executive which some of them established at the time of their earlier independence.

Under the Weimar Republic the German President was elected for a period of seven years by the vote of the people, all of whom, of either sex of twenty years or more, were, by the Constitution, enfranchised. The President was eligible for re-election for a further term, or he might, before the expiration of the period, be removed from office by the vote of the people on a motion of the *Reichstag* passed by a two-thirds majority. If then the popular vote went against the *Reichstag*, that vote achieved two things, first a re-election of the President and secondly a dissolution of the *Reichstag*.

The German Constitution, like the French, set out a long array of powers belonging to the President, but in practice he could not exert them because the Federal Chancellor and his Cabinet were made responsible for all acts. The parliamentary nature of the executive was very clearly established by certain clauses in the Constitution. Thus Article 50 said that all orders and decrees of the President required the counter-signature of a minister, which counter-signature implied responsibility. Article 54 stated that "the Chancellor of the Federation and the Federal Ministers require, for the administration of their office, the confidence of the *Reichstag*. Any one of them must resign, should the confidence of the House be withdrawn by an express resolution." Articles 55 and 56 emphasised the Cabinet system and the office of Prime Minister (*i.e.*, Federal Chancellor) by saying that the Federal Chancellor presided over the Federal Government and directed its business, and that he determined the main lines of policy for which he was responsible to the *Reichstag*. Finally, the *Reichstag*, by Article 59, was entitled to arraign any or all of the members of the Federal Executive, including the President of the Republic, before the Supreme

Court of the Republic, for "culpable violation of the Federal Constitution, or of a Federal law."

What an enormous change, then, had come about in Germany through the break-up of the old Imperial power resultant upon the war! Until the changes of 1918 the Emperor had been both the nominal and the real executive. His chief minister, the Imperial Chancellor, was responsible to him alone, and nothing that the *Reichstag* was enabled by the old Constitution to do could disturb him. But under the Republican Constitution, not only was the hereditary Emperor with real executive powers replaced by an elected President with only nominal ones, but the Imperial Chancellor, instead of being the direct servant of the Emperor, removable at his pleasure, became the servant of the elected Chamber, the *Reichstag*, which thus acquired a real political force, whereas formerly it had existed merely as an advisory body, notwithstanding that it was elected upon a very broad franchise.

As to Rumania, the old pre-war Constitution continued to apply to the enlarged state with its hereditary monarch whose acts were actually performed by a Cabinet of ministers responsible to the elected assembly. In the case of Yugoslavia, or the Kingdom of the Serbs, Croats and Slovenes, as it was then called, a new Constitution was drawn up by a constituent assembly in 1920 and became operative in 1921. But in some respects it was not really a new Constitution at all; nothing more than an extension of the original Constitution of Serbia of 1886 which had been re-enacted in 1903. Article 47 stated simply that "executive power is administered by the King through his responsible ministers." The Constitution of 1920 was amended in 1931 but has now, as we saw in Chapter V, been entirely superseded by the Soviet-inspired Constitution of the Federal People's Republic of 1946.

As to the new republics constituted after the First World War, four are of interest: namely, Austria, Czechoslovakia, Poland, and Finland. In the case of Austria the Constitution of 1920 was drawn up by a constituent assembly which looked to the ultimate incorporation of the new Austria into the new German Federal Republic. Meanwhile, the Constitution was to apply to eight provinces, themselves forming a quasi-federal state. But then the Peace Treaties prohibited the incorporation

8*

of Austria in Germany, and the Austrian Constitution of 1920 ceased to have a merely provisional character. The President was elected, as in France but for a period of only four years, by the two Houses (the *Nationalrat* and the *Bundesrat*) in joint session. He actually performed certain important executive functions, the rest of which were discharged by a federal ministry deliberately elected by the Lower House (*Nationalrat*). Thus, if that House withdrew its confidence from the minister or the ministry as a whole, he or it immediately had to resign and a new ministerial election took place. All this was, of course, undone in the period of Nazification which preceded the German annexation in 1938 and naturally had no force thereafter. But the characteristic features of the former constitution reappear in that of the now restored independent Republic.

In Czechoslovakia before the Nazi rape the President was elected for seven years by the Chamber of Deputies and Senate in joint session, provided that an absolute majority of both Houses was present and that the candidate secured a three-fifths majority. The President could not submit himself for a third term of office, though this proviso was not to apply to the first President, Masaryk, whose venerability and services to his country marked him out for the signal honour of the possibility of holding the office for life. There was a Prime Minister and Cabinet which was responsible to the Chamber of Deputies. But an interesting safeguard against government instability was introduced by Articles 75 and 76 of the Constitution of February, 1920. These articles stated that a vote of "no confidence" in the Ministry by the Chamber of Deputies should be valid only when more than half the members were present, if there were an absolute majority, and if the vote were taken by roll call. Further, such a motion for a vote of "no confidence" had to be signed by not less than a hundred deputies before it could be introduced. The object of this elaborate scheme was, obviously, to save the government from overthrow by merely factious attacks during the critical early days of the Czechoslovakian Republic.

This constitution was gravely weakened when Czechoslovakia was forced to surrender the Sudetenlands to Germany by the fateful capitulation at Munich in September, 1938, and was completely overthrown in the following March when Hitler annexed the provinces of Bohemia and Moravia. But in the period immediately following Czechoslovakia's liberation in the Second World War it was provisionally revived in a modified form, pending a definitive constitutional reconstruction. The reconstruction, when it came, bore little resemblance to the older constitutional forms, for the new Constitution of 1948 was promulgated in the heavy shadow of the Soviet power. So far, indeed, were its essential principles from the spirit of the founders of the Republic of 1918 that President Benes could not bring himself to endorse it, and he retired from public life. Under the new Constitution there is still a President elected for seven years by the National Assembly, which is a Parliament of one Chamber, but he must act through a Ministry of twenty-four members with the ominous name of Presidium. It would be too much to say that, on paper at least, the Czechoslovak Constitution of 1948 establishes a Soviet system, but it is undoubtedly true that, although the state is called a "Democratic People's Republic," it manifests a marked apostasy from the Western models which the earlier Constitution followed and a strong tendency towards a political authoritarianism of the Russian type.

Again, in the case of Poland the President was elected for seven years by both the Senate and the Diet, sitting together. Article 43 of the Constitution of 1921 stated that the President exercised the executive power through Ministers responsible to the Lower House, and the Ministers, it added, were responsible not only for the acts of the President but for those also of the subordinates whom he appointed. But this liberal constitution had already been for some time in suspense when in 1935 it was replaced by a new one. Under the Polish constitution of 1935 the President was specifically invested with quasi-dictatorial powers including the right to nominate a third of the Senate, while a new electoral law practically disfranchised the parties opposed to the government. Thus the parliamentary executive in Poland had disappeared when the German onslaught came in September, 1939. But as soon as Poland had been liberated in the Second World War through Russia's westward sweep, a struggle began between a Provisional Government under Russian influence and those Poles, mainly in exile, who wished to restore the parliamentary democracy of the original constitution. But it was soon evident that the anti-Russian Poles were fighting a losing battle, and the victory of the protagonists of the Russian type of political organisation would now seem to be complete. Nor, in view of the propinquity of the Soviet system and its many ardent Polish adherents, is it easy to see how constitutionalism of the Western type, and particularly the principle of the parliamentary executive, can be successfully revived in Poland.

In Finland the Constitution of July, 1919, replaced the old Swedish Constitution of 1772, as revised in 1789, and a later Parliament Act of 1928 modified the Law of 1906 which had established the Diet. Under this Constitution, which is thus documentary, though fragmentary, there is a representative single-chamber legislature and a President popularly, but not directly, elected (though the first President was elected by the Chamber). The permanent plan adopted followed the system laid down in the Constitution of the United States, where, however, it is not in practice any longer carried out. The people, said Article 23 of the Finnish Constitution, should elect three hundred Presidential Electors, and the right to vote for these should be the same as that for members of the Chamber of Deputies, namely, by universal adult suffrage and under a system of P.R. The voting of the three hundred was secret, and if no candidate for the Presidency secured more than half the votes cast, there should be a second ballot, and if, as a result of this, no one gained an absolute majority, the two candidates with the highest number of votes should be voted for again. The President thus elected had certain real powers, but most of his acts, to be valid, required the counter-signature of a minister who had to be a member of the Council of State, or Cabinet, enjoying the confidence of the elected Chamber (Articles 36 and 43). In cases of conflict between the President and the Council of State, the latter had the final decision, so long as it was thus acting within the terms of the Constitution, which was ultimately to be interpreted by a Supreme Court of Law. There were slight Fascist disturbances in the early 1930's, but they ended in 1932 without seriously affecting the Cabinet system, and, even when the Finns were led into their disastrous alliance with Germany, the Nazis had little influence on their governmental practice.   After 1944, under Russian pressure some elements of authoritarianism manifested themselves, but these were removed in 1947, and the Finns managed to maintain their parliamentary executive.

Thus the states created as a result of the First World War universally adopted the principle of the parliamentary executive. But after their brief experience of its working between the wars virtually all have failed to restore it in the conditions created by the consequences of the second. Yugoslavia has adopted a constitution with an executive frankly modelled on the Russian Presidium, and Czechoslovakia and Poland seem equally to have succumbed to Russian influences in this respect. Finland alone has so far resisted a similar fate, but the three Baltic States—Estonia, Latvia and Lithuania—have had no choice but to be incorporated in the federal system of the U.S.S.R. As to Germany and Austria, so far as the Western Powers could influence them, both have been encouraged to revive their earlier Parliamentary institutions and to restore the Parliamentary Executive which characterised their pre-Nazi constitutions. The Bonn Constitution, inaugurated in Western Germany in 1949, is, as we have seen, based on a Cabinet system of Ministers responsible to Parliament, while in Austria the Executive is similarly responsible to the National Assembly.

READING

BAGEHOT: *English Constitution*, Essays i, vi–ix.
BARKER: *Essays on Government*, Essays i, iv, v.
BRYCE: *Modern Democracies*, Vol. I, Ch. xxi, pp. 535–8; Vol. II, Chs. xlviii, lx.
DICEY: *Law of Constitution*, Ch. xi.
FINER: *Modern Government*, Vol. II, Chs. xxii, xxiv, xxv. *Future of Government*, Chs. i, iv, v.
GETTELL: *Readings in Political Science*, Ch. xix.
JENKS: *Government of British Empire*, Chs. v, ix, x, pp. 64–70.
JENNINGS: *Cabinet Government*, Chs. ii, iii, viii, ix, xiv. *Law and Constitution*, Ch. i, Sections 2 and 3.
KEITH: *Responsible Government in the Dominions*, Vol. I, Pt. ii, Ch. vii; Vol. II, pp. 621–3, 710–12.
LASKI: *Grammar of Politics*, pp. 295–303, 356–410,
LOWELL: *Government of England*, Vol. I, Chs. i–viii and xvii–xviii. *Governments and Parties*, Vol. I, pp. 26–34, 161–7. *Greater European Governments*, Ch. i, pp. 287–292.
MARRIOTT: *English Political Institutions*, Chs. iii–v. *Mechanism of the Modern State*, Vol. I, Ch. xiii; Vol. II, Chs. xxiii–xxx.
SAIT: *Government and Politics of France*. Chs. ii–iv.
SIDGWICK: *Element of Politics*, Chs. xxi, xxii.
WILSON: *State*, pp. 155–162, 181–206, 262–3, 425.

BOOKS FOR FURTHER STUDY

ANSON: *Law and Custom.*
FINER: *Governments of Greater European Powers.*
JACKSON: *Finland.*
KEITH: *Dominion Home Rule in Practice.*
LASKI: *Parliamentary Government in England.*
LIDDERDALE: *Parliament of France.*
LOWELL: *Essays on Government.*
MCKENZIE: *British Political Parties.*
PICKLES: *France: The Fourth Republic.*

SUBJECTS FOR ESSAYS

1. "The great overruling power in every free community." Discuss this description of the legislature as compared with the executive in the modern state.

2. Distinguish between nominal and real executives, whether hereditary or elective.

3. Discuss the theory of the "Separation of Powers" and show its influence on the development of the executive in modern states.

4. What are the essential characteristics of a parliamentary executive?

5. Trace the growth of the Cabinet system in Great Britain.

6. Summarise the main features of British Cabinet government as it exists to-day.

7. Explain the significance of the application of the principle of Cabinet government to the British Dominions.

8. What part is played by the Cabinet in the executive system of the Fourth French Republic?

9. How far has Italy under the new Republic restored the Cabinet system as it existed before Mussolini's Dictatorship?

10. Give some examples of states which introduced the Cabinet system after the First World War and say what has happened in them in this respect since the Second World War.

CHAPTER XI

THE NON-PARLIAMENTARY OR FIXED EXECUTIVE

I. GENERAL CONCEPTION OF THE DEMOCRATIC VALUE OF A FIXED EXECUTIVE

UNLESS carefully watched, the terms Cabinet and Presidential Government may be misleading. As we have already shown, an elected President may not be the real executive, and in that case the executive is actually in the hands of a Cabinet, with a Prime Minister at its head, responsible to Parliament. But again, Cabinet Government does not necessarily mean the rule of a body as opposed to the rule of one man. As we pointed out, the Cabinet in England is virtually controlled by the Prime Minister, and beyond the necessity that all members of his Cabinet must sit in one or other of the Houses of Parliament, and that they will normally be members of his party, there is no restriction upon his choice. Furthermore, Presidential Government also involves a body of ministers who, in the United States at any rate, are known as Cabinet Officers. It is very difficult, of course, to achieve a diffusion of executive power among a body of men. The whole trend of executive power is towards concentration in the hands of one, and a mere elective system is no guarantee that it will be diffused. In Britain, for instance, since it is the practice that the very great majority of the members of the Cabinet shall be members of the House of Commons (only two or three nowadays sitting in the Lords), it follows that the Cabinet is largely made up of representatives of the people. And yet it is by no means an *ad hoc* elected body. In this respect, then, Cabinet and Presidential Government or parliamentary and non-parliamentary executives may be alike. There are cases of republics—Switzerland, for example—where the executive is actually elected by the legislature, but such election is obviously not an inherent

239

characteristic of either a parliamentary or a fixed executive. The only sort of truly fixed executive is that which is either a real hereditary executive or an elected executive unmovable by the action of the legislature. Hence it follows that a fixed executive is not necessarily democratic. But since in the Western world of to-day there no longer exists an example of a real hereditary executive, we are driven to examine the fixed executive conceived as a democratic device. The most important case of this is the executive of the United States, but it has been copied in most states of Latin America.[1] The significance of an elected executive which is real is that the elected person is in fact what he is in name. There is no case where the elected real executive becomes a parliamentary executive (though Turkey now offers an apparent rebuttal of this absolute statement), just as there is no case where an executive which arises out of a body of men elected to the legislature is other than a parliamentary executive. For if the executive is elected as such, then it is either the executive without the interference of the legislature, in which case it is non-parliamentary or fixed, or else it is not the executive at all in fact, and the real executive power is in the hands of a man or body responsible to the assembly.

The democratic value which is conceived to lie in this fixed executive is traceable back to the old theory of the separation of powers. The argument runs that, if a president is popularly elected to perform executive functions, he should not be subject to limitation in his executive acts by a body elected for another purpose.[2] It is only in theory that such an absolute division of functions is possible, for, after all, part of the work of the executive is concerned with the execution of the decrees of the legislative power. But where the executive is non-parliamentary, what the constitution states as belonging to the executive branch really does belong to the office of the person elected to carry it out; whereas, where the executive is a parliamentary one the powers stated in the constitution as belonging to the

---

[1] In the Argentine a new Constitution of 1949, inspired by the Dictatorship of Juan Perón, provided for the direct popular election of the President, instead of through an Electoral College, as under the Constitution of 1857, and for his permanent re-eligibility. After Perón's fall in 1955, a provisional, but hardly less authoritarian régime established itself, and as late as 1958 the reform of the Constitution was still being debated.

[2] This is the position of the Gaullists and other opponents of the parliamentary executive in France. See earlier, pp. 229–230.

executive do not in fact belong to the person called by heredity or chosen by election to execute them.

The constitutions that we are now to examine from this point of view vary very considerably. The first—that of the United States—is a true case of a fixed executive. The second— that of Switzerland—offers an example quite unique among the constitutional systems of the world, having an executive which is in appearance a parliamentary one, but, in practice, shows the separation of functions. As to the third—that of the Turkish Republic—this offers a new type of executive which appears to combine the characteristics of both the parliamentary and fixed types.

II. APPLICATION OF THE PRINCIPLE IN THE UNITED STATES

The principle of the non-parliamentary or fixed executive is most perfectly illustrated in the case of the United States of America. The Fathers of the Constitution applied, to its extreme practical limit, the conception of the independence of the executive from the legislature. Although in one important particular, which we shall note in a moment, the machinery which they originally set up has been considerably modified in its working by custom and practice, the principle of separation remains intact. The Constitution says that "the executive power shall be vested in a President of the United States of America" and that "he shall hold his office during the term of four years . . . together with the Vice-President chosen for the same term." The original arrangements for the election of these two officers were laid down in Article 2, Section 1, of the Constitution, but were superseded in 1804 by the Twelfth Amendment which, instead of making Vice-President that candidate who secured the next highest number of votes to the President, caused two distinct ballots to be taken, one for each office.

As we stated in Chapter III, the elaborate arrangements detailed in the original clause and in the amendment have ceased to operate, and the high-minded intentions of the founders to keep the election free from direct popular influences have been utterly foiled. The Constitution says that electors shall be chosen in each state to a number equal to the number of members of the House of Representatives and of the Senate for that state; in other words, equal to the state's representation in Congress. These electors shall meet in each state and nominate and cast votes for Presidential and Vice-Presidential candidates. When they have so chosen, they shall send the names with the votes recorded for each to the President of the Senate who, in the presence of both Houses of Congress, shall unseal and count the votes.

This does not happen at all in practice. In fact, the two occasions on which Washington (the first President) was elected were the only times that it occurred. Since then the growth of party conventions has made the election of the President entirely popular. What happens, in fact, is that the various parties hold meetings long before the date fixed for elections and each selects a candidate for each office. When, therefore, the people in each state elect electors, they know for which Presidential and Vice-Presidential candidate they are voting, and hence the meeting of those electors afterwards is a mere form. The candidate for each office for whom a majority of votes is cast in any one state is the candidate for that state, and therefore scores as many electoral votes as there are members of Congress from that state, quite irrespectively of the largeness or smallness of the majority; for, under this system of electing electors, all the voters in a state have as many votes as there are electors to be elected in that state. Thus the whole state, in this case, is the constituency, and electors are elected *en bloc* according to the candidate they are pledged to vote for.

Two examples will make the practical working of the plan clear. Let us take a state with a large population, New York, and one with a small population, Maine, and suppose that the Presidential candidates are A and B, and the Vice-Presidential candidates X and Y. The State of New York has approximately nine million inhabitants, and returns forty-three members to the House of Representatives, and therefore elects forty-five Presidential Electors (adding two for its senatorial representation); the State of Maine has a population of approximately three-quarters of a million and therefore elects six Presidential Electors. Now, if a majority of the voting portion of the nine millions in New York State vote for A as President and X as Vice-President, then A and X carry all the forty-five votes for New York State as Presidential and Vice-Presidential candidates respectively. Similarly, if a majority of the voting portion of Maine's three-quarters of a million inhabitants vote for B as President and Y as Vice-President, then B and Y carry all the six votes for the State of Maine as Presidential and Vice-Presidential candidates respectively. But from this it is not difficult to realise how much more important it is for a Presidential candidate to carry the large than the small states. It would be possible, indeed, for a candidate to carry the eleven smallest states in the Union and still be outvoted by the candidate who carries New York.

This particular arrangement often has the effect of showing a marked discrepancy between the total of original popular votes recorded and the final result. President Lincoln, for example, was elected in 1860 in a tri-angular contest by 180 electoral votes to 123 recorded by his three opponents, but the people who voted for those electors who stood for him numbered 1,860,000 while those who voted for his opponents numbered 2,810,000. In other words, he was the choice of only 40 per cent of the voters of the country. In a complex four-cornered election in 1912 President Wilson obtained 435 electoral votes to his three opponents' 96 combined, but his popular vote was only 6,298,859 to his opponents' 8,511,312. In the Presidential Election of 1928 the figures were even more remarkable, for in that case there was a straight fight between two candidates. While Mr. Hoover's electoral vote was 444 (40 states) to Governor Smith's 87 (8 states), the figures for the popular vote were: Hoover, about 21,000,000; Smith, over 16,000,000, and while Mr. Hoover's electoral vote was the greatest ever gained by any party in the history of the United States, up to that time, Governor Smith's popular vote was the greatest ever gained by the Democratic Party to that year. More recent elections have shown a similar discrepancy. In the Presidential Election of 1932, although Hoover polled nearly 16,000,000 votes against Roosevelt's 23,000,000, he gained only 59 electoral votes against Roosevelt's 472. Again in 1936 when Landon's popular vote was more than half as large as Roosevelt's, Roosevelt carried every state but two, scoring an electoral vote of 523 against his opponent's 8. In 1940 Roosevelt's popular majority against Wendell Wilkie was only 5,000,000 in a total poll of 49,000,000, and yet his electoral vote was 449 to 82. In 1944 Roosevelt's corresponding figures were 3,500,000, and 432 to 99. In 1948

Truman's popular majority was 2,100,000, and his electoral vote 304 to 189. In 1952 Eisenhower's popular majority was 6,600,000, and his electoral vote 442 to 89. In 1956 his corresponding figures were 9,500,000 and 457 to 74.

None the less, it remains the fact that the President in the United States is now popularly elected (that is, directly instead of indirectly, as was the intention of the Fathers of the Constitution), but this is the only case among the foremost states of the world in which the President at the same time is popularly elected and is the real executive. These two facts in combination make inevitable a non-parliamentary executive, for if Congress could remove the President at will (he can be removed only by impeachment), the electoral machinery would be utterly unreal, whether in its original form as stated in the Constitution or in the popular form it has in practice assumed.

The powers of the President are very real, though the exercise of them varies greatly with the personality of the President, and in times of crisis they can become greater still. While it is his business to execute the laws passed by Congress, he can and does influence the actions of Congress in its legislation. First, he delivers to Congress an Annual Message, either in person or through a deputy who reads it. But he may call Congress together for the purpose of delivering a message more often if he considers that the gravity of circumstances demands it. This right can have a tremendous bearing upon the course of legislation, especially if used by an orator who chooses to address Congress in person, as, for example, did both Woodrow Wilson and Franklin Roosevelt. Secondly, the President can get a member of Congress to embody his ideas on a certain subject in a bill. But it must be remembered that neither the President nor any of his Cabinet Officers is allowed to take part in the business of either the Senate or the House of Representatives, and therefore the power of the President to influence Congress is largely conditioned by the state of parties in the Houses. While the President is elected every four years, the House of Representatives and a third of the Senate are elected every two; so that, while it is probable that the wave of favour towards a certain party which has brought a particular man into the Presidential Chair will also bring him a majority in the Houses, it may well be that, at the next Congressional election, the President, who has still two years to run, will lose this backing.[1]

But then the President has an important power at the other end of the legislative process, which may easily neutralise the effects of a minority of his party in the Houses. After a bill has passed both Houses, it cannot become law until the President has signed it. This signature he may refuse (he must notify his refusal within ten days), and if he does, the bill must go back to Congress and be passed in each House by a clear two-thirds majority. Such a majority, as may be imagined, is very difficult to achieve unless the President's party is hopelessly outnumbered. In practice, a bill vetoed by the President seldom gains the necessary majority afterwards, and so the President's veto is a very potent weapon in his hands.

Further than this, the President is Commander-in-Chief of the Army and Navy; he has the function of making all the important appointments in the federal government; and the conduct of foreign affairs is in his hands, though the Senate may refuse its assent to certain appointments, and a treaty made by the President requires the ratification of two-thirds of the Senate. Finally, the power to declare war belongs to Congress as a whole, but clearly executive action may bring negotiation to such a pass as to make war almost inevitable.

Thus, though relations exist in the United States between the executive and legislature, the intimacy of which varies with party strength and the personality of the President, the two powers are quite distinct, and it is safe to say that in no constitutional state in the world to-day does there exist an officer with such vast powers as those of the President of the American Union. If he proposes to seek re-election, he is, of course, subject, as the time approaches, to the great party caucuses which control the politics of America, but no more so than any other politician in the country. But actually, during his four years of office, so long as he does not act unconstitutionally, his power remains unchecked, except in the ways we have mentioned, and his position unchallenged. And if, at the last, public opinion is

[1]This is exactly what happened as a result of the Congressional Election of 1946, when the Republicans were returned with a majority in both the Senate and the House of Representatives while the Democratic President Truman, who as Vice-President had succeeded Franklin Roosevelt on his death in 1945, had still two years of his term to run.

with him, he may frequently prevail over the opposition even of an antipathetic Congress.

III. THE PECULIAR EXECUTIVE OF THE SWISS CONFEDERATION

No executive system in the world is so deserving of attention as that of Switzerland, for the founders of the Swiss Constitutions of 1848 and 1874 would appear to have succeeded in a project which has baffled the ingenuity of all previous statesmanship, and especially that of France, namely, to combine the merits and exclude the defects of both the parliamentary and the non-parliamentary executive systems. The Swiss executive, the Federal Council, is a ministry elected, but not dismissible, by each Federal Assembly. The actual Swiss executive thus resembles at the same time both the nominal and real executive of France; for, like the French President, the Swiss Federal Council is elected by the legislature, and, like the French Cabinet, it is the real executive. But again, in its immovability over a certain period, once chosen by the Assembly, it resembles the American Presidency.

Who, then, is the President of the Swiss Republic? The answer is, there is no such person because there is no such office. The Swiss Federal Council is a body of seven ministers elected by the two houses of the legislature—the National Council and the Council of States—sitting together to form a National Assembly. They are elected at the beginning of each new National Council for the duration of that assembly, namely, four years. This is an attempt to secure an executive power diffused or dispersed among a body of men, as distinct from such a power concentrated in the hands of one. And the attempt appears to be successful; for, in the strictest sense of the term, these seven hold the power equally among them. But because there are certain duties, such as receiving foreign potentates and ministers, that it is manifestly impossible for seven men to perform simultaneously, one of the seven is chosen by the National Assembly to act as Chairman of the Council for one year only. Swiss democracy insists upon the principle of rotation, and no man is allowed to hold the chairmanship for two years in succession. He gets a salary equal to about £60 a year more than each of the other six during his year of office. This Chairman of the Federal Council of Ministers is often familiarly referred to as the President of the Republic, but his precedence over the rest is "a merely formal precedence: he is in no sense the Chief Executive."

Thus the Swiss Council of Ministers is, at first sight, a parliamentary executive in a very emphatic sense. But, if we look more deeply into its working, we find that it turns out in practice to be fixed. The seven members of the Council elected by the House need not be members of one of these Houses before being chosen, though they generally are, but, if they are, as soon as they are elected to the Council they must resign their seat in the Chamber. In other words, the election to a place in the executive involves the resignation of the legislative function. The members of the Council at the expiration of their three-year term are frequently re-elected, and some of them have held office successively for as long as fifteen years.

But in the matter of the relationship between the executive and the legislature, Swiss practice offers a strong contrast to the American. Whereas in the United States the only contact between executive and legislature is through the President's Messages, and none of his Ministers is allowed in either House of the Legislature, in Switzerland the Ministers, as heads of departments, may attend the sittings of either House, and may take part freely in debate. And, indeed, Parliament looks to them for guidance in its business of passing laws. Nevertheless, the Ministers are not the leaders of the Houses, but their servants. The Ministry has no partisan character; it stands outside party; it does not do party work; and it does not determine the policy of the various parties in the Houses. Its business is purely administrative, being concerned chiefly with such federal affairs as the collection of national revenue and the management of national undertakings, such as railways.

The most remarkable feature about the Executive in Switzerland is its stability. As we have said, though the Houses elect the Ministers, they cannot dismiss them within the term of the Lower House, and, further, it is the common practice to re-elect them if they desire it. If the National Council is dissolved before the end of its normal three-year term, the first business of the new one and of the Council of States is to elect the Federal Council, but in practice this generally means re-electing the members of the last one. Thus the Federal Council has a permanence and stability far more like that which characterises a fixed executive, such as that of the United States, than that which characterises Cabinet government as it exists, for example, in Belgium and France. And yet, though it is elected by Parliament, it is more permanent even than the executive of the United States. Dicey, indeed, likened the Swiss Federal Council to a board of directors of a joint-stock company, adding that there is no more reason for altering its composition if it is doing its work efficiently in the general interest than there is to alter the membership of such a board under similar circumstances.

It is said that the only serious reform in the executive department suggested in Switzerland is that the election of the Ministers should be taken out of the hands of the National Assembly and placed in those of the people. If this were to happen, the only reason which we now have for calling the Swiss executive a parliamentary one would disappear, for it would in that case become, to all intents and purposes, a fixed executive in the American sense, except that the austere republicanism of Switzerland would retain the diffused character of its executive and popularly elect a body instead of an individual to whom the choice of his cabinet is left. So, while the semi-parliamentary executive which the founders of the Third French Republic intended to establish turned out to be a parliamentary executive of a very extreme type,[1] the parliamentary executive which the Swiss Constitution contemplates is found on examination to be more fixed and non-parliamentary in its working than any other in Europe.

IV. THE INTERESTING CASE OF TURKEY

The Turkey of to-day is very different from the Turkey of the days before the First World War. The Turkish Empire was, as a result of that war, dissolved, its former external dominions being partitioned into new states under a tutelage other than Turkish and mandated areas controlled by one or other of the successful Allies. Turkey is now a fairly closely-knit, almost national, state, confined very largely to its original Near-Eastern home, Anatolia, with its true capital at Angora. But more than this, an ancient despotism, the Sultanate, has been superseded by a republican form of government, and the ancient

[1] This characteristic, as we have shown, has been revived in the Constitution of the Fourth Republic (1946).

headship of the Mohammedan religion, the Caliphate, which was vested in the Sultan, has gone the way of the secular office. Though the old régime in Turkey was always regarded as an absolute monarchy, attempts were made to constitutionalise it. In 1876, Abdul Hamid II, under pressure from the Powers, proclaimed a Constitution, but it remained a dead letter until the Young Turk Revolution of 1908 overthrew Abdul Hamid, when the Constitution was set to work. But though a Parliament met thereafter, the government remained, in fact, an autocracy, and no real control was exercised by the Chamber of Deputies. The chagrin of the Turks at having "backed the wrong horse" in the First World War, and their sentiment of disgust at what they regarded as the feebleness of the Sultan in failing to resist the indignities to which he was subjected during the peace negotiations, spurred them into renewed action. When the Sultan, at Constantinople, signed the Treaty of Sèvres in 1919, the Turkish nation refused to ratify it, and from their new centre at Angora they organised so vigorous a resistance that they forced the Allies to agree to a new treaty after two conferences at Lausanne in 1922–3. This latter treaty brought the Turks back into Constantinople and Thrace.

Meanwhile, a Parliament, under the arrangements of the Constitution revived in 1908, assembled at Angora, and it assumed a constituent mandate which it did not by right possess. It worked directly under the influence of one of the few great men that modern Turkey has produced, Mustapha Kemal (later known as Kemal Ataturk, a title of the highest honour in Turkey), a soldier and statesman whose views were very markedly coloured by Western ideas. This Assembly so amended the original Constitution as in fact to abolish it and write a new one. On 29th October, 1923, with only half (158) of the members present, it unanimously elected Kemal President of the Turkish Republic.

The President under that Constitution was granted a remarkable sweep of powers. Having been elected by the legislature— the Grand National Assembly, consisting of one Chamber— he holds office during its term, which is four years, but is eligible for re-election. So far, he resembles, in some respects, the President in France, and in others the Federal Council in Switzerland. Next, he works through a Cabinet with a Prime

Minister, but he chooses the Premier and approves the appointment of every member of the Cabinet. Again, on all legislation passed by the Assembly he has a veto, which, however, he must exercise, like the American President, within ten days; but, as the Assembly can override his objections by passing the law again by a bare majority, in this respect the Turkish President is not so powerful as the American President, whose veto, it will be recalled, requires a two-thirds negative majority in both Houses to make it ineffective. But in practice the Turkish President may be more powerful, for, since he is the leader of the party organisation of the majority party in the Assembly which elects him, he can, in fact, effectively sway that Assembly. Besides this, he selects the President of the Assembly, the holder of an office equivalent to that of the Speaker in the British House of Commons, and thus may hold what is virtually a four-fold presidency—of the Republic, of the Cabinet, of the Assembly, and of the majority Party therein. This is something unique among constitutions with cabinet governments, for it is the only one where the elected President, working through a cabinet of ministers, yet remains the real executive. Yet it is hardly a fixed executive, in the American sense, since the dissolution of the Assembly ends the term of the Presidency.

Under Kemal Ataturk, who died in 1938, the Turkish Republic was an enlightened despotism, if not a dictatorship. Nor did it change much in this respect under his successor, General Ismet Inönü, though the latter was hardly of Ataturk's stature. For a long time one-party government remained, with an increasing tendency towards a totalitarian system. The result was such a profound electoral apathy that in the late 1930's an official opposition was permitted in the National Assembly. At first the numbers of the Opposition were strictly limited, but the restriction was afterwards removed. This new freedom had a vitalising effect on Turkish political life, as was proved at the election of 1950 when the Democrats scored a remarkable victory over the People's Republican Party, which Ataturk had founded, obtaining 434 seats in the Assembly; whereupon President Inönü resigned in favour of the leader of the Democrats. Here was the first example in modern history of a Dictatorship voluntarily surrendering its power in response to the popular will—a triumph indeed for constitutionalism.

V. COMPARATIVE ADVANTAGES OF PARLIAMENTARY AND FIXED
EXECUTIVES

From this discussion of the two fundamentally distinct types of executive in the modern world there emerge one or two points which need emphasis. First, we observe that our own country is the general inspirer of the parliamentary executive wherever it appears, being the model upon which all the others are based. It is interesting, therefore, to note that in England the executive was originally a non-parliamentary one and in name remains so, for every minister is the servant of the Crown, and is still nominally appointed and dismissible thereby. But, as we have seen, the modern democratic electorate has come, in effect, to elect the Prime Minister as well as the House of Commons, for, though it is true that the Prime Minister-to-be is elected not as such but as a Member of Parliament, the conventional operation of the constitution assures that the leader of the majority party will, in fact, be the head of the government.

Which, then, of these types of executive, we may usefully ask, better serves the purposes and the good of democracy? As to the parliamentary executive, since it is founded, where it is most real, on a party system, there is a danger that it may become the slave of the legislature which creates it. While this system implies that the legislature and executive can hardly ever come into serious conflict, the executive may come to reflect not only the permanent will of the legislature but its transient moods and passions, and hence those also of the electorate, which may be even more fickle. Freedom from this danger is the advantage of the fixed executive, for, in the first place, executive action often demands that, for the good of the state, it shall be untrammelled, and in the second, a man in the position, for example, of the President of the United States may, in his independence of such control, become a true leader and thus save democracy from its greatest peril—that of being no better as a whole than the lowest member of it.[1]

Yet a fixed executive, which is popularly elected, as in the United States, is clearly more directly subject to popular passion than is an executive dependent upon the legislature. But its

[1]See, for example, Émile Faguet: *The Cult of Incompetence.*

great advantage is that, once elected, it cannot be disturbed by the whims of party feeling and the shifting criterion of bye-elections. As we have said, a parliamentary executive, to be stable, requires an established and well-defined party system. Where it has this, as in Britain, it works well. Where it has not, as in France, the composition of the executive is constantly changing, which is a bad feature in any government. The safeguard we have noticed in the original constitution of Czecho-slovakia, where a serious government defeat in itself could not force a resignation, is a good plan, especially in a newly-founded political organisation, which requires, more than anything else, practice in the working of democratic machinery. But constitutional safeguards in themselves are of little value. A parliamentary executive can easily become corrupt, with the connivance of an assembly itself not above corruption, which was to some extent true in England under Walpole. Again, it is evident from the political history of Europe between the two world wars that in a state where the constitution is a dead letter a parliamentary executive becomes first fixed and then tyrannical, which is what happened both in Italy under Mussolini and in Germany under Hitler.

Mussolini, in fact, soon after he became Prime Minister, passed a law giving himself the title of Head of the Government and making himself, as such, independent of any parliamentary vote of censure or no-confidence. Moreover, by establishing the Fascist Grand Council in 1928 as "the supreme organ co-ordinating all the activities of the régime which arose out of the Revolution of 1922" he, in effect, abolished the Cabinet as the responsible body of Ministers. In short, the legislature in Fascist Italy became a mere registry office of the despot's decrees, akin to the "packed" parliaments of the Tudors in England or to the *Parlements* of the French kings of the pre-Revolutionary epoch. Something similar happened in Germany under Hitler. What was known as Hitler's Cabinet was not a "collegial body," in which the Chancellor of the Reich was *primus inter pares*, as he had been in the Weimar Republic, but a council of leaders (*Führerrat*) which the *Führer* gathered round him in order to keep himself informed of what was happening in the major departments of state without reference to an elected assembly or the electorate. These two examples of the way in which a parliamentary executive can be perverted to a dictatorship show how easily constitutional rights can be lost if the electorate and the legislature do not exercise that eternal vigilance over the executive which is the price of liberty.

The conclusion to which we are driven is that both types of executive require, for their proper working, a political experience which is necessarily lacking in the newer states of the world. The problem for such new states, therefore, is to find the most stable form of government, consistently with the security of popular rights, during the period necessary for experience to be gained. And it is probable that this stability is to be secured more certainly through the device of the parliamentary executive than through that of the non-parliamentary. For a parliamentary system imposes a check upon the executive at one remove from the politically ill-educated mass. The representative House, which supplies the check on the executive in this case, meanwhile gains experience by the constant exercise of parliamentary functions. And when at length the parliamentary electorate has settled down to a proper working of elections, it will probably be in a better position to destroy a corrupt house of deputies, conniving at an inefficient executive, than it would be, after the same lapse of time, to prevent the practice of tyranny by an executive free from control over the period for which it is elected.

READING

BAGEHOT: *English Constitution.* Introduction to, by the Earl of Balfour.
BASSETT: *Essentials of Parliamentary Democracy,* pp. 240–252.
BRYCE: *American Commonwealth,* Vol. I, Chs. v–ix, xx–xxi, xxv. *Modern Democracies,* Vol. I, pp. 393–99; Vol. II, pp. 71–82 and Ch. lxviii.
DICEY: *Law of the Constitution,* Appendix, Note iii.
FINER: *Modern Government,* Vol. II, Chs. xxiii and xxvi. *The Future of Government,* Chs. ii, iii, vi.
GETTELL: *Readings in Political Science,* Chs. xvii, xix.
LOWELL: *Governments and Parties,* Vol. II, pp. 193–207.
REED: *Form and Functions of American Government,* Chs. xix–xx and xxiv–xxv.
WILSON: *State,* pp. 327–330, 373–382, 401–408, 459–461.

BOOKS FOR FURTHER STUDY

BROGAN: (1) *The American Political System.* (2) *Introduction to American Politics.*
FINER: *Governments of Greater European Powers.*
SILONI: *The School for Dictators.*
LASKI: (1) *The American Presidency.* (2) *The American Democracy.*
LICHTENBERGER: *The Third Reich.*
HILLER: *After Nazism—Democracy?*

SUBJECTS FOR ESSAYS

1. Show how a fixed executive may have either a democratic or a despotic tendency.

2. What changes has usage introduced in the system of Presidential Election, as originally stated in the Constitution of the United States?

3. Explain the powers of the President in the United States. In what sense is he a real executive?

4. "An American President can, if he chooses, run counter to the opinion of Congress." Elucidate this statement.

5. Explain what is meant by a diffused executive power and show how this is more nearly achieved in the Swiss Republic than in any other modern state.

6. In what respects is the Swiss Executive unique among executives in modern states?

7. Discuss the powers of the President in the Turkish Republic.

8. Compare and contrast Cabinet Government in the United Kingdom with Presidential Government in the United States.

9. In what sense did the Fascist and Nazi Dictatorships establish a fixed executive?

10. Which of the two sorts of executive—parliamentary and non-parliamentary—do you consider the more compatible with popular sovereignty?

CHAPTER XII

THE JUDICIARY

I. THE INDEPENDENCE OF THE JUDICIAL DEPARTMENT OF GOVERNMENT

A DISCUSSION of judicial systems, classified, as we have classified them, on the ground of the difference between the Rule of Law and Administrative Law, arises directly out of an examination of executive systems, for it is especially on account of the distinction between the judiciary and the executive that this division is made. What we have called Common Law States, like our own, which have developed this Rule of Law, are identified by the complete freedom of the judicial body from administrative (or executive) interference, while those we have designated Prerogative States allow a certain branch of law, called Administrative Law, to be controlled by the executive. It is with this distinction that this chapter will be chiefly concerned, but before coming to this in detail it will be well for us to deal with some more general features of the judiciary. A study of the judicial department of government, as such, is a highly technical matter and belongs rather to jurisprudence than to politics. But, clearly, an introduction to comparative politics would be incomplete without some treatment of the judiciary, inasmuch as it is everywhere one of the three great organs of government and is closely associated with the powers of the other two and with the rights and duties of the governed.

In discussing, in Chapter X, the theory of the separation of powers, we pointed out, it will be remembered, that in its extreme interpretation this doctrine means the complete isolation of the three departments from one another, but that, in a broader sense, it means merely that the three powers shall be in separate hands. The extreme interpretation is impossible of achievement in practice under modern conditions, since the business of a constitutional government is so complex that it cannot define the area of each department in such a manner as to leave each independent and supreme in its allotted sphere; for, as H. J. Laski said, "the separation of powers does not mean the equal balance of powers." In a truly constitutional state, even where the executive is a non-parliamentary one, the legislature ought to be and is able to secure that executive acts broadly carry out its will, and we have seen that in the very state where the doctrine of the separation of powers was of the essence of its first Constitution—namely, France—that doctrine has since been so far modified as to introduce in the Constitution of both the Third and the Fourth Republics the system of the parliamentary executive which makes the executive a part—a committee, in fact—of the legislature. Again, there should, and does exist, under a good system of government, a prerogative of pardon or reprieve in the hands of the executive which may hereby check or undo the too harsh decisions of the judiciary. And, further, it is always the business of a legislature, within the limits of its competence, to secure that, if the tendency of the judiciary is deemed to be against good policy, it shall be reversed by legislation. These instances show the interaction of the three departments.

But in the broader sense—that the three powers shall be in separate hands—all modern constitutional states conform to the ideal of separation of powers, for in no case to-day is the body that performs one function identical with those that perform the other two. As to the legislature and executive, the separation obviously exists in the case of a state with a non-parliamentary executive. It also exists to a certain degree in a state whose executive is a parliamentary one, for the executive is only a part of the legislature and not the whole of it. As to the executive and the judiciary, there are one or two exceptions which hardly touch the main truth that they are different bodies. For example, in Britain the Lord Chancellor, the highest judicial dignitary in the land, is a member of the Cabinet, besides being, *ex officio*, Chairman of the House of Lords, and hence the occupancy of the Woolsack changes with a change of government. Also the Lords of Appeal are members of the House of Lords, but this is due to the fact that the House of Lords is still the final Court of Appeal; and just as an ordinary peer has nothing to do with the work of this judicial body, so the Lords of Appeal ordinarily take no part in the political business of the Lords. In most Cabinets on the Continent, too, there is a Minister of Justice, but he is not always a judge. Only in the United States is it true that there is no representative of the judicial body in the executive and vice-versa. But these are exceptions which prove the rule, and it remains one of the maxims of constitutionalism that the judiciary ought to be free from control in its own department, though the question arises, what are the limits of that department?

In pursuance of this maxim of independence, the tenure of judges in most constitutional states is permanent, that is to say, they hold office while they are "of good behaviour"—*i.e.*, not guilty of any crime known to the law—and their tenure is therefore not subject to the fluctuations of electoral results as are the other two branches of government. Two great exceptions to this are Switzerland, where the judges are elected by the two Federal Chambers, sitting together, for six years (but even here re-election is so frequent as in many cases to achieve, to all intents and purposes, a permanent tenure of office), and some of the individual states of the United States in America, where the system of popular election for a term (in some cases as short as two years) obtains. Such a system leads to all sorts of abuses and corruptions. It does not, of course, apply to the Federal Judiciary in the United States, where the appointment, made by the President with the advice and sanction of the Senate, is for life.

In France candidates for the Bench of Judges are selected by competitive examination (a system of appointment which obtains universally in France for all permanent government posts—even for school teachers) under the direction of the Minister of Justice, and they pass from one grade to another of the courts by seniority and merit. They cannot be removed by either the legislature or the executive, but only by a superior court (*Conseil Supérieur de la Magistrature*) of which the President of the Republic is president and which, under the Constitution of the Fourth Republic, consists of fourteen members. In Great Britain judges are appointed in theory by the Queen, in practice by the Lord Chancellor, and their right to

9

hold office while of good behaviour was definitely established by the Act of Settlement (1701). They can be removed only as the result of an address of both Houses of Parliament to that end, but as no such address has ever been presented since the passing of the Act the permanency of their tenure is manifest. In the United States judges of the Supreme Court can be removed only by the process of impeachment before Congress.[1]

Thus, though the executive, or a part of it, in most cases appoints judges, generally speaking their removal is in the hands of the legislature, or, at any rate, it is entirely outside the control of the executive. Thus are the ultimate rights of the governed in most constitutional states doubly secured, since the judges, on whom largely rests in the last resort the guarantee of those rights, are not appointed by a process in which the notorious fickleness of democracies plays any part, and they are given a security of tenure which raises them above the exigencies of political expediency. Having shown in what respects the judiciary is independent of the other two departments, we have now to examine what influence the judiciary can bring to bear on (i) the legislature and (ii) the executive.

II. THE JUDICIARY AND THE LEGISLATURE

We have said that the business of the legislature is to make the law, and that of the judiciary to "decide upon the application of the existing law in individual cases"; in other words, to punish the transgressors of the law. But we have also seen that in many states the judges actually make law by their decisions. This case-law or judge-made law is characteristic rather of Common Law States, like Great Britain, than of Prerogative States, like France (though it is a curious fact that the administrative courts, as distinct from the judicial courts, in France, do actually use this process).

The principle of judge-made law is founded upon the force of precedent; that is to say, the previous decisions of judges are generally regarded as binding on later judges in similar cases, though variations on these decisions accrue with time, the previous decision merely standing as a guide. In this way, in Anglo-Saxon states, new law is grafted on the old, entirely apart

[1]President Roosevelt's attempt in 1937 to fix a retiring age at 70 completely failed. See earlier, p. 108.

from the work of the legislature, so that whether the judge
follows a precedent or creates one he may fairly be said to make
law. Thus, a great English authority, the late Professor Dicey,
spoke of the "essentially legislative authority" of judges, and a
great American judge, the late Mr. Justice Holmes, said "judges
do and must legislate."

This case-law implies an important characteristic of Common
Law States, that in such there is no codification of the law; that
is to say, no organised system of law, fixed in extent at one time
beyond the limits of which the judges may not act, except in
special circumstances. But in those states where the law has, as
in most Continental states, long been codified, this building-up
of law by the judges is not possible. In France, for example,
where the law has been codified since the time of Napoleon, the
judges are expressly forbidden to build up case-law. They have
the code to guide them, and if the code is defective as to the
particular case before the court, the judge may give a decision,
but it will in no sense be binding in future cases. Now, under the
Common Law system such a decision would be held to be good
law for the future. There are advantages and disadvantages in
both systems. In Common Law States, the lawyer is certain of
his ground where he is dealing with precedents and is not subject
to the whim of a judge or the ambiguous phrasing of a codified
law. On the other hand, the mass of precedent decisions has
become so tangled, confused and conflicting that it is often
difficult for lawyers to discover what the law really is. In states
with a codified law, judges are in one sense freer than ours, since
they are not controlled by precedents, and when a case arises
outside the existing code they can concentrate on doing justice
without having to watch that the precedent of a learned predecessor is followed. At the same time, judges in such states
are more circumscribed, since only the legislature can alter the
law, either by the passage of special laws, or by permitting a
new codification; whereas Common Law judges can by their
reasoning and judgments make new law so long as their
decisions are not in conflict with Statute Law. All this, of course,
does not affect the power of the legislature to alter by statute
any previous decisions, however venerable, of any judges, however eminent, or to modify a legal code, always provided that
the legislature is acting within the powers granted to it by the

constitution, and a study of the relation between the judiciary and the legislature in connection with some of the subjects we have earlier touched upon—the unitary and federal state, the flexible and rigid constitution—is extremely helpful here.

We have said that in a unitary state the central legislature is supreme, except for restrictions, if any, placed upon it by the constitution, while in a federal state the federal legislature is limited both by the fact that it shares its powers with the states and by the fact that the constitution is rigid. As to the constitution, we have shown that where it is flexible the supremacy of the legislature is undisputed, and where it is rigid its supremacy is modified to the extent of restrictions placed upon it in the matter of constitutional law-making. What part does the judiciary play in seeing that these conditions are fulfilled? In examining the unitary state, we saw that in the case of the United Kingdom, for example, the judges are bound to apply laws passed by Parliament, without question. If statute law conflicts with common law, the common law must go in that particular case. The judges have, of course, a certain power of interpretation with regard to any statute, since the "powers, however extraordinary, which are conferred or sanctioned by statute, are never really unlimited, for they are confined by the words of the Act itself," but the judges may not go outside the words; and if the words badly express the intention of Parliament, then the application of the Act may be something quite different from what was intended by those who passed it. Again, in a unitary state there is no possibility of the judges being called upon to decide disputes between the central parliament and other bodies within the state, because those other bodies have no rights except those bestowed upon them by the central legislature.

But in federal states the position is different. In most of these the powers of the judiciary, as compared with the legislature, are much greater than in unitary states. In the United States, for example, not the legislature but the Constitution is supreme, and this fact gives the judiciary a power which makes it a co-ordinate organ with the legislature and the executive. The federal judges—and, for that matter, the state judges, too— have it as their prime duty to safeguard the Constitution and to treat as void every legislative act, of either Congress or a state legislature, which is inconsistent with the Constitution. They cannot, indeed, abolish such a law, but they are bound to treat it as void in all cases before the Court arising out of it. Thus the judicial department of government in the United States has a competence far beyond that of the judiciary in the United Kingdom.

The powers of the judiciary vary greatly from one federal state to another. In Australia, for instance, where the position of the federal judiciary approaches most closely to that of the United States, most of the powers of the Commonwealth and the states are concurrent, and consequently quite a large proportion of constitutional issues determined by the High Court relate to the demarcation of the boundary line between federal and state powers. In fact, the main difference between Australia and the United States in this respect is that the Australian High Court may entertain appeals concerning state law, which the United States Supreme Court has no power to do. In Germany under the Weimar Republic the powers of the federal judges to interpret the Constitution were not nearly so great as they are in U.S.A. and Australia, because the Constitution said that the federal law overrode state law, but where a question arose whether a certain state law was incompatible with federal law, an appeal lay to the federal judiciary. In Switzerland no such interpretative power exists, and in this impotence of its judiciary Switzerland is unique among federal states.

As to flexible constitutions, we have shown that under them there is no place for a judicial power above the legislative power. In such states as Great Britain and New Zealand, no Act of Parliament can be unconstitutional. In the case of rigid constitutions in unitary states, as in France and Belgium, we might expect to find a court with power to decide on the unconstitutionality of the acts of their legislatures, in the event of their being deemed to have contravened the conditions of the constitution and the parliament to have acted beyond its competence as laid down therein. If, for example, a law were passed by the French Chambers extending the term of the Presidency, this would certainly be a breach of the Constitution, which cannot be altered except by the special process of amendment laid down in the Constitution, as already described. Yet the fact remains that there is no such court either in France or in Belgium, no judge in either state ever having pronounced a statute unconstitutional. Dicey explains this absence of judicial power by saying that most French (and Belgian) statesmen "may well have thought . . . that . . . possible parliamentary invasions of the Constitution were a less evil than the participation of the judges in political conflicts." Yet many French critics have urged that a power to restrict the competence of Parliament should be bestowed upon the judiciary, which should have the final right to declare a law unconstitutional, a power that was, for example, granted to the judiciary in Norway in 1904, in Rumania in 1912, and in Italy under the Republican Constitution of 1947.

The conclusion from these remarks is irresistible. It is that in all constitutional states the judicial body is given a status free from capricious or whimsical interferences and a security of tenure that lifts it above the fear of acting against its conscience; that, except in federal states for the most part, the judicial department of government is bound to impose the laws passed by the legislative department; and that in most federal states it has the power either to refuse to impose any law passed by the federal legislature which it considers to be beyond that body's constitutional competence, or to decide in cases where the federal and state legislatures are in conflict. The connection between the judiciary and the executive is not so easily stated, as we shall now see.

III. THE RULE OF LAW

We have said in an earlier chapter that one of the fundamental legal safeguards enjoyed by citizens of what we may call the Anglo-Saxon states—*i.e.*, the United Kingdom, the British Self-governing Dominions, and the United States—is that principle which is summed up in the expression, the Rule of Law. Dicey, a great authority, said that we mean by this "not only that with us no man is above the law, but (what is a different thing) that here every man, whatever be his rank or condition, is subject to the ordinary law of the realm and amenable to the jurisdiction of the ordinary tribunals." Now, this is by no means a right enjoyed in common by the citizens of all modern constitutional states, as we shall show in this and the next section. We have distinguished the states which enjoy this right from the rest by calling the first Common Law States and the second Prerogative States, and in examining the two types we shall take Britain as typical of the one and France as typical of the other.

This Rule of Law is at the base of the British Constitution, not because it is guaranteed by the Constitution (as rights are frequently secured in documents) but because the Constitution has gradually grown up out of the constant recognition of it. As Dicey puts it, "the rules which in foreign countries naturally form part of a constitutional code, are, in English-speaking states, not the source, but the consequence of the rights of individuals, as defined and enforced by the Courts." This Rule, then, places the judiciary not only in a condition of freedom from interference on the part of the executive, but in a positive superiority to it in respect of its individual members, since "every official from the Prime Minister down to a constable or a collector of taxes is under the same responsibility for every act done without legal justification as any other citizen." Officials in this country are constantly brought before the Courts and made liable to punishment or the payment of damages for acts done in their legal capacity, but in excess of their lawful authority. This fact was implicit among the rights of Englishmen from very early days. We find it broadly present in Magna Carta (1215) and still more distinctly in the Petition of Right (1628) and in the Habeas Corpus Act (1679). The reason for this recurrent enforcement was that the Crown in earlier days always tried to arrogate to itself an executive prerogative inimical to the Common Law—*i.e.*, contrary to the decisions of the judges —or to make the tenure of judges dependent on its will. This prerogative, to which the Crown from time to time laid claim, it was allowed to hold under the Tudors, but against the Stuart abuses Parliament became extremely vocal in its defence of traditional rights. The Rule of Law was established beyond dispute in the face of the last attempt to restore the Crown prerogative by George III, for in 1763 John Wilkes, who had attacked the King's Speech in his paper, *The North Briton*, gained £1,000 damages from the Home Secretary for wrongful arrest on a General Warrant. In this last case, not only was the private citizen secured against arbitrary action on the part of a government official, but that government official found himself entirely unprotected against the processes of ordinary law, even though he may have been conceived to be acting in his purely official capacity or in the interests of the state.

In those states which enjoy the Rule of Law, therefore, the judges are the ultimate guardians of individual rights in every case that may arise under Common Law, Statute Law and (under rigid constitutions which make this a separate branch) Constitutional Law. Nothing that the executive of itself can do can affect the attitude of the Courts towards breaches of the law by state officials. It is true that at any moment certain rights, hitherto existing, may be abrogated by Act of Parliament (which indeed may be and probably is passed at the instigation of the executive) and that it would then be the business of the judges to enforce the law so made. It may even be that such a statute would deprive the judges of power to control executive acts in certain cases. But the point is that not until such a law is passed and only in respect of the particular class of acts indicated in the statute could the independence of the judiciary be affected. Such modifications of the Rule of Law we shall discuss in the last section of this chapter.

Britain is not alone, as we have already remarked, in the enjoyment of this Rule of Law, for, besides the Self-governing Dominions and the United States, it exists in Belgium and, on paper at least, in most states of Latin America. In all these states the Rule belongs to the Constitution in spite of the greatest differences between them, for some are unitary and some federal states, not all have rigid constitutions, and some have parliamentary, while others have non-parliamentary, executives. The existence of the Rule of Law in the case of the Anglo-Saxon states is explained by the fact of their common English origin. Its existence in Belgium, which in this respect is unique on the Continent of Europe, is due to British influence upon the state during the critical period of the establishment of its independent sovereignty which was finally achieved in 1839. In the case of the Latin-American states, it is due to the fact that they have rather imitated the United States than perpetuated the tradition of the Latin states of their origin. In all other cases the reason for the existence of the Rule of Law is clear. The original English colonists in various parts of the globe carried with them the tradition of the English Common Law, and this was a part of their very social substance long before their constitutions came to be written. So that, where Continental states which know nothing of this Rule of Law have secured the rights of the individual through their constitutions, these original British Dominions had no need so to safeguard them. Thus the constitution in each of these latter states has not affected the Rule of Law, or else it has only strengthened it, as, for example, in the United States where the Constitution categorically asserts that "the judicial power shall extend to all cases in law and equity, arising under the Constitution."

We shall now examine how, in those states where the Rule of Law does not obtain—*i.e.*, those which we have called Prerogative States—a special type of law protects state officials in the execution of their official duty.

IV. ADMINISTRATIVE LAW

We speak of Administrative Law by way of translating the French term, *Droit Administratif*, which is, strictly, untranslatable into English, and the want of a true English equivalent for it, as Dicey has said, is due to the non-recognition of the thing itself. The language of the French authorities on the subject describes something which is quite foreign to an Englishman. Administrative Law, says one, is the body of rules which regulate the relations of the administrative authority towards private citizens, and determines the position of state officials, the rights and liabilities of private citizens in their dealings with these officials as representatives of the state, and the procedure by which these rights and liabilities are enforced. In short, we may say that in France there is a distinction between public and private law, and that the effect of this division of law on the judiciary is that the ordinary courts are not competent to deal with cases arising out of acts of the executive (or administrative) department of government, whether concerning the rights and liabilities of state officials or the rights and liabilities of the citizen in his relations with them.

The effect of this system is to make the "administration the arbitrary judge of its own conduct." The system is inherent in French history. In the eighteenth century there were such frequent conflicts between the royal administration and the law courts that by the time of the Revolution the interference of the courts to the detriment of good government was regarded with justifiable suspicion; and under the influence of the doctrine of the separation of powers, the various constitutions of the revolutionary period made the executive and judicial functions quite distinct and forbade the courts to take any action that invaded the executive field. Napoleon maintained this distinction, which has with variations survived to this day.

Thus in France there grew up two distinct sets of courts—judicial courts and administrative courts. Before the first came criminal cases and cases of private law—*i.e.*, between one private citizen and another. Before the second came cases of public law—*i.e.*, between the government and its officials, or between private citizens and government officials. This apparently left the private citizen without protection against the state official, but, in view of certain modifications of the original position in France, the words of Lowell on the subject—that "the government has always a free hand and can violate the law if it wants to do so without having anything to fear from the ordinary courts"—require some qualification. For in 1872 there was established in France an independent Conflict Court to decide in doubtful cases whether the judicial or the administrative department had jurisdiction, so that the judicial court might not of its own authority encroach on the administration and the administrative court should not have the judicial court at its mercy. To secure impartiality this Conflict Court was composed of nine members—three chosen by the highest judicial court (the Court of Cassation), three by the highest administrative court (the Council of State), and two more chosen by these six, the ninth member being the Minister of Justice (a member of the Cabinet) who acted as president. The eight members held office for three years, but were eligible to be and generally were re-elected. The term of the Minister of Justice, of course, coincided with that of the Cabinet to which he belonged.

This system of administrative law, as we have said, has been adopted in most Continental states whose judiciaries manifest in this respect narrower or wider variations of the French model. In Germany, for example, in each of the separate states

which went to form the Empire there was already an administrative law to protect public servants, and, under the Imperial
Constitution of 1871, the *Bundesrat* (as the Upper Chamber
was then called) was made the chief administrative council of
the Empire. Under the Constitution of the Weimar Republic
the distinction between administrative and judicial courts was
retained. In Switzerland also the distinction is made, but here
the judiciary is completely subordinated to the legislature and
executive, and administrative jurisdiction is in the hands of the
Federal Council (Executive) with an appeal lying to the Federal
Assembly (Legislature). In Italy administrative and judicial
courts have also been traditionally differentiated, but not so
sharply as in France.

V. JUDICIARIES UNDER THE TWO SYSTEMS COMPARED

If we closely examine these two legal systems, as they were
and as they are, we are struck by some of their ultimate likenesses no less than by their superficial differences. With the
passage of time and the progress of constitutional checks, the
administrative courts in Continental states, and particularly
in France, have lost much of their former absoluteness. Under
Napoleon, for example, the powers of the Council of State were
all but despotic in deciding administrative cases, and in spite
of revolutions in a democratic direction—*e.g.*, in 1830 and 1848
—the immunity of the executive from the ordinary processes
of law remained almost untouched. But after the fall of the
Second Empire (1852–1871) and during the existence of the
Third Republic, much modification went on. As we showed, the
Conflict Court was equally representative of the ordinary
judicial body and of the administrative judiciary, though the
fact that its president was a member of the government of the
day ensured to the executive that its interests would be
safeguarded. After the Liberation in the Second World War
the system was revived and consolidated by a special Decree
of July 31, 1945, which reconstituted the Council of State.

Again, looking at the English system historically, we find
that ideas current in the sixteenth and seventeenth centuries
were not altogether opposed to the establishment of something
very like an administrative system of law. The Tudors and the
Stuarts were supported by those who were ready to assert that

the administration had a discretionary power which could not be controlled by any court of judges. Such courts as Star Chamber, the Council of the North, and the Court of High Commission, for example, were, to all intents and purposes, administrative courts completely in the hands of the executive, which in those days was actually the Crown. Lawyers, like Sir Francis Bacon, if they had had their way, would have succeeded in establishing in England an administrative system distinct from the ordinary law. Their object was defeated by the failure of the Stuarts in the Civil War and the triumph of the traditional respect for the principle of equality before the law which was reinforced by the statutory arrangements arising out of the Revolution of 1688.

We have observed earlier that the progress of collectivist legislation, establishing new social services—*e.g.*, National Insurance—tends to give new powers to the executive branch of government in Britain. This drift, indeed, is inevitable under modern democracy. Legislatures in great industrial communities, like Britain and the U.S.A., with an ever-increasing burden of social law-making imposed upon them, simply cannot compile statutes in such detail as to meet every possible contingency in operation. The result is that "administrative bodies find themselves compelled not only to undertake judicial duties but also to perform them in such a way that the courts are excluded from scrutiny in their operations." For example, in Britain it has been decided that, if no particular method is detailed in a statute, the government department concerned with its execution may adopt what procedure it thinks best without interference from the Courts. Or where a method is outlined it often equally results in the virtual independence of the executive from judicial interference. For example, the National Insurance Act of 1911 (the first of a series of such statutes, culminating in the Comprehensive Act which came into effect in 1948) established a body of Insurance Commissioners, appointed by the Treasury, with powers to make regulations and with judicial authority. Under the Act any disputed claim was to be decided by the Commissioners, with an appeal to a court of Referees and a final appeal to an Umpire. Thus the ordinary law courts were excluded, and no Commissioner or Referee or Umpire was a judge. Similarly, in the United States, it has been decided by the highest Court that "the decisions of the Secretary of Labour in all immigration cases are final."

These developments are an unavoidable concomitant of this sort of legislation which demands an expert administrative knowledge to which judges in the ordinary way cannot pretend. Moreover, the extension of the duties of the state, discharged by the administration, necessitates the grant to that department of powers which allow for the expeditious treatment and quick decisions demanded by the multifarious claims involved. The weakness, through its ponderousness, of the Rule of Law, is again seen in times of stress, as, for example, during the two World Wars, when, under the Defence Regulations in Britain, many new tribunals, outside the judiciary, were set up. This manifestation, as it has been called, of "the encroaching temper of the ever-expanding executive" is clearly a danger, and unless carefully watched, obviously threatens the ramparts of liberty. "It would be strange," as a great English judge, the late Lord Sankey, once said, "if we had escaped the frying-pan of the prerogative to fall into the fire of a Minister's Regulations."

In those states, on the other hand, where a distinction is admitted between the two departments of administrative and judicial law, there exists protection not only for the official but for the private citizen, and the latter knows where he stands with regard to the official. In France, at any rate up to the outbreak of the Second World War, litigation in the administrative court was cheap and was executed rapidly; the procedure was simple, and Frenchmen preferred it for such cases, just as a soldier is said to prefer the direct and expeditious methods of a court-martial, though he thereby loses the safeguards of trial by jury. The lack of protection afforded, under modern conditions, to the citizen of a state with an administrative law can easily be overstated. The very clear distinction made in France between a "fault of service" and "a personal fault," on the part of the official, at the same time protects the citizen against the evil consequences of too much official zeal and gives the official less cause for fear in acting as an efficient servant of the state.

It is admitted, then, that in Common Law States the Rule of Law is bound to be relaxed under the weight of modern social legislation. If, by being forced to grant judicial powers to heads of departments, we suffer the disadvantage of a sort of administrative law, we do not enjoy the compensating advantages of a recognised distinction between this and the judicial law. Two lines of reform have, therefore, been suggested by critics of the administrative tendency in Britain. The first is that the administrative tribunals, where they must exist, should be completely judicialised and made entirely independent of the executive; that is to say, there should be established for such purposes special courts whose judges would be experts in the matter concerned. The second is that in certain cases there should be an appeal from the administrative tribunal or the decision of a minister to a judicial court. In this way we should diminish the danger to individual liberty which lurks in these modern qualifications of the Rule of Law.

We come to the conclusion, then, that, in spite of differences in legal attitude and historical development, constitutional states do not nowadays greatly differ in the ultimate rights secured to citizens through the judicial department. They all ensure the impartiality of the judge by placing him above fluctuations of party feeling and giving him security of tenure without making it impossible to remove him for crime or corruption. In states whose legal systems are founded on Common Law, the Rule of Law puts the executive on an equality with all other bodies and makes it answerable for its actions by refusing to admit reasons of state for executive acts. In Prerogative States, which have an Administrative Law, the executive is placed to some extent above the processes of ordinary justice by making the official answerable to an administrative court. But the Rule of Law under modern conditions suffers somewhat through the exigencies of latter-day collectivist legislation which perforce grants to officials absolute powers that in practice place heads of government departments above the law, though, of course, this is only in so far as the statute concerned permits it; while, in the case of Prerogative States, although a special procedure protects the official, it is now so hedged about with restrictions that the ordinary citizen has little complaint against it.

In general, we may say that Common Law States have a greater air of legalism than those whose law is codified and which have an administrative law. The reason for this is that in the former the judges can make law, whereas in the latter the code restricts the judges in this respect and leaves a wide area for decision in the administrative courts, where, in fact, the judges do make the law under the direction of the executive, with the result that there is a sort of judicial legislation going on in Prerogative States, and this defies codification. Putting it another way, we may say that jurisprudence (*i.e.*, law on the basis of precedent) characterises Common Law States, and that political decisions (as distinct from judicial decisions) have wider scope in Prerogative States. Whether judges or politicians are the better custodians of democratic rights is a question not easy to answer. But as, in all modern democratic constitutional states, the ultimate power to alter any of these decisions lies with the people, through its power either to force the hand of the legislature or change it, or through its right to bring about a constitutional amendment, or through its ability to effect changes through a referendum, the question, after all, has perhaps now become little more than academic.

READING

BRYCE: *American Commonwealth*, Vol. I, Chs. xxii-xxiv. *History and Jurisprudence*, Vol. II, Essays xi, xiv, xv. *Modern Democracies*, Vol. I, Ch. xxii; Vol. II, Chs. xliii, lxii.
DICEY: *Law and Opinion*, Lecture xi. *Law of Constitution*, pp. 151–167, Ch. xii, Appendix, Note xi.
GETTELL: *Readings in Political Science*, Ch. xx.
JENKS: *Government of British Empire*, Ch. xi.
JENNINGS: *Law and Constitution*, Chs. vi and vii.
KEITH: *Responsible Government in Dominions*, Vol. I, pp. 570–4; Vol. II, pp. 661–72, 727–31.
LASKI: *Grammar of Politics*, Pt. II, Ch. x.
LOWELL: *Government of England*, Vol. I, Ch. xix; Vol. II, Chs. lix-lxii. *Governments and Parties*, Vol. I, pp. 44–65, 170–77, 214–19.
MARRIOTT: *English Political Institutions*, Ch. xiv. *Mechanism of Modern State*, Vol. II, Chs. xxxi-xxxiv.
REED: *Form and Functions of American Government*, Ch. xxiii.
SAIT: *Government and Politics of France*, Chs. xi and xii.
SIDGWICK: *Elements of Politics*, Ch. xxiv.
WILSON: *State*, pp. 164–5, 173–5, 216–222, 321–27, 366–73, 407–9, 413-18, 428, 486–89.

BOOKS FOR FURTHER STUDY

ALLEN: *Law and Orders.*
BOUTMY: *Studies in Constitutional Law.*
GOODNOW: *Comparative Administrative Law.*
HEWART: *The New Despotism.*
RIDGES: *Constitutional Law of England.*

SUBJECTS FOR ESSAYS

1. "The separation of powers does not mean the equal balance of powers." Discuss this statement with reference to the judicial department of government in comparison with the other two.

2. Why is it a good rule that judges should continue to hold office "while of good behaviour"?

3. "Judges do and must legislate." Show how far this statement is true of Anglo-Saxon states.

4. Compare the powers of the judiciary in the average unitary state with those in the average federal state.

5. What is meant by the term "Rule of Law"? Show how it operates in Britain, the Self-governing Dominions, and the United States.

6. What is the significance of the following words in the Constitution of the United States: "The judicial power shall extend to all cases in law and equity arising under this Constitution"?

7. Attempt a definition of the term "Administrative Law," and explain how it works.

8. How do you account for the fact that in England attempts made at various epochs to establish an Administrative Law have been frustrated, while in France the system remains to this day?

9. Explain how it is that elements of Administrative Law tend to creep into the Anglo-Saxon legal system under the stress of modern social legislation.

10. Discuss the comparative advantages and disadvantages of the "Rule of Law" and *Droit Administratif.*

PART III

ADDITIONAL CONSIDERATIONS

CHAPTER XIII

DIRECT DEMOCRATIC CHECKS

I. THE PLEBISCITE AND THE PROBLEM OF MINORITIES

IN this part of the book we shall be chiefly concerned with an examination of the United Nations Organisation, without which no study of constitutional politics would now be complete. As such an examination is the logical outcome and end of an analysis of modern political institutions, we should not neglect first to deal with any topics which, though they lie on the edge of the subjects already discussed, nevertheless arise out of them. This will serve the double purpose of completing our comparative study of the machinery of existing states and of helping us to approach, with a fuller appreciation of its difficulties, the problem of international political organisation. Among the outstanding topics of interest to students of comparative politics are first what may be called Direct Democratic Checks —viz. the Plebiscite, the Referendum, the Popular initiative, and the Recall; secondly, Constitutional Experiments among non-European Peoples; and thirdly, Economic Democracy in its relation to Political Democracy. These three topics expand or amplify one or more of our earlier divisions of the subject, and to each of them we shall devote a chapter.

The four direct democratic checks are connected in the sense that they are designed to give to the voting mass of the people a direct control of their political destiny by granting them the power to approve or reject measures for their well-being, to institute legislation, and to remove unsatisfactory representatives. They are thus what we may call ultra-democratic developments. But, though they mark to some extent an advance on the normal parliamentary methods which we have so far discussed, they are, nevertheless, perfectly constitutional schemes and therefore find a place here. The terms plebiscite and referendum are similar in meaning, but refer to practices somewhat different in purpose. Of the referendum in connection with the amendment of rigid constitutions we have already said something in Chapter VII. Its reference to ordinary legislation we shall discuss in the next section. In this we shall confine ourselves to the plebiscite with particular reference to its connection with the problem of minorities.

The term plebiscite means literally decree of the people. The plebiscite is a device to obtain a direct popular vote on a matter of political importance, but chiefly in order to create some more or less permanent political condition. It was freely used by Napoleon Bonaparte at the various stages of his rise to power, as a means of getting behind the machinery of government already existing. Thus in 1799, having overthrown the Directory by a *coup d'état*, he prepared a constitution by which he made himself one of three Consuls, and submitted it to the vote of the whole people, who accepted it by an overwhelming majority. Again, in 1802, when he made himself Consul for life, and in 1804 when he proclaimed himself Emperor, he appealed to the people for their approval of these changes. The same plan was associated with the rise of his nephew, Napoleon III, who, by a similar succession of popular votes, secured first his election as President of the Second Republic in 1848, next an acceptance of the *coup d'état* of 1851 which ended that Republic, and lastly approval of the Second Empire in the following year.

The evil of such a popular vote is that it is democratic only in appearance, for, once it is given, the people must bear all the consequences without means of redress. In view of the unhappy consequences of the Second Empire in France, it is not surprising that the plebiscite became thoroughly discredited there after the Franco-German War, and that the framers of the Constitution of the Third Republic in 1875 were concerned to save the state from its abuse by subjecting the executive to parliamentary control. But the idea of the plebiscitary executive has continued to have its adherents since that day. As we have seen, the political crisis of 1886 arose out of the attempt of General Boulanger and his supporters to liberate the Presidency from the shackles of Parliament and to-day the Constitution of the Fourth Republic, adhering to the principle of a President elected by the Chambers and responsible to the National Assembly through a Prime Minister and Cabinet, still struggles to justify itself against those who wish the President to be popularly elected and granted real executive powers.

The same abuse of the plebiscite as marked the tactics of the two Napoleons accompanied Hitler's rise to power in Germany, for Hitler held a succession of such plebiscites to secure popular consent *ex post facto* to his political actions. The first was held in November, 1933, to gain the people's approval to Germany's leaving the League of Nations and the Disarmament Conference. The second took place in August, 1934, when the nation was asked to approve Hitler's action in combining in the person of the *Führer* the offices of Chancellor and President on the death of Hindenburg. In both cases enormous majorities of over 90 per cent were recorded in Hitler's favour. It was on the result of these popular votes that the Nazis based their assertion that Hitler's triumph was the effect not of a *coup d'état* but of a legal vote of the people, and it cannot be denied that the Germans thereby gave an air of legality to the Nazi tyranny. Nor was the argument weakened four years later when, in 1938, the Germans and Austrians approved the annexation of Austria by popular majorities in plebiscites of more than 99 per cent. In the United States the Presidency is now in practice, though not in theory, to some extent of a plebiscitary kind, yet with one great difference. Unlike the French and German plebiscites to which we have referred, an American Presidential election, though it does indeed establish a real executive, does so for a fixed short term of years, and thus ensures a recurrent popular control, instead of condemning the people to a perpetual acceptance of the régime which their single exercise of the vote has established. The German Presidential election under the Weimar Republic was also of this order, but in this case, as we have seen, the President was not the real but only the nominal executive. From these examples it should be obvious that if democracy is to use this means of establishing a real executive it must watch carefully that it secures the constitutional means of controlling it.

The device of the plebiscite was also freely used after the First World War to decide the political destiny of those small groups of people which, liberated by the war, were yet unable to establish their complete political independence. This was a logical outcome of the cry of self-determination which formed so vital a part of President Wilson's Peace programme in the days of the Armistice. If, as he said, there were to be no annexations, it followed that certain groups of people must decide for themselves to which state they should be attached, supposing it to be impossible, as it was in many cases, for them to establish themselves as sovereign political entities. In the case of areas like Poland and Czechoslovakia independent states were set up. In the case of such areas as Alsace-Lorraine, the Trentino and Transylvania, there was no question as to which state they wished to join, for they had long aimed at incorporation or reincorporation with their respective national groups— France, Italy or Rumania, as the case might be. But in certain other cases the issue was not so straightforward. Schleswig, formerly belonging to Prussia, had to decide whether it wished to remain under that allegiance or change it to that of Denmark; Allenstein, formerly German, had to decide between East Prussia and Poland; Southern Silesia, formerly Prussian, between Germany and Poland; the district called Klagenfurt, between Austria and Yugoslavia. The plebiscites were held and the results were honoured by the Powers, except in one case, Southern Silesia, in connection with which a division was afterwards made between Germany and Poland by an arbitration.

But though such a popular vote might settle the immediate question of political allegiance, it by no means solved the problem of minorities within the new or enlarged states of Europe. The plebiscite showed here the same sort of weakness as we saw that it possessed in the case of the earlier French plebiscites. The voting having been held, it appeared that the people must continue in perpetuity to stand by the arrangement so made. Diplomacy might arrange for a popular decision to be once taken, but how could it secure to the minorities the enjoyment of an equality of rights with the original citizens of the state so joined? This problem arose not only in the case of those areas where a plebiscite was held but also in those about which there was no dispute either in the area as a whole or in some part of it. For example, there was no question whether the provinces of Alsace and Lorraine, as a whole, wished to be reincorporated with France; yet there emerged there one of the acutest political problems in Europe, largely owing to religious differences. Again, in Transylvania the majority were Rumanians, but there came over to Rumania with them no fewer than two million Magyars. How were the latter's rights to be secured? The same question arose in other states. For instance, as a result of the new boundary-making carried out by the Peace Treaties, vast collections of Germans were dispersed outside the borders of Germany. There were three and a half millions of them in Czechoslovakia, two millions in Poland, half a million in Rumania, and 300,000 in the Italian Tyrol. Austria itself was a sort of isolated German minority of about seven millions, demanding entrance into the German Reich, a right which the Peace Treaties denied them. To take other examples, there were two million Russians in Poland and one million in Rumania, while Yugoslavia was a hopeless jumble of minorities, for of its population of twelve millions only six millions were Serbs.

Indeed, the question of minorities was one of the most acute political problems left over by the First World War, and bitterly did Europe and the world pay for their failure to solve it. The plebiscites at that time seemed an ideal instrument of self-determination and a sure means of making the world safe for democracy. But, in fact, their results were vitiated by the aggressions of the very tyrant who had used the same method to legalise his tyranny.

II. THE REFERENDUM

In discussing, in Chapter VIII, the general question of representative government, we said that the system of representation by itself has in some states been found inadequate, and that the distrust of this method alone has led to the adoption of supplementary plans by which the citizens could share directly with the representatives the business of law-making. This is what the three ultra-democratic developments which we are now to discuss, namely, the Referendum, the Popular Initiative and the Recall, set out to do.

These three devices have this in common with the plebiscite, that they imply a direct consultation of the people; but they differ radically from it in both method and purpose. For whereas the plebiscite is a vote held on one occasion to create a régime which the voters must afterwards endure without redress, the other three contrive to establish, by means of a recurrent vote, a perpetual popular check upon the political machine, since the referendum allows the electorate to review the acts of the legislature before they actually pass into law, the popular initiative gives the voters the right to propose measures to be passed by their representatives, and the recall grants them the power to remove an unsatisfactory representative before the expiration of his term of office.

These three direct democratic checks, then, mark a reversion to the earlier types of direct or primary democracy, as it existed in many of the city states of Ancient Greece. In their modern form these methods derive theoretically from the teaching of Rousseau, whose doctrine of popular sovereignty, inalienable, indivisible and inerrant, applied essentially to small states, in which the possible abuse of representation would be reduced to a minimum; and it is in small states, such as Switzerland and the less crowded individual states of the American Commonwealth, that they have principally been put into practice. But, though these methods have not yet been generally adopted, they have been widely advocated as a means of counteracting some of the evils which undoubtedly lurk in the practice of representative democracy.

Practically, therefore, these devices have grown out of a keen sense of dissatisfaction with the conduct of representative bodies. In the first place, while the action of opinion is continuous, that of voting is only occasional, and many changes of opinion can take place between one general election and another. Secondly, when a general election shall be held is a matter entirely outside the power of the people to decide at any moment. Thirdly, the representative elected may either honestly misconceive the desires of his constituents or deliberately misrepresent their views. Fourthly, in most large states to-day the private member has very little time or opportunity allowed him to initiate legislation or, indeed, to do anything else than support or oppose the policies of the government of the day. Fifthly, the party caucus, or machine, is a thing generally so strong as virtually to destroy the independence of the individual representative.

Some or all of these difficulties are present in all modern constitutional states. They are most apparent in large states, but it is precisely in these that they are hardest to overcome.

As to the ways of surmounting these difficulties, we have already spoken of the referendum in connection with certain rigid constitutions whose amendment requires a vote of the people before it can be carried into effect, as happens, for instance, in Switzerland, Australia, and, more recently, in the Fourth Republic in France and in the new Italian Republic. In some states its use is carried much farther than this into the realm of ordinary legislation. In Switzerland, for example, in the case of all laws passed and resolutions carried by the federal legislature, a referendum must be held if a demand for it is made either by 30,000 citizens or by the legislatures of any eight cantons, unless the resolution is declared by the federal legislature to be "urgent." If a referendum is held and a majority of the people vote against the law in question, it is thereby void. Similarly, in eight of the cantons all laws whatsoever must be so submitted. This is called the Obligatory Referendum. In seven other cantons, if a certain number (which varies from one canton to another) of citizens demand a referendum, it must be held. This is called the Facultative or Optional Referendum. In a further three cantons some laws of a specified kind must be submitted to the people in any case, and others if a certain proportion of citizens demand it. In most of the remaining cantons the population is so small that primary democracy exists (that is, the whole people forms the legislature) and in such cases, of course, a referendum would be superfluous.

In the United States the referendum is not used for any purpose in federal matters, but in some of the individual states legislative abuses have become so glaring and widespread that the referendum, as well as the popular initiative and recall, have been adopted in recent years, in an endeavour to counteract those evils. The referendum, in one form, is no new thing in American States, for state constitutions were often enacted by popular vote in the early days of the Republic, and the practice of submitting to the people amendments proposed by the legislature or by a special convention has gone on ever since. But it has in later days developed much farther, and in several states a provision is now made permitting a prescribed number of citizens (varying from five to ten per cent of the electorate) to demand that an act passed by the legislature shall be submitted to the people for its approval or rejection. This provision exists in twenty-one out of the forty-eight states, but they are mostly the newer and more westerly states, such as Oregon, Colorado and California, though so old a state as Massachusetts has adopted this as well as the popular initiative. As in Switzerland, most of the American states exempt from the operation of the referendum any acts deemed by the legislature to be urgent. This power is often abused, and the label of urgency has frequently been attached to a measure without justification, to save it from the possibility of popular rejection.

In Germany under the Weimar Republic also the referendum could be used for laws besides those amending the Constitution. Any law passed by the *Reichstag* and going to the President for signature had, within one month of its passage, if the President so ordered, to be referred to the people. The promulgation of any law passed by the *Reichstag* (except laws declared by both Houses to be urgent) was deferred for two months, if one-third of the *Reichstag* so demanded, and if, during that period, one-twentieth of those entitled to the franchise expressed the desire, it had then to be submitted to the people. The *Reichsrat* could force the submission of a law to a referendum but such a law could be annulled by a popular majority only if a majority of the electorate took part in the vote. The practice was not revived under the Bonn Constitution, which makes no mention of the referendum. The Referendum in the new Italian Republic applies not only, as we saw, to constitutional amendments but also to ordinary laws; *e.g.* a proposal to determine the abrogation of a law made by 500,000 electors or five regional councils has to be submitted to the people for their decision. In some other states the referendum has been used on very rare occasions, as, for example, in New Zealand, where the legislature voluntarily submitted to the people the question of the prohibition of the sale of intoxicating liquor; and in Australia (apart, of course, from constitutional amendments) where, in 1915 and 1917, on the subject of compulsory military service, and again in 1928, on that of prohibition, the opinion of the people was sought by this means.

III. THE POPULAR INITIATIVE AND THE RECALL

The Popular Initiative, whose object is to place in the hands of the people a direct power of initiating or proposing legislation which must be taken up by the legislature, is a development of ultra-democratic practice, within the area of constitutionalism, even more advanced than the referendum. It is necessary to study the initiative apart from the referendum, because, although the theoretical foundations of the two are the same, the conditions under which they are applied differ, for, as one authority has said, while the referendum protects the people against the legislature's sins of commission, the initiative offers them a remedy for its sins of omission. The argument for the initiative, beyond that for the referendum, is that legislatures do not adequately represent the people's point of view and that, as a referendum only concerns proposals made by the legislature, it is not by itself a sufficient guarantee against abuse. But we sometimes find the initiative and the referendum working in combination, so that the proposals initiated by the people come back to them, after passing through the legislature, for their final approval. And in no country in the world do we find the initiative in existence without the referendum also.

In Switzerland, where, as we have shown, the referendum exists for constitutional amendments, laws and resolutions, for both cantonal and federal affairs, the popular initiative is also used for both, but not quite so fully in federal as in cantonal matters. As to the Confederation as a whole, any 50,000 citizens may propose an amendment to the Federal Constitution either as a specific proposal or as a request that such be drawn up by the Assembly. Or the citizens may propose total revision. In this case, as explained earlier, if the Assembly disagrees but the people in a referendum approve the principle of the proposal, the amendment must be drawn up and finally submitted for acceptance or rejection. In the cantons the regulations for the use of the initiative go farther and include not only constitutional matters but ordinary laws and resolutions. In all cantons, except Geneva (whose constitution is automatically revised every fifteen years), a prescribed number of citizens, which varies from one canton to another, may either demand a general revision of the constitution or propose specific amendments to it. Again, in all the cantons except three a prescribed number of citizens may either propose a new law or resolution fully drafted or submit the principle of some law or resolution to be drafted by the Cantonal Council. In the former case, the bill is submitted direct to the people; in the latter, the Council asks the people by a referendum whether it shall proceed with the drafting of the bill, and, if they agree, the bill in its completed form is finally submitted for their approval or rejection.

In the United States, not so many states use the initiative as use the referendum. At present the initiative is in force in nineteen states for laws and in fourteen states for constitutional amendments. The number of citizens which may submit a proposal under the initiative arrangements ranges from five to fifteen per cent of the electorate of any given state, while in some states a fixed number is prescribed. But these rights are much abused in America. Agents of political associations are sent round to obtain, even to purchase, signatures to some measure which it is proposed to initiate, and often many of the signatures are forged. In those states which use the initiative for constitutional, as well as for ordinary, laws, there is no distinction in procedure, and thus ordinary laws are often put in the form of constitutional amendments, and so, if passed, cannot later be repealed by the ordinary action of the legislature. The result is that in some states the constitution, which in all cases was intended to be a fundamental instrument of special sanctity, is in danger of becoming a mere jumble of minor and trivial provisions entirely unsuited to such a document. This is hardly the outcome intended by the founders of a scheme whose professed object is the purification of politics.

In Germany under the Weimar Republic there was an interesting clause (the 73rd) in the Constitution establishing the principle of the initiative. It stated that if one-tenth of those entitled to vote initiated a request for the introduction of a bill (which had to be fully drafted) the government was obliged to present it to the *Reichstag*. If the *Reichstag* passed it, the law was promulgated without further ado; if it did not, the bill had to be submitted to a referendum. A similar example of the initiative appears in the new Constitution of the Italian Republic. According to Article 71 of that Constitution any fifty thousand electors may submit a bill, which must be properly drawn, for consideration.

The Recall of representatives or other elected officials is a popular power very recent in modern politics, though it is not altogether a new device. During the course of the French

Revolution, for example, a proposal was made, though it never materialised, to provide for the removal of an unsatisfactory deputy by those who had elected him. But in recent times it is only in certain states of the United States that it has been completely carried out. The law in the state of Oregon, for example, provides that, where a prescribed number of citizens sends up a petition demanding the dismissal of an elected officer, whether legislative or executive, a popular vote shall be held on the matter, and if the vote by a majority goes against the official he shall be dismissed and a new election shall be held to fill his place for the unexpired portion of his term of office. This procedure has been adopted by other American states and has been frequently successful, though very rarely in the case of members of the legislature. In other states it has been carried farther and applied to judges, where they are elected, and even in one case (Colorado) to the decisions of such judges. In the last-mentioned use of this plan the actual practice was, however, declared unconstitutional. The recall of all elected officers, including judges, is in use in eight states of the American Union; that of such officers, excluding judges, in four. As in the case of the referendum and the initiative, the recall is, generally speaking, confined to the Western American states, and those few Eastern states which have adopted the other two devices have continued to look askance at this one.

No other nation in the world to-day has adopted the recall in this way. It was, it is true, provided for in the original Constitution of the Russian Soviet Republic, but it finds no place in the 1936 Constitution of the U.S.S.R. In Switzerland there is a scheme which somewhat resembles the recall in action. There, in seven cantons, the people, by a specified majority, may demand the dissolution and re-election of the cantonal legislature before the expiration of its term. This is as far as the recall has gone outside the United States, though there are reformers who urge its adoption in states where it has never been attempted.

The referendum, the popular initiative and the recall seem, at first sight, such a logical development of democracy that it may strike one as strange that their adoption has not been more widely demanded. As we have said, they are more applicable to small states than to large and have only been adopted to any extent in Switzerland and certain individual states of the American Union. In Switzerland the referendum is more in use than the initiative, because the people are inspired rather by a democratic dogma than by an active spirit of discontent, and therefore wish more to check than to direct their law-makers. In the American states the reverse is the case, these devices having been adopted there as a deliberate means of counteracting the evils of corrupt legislatures. Even so, the referendum in Switzerland, though it is a thoroughly live institution, has always been sparingly used. In American states it is less used now than formerly. As to the initiative, it is much more freely used in the cantons of Switzerland than in the Confederation as a whole, where its use is confined to constitutional amendments. In the American states, on the other hand, the initiative is used constantly, and its introduction, from the popular point of view, has certainly been justified by the amount of use made of it.

IV. ARGUMENTS FOR AND AGAINST THE USE OF THESE DEVICES

What conclusions, then, can we draw from the working of the referendum, the initiative and the recall in those states which have tried them, and what can be suggested as to their applicability to large states? First, the referendum corrects the faults of legislatures which may act corruptly or in defiance of their mandate. Secondly, it keeps up a useful and healthy contact between the elected and the electors, a contact not always assured by infrequent general elections. Thirdly, it secures that no law which is opposed to popular feeling shall be passed. As to the initiative, the same arguments may be advanced in its favour. But there is a further reason for its use; namely, that, while the referendum only permits a vote of the people on matters already dealt with by the legislature, it gives no scope for popular proposals independently of the representative body. If the people, the argument runs, are capable of approving or disapproving a measure, why should they not be deemed also capable of proposing one themselves? Similarly with the recall: if the people are given the power to choose a deputy, should they not have the right also to remove him if in their view he fails in his duty? Is not the one right the corollary of the other?

On the other hand, many arguments may be brought forward

against the use of these devices. As to the referendum, if generally adopted in a large state, it would probably cause such delay in the promulgation of laws as might deprive society of the benefits they were designed to bestow, or permit the perpetuation of the evils they were intended to remove. Another objection is that, in a crowded community like our own, the various voices which it would allow to express themselves would, over a long series of measures submitted, probably neutralise one another and so lead to a complete nullification of all progressive legislation. Again, under modern conditions, legislation has become so highly specialised that even a well-informed citizen could hardly hope to grasp the details of all the bills submitted for popular consideration—which, moreover, would already have enjoyed the great advantage of being carefully weighed and debated in a legislature—and this would lead either to the enthronement of ignorance or to an indifference which would render the practice futile. Other objections besides these apply to the initiative. "It brings before the people," as one writer says, "bills that have never run the gauntlet of parliamentary criticism, which, if they have been carelessly or clumsily drafted, will, if enacted, confuse the law, creating uncertainty and inviting litigation." Further, the initiative gives opportunities to unscrupulous leaders or corrupt factions to do great harm to the state by playing upon the ignorance and irresponsibility of the crowd.

These objections to the initiative apply even more strongly when it is used in connection with constitutional law. As we have shown in Chapters VI and VII, a Constitution is something fundamental, only to be changed after great deliberation. If it became a mass of laws inserted by popular drafting and voting, it would lose its essential character and become a conglomeration of unworkable provisions. Such a condition of things would probably lead first to anarchy and then to despotism, in which case this popular device would entirely defeat its own end. The referendum is more suited to constitutional questions than is the initiative, and a further useful purpose to which it might be put is for resolving deadlocks between the Houses in those states where the legislature consists of two Chambers and the constitution does not provide that the voice of one shall prevail. This device was proposed but rejected in Australia, appeared in the Constitution of the Weimar Republic, and has been suggested in Norway and Belgium. It was once proposed in Great Britain during the deadlock arising out of the refusal of the Lords to pass the Budget of 1909.

As to the recall, the objections are fewer. There have been instances in America in which it has worked well and to the state's advantage. But it is said by its opponents to create in officials a timorous and servile spirit. If it is applied to legislators, there is a danger of turning the representative into a mere delegate, making him the victim of the corrupt attacks of any active and intriguing clique, and this would tend to drive public-spirited men out of public life. If it is applied to the executive, it clearly tends to weaken authority and would prevent the best men from taking public office. There is no case at all for applying its use to judges, for here we enter a domain even more specialised than either of the other two departments of government. The recall, as applied to judges, subjects them to popular caprice and so destroys that security of tenure which, as we have said, is essential to the well-being of the state. Logically, of course, the recall of judges can only apply where they are popularly elected, and it is only in those American states where this happens that the recall of judges has been put into practice. The recall of judicial decisions, which, as we have said, had been adopted in Colorado and has been proposed in some other Western American states, is even more politically unsound. A more general adoption of the system of popular election as applied to judges, and the use of the recall in connection with their tenure of office and decisions, would undoubtedly tend to a widespread looseness in the administration of justice in certain American states, by making the judges afraid to render unpopular decisions and causing them to hear and decide cases with a view rather to preserving themselves than to serving the ends of justice.

Our conclusion from this part of our inquiry is that constitutional democracy can, in the present state of civilisation, easily have put upon it a greater burden than it is yet qualified to bear. "To raise the standard of civic duty," as Lord Bryce truly wrote, "is a harder and longer task than to alter institutions." The utility and stability of political institutions depend upon the state of the community to which they apply, and it is important that institutions should not be in advance of the capacity of the people to operate them. The one should develop as the other justifies the development. If a too rapid progress is a danger with advanced communities, it is an even greater one with backward peoples, and it will be worth while now to turn to a brief examination of those constitutional experiments which have been and are being tried among certain more backward communities and especially those under the British Crown.

READING

BRYCE: *American Commonwealth,* Vol. I, Ch. xxxix. *Modern Democracies,* Vol. I, Ch. xxix; Vol. II, Ch. lxv.
DICEY: *Law of the Constitution,* pp. xci–c.
FINER: *Modern Government,* Vol. II, Ch. xxi.
GETTELL: *Readings in Political Science,* pp. 317–325.
KEITH: *Responsible Government in Dominions,* Vol. I, Pt. iii, Ch. i.
MARRIOTT: *Mechanism of Modern State,* Vol. I, Chs. iii, iv, xvii.
LOWELL: *Government of England,* Vol. II, Ch. xii.
WILSON: *State,* pp. 303–5, 396–400.

SUBJECTS FOR ESSAYS

1. Explain how the Plebiscite has been used in French internal politics in the past, and discuss its value for similar purposes in other states to-day.
2. What use was made of the Plebiscite at the end of the First World War and with what effect?
3. Discuss Hitler's use of the Plebiscite in the 1930's as an abuse of democracy and an instrument for the establishment of tyranny.
4. Explain the working of the Referendum in Switzerland.
5. To what extent is the Referendum in use in the United States of America?
6. From the use made of the Referendum in certain Self-governing Dominions, discuss its applicability to Great Britain.
7. What is the object of the Popular Initiative and how far does it achieve its purposes in those states which have adopted it?
8. Compare the advantages of the Recall in modern democratic states as applied to the three departments of government respectively.
9. Compare the value of the Referendum and Initiative as applied to ordinary laws with their value as applied to constitutional amendments.
10. Do you consider that the advantages of these direct democratic devices are more apparent than real?

CHAPTER XIV

CONSTITUTIONAL EXPERIMENTS AMONG NON-EUROPEAN PEOPLES

I. NEAR AND FAR EAST

In its expansion and adaptation the political constitutionalism of the Western World has, as we have shown in Chapter II, gone far afield. The dissemination of the national democratic seed has sometimes borne fruit, sometimes only reaped a harvest of tares. It might, indeed, be fairly argued that the amount of ground that has so far actually proved suited to this particular form of political culture, both in the Old World and in the New, is not so great as that which has been deemed fitted for experiments in it. But political man goes on inventing methods of intensive cultivation, and his proclivity to do this produces a political problem of the first importance; namely, how far methods of self-government can be applied to politically backward peoples. And it is a problem which affects the future not only of those backward races and of Europeans in contact with them, but also of international government, in which, if it is to be really effective, they must all play a part.

The application of the principle of self-government has proved easy enough in what we may call white colonies. The British people, settling in largely uninhabited temperate areas in various parts of the world, have learned how to evolve by stages their self-governing institutions. At no time, indeed, after the first few years of settlement, were these colonies in the Western Hemisphere, in the Antipodes and in South Africa, subject to the complete political domination of the Mother Country. This is seen very clearly in the case of the American Colonies before the War of Independence, when, as the late Professor Seeley once remarked, while Britain treated the colonists economically like a pack of conquered Indians, she regarded them politically as free men. In truth, nothing in the political history of the world is more instructive than the way in which British colonists carried with them the political spirit of the people from which they had sprung and gave it play until at last it produced one of two things: either complete sovereign independence with a political constitution which, for stability at least, may challenge comparison with any in the world, as it did in the case of the United States, or that type of autonomous political organisation which we now see in Canada, Australia, New Zealand, South Africa, and the rest in the British Commonwealth.

But another question altogether was raised when it came to applying these ideals and establishing these institutions in those areas in tropical zones where no considerable colonies of white men could settle and where European governments had become the paramount power among vast native populations far behind the Western nations in potentiality for progress. Even among the more backwards peoples of Europe the difficulties in the way of building up self-governing institutions have often proved very great. The experiment, for example, of suddenly creating constitutional monarchies out of the ruins of a part of the despotic Turkish Empire in 1878, in states like Serbia and Rumania, was, to say the least, highly speculative, and proved far from successful in the event. Again, Russia, in the opening years of the present century, failed to establish a working political constitution, largely because it was a vast country with a preponderantly ignorant peasant population. Further, some of the eastern and south-eastern European states created or enlarged by the First World War failed to adapt themselves peacefully to the constitutionalism which we have examined in these pages, and fell an easy prey to totalitarian régimes, first of a Fascist and later of a Communist sort.

When we contemplate the failure of political constitution-alism to establish itself even in certain parts of Europe, we are not surprised to find an incapacity successfully to adopt it in some countries outside Europe, even though there might exist in some of these, as in the European states mentioned, a genuine national sentiment. For instance, the attempts to set up a constitutional régime in Turkey from 1876 onwards were a complete failure, and only since the First World War has she begun to show the slightest capacity for political advancement. In Persia, again, a revolution in 1906 created a representative assembly, but, there being no executive sufficiently strong to carry out its will, it failed as an effective body.

These remarks suggest the value of a gradual policy in the establishment of self-governing institutions among the politically backward peoples. But it appears to be possible only under the directive force of a Great Power in control of the situation and sympathising with the aim of the ultimate political liberation of the people under its tutelage. The case of Egypt, in this respect, offers a strong contrast to that of Persia, for Egypt seems to have gained considerable political advantage from the presence of a progressive foreign Power. From the time that Britain assumed the virtual Protectorate of Egypt in 1882 (a Protectorate formally declared in 1914), opportunities were given to the Egyptians to educate themselves politically through a representative assembly which was established in 1883 and whose powers were considerably widened in 1913. After the First World War, and with the collapse of Turkey, Britain considered herself free to redeem the pledge originally given by Mr. Gladstone that our occupation of Egypt should be only temporary. In response to the demands of the Egyptian Nationalist Party, which cried, "Egypt for the Egyptians," Britain, in 1922, agreed to the establishment of a constitutional monarchy, with a descendant of the original Khedive family as King. By the Anglo-Egyptian Act of 1936 Egypt became a sovereign state, and the British military occupation was terminated, subject to certain safeguards connected with British interests in the Sudan and the Suez Canal. The treaty was to last for twenty years but could be reconsidered in 1946. This mid-point in the operative period happened to coincide with the months following the close of the Second World War, and the re-opening of the question of withdrawal became inextricably involved in the post-war nationalist revolution which shook Egypt and the Arab world.

The Egyptian Constitution which came into force in 1923 established a constitutional monarchy of the British type with the King as the nominal executive, acting through a Prime Minister and Cabinet responsible to Parliament made up of two Houses: the Senate, partly nominated and partly elected, and the Chamber of Deputies. This constitution had a chequered career until in 1952 the monarchy was overthrown by a military *coup d'état* and a republic was set up. In 1956 Colonel Nasser was elected President of the Republic in a plebiscite at which he was the only candidate. In 1957 there was an election for a new Parliament (the General Assembly). The list of candidates, which was officially pruned, included women, and at the election women voted for the first time. Yet the régime remained authoritarian, for the new constitution left unchecked executive power in the hands of the President, aided by a Council of Ministers. In fact, in the new Egyptian Republic the President is also the Prime Minister.

Meanwhile, the Anglo-Egyptian Condominium in the Sudan came to an end with the establishment of the Republic of the Sudan in 1956. The new Republic is governed by a Council of State and a bi-cameral legislature comprising a fully-elected House of Representatives and a partially elective Senate.

In the Far East it seemed for a time that Japan might successfully assimilate and apply European political ideas, for in 1889 she established under the Emperor a constitution on the Western model, with a Prime Minister and Cabinet responsible to a Parliament (Diet) consisting of two Chambers: a House of Peers, partly hereditary, partly nominated and partly elected, and a House of Representatives elected for four years by universal male suffrage. But the hope of steady constitutional progress, which this charter seemed to justify, faded in face of the expansionist policy of the dominant party in Japan, which, like its German and Italian counterparts in Europe, used the success of its aggressions beyond the state to strengthen the totalitarian régime within. With the overthrow of the Japanese Empire in the Second World War, the Japanese people, under the influence of America, the chief Occupying Power, have a second opportunity to prove their ability to govern themselves by a democratic system. In 1947 there came into force a new constitution based broadly on the old, except that the Second Chamber, now called the House of Councillors, is fully elective. It cannot be said, however, that at the elections held in April, 1947, for both the House of Councillors and the House of Representatives, the people displayed any very great enthusiasm for their regained rights, despite the fact that women were for the first time enfranchised, but it will be interesting to watch the working of this revived experiment as the Japanese gradually re-build their new economic and political life within the natural boundaries of the national state.

Nor has the attempt to establish constitutional government been any more successful in China than in Japan, though in China the circumstances in which a constitution was first promulgated were much more revolutionary. For in 1911 the age-old imperium of the Manchu dynasty was violently over-thrown and a republic set up in its place. The Constitution of the Republic which was promulgated in February, 1912, established an elective presidency, an executive ministry, or Cabinet, with a Premier at its head, and a bicameral legislature made up of a Senate and a House of Representatives. But this constitution failed to work from the beginning. The results of Presidential elections were disputed and the laws passed by Parliament were ignored. Meanwhile, a new party, the People's National Party (the Kuomentung), opposed to the government, was formed and became so powerful that in 1928, under the leadership of Chiang Kai-Shek, it captured Peking and promul-gated a new constitution which established an oligarchical type of government by five councils, with the President of the Republic at their head. From 1937 this government had to face both the aggressions of Japan and the opposition of the Com-munist Party which set up a separate government and fought the Japanese with a military organisation entirely distinct from that of the National Government. If the common peril of Japanese imperialism could not unite the Chinese, it is not surprising that they were unable to settle their differences when the Second World War had destroyed the power of their mighty eastern neighbour, and that China remained divided. In 1945, Chiang Kai-Shek promised to summon a People's Congress to draft a new constitution which would re-establish the sover-eignty of the people. But meanwhile the Communists, under Mao Tse-tung, gradually gained control of the whole of China, and in September, 1949, proclaimed the People's Republic, with a constitution modelled largely on that of Soviet Russia.

II. INDIA AND PAKISTAN

Nowhere is the grant of political rights by stages better illustrated than in the history of the growth of the British Self-governing Dominions, and it is of special interest in the

case of India, where the successive steps—from the faint
beginnings of partial self-governing institutions to the achievement of Dominion Status—covered a period of ninety years,
though the ultimate pattern of responsible self-government,
when it finally emerged in 1947, turned out to be very different
from that foreshadowed in the earlier Acts. The earlier history of
the British in India is the story of the assumption of political
responsibilities by the East India Company and their gradual
transference to the British Crown. Beginning as a purely
commercial venture, the East India Company, under a Charter
granted by the Crown in 1600, found itself faced with greater
and greater political difficulties resulting from the combined
effect of the break-up of the Mogul Empire and the struggle
for supremacy with the French. When the French power had
been destroyed in the Seven Years' War (1756–63), the government at home was forced to intervene and two Acts were
carried in fairly rapid succession—North's Regulating Act
(1773) and Pitt's India Act (1784)—which attempted to order
the government of those parts of India which had up to those
dates passed under British sovereignty, and laid the foundations
of the office of Governor-General of India as an Imperial officer
rather than as a servant of the Company, while Pitt's Act
established in London a Board of Control which was the beginning of the India Office.

This Act lasted for more than seventy years, when the outbreak of the Indian Mutiny in 1857 necessitated its repeal and
the passing of a new Act in the following year. That Act abolished the East India Company, proclaimed Queen Victoria
Sovereign of India (the Imperial title was not assumed till
1877), created the office of Secretary of State for India as a
separate post, and arranged that one Indian native should sit
on the Board at the India Office in London, a second native
seat being added later. The main features of that Act continued
to be the basis of the government of British India, though it
was modified by a number of statutes, passed from time to time,
calculated gradually to evolve a less absolute form of government. The Governor-General of British India and the Governors
of the various Provinces into which it was divided came to be
assisted in legislation and even in administration by a body
drawn from an ever-widening area of recruitment in Indian

society. A series of Indian Councils Acts in 1861, 1892, 1909, and during the First World War, gradually developed the practice of a participation by the Indians, through partially representative assemblies, in the government of their country, both in the Viceroy's Council and in those of the Provincial Governors. These measures culminated in the Government of India Act of 1919, passed under the ægis of Lord Chelmsford, as Viceroy, and Edwin Montagu, as Secretary of State.

The preamble to this Act stated that it was the intention of Britain to bring about an increasing association of Indians in the administration and a gradual development of self-governing institutions in British India as an integral part of the Empire, and to give the Provinces of India the largest measure of independence of the government of India compatible with the latter's due discharge of its responsibilities. For the Central Government the Act set up an Upper House, called a Council of State, of sixty members, a proportion of whom were elected, the rest nominated (not more than twenty of these latter were to be officials), and a Legislative Assembly of 140 members, of whom one hundred were elected and the rest nominated (not more than twenty-six officials). The term of the Council was five years, of the Assembly three, but either or both might be previously dissolved by the Viceroy. Their powers were at first very shadowy. The Executive Council, which was the real force with which the Governor-General acted, was not responsible to them, but every member of it had to have a seat in either the Council of State or the Legislative Assembly. Ordinary legislation passed through both Houses, including certain branches of finance. But the Viceroy might enact anything to which they refused their assent and veto anything which they might enact.

It was in the eight principal Provinces, in each of which the Governor administered those affairs not in the hands of the Governor-General, that a real measure of self-government was inaugurated by the Act of 1919. In each of the Provinces the principle of Responsible Government, as we have seen it at work in the Dominions whose constitutions we have studied, was, though in a modified form, introduced. Each Province had a Governor, an Executive Council, and a Legislative Council. At least 70 per cent of the membership of each Council (the number varying from 125 in Bengal to 53 in Assam) was to be elected, the rest nominated. The term was three years, if the Council was not dissolved earlier. The affairs of the Provinces were divided into two sorts; namely, reserved subjects and transferred subjects. The first were administered, as before, by the Governor and the Executive Council, but the second were administered by the Governor on the advice of Ministers drawn from the elected members of the Legislative Council who were responsible to the Council. This Act was to stand for ten years, after which its working was to be reviewed, to see in what ways it might be changed in a progressive direction.

To liberal-minded men and women in Britain the Government of India Act of 1919 seemed to contain a seed which might ultimately blossom into a fine flower of responsible federal government. It is true that the powers of the Governor-General remained very great, but under the then existing conditions it would have been dangerous to place him in a position of complete responsibility to a fully elective legislature, which is the essence of responsible government as we know it in the Self-governing Dominions. But India was, and is, very different from those Dominions. It is rather a continent than a mere country, inhabited by more than four hundred million native peoples living in a welter of antagonisms, social, religious and political. The vast mass of its people were, and remain, illiterates, some of them, the Untouchables, having until recently[1] been regarded, under the caste system, as almost less than human. It, therefore, lacked, and still lacks, the essential elements which go to compose a nation-state.

Nevertheless, the British Government was ready to redeem its promise to review the situation within ten years of the passage of the Act of 1919, and in 1928 the Simon Commission was sent to India to enquire into the possibilities of revision. Out of the report of that Commission, and the discussions which followed it, arose a new adventure in the self-government of a vast native population which seemed at the time to constitute the most daring political experiment in the history of the world. For after seven years of discussion in India and in Britain, a new Government of India Act was passed in 1935. It is a monumental document filling nearly 100 pages of close print. In one

---

[1] Untouchability is abolished, and its continued practice made punishable, under the Constitution of the Union of India of 1950. (See pp. 302-303.)

respect the Act introduced an entirely novel experiment, namely, the principle of an All-India Federation. In another, with reference to the Provinces, it marked a development and enlargement of political rights and powers already granted and exercised under the Act of 1919. The Act, so far as it concerned Provincial autonomy, came into operation in April, 1937. The Provinces granted autonomy were called Governor's Provinces (of which there were then eleven), and these were divided into two classes, one class comprising Madras, Bombay, Bengal, the United Provinces, Behar, and Assam, and the other class the remaining five Provinces. The six named had two legislative chambers, the Legislative Council and the Legislative Assembly, and the remainder only one, the Legislative Assembly. In each of these the Governor represented the King and was aided and advised by a Council of Ministers responsible to the legislature. The Governor was to choose his Ministers according to his view of their likelihood of being supported in the legislature. He was to take the Ministers' advice on all Provincial matters except those for which he was directly responsible, such as the safety of the Province or orders from the Governor-General which might conflict with the views of his Ministers.

The Act laid down how the Provincial Assemblies were to be constituted and who should form the electorate. The franchise was granted to men and women of twenty-one years or more with certain qualifications based mainly on property, and the electorates in each Province were so arranged as to give representation to the various races, communities and special interests. The franchise was thus granted to over thirty millions of the native population of India, including more than four million women. The first general election under the Act was held in 1937, and although the vast majority of the electorate was illiterate, the election aroused great popular interest and over 50 per cent went to the polls, a proportion that compares very favourably with that of some elections in this country.

It is evident that this scheme was much more far-reaching than that under the Act of 1919 and that it came very near to what we know as Responsible Government as applied to the Dominions. It will be observed that, whereas under the Act of 1919 the powers were divided into reserved and transferred, and only the latter were within the purview of the responsible ministries, in the Act of 1935 the scope was much wider, including as it did all matters other than those reserved for the Governor's discretion. It is clear, therefore, that here was an incipient form of Cabinet Government, such as that which existed in Canada after 1840 as a result of the Durham Report,[1] in which the full stature of responsible government might gradually be reached with the help and guidance of sympathetic Governors, and given the readiness of parties in the legislature to learn and co-operate.

The idea of an Indian Federation was something quite new. The membership of the All-India Federation under the Act was to consist of Governors' Provinces, Commissioners' Provinces (parts of British India other than the eleven Provinces referred to above), and the Native States which might agree to join it. The Federation was to come into being on a date to be announced by Royal Proclamation, and it appeared to be the intention to launch the federal plan as soon as the rulers of states representing not less than half the aggregate population of the Native States, and entitled to not less than half the seats in the Federal Legislature, should have agreed to come in.

Under the Act the Federal Government was to consist of the Governor-General and a legislature of two Chambers, namely, the Council of State and the House of Assembly. The Upper House was to consist of 156 representatives of British India, mostly elected by an electorate of about 100,000 persons, and not more than 104 representatives of Native States nominated by the Rulers. The House of Assembly was to consist of 250 representatives of British India, chosen by the Provincial Legislatures, and not more than 125 representatives of the Indian States, the allocation of the seats to each state or group of states to be in proportion to their population. The franchise for the election of the Lower House, so far as the representatives of British India were concerned, was to be substantially that for Provincial Legislatures, with an added educational qualification, thus constituting a total native electorate of several millions of men and women.

The executive power of the Federation was to be exercised by the Governor-General, as the Representative of the King-

[1] See earlier, pp. 222-223.

Emperor, aided and advised by a Council of Ministers responsible to the legislature. But certain departments—namely
defence, external affairs and ecclesiastical administration—
were to remain in the personal control of the Governor-General.
Also the Governor-General was to continue to be charged with
"special responsibility" in respect of certain matters, such as
menace to internal peace, financial stability, interests of minorities, protection of rights of any Indian States, and prevention
of commercial discrimination, but only where he felt it contrary
to the general good would he even in those cases decline to be
advised by the Council of Ministers. For the rest, Cabinet
Government, as normally understood, was to operate in the
Federal State of India under the Act of 1935.

The federal system thus projected had a background very
different from that on which federations, as we have seen earlier,
have generally been based. For the units to be federated were
not only utterly dissimilar in their history and existing form,
but entirely different in their relationship to the Imperial
Government, and, whereas the Provinces of British India had
only such powers and functions as had been delegated to them,
the control of the Imperial Authority over the Native States
was generally confined to external relations. In fact, an All-
India Federation implied the union of a continent even more
multifarious in race, history, language, culture and religion
than, say, the continent of Europe.

The plan to make British India one Self-governing Dominion
and to establish an All-India Federation as adumbrated in the
Act of 1935 was fated never to be realised. Rendered obsolete
in the aftermath of the war, it was then superseded by the
demand for something much more far-reaching: nothing less,
in fact, than complete independence. This had always been in
the minds of extreme Indian nationalists who from the beginning boycotted the Provincial Assemblies established by the
Act of 1935, and the demand was precipitated by the Second
World War which produced a fresh surge of nationalism
throughout Asia.

Seeing that the plan of 1935 was out of date, the British
Government sent to India in 1946 a Cabinet Mission, which,
after three months of consultation with Indian leaders of all
parties, recommended that the future constitution of India

should be settled by a Constituent Assembly composed of representatives of all communities and interests in British India and of the Indian States. Under the stimulus of this new British attitude, an Interim Government was formed at the centre composed of the political leaders of the major communities, exercising wide powers within the existing constitution, and Indians at first seemed ready to co-operate in the working of Indian governments responsible to legislatures in all the Provinces. But a fundamental rift soon manifested itself between the two main Indian Parties: the Hindus (Congress Party) and the Muslims (Muslim League). The Muslim League withdrew from the Interim Government and announced that they would accept nothing short of partition and the formation of a separate Muslim state (Pakistan) so as to secure the liberty of Muslims in those areas where they were in a majority. In February, 1947, the Prime Minister announced to the House of Commons the definite intention of the British Government to "take the necessary steps to effect the transference of power into responsible Indian hands by a date not later than June, 1948."

This announcement caused the Indian leaders to hasten a settlement of their differences, with the wholly unexpected result that they abandoned the idea of complete independence and agreed instead to divide the country into two Self-governing Dominions (India and Pakistan) under the British Crown. The British Parliament immediately passed the necessary legislation and the two Dominions were established in August, 1947.[1] The immediate question was how to introduce constitutional procedure in states so precipitately created as to be without constitutions. All that existed at that moment were two Constituent Assembles, one for India set up under the plan proposed by the Cabinet Mission of 1946 and the other formed by the Muslims when they decided not to co-operate with the Hindus in the creation of a united India. The difficulty was surmounted by adopting the India Act of 1935, with necessary modifications, as the basic constitution for the time being of both new

[1]One interesting consequence of the establishment of the two Self-governing Dominions in India was the abolition of the ninety-year-old office of Secretary of State for India, and the incorporation of such Indian functions as remained in the office, newly created in 1947, of the Secretary of State for Commonwealth Relations. Also the title of Emperor was dropped from the royal style.

Dominions, and giving the two Constituent Assemblies the status of Parliaments.

The Indian Constituent Assembly, having become the Provisional Parliament of the Dominion of India, lost little time in considering a new constitution, the draft of which was introduced in the Assembly in November, 1948. In the autumn of 1949, however, India declared her intention of becoming a Republic, though expressing at the same time a desire to remain a member of the British Commonwealth, a proposal to which the British Parliament raised no objection. The result was that, when the new constitution was approved in November, 1949, and came into force in January, 1950, it applied not to a Self-governing Dominion with a Governor-General representing the King but to an independent Republic with an elected President. The President of the former Constituent Assembly was unanimously elected first President of the Republic, and the Governor-Generalship was abolished. From that day also the British Commonwealth of Nations assumed a new form, for, since India was to remain a member, it then for the first time included a republic in its membership.

This federal Union of India comprises fourteen States and six Union Territories. Each State has a Governor, appointed by the President of the Republic, and a unicameral or bicameral legislature whose powers are defined in the Constitution. The federal legislature is composed of a Second Chamber called the Council of States and a lower called the House of the People. The Council has 250 members, twelve nominated and the rest elected proportionately by the various state legislatures, though in the case of bicameral legislatures by the lower House only. It is a permanent body not liable to dissolution, one-third of the members retiring, like American Senators, every two years. The House of the People consists of not more than 520 members elected by voters of both sexes of twenty-one and over, making a total electorate of about 180 millions, or about one in two of the whole population. The life of the House is five years, though subject to earlier dissolution.

The President and Vice-President (who is *ex-officio* Chairman of the Council of States) are nominal heads of the executive. The President is elected by an Electoral College made up of all members of federal and state legislatures. His tenure is five years, but he is eligible for re-election. Like the President of the French and German Republics, he acts through a Prime Minister and Cabinet responsible to the elected legislature. The first General Election for the Union Parliament was held in 1952. Of the total register of nearly 180 million voters, 107 million went to the polls. At the second election, in 1957, the numbers were even larger. Both were remarkable spectacles of liberty and tolerance in an Asiatic nation so largely illiterate and so recently enfranchised.

Like the Union of India, Pakistan is a federation of former British Provinces and Indian Native States. These include West Punjab, Sind, the North-West Frontier, East Bengal and Beluchistan, and Bahawalpur and Khaipur. For about eight years it continued to be a self-governing Dominion under the British Crown, as it became by the Indian Independence Act of 1947, and, as such, had a Governor-General, a Muslim, who acted through a Prime Minister and Cabinet responsible to the legislature. As in the Union of India, the Constituent Assembly of the Federation of Pakistan had full legislative powers until a Parliament was convened under a new constitution. The constitution, which was promulgated in 1956, established the Islamic Republic of Pakistan.

Under the new constitution the federal legislature, called the National Assembly, consists of only one House of 300 members, elected for five years (unless previously dissolved) by adult suffrage. Half the members are drawn from each of the two Provinces (West Pakistan and East Pakistan) which constitute the federation. The President is elected for five years by the members of the National and Provincial Assemblies. His powers are wide, and he acts only to a limited extent through a Cabinet reponsible to Parliament. Each Province has a Governor who acts through Ministers responsible to the provincial legislature, which consists of one Chamber, known as the Provincial Assembly. Its period of office is five years, unless dissolved earlier. The seats in each Assembly are distributed, in varying proportions, among scheduled castes, including some seats specifically allotted to women.

The constitutional difficulties confronting these two new states are manifestly formidable, but Pakistan's problems are more complicated than those of India, not only for economic reasons but also because its two main parts are separated by about two thousand miles of Indian territory.

III. BRITISH COLONIES

A Fabian policy of political education and practice similar to that which characterised the later history of British India is being followed also in various parts of the British Colonial Empire. This Empire is made up of forty-five territories, lying almost wholly in the tropics, under thirty-five separate Governors and with a total population estimated to be between 60 and 70 millions. The territories vary greatly in area, from the vast region of Nigeria, with nearly 400,000 square miles, to Gibraltar, with only $2\frac{1}{4}$. The general political pattern of the contemporary Colonial system is one of progressive devolution to self-government. In most of the Colonies we may observe the germ of constitutionalism, although some have already passed well beyond the embryonic stage. In these we may examine the three departments of government and note how they are related to one another. Each has a legislature composed in some cases of one chamber, partly or wholly elected, and in others of two chambers, the lower of which is wholly elected. The executive consists of a Governor assisted by an Executive Council, which in some cases is wholly appointed by the Crown, in others partly nominated by local interests, and in yet others partly elected by the legislature, a reform recently carried, for example, in Trinidad, where the elected members are in a majority; in Jamaica, where they are now in a very large majority; and in Mauritius, where they are in a minority. Each Colony, again, has a judiciary whose members are appointed by the Crown and hold office "while of good behaviour", for in all the Colonies the Rule of Law holds as it does in Britain and in all the Self-governing Dominions.

We may follow these constitutional developments in the Colonies through a rising scale of local representation in the Colonial legislatures. The lower end of this scale is found, for instance, in North Borneo, which has a legislative Council of twenty-three members, of whom three are ex-officio, nine official and ten nominated. The racial interests represented include Chinese. Next in order comes a case like Hong Kong which has a Legislative Council of seventeen members, of whom nine are official and eight non-official. Slightly higher up the scale in different parts of the world are a number of Colonies with a Legislative Council in which a majority are official and nominated, and a minority elected members. Examples of this type, in ascending order of numbers elected in proportion to the whole body, are Fiji, Kenya and the Leeward Islands.

The next class is one in which each Colony has a Legislative Council with a majority of elected members. Examples of this type are Mauritius, Grenada, British Honduras and Singapore. In the same way there have been some striking examples of constitutional progress in Colonial Africa. One is that of Sierra Leone, which, under its new Constitution of 1948, has a single-chamber legislature in which all thirty members are elected. An even more remarkable case is that of Nigeria. This colony is divided into three regions, each with its own Assembly. For the whole colony there was until recently a Legislative Council, of whose forty members only four were elected. But by an Act passed in 1954 the three regions were joined in the Federation of Nigeria. The Federation has a House of Representatives of 193 members, of whom only nine are officially appointed. The remaining 184 members are all elected. There remain four examples of Colonies in the West Indies, each having a bi-cameral legislature, the Upper House of which is nominated (or else indirectly elected) but whose Lower House (variously called the Representative Assembly, the House of Assembly, and the House of Representatives) is wholly elected. These are Jamaica, Barbados, Bermuda, and the Bahamas. Having advanced so far separately, the peoples of the British Islands in the Caribbean are now, like the Nigerians, experimenting with a scheme of common government. In 1957, after much discussion, the project to form a West Indies Federation was approved, and in 1958 this new constitutional experiment was finally launched with the formal opening of the first Federal Parliament in Trinidad.

This process of evolution from Colonial to Dominion status is well exemplified in the case of Ceylon, where, between 1923 and 1931, there was a Legislative Council with very restricted powers. In the latter year, however, by an order in Council, a new State Council was constituted. The State Council was composed of three Officers of State, eight nominated members and fifty elected members. Under this single-Chamber system (known as the Donoughmore Constitution) the people of Ceylon gained useful political experience, and when they demanded further reforms the British Government instituted an enquiry under Lord Soulbury and in 1945 offered Ceylon a constitution on the British model, with a Cabinet responsible to Parliament for all internal affairs. Having been accepted by the State Council, the new constitution came into force in 1947.

This was regarded on all sides as a deliberate preparation for the assumption by Ceylon of complete responsible self-government, and in the same year elections were held, as a result of which there came into being a government regarded as capable of assuming full responsibility. Consequently the Soulbury Constitution was amended so as to confer full Dominion Status on Ceylon, and the British Parliament passed the Ceylon Independence Act to give it effect. In January, 1948, the new Parliament was opened at Colombo. It is a legislature of two Chambers (the House of Representatives and the Senate) to which the Prime Minister and his Cabinet are responsible. So in the year 1948 Ceylon became a fully Self-governing Dominion within the British Commonwealth of Nations.

A more recent and striking example of this kind of political evolution is supplied by the former colony of the Gold Coast. Having passed rapidly though various stages of self-government, it became in 1957 the independent state of Ghana.

IV. MANDATE AND TRUSTEESHIP

The policy of granting self-governing institutions by progressive stages to politically backward peoples is one which the Colonial powers must bring more and more into consideration both in the interest of those peoples and as part of the necessary machinery of world security. This is what the Americans have done in their conduct towards the Philippines, conquered from the Spanish in 1898-9. There a beginning was made in 1907 when the United States established a form of government in which the Filipinos had some share, with a pledge that they should have their independence when they were fit for it. In pursuance of this policy the islands were granted in 1935 a constitution under what was called Commonwealth Status, with a President and a National Assembly of their own, though with certain safeguards for American naval bases, and a promise of full independence in 1946, a promise which the Americans redeemed after the reconquest of the Philippines from the Japanese in the Second World War.

The Mandate system, which was incorporated in Article 22 of the Covenant of the League of Nations after the First World War, had, for certain types of areas, the same purpose in view, and, although the League is a thing of the past, this aspect of its constitution largely reappears in the Trusteeship system formulated as part of the Charter of the United Nations Organisation set up at the end of the Second World War. As a matter of background, therefore, it is well worth a brief examination. Article 22 of the Covenant provided that the more advanced nations, as members of the League, should accept as a sacred trust the tutelage of the people of any territory not able to stand by themselves. Mandates under the League were divided into three classes officially described as A, B and C.

Class A Mandates included all those former Turkish territories whose peoples had reached such a stage of development that their independence could be provisionally recognised, subject to assistance and advice by a Mandatory until such time as they could stand alone. There were five such Mandates: Syria[1] and Lebanon under France, and Iraq, Transjordan and Palestine under Britain. Iraq and Transjordan (now Jordan) became sovereign states in 1935 and 1946 respectively. In Palestine conditions became so intolerable that in 1948 Britain withdrew, and, after a further period of disorder and war, the independent Republic of Israel was established in 1949.

Class B Mandates were territories of tropical Africa and included three of the former German colonies: Togoland, the Cameroons and Tanganyika, the first two of which were divided between France and Britain, the third going to Britain. In these cases the Covenant said nothing about political institutions but merely required the Mandatory to maintain public order and morals, to guarantee freedom of conscience and religion, to prohibit the slave trade and traffic in arms and liquor, to

[1]Syria, independent in 1943, formed with Egypt a united Arab Republic in 1958.

prevent the establishment of fortifications and the training of natives except for police purposes, and to secure equal trading opportunities among members of the League.

Class C Mandates were territories so remote from civilisation and so sparsely populated as to be best administered as integral parts of the territory of the Mandatory. They included the former German possessions in the Pacific, one of which went to Australia, another to New Zealand, and the remainder to Japan. These Mandates have remained as they were originally allocated, except, of course, that those allotted to the Japanese passed out of their hands with their defeat in the Second World War, and are now under the "strategic trusteeship" of the United States.

The League of Nations set up a permanent Commission to examine the annual reports of the Mandatories, which were all that was required of them by way of answerability to the League. And now the whole question has passed to the United Nations Organisation, whose attitude to the problem of the trusteeship of politically backward peoples is expressed in no fewer than three Chapters (XI-XIII), containing nineteen Articles (73–91) of the Charter. Chapter XI begins with a Declaration regarding Non-Self-governing Territories, which states that members of the United Nations which have responsibility for the administration of territories whose peoples have not yet attained a full measure of self-government must recognise that "the interests of the inhabitants of these territories are paramount" and "accept as a sacred trust" the obligation to promote their well-being. Such members, continues the Article, accordingly undertake, among other things, "to develop self-government, to take due account of the political aspirations of the peoples, and to assist them in the progressive development of their free political institutions, according to the particular circumstances of each territory and its peoples and their various stages of advancement."

The principle of trusteeship, as enunciated in the Charter of the United Nations, places the conception of the relationship of Colonial Powers to their subject peoples on an entirely new plane in what might be called the public law of the world. The United Nations for this purpose has established a Trusteeship Council, which was the last of its main organs to be constituted and did not hold its first meeting until April, 1947. But to realise this principle in practice mere machinery is not enough. In 1947 Soviet Russia refused to appoint a representative to the Trusteeship Council. On the other hand, Britain, France, Belgium, Australia, and New Zealand had already submitted to the United Nations trusteeship agreements for certain of their mandated territories. Perhaps the most interesting solution of a post-war problem in this sphere was in the case of Libya, a former Italian colony, which in 1951 became an independent kingdom. This was the first example of a state created by a decision of the United Nations. But in the long run the success or failure of the idea of trusteeship must depend more on the readiness of the Colonial Power to grant its backward peoples progressive rights towards the ultimate achievement of self-government than on the existence of an international body that can do little more than exert a moral influence and focus attention on this vital aspect of the well-being of mankind and the future of world peace.

READING

BOYD: *UNO Handbook*, pp. 41–2, Ch. vii.
BRYCE: *Modern Democracies*, Vol. II, Ch. lxxi.
DICEY: *Law of Constitution*, pp. 95–98.
HAYES: *Political and Social History of Modern Europe*, Vol. II, pp. 592–6.
JENKS: *Government of British Empire*, Ch. iv.
KEITH: *Constitution, Administration and Laws of the Empire*, Pt. ii, Chs. v–viii.
LOWELL: *Government of England*, Vol. II, Chs. lvi–lvii. *Greater European Governments*, pp. 87–96.
NEWTON: *Federal and Unified Constitutions*, pp. 263–9.
REED: *Form and Functions of American Government*, Ch. xxvi.
WILLIAMSON: *Short History of British Expansion*, pp. 574–615.
WILSON: *State*, pp. 262–5.

BOOKS FOR FURTHER STUDY

CARRINGTON: *British Overseas*.
KEITH: *Governments of the British Empire*.
MELLOR: *India Since Partition*.
Constitutions of All Countries, I, *British Empire*. (*For Government of India Act*, 1935.) *World Survey* and *Whitaker* (for Colonial *Constitutions*).

SUBJECTS FOR ESSAYS

1. Trace the rise of self-governing institutions in the states of eastern and south-eastern Europe during the second half of the nineteenth century, and suggest any lessons that can be learned from it.
2. How far do you consider Western constitutional methods of government adaptable to the countries of the Middle East?
3. Explain the nature of the former British Protectorate of Egypt and the constitutional position in that country following the Second World War.
4. Examine the attempts so far made to establish constitutional government in Japan and China, and discuss the problems facing these two countries in this connection since the Second World War.

5. Give some account of the legislation leading up to the Government of India Act of 1919 and show what measure of self-government was granted to the Indians by that Act.

6. How far is it true to say that the intention of the Government of India Act of 1935 was to give to British India the status of a Self-governing Dominion?

7. What are the constitutional difficulties to be overcome by the peoples of India and Pakistan now that they have become independent Republics, while remaining in membership of the British Commonwealth of Nations?

8. Distinguish, from the point of view of their government, between the various types of British Colonies.

9. Taking the growth of self-governing institutions in Ceylon as an example, discuss the prospects of other British Colonies achieving full Dominion Status, as Ghana (Gold Coast) did in 1957.

10. In what respect does the Trusteeship principle projected by the United Nations Organisation constitute an advance on the Mandate system under the League of Nations as a means of developing self-government among politically backward peoples?

CHAPTER XV

THE ECONOMIC ORGANISATION OF THE STATE

I. DEMOCRACY, POLITICAL AND ECONOMIC

So far we have discussed only the political organs of the constitutional state, but something remains to be said of its economic organisation which now plays such an important part in both national and international questions. It is not our intention here to go deeply into economic problems but merely to indicate what has been and what might be done in the constitutional state to establish a real economic democracy, by which we mean not only the attempt to control through political democracy the material conditions of life, but also the constitution of organs of economic control comparable to those already existing for political purposes. In so far as this is an extra-constitutional question—and in many respects it is by its nature bound to be so—it is beyond our province to discuss it here. But to the extent that it is either within, or capable of being brought into, the sphere of practical constitutional politics, it is necessary that we should examine it.

In the early days of the modern state the economic functions of government were fully recognised, and statesmen considered it their business to control society's economic activities, by means of laws and regulations, for the sake of national power. This condition of things was known as the Mercantile System, and it was founded on the belief that wealth consisted solely of money or precious metals whose possession meant national power. This view was universally accepted in Western Europe from the seventeenth century onward, and was the mainspring of almost all political action in those days. In external politics it was responsible for the European and Colonial wars which filled the eighteenth century, and in internal politics led to the building up of a mass of restrictions upon trade and industry with which the state was encumbered. Then, towards the end of the century, the grand attack upon it began in Adam Smith's *Wealth of Nations*. His argument that the individual was the best judge of his own economic interests found its counterpart in the political philosophy of the late eighteenth and early nineteenth century. The theorists of the American and French Revolutions and writers like Thomas Paine, Jeremy Bentham and William von Humboldt, in their different ways, assumed that government was a necessary evil. They therefore argued that its interference with the individual should be reduced to a minimum and that, in fact, its sole duty was to protect the individual from violence and fraud. They maintained that, government being merely a justice-dispensing institution, any economic activities on its part were entirely unjustified.

These theories seemed to be supported by the facts of the moment. In England the dissolving force of the Industrial Revolution, whose effects began to be seriously felt at the beginning of the nineteenth century, rendered all the state regulations obsolete, and, after a period of Tory reaction, occasioned by the Napoleonic War and its aftermath, an epoch of reform set in which swept them all away and inaugurated the policy of *Laissez-faire*, or non-interference of the state, in the economic activities of society. This epoch, broadly speaking, covered the years 1825–1870, a time which Dicey has called the "Period of Benthamite Individualism." This nineteenth-century individualism largely inspired the rapid development of that political constitutionalism which we have examined in these pages. But the practice of *Laissez-faire* led to such abysmal misery in this period that a new conception of the economic functions of the state at last dawned, and the conviction grew that governments should take a greater and greater share in ordering the economic welfare of society, which was now shown to be unable to take care of itself in such matters. Thus was ushered in that policy which is generally called Collectivism. This looks, at first sight, like a reaction to an earlier political practice, and the wheel might appear to have turned full circle. But the resemblance is more apparent than real; for not only was this new policy inspired by motives of humanitarianism, with which the Mercantile System certainly had nothing to do, but it continues to expand in an endeavour to save the state from disruption by forces (unknown to an earlier age) which consider political democracy in itself worthless, and deny its ability to achieve the true material interests of the mass of the people because by its nature it is already controlled by economic interests which it is hopeless to try to combat by means of the ballot box.

This policy of Collectivism, which means in essence the use of the coercive machinery of the state in the economic interests of the community, has resulted in a multiplication of the organs, because it has meant a great expansion of the functions, of government. Hence the establishment in every progressive state in the world to-day of new government departments like those we have in Britain, such as the Ministries of Agriculture, Labour, Health, Food, and Fuel and Power. Collectivism is now accepted as a principle of action, in a greater or less degree, by all political parties. The only question that divides the constitutionalists in this matter is how far the policy of collectivist action should be carried. What may be called the older political parties, while admitting the need for a certain amount of state action, remain individualist in their main tenets, and decline to accept the dogma that the state should assume the ownership of the means of production. The Socialists, on the other hand, believe that this should be done and that it is possible to do it without fundamentally changing the constitution of the state, as we know it. Furthermore, they assert that, if the constitutional state proves itself incapable of satisfying this economic demand which will be made upon it more and more insistently, it must give way before some other form of coercive social organisation.

The extreme form of the economic organisation of the state is found under the Communist régime in Russia and, though to a less extent, in the People's Republic of Yugoslavia, whose constitution of 1946 is, as we have seen, largely modelled on that of the U.S.S.R., as is also in some respects the constitution of the People's Republic of Czechoslovakia of 1948. Indeed, Lenin's original Soviet constitution was concerned more directly with the economic than with the political organisation of the state. But it was no less coercive. What the Russian revolution established, according to Lenin, was not socialism or democracy but a transitional state, maintained by the dictatorship of the proletariat, which would wither away as the purposes of the revolution were gradually accomplished. Ultimately, said Lenin, there was to be a classless society which would render any form of state unnecessary. But clearly that condition has not yet been reached, for, despite the Constitution of 1936, the authoritarian emphasis of Stalin's government is certainly no less marked than Lenin's.

II. ECONOMIC COUNCILS AND THE SOVIETS

A common factor of all Western constitutional states which we have discussed is that the territorial constituency is the basis of all their electoral systems. It is this that reformers have frequently pointed to as one of the weaknesses of political democracy, and many of them feel that the territorial constituency should be, if not supplanted, at least supplemented by a functional or occupational one. Under such a system an elector would vote in the trade or profession in which he works instead of, as now, the district in which he lives, thereby securing such a representation of economic interests as a mere division into areas can never hope to achieve. One way which suggests itself of achieving this end is by means of a reformed Second Chamber which might be made to represent this side of a nation's activities, drawing its members from occupational constituencies, while the Lower House continued, as at present, to be drawn from territorial divisions. As we have seen, the Senate in Eire under the Constitution of 1937, may contain representatives directly elected by any functional or vocational group or association, and a similar arrangement allowed for the election of five such Senators in Spain under the original Constitution of 1876, though naturally this did not appear in the Spanish Republican Constitution of 1932 which established a unicameral legislature, and is, in any case, now abolished by the Dictatorship.

Another way of achieving the same end is by means of Economic Councils such as were tried under the original constitution of the Irish Free State (1922) and in the Weimar Republic (1919), and of the type that is set up under the constitution of the Fourth Republic in France.

Article 45 of the Constitution of the Irish Free State stated that Parliament

" may provide for the establishment of Functional or Vocational Councils representing branches of the social and economic life of the nation. A law establishing any such Council shall determine its powers, rights, and duties, and its relation to the government of the Irish Free State."

The Weimar Constitution went farther. In Article 165 it stated:

"For the protection of their social and economic interests, workers and salaried employees shall have legal representation in Workers' Councils for individual undertakings and in District Workers' Councils grouped according to economic districts and in a Workers' Council of the Reich.

"The District Workers' Council and the Workers' Council of the Reich shall combine with representatives of the employers and other classes of the population concerned so as to form District Economic Councils and an Economic Council of the Reich for the discharge of their joint economic functions and for co-operation in the carrying-out of laws relating to socialisation. The District Economic Councils and the Economic Council of the Reich shall be so constituted as to give representation thereon to all important vocational groups in proportion to their economic and social importance.

"All Bills of fundamental importance dealing with matters of social and economic legislation shall, before being introduced, be submitted by the Government of the Reich to the Economic Council of the Reich for its opinion thereon. The Economic Council of the Reich shall have the right itself to propose such legislation. Should the Government of the Reich not agree with any such proposal, it must nevertheless introduce it in the Reichstag, accompanied by a statement of its own views thereon. The Economic Council of the Reich may arrange for one of its own members to advocate the proposal of the Reichstag.

"Powers of control and administration in any matters falling within their province may be conferred upon Workers' Councils and Economic Councils.

"The Constitution and functions of the Workers' and Economic Councils and their relations with other autonomous social organisations are within the exclusive jurisdiction of the Reich."

In Ireland the plan was abandoned in the Constitution of 1937. In Germany the Economic Councils seemed to be making some headway before Hitler destroyed them with the rest of the Weimar Constitution. What place the Economic Council is to have in French political life is yet to be seen.

Article 25 of the Constitution of the French Fourth Republic (1946) says:

"The Economic Council, whose status is fixed by law, examines, in an advisory capacity, the projects and proposals of laws which are within its province. These projects are submitted to it by the National Assembly before the latter debates them.

"In addition, the Economic Council may be consulted by the Council of Ministers. It must be consulted on the establishment of a national economic plan, the object of which is the full employment of men and the rational use of material resources."

Such councils, it must be understood, are something quite different from bodies like the Chamber of Commerce in England and the National Association of Manufacturers in America, which have become merely trade-protecting societies, and which, far from combining with the government for their common advantage, are chiefly concerned with preventing government enterprise. In Germany, the Economic Council of the Reich was called by one authority "a Parliament of Industry," and the question seriously arises whether such a Parliament of Industry can be given any sovereign powers, and, if not, whether it can be really effective. The German plan was described as a "parastatal" system, by which term was meant a régime of two equal forces within the state—one political, the other economic. This recalls the plan suggested by the Guild-Socialists in England during the decade preceding the First World War. This was a variant of the Syndicalist proposals, but, whereas Syndicalism demanded the complete abolition of political organs, Guild-Socialism proposed to retain the state, as we know it, for all non-economic purposes. The organs of economic government, however, were, according to this school of thought, of such prime importance that they must be not subordinate to but co-ordinate with those of political life. In other words, there must be two Parliaments with equal power, one guarding society's political interests, the other its economic welfare.

Here, then, is raised the whole question whether it is possible thus to divide the sovereignty of the state. One writer categorically asserts that there is no *via media* between State-Socialism and Syndicalism, meaning that sovereignty, being indivisible, must work its will either through Parliament as a political organ, which will brook no interference from economic associations,[1] except in so far as it freely accepts them, or else through a Parliament of Industry with absolute powers, which is the essence of Syndicalism. The same question arises also in

---

[1] This was the point at issue between the Government and the Trade Unions in England in the General Strike of 1926.

the case of two Chambers, one political, the other economic. Could they, that is to say, be truly co-ordinate bodies? The point, then, is whether the constitutional state can voluntarily share its sovereignty with a co-equal force, and whether, if it submits to violence, it can be said to exist any longer. Violence was not lacking even in the doctrine of the Guild-Socialists (an otherwise very pacific body of citizens), but only for the purpose of setting their programme to work. A general strike, they argued, would force the state to take over the ownership of the means of production which it would then hire out at a rent to the appropriate guilds or unions. The latter would, thereafter, control everything economic (wages, prices, conditions of labour, etc.) connected with their own trades.

The scheme which appeared in the Weimar Constitution arrived in a rather different way. There was violence, indeed, but it arose fortuitously, so to speak, out of the circumstances attending the end of the First World War. In the German Revolution of 1918, Councils of Soldiers and Workers were set up and for a moment very nearly succeeded in overthrowing the parallel political revolution. The latter, however, was destined to prevail, and evolved the Republican Constitution whose various aspects we have examined. Yet the Councils proved sufficiently influential to bring Article 165 into the German Constitution, though, as the last paragraph of that Article shows, they were completely within the jurisdiction of the political authority.

In Russia, on the other hand, through the Bolshevik Revolution of 1917, although similar parallel régimes existed for a time, each struggling for supremacy, the leaders of the Workers' Councils, or Soviets, did succeed in overwhelming the ordinary political organs. In the Constituent Assembly of January, 1918, which had been elected to promulgate a new political constitution, the Bolshevists moved that "Russia is a republic of Soviets," and when this was heavily defeated, Lenin, by means of a *coup d'état*, dissolved the Assembly, on the ground that it was "too bourgeois." Since that moment the Communists have remained supreme in Russia without any fundamental change in their outlook on the economic organisation of the state. It is true that, as we have seen, the Constitution of 1936 reveals certain Western influences, particularly in the language of the

Articles dealing with the federal structure. But, according to the Stalin Constitution, it is still true also that the U.S.S.R. is "a Socialist State of Workers and Peasants" (Article 1), that its political foundation is "formed by the soviets of toilers' deputies which have grown and become strong as a result of the overthrow of the power of the landlords and capitalists, and the conquest of the dictatorship of the proletariat" (Article 2), and that "all power belongs to the toilers of the town and village in the form of soviets of toilers' deputies" (Article 3). Certainly Stalin had modified the original conception to the extent of his adoption of the policy of "socialism in one country," as against the opposite theory of "continuous revolution," to which the Trotskyists clung after Lenin's death and which Stalin publicly declared to be "incompatible with Bolshevism." But since then Communist Russia's power to influence the political and economic organisation of neighbouring nations has been vastly strengthened, in a way which the founders of the socialist state could never have foreseen, by her triumph in the Second World War. Heavy though the price of victory was that Russia paid in lives, property and resources, she now, for good or evil, dominates the states of Eastern Europe, which, in their need to use the political machine as the means of economic reconstruction, are thus torn between the differing methods of Western constitutionalism and Soviet totalitarianism.

III. THE CORPORATE STATE

There remains one further type of politico-economic organisation for us to examine. This is the experiment of the Corporate State as devised by Mussolini in Fascist Italy and by Antonio de Salazar in Portugal. Mussolini's plan, though it fell with him and no element of it is revived in the Constitution of the Italian Republic of 1947, had points of considerable interest which, in spite of his anti-democratic motives in formulating it, are not unworthy of study by democrats. The Corporate State was based on what Mussolini called National Syndicalism, and there is no doubt that the Dictator's earlier association with syndicalism, in the days before his rise to political power, was largely responsible for this conception, though what he was concerned to establish was not self-government in industry, as the syndicalists desired, but national control of industry.

The practical origins of the scheme went back to 1924, when a special Commission was appointed to explore its possibilities. In its report the Commission reviewed the methods used in other states for dealing with the industrial problem: trade unionism in Britain, the trust in the United States, the Marxist theory as applied in Russian Communism, the Economic Councils established in Germany under the constitution of the Weimar Republic, and Liberal Democracy. The defect common to all of them, according to this report, was that they tended to weaken the supremacy of the state, a tendency which the new Corporate State must at all costs avoid. The old Italian Syndicalists, the argument ran, aimed exclusively at safeguarding and advancing the interests of the proletariat, while capital, manual labour and intellectual labour had always regarded themselves as separate and mutually antagonistic entities, outside, if not indeed above, the state. National Fascist Syndicalism would end this opposition by subordinating all three sections equally to the national interest. But it was not pretended that the state was capable of taking over production. Capitalism and private initiative were to remain, as necessary to the economic progress of society, but its rights and liberties must be made consistent with the supremacy of the state.

On the basis of the report a new Syndical or Trades Union Law was passed and came into force in April, 1926. This was followed by a decree of July, 1926, which filled in the details of the new Act. Finally, in April, 1927, a Labour Charter was published. The law was divided into three parts. The first arranged for the constitution and control of syndicates or unions of three sorts: of the employers, of the manual workers, and of the intellectual workers. Six national confederations of employers, six of employees, and one of the professional classes were to be set up, each of the thirteen under a general council and all three collateral structures under the control of a new Ministry of Corporations. No citizen was forced to join a syndicate, but he had to pay the annual contribution—one day's pay—whether a member or not, and, as no worker would have any protection except through his appropriate official guild, it followed that all non-official unions would die of inanition. The second part of the Act established special courts, known as the Magistracy of

Labour, to which recourse in the case of all disputes was obligatory. The third part of the Act prohibited all strikes and lock-outs, under pain of the most rigorous penalties for its breach.

The Decree of July, 1926, stated that any person over the age of eighteen might join a syndicate "if of good moral and political conduct": a plain indication of the intention of the authorities to secure that all young workers were good Fascists. On the day after the publication of the Decree the new Ministry of Corporations was set up. The Charter of Labour, issued in April, 1927, was, it seemed, to be the very bible of the Fascist Corporate State. The purpose of labour, it said, "may be summed up as the well-being of the producers and the development of the national strength." "Professional or syndical organisation," it added, "is free, but the recognised syndicate alone, under the control of the state, has the right of legally representing the employers and employed, of stipulating for collective labour contracts for all belonging to its category, and of imposing contributions on them."

By 1927, then, the foundations of the new economic structure seemed well and truly laid. It remained to build the superstructure. For the moment the Chamber of Deputies was permitted to remain but in a yet more emasculated form than that to which it had already been reduced by the electoral law of 1924, which had made the whole country one vast constituency and had laid down that any party gaining a majority in the election, however small, should take two-thirds of the seats. By a new law of 1928, designed to bring the Chamber into line with the new economic set-up, deputies were to be drawn exclusively from the syndicates. Under the procedure laid down in this law the general councils of the thirteen National Syndicates met in Rome and nominated a list of 800, which was reduced to 400 by the Fascist Grand Council. Then the whole list of 400 was submitted to the country for a simple yes or no to the question on the ballot paper: "Do you approve the list of deputies designated by the National Grand Council of Fascism?" In view of the art and craft employed to secure it, one is not surprised that in the election of 1929 the official list received an overwhelming majority.

Things remained in this state for the next four years while

the syndicates were being established and tried out. Then in
1933 Mussolini announced that, the syndical phase having been
accomplished, the corporate phase might now be entered upon.
This meant that the time had come for the establishment of the
national connecting-links between the syndicates of employers
and the syndicates of employees set up under the law of 1926.
These were called Corporations, and were to be composed of an
equal number of employers and employees in twenty-two
nation-wide economic activities: eight for agriculture, eight for
industry and commerce, and six for various services, such as
transport, and the professions. The Corporation was to cover
all concerned in the cycle of production in any given under-
taking: employing and employed, producers of raw materials,
masters and workers in the processing industries, traders in the
finished product, and technical and scientific experts. The
Councils of the twenty-two Corporations were solemnly installed
by Mussolini in November, 1934.

The final step in the process of creating the Corporate State
was taken in 1939, when the Chamber of Deputies was abolished
and replaced by the Chamber of Fascios and Corporations,
which was opened by the King. It had 682 members, called
National Counsellors. Rather more than two-thirds of the
members were delegates of the Corporations, generally leading
officials of the syndicates. The remainder were officials of the
Fascist Party. There was no sort of election to the Chamber,
most of the members being there *ex-officio*, though they all had
to be approved by the *Duce*. The Chamber of Fascios and
Corporations bore the same relation to the Senate as the former
Chamber of Deputies. The Senate was still, as under the original
constitution, made up of nominees of the Crown, but the King
had "obligingly swamped it with Fascists." There was no
longer any pretence of legislative power left to the Chambers.
The function of the new Chamber was purely advisory, and
whether any measure to which it gave consideration should go
to the King for signature was a matter entirely for the decision
of the *Duce*, whose powers were not in the least diminished, for
he was in no way responsible to the new Chamber.

There was little chance to judge of the success or failure of
Mussolini's Corporate State, for in the very year in which it was
finally launched Italy, like the rest of Europe, was caught in

II

the toils of Hitler's war. But certainly it can be said that it did nothing to save Italy from her débâcle. The Corporate State was hailed as an original panacea for correcting the disorders of an effete democracy and as an inspiration to the democratic states of the world for the remodelling of their institutions. These trumpetings were far from justified, but the plan certainly had some constructive features. The weakness of political democracy, as we have known it in the West, is that it leaves the economic structure of society very largely to its own devices, and even where economic planning is undertaken on a large scale, as, for example, in Britain after the Second World War, it has used the existing political organs. The virtue of Mussolini's scheme was that it at least brought the representation of economic interests into the national assembly. It is true that the Chamber of Fascios and Corporations was denied any real legislative power, but such denial of authority to a Chamber elected on the basis of occupational interests rather than in territorial constituencies is obviously not essential to it. In some such Chamber with real powers might conceivably be found a *via media* between the Soviet organisation, with its almost purely economic emphasis, and the Parliamentary system which entirely neglects economic representation.

If the Corporate State is dead in Italy, it is still alive in Portugal, where it is also associated with a form of dictatorship, as evolved by Dr. Salazar. In Portugal the Republic was instituted in 1910, when an armed rising drove the Royal Family into exile. Under the Constitution of 1933 there is a President elected for seven years and a Prime Minister and Cabinet responsible to a legislature of a single chamber (the National Assembly) of 90 members elected by the head of each family, whether man or woman. There is, besides, a Corporative Chamber consisting of representatives of local authorities and industrial, commercial and other corporations, including organisations of employers and employees. This body is not strictly a Second Chamber, because it has no legislative power, but, under the constitution, all bills must be submitted to it for its opinion before the National Assembly can give a final vote on them.

In practice the parliamentary candidates are exclusively those put forward by the Government party, and in the long recesses between the meetings of the National Assembly the Government legislates by decree. In Portugal, Dr. Salazar, who became Prime Minister in 1928, holds undisputed sway. The theory of Salazar's Corporative State has been described as an attempt to find a middle way between Marxist Communism and Liberal Democracy by means of vocational groups under the general supervision of the Government. Strikes and lock-outs are prohibited, but, on the other hand, the Portuguese have been given labour laws, under the Statute of Labour, which they never enjoyed before. In other words, trade unionism and collective bargaining have been introduced but under a dicta-torial régime which, however enlightened it may be, the workers in most Western European states would not tolerate.

READING

BRYCE: *Modern Democracies*, Vol. II, Chs. lxxviii–lxxix.
DURNS: *Political Ideals*, Chs. x and xi.
DICEY: *Law and Opinion*, Introduction and Lectures iii–iv.
DUNNING: *Political Theories*, Vol. IV, Chs. ii, iii, vi.
FINER: *Modern Government*, Vol. I, Ch. ii.
JENKS: *State and Nation*, Ch. xvi.
LASKI: *Grammar of Politics*, Pt. I, Ch. vii; Pt. II, Ch. ix.
MACIVER: *Modern State*, Ch. ix.
SIDGWICK: *Elements of Politics*, Chs. iv, v, xxviii.
The Annual Register, 1927 and 1939 (for Mussolini's Corporate State).
Whitaker's Almanack for 1947 (for details of Corporative State in Portugal).

BOOKS FOR FURTHER STUDY

CARR: *The New Society.*
COLE: (1) *Guild Socialism Restated.* (2) *Social Theory.*
FINER: *Representative Government and a Parliament of Industry.*
HOLLIS: *Can Parliament Survive?*
LASKI: (1) *Foundations of Sovereignty.* (2) *Communism.*
LIDDERDALE: *Parliament of France.*
RUSSELL: (1) *Prospects of Industrial Civilisation.* (2) *Roads to Freedom.*
WEBB: (1) *Industrial Democracy.* (2) *Soviet Communism.*

SUBJECTS FOR ESSAYS

1. Examine the statement that political democracy by itself is worthless.
2. Account for the growth of modern Collectivism and explain the circum-stances in which it gradually replaced the policy of *Laissez-faire*.
3. Suggest ways in which Second Chambers might be made to represent economic interests in the modern state.
4. Explain the proposals in the German Constitution of 1919 for establishing economic councils, and compare them with those in the Constitution of the Irish Free State of 1922 and in that of the Fourth French Republic (1946).
5. How far is it true to say that the Russian Revolution has achieved an economic democracy?

6. "There is no *via media* between State Socialism and Syndicalism." Discuss this statement in reference to the proposals of Guild Socialists for the establishment of a Parliament of Industry having co-ordinate powers with those of the political Parliament.

7. Discuss the scheme of the Corporate State as conceived by Mussolini and suggest any lessons that democrats may learn from it.

8. Describe the position of Salazar and his corporative system in Portugal.

9. Do you consider it possible to replace the territorial constituency, as it exists in most constitutional states to-day, by an occupational one?

10. Compare the prospects of the economic reorganisation of Europe after the Second World War through the methods of Parliamentary constitutionalism with those by way of the Soviet system.

CHAPTER XVI

THE CHARTER OF THE UNITED NATIONS

I. PROJECTS OF INTERNATIONALISM

WHEN we consider the external relations of states we touch the most vital aspect of contemporary political organisation. Clearly, it is idle for any nation under modern conditions to attempt to work out the means of its own welfare without regard to its intercourse with other nations. For not only are states to-day economically interdependent but at any moment a conflict between them may in a flash place the whole of their internal political machinery in jeopardy, and, as recent events have shown, bring it crashing down in ruins. It is, therefore, ultimately on a solution of the problem of international relations that the future well-being of every nation depends. Hence, a study of the methods proposed or adopted for regulating the external relations of states arises naturally out of a study of their internal political constitutions.

President Wilson, in his message to the Provisional Government of Russia in May, 1917, expressed the hope that, as a result of the war then raging, the brotherhood of mankind might cease to be a fair but empty phrase and be given a structure of force and reality. In January, 1918, Wilson issued his Fourteen Points. The Fourteenth Point demanded the creation of a League of Nations, an attempt to embody the ideal of international peace in a set of permanent organs; in short, a political constitution designed to adjust the relations between states comparable to those constitutions we have here examined which define the relations between the government and the governed within a single state. The failure of the League experiment led to the Second World War and so to another attempt to establish an international constitution; this time through the United Nations Organisation. But the United

Nations plan, like that of the League of Nations, is only a phase in an age-long evolution of projects of internationalism. The truth is that the ideal of unity and fellowship derives from two traditions at the very roots of Western Civilisation; the actual unity of the Roman Empire and the Christian message of "peace on earth, good will towards men." And so we find that some demand for the formulation of the means to prevent war has followed almost every major conflict since the modern system of states emerged. The general burden of such demands has always been that states ought to be subjected among themselves to a system of law and order analogous to that to which individual citizens are subjected in the smaller political units in which they live. At first such ideals did not get beyond the pages of the books of a few intellectuals, and there is a long succession of writers who have worked out paper-schemes for such ends: for example, Pierre Dubois as early as the fourteenth century, Erasmus in the sixteenth, Henry of Navarre in the seventeenth, the Abbé de St. Pierre, Rousseau and Kant in the eighteenth. The next stage, following the Napoleonic Wars, was much more closely in touch with reality, and, ceasing to be confined to a few idealists, practical schemes of international organisation passed under the control of dominant personalities and powers.

Thus it was that the Concert of Europe came into being. It began as a Christian Brotherhood of Monarchs, inspired by the Emperor of Russia, under the title of the Holy Alliance, but, confined as it was to three Powers—Austria, Russia, and Prussia—it soon degenerated into a mere engine of repression to crush the dawning Liberalism of the smaller states of Europe. But in the form in which it was strongly supported by the British Foreign Minister, Castlereagh, the Concert of Europe might have become much more effectual as a way of maintaining peace through a system of occasional conferences of the Great Powers. From this scheme, which lasted from 1814 to 1822, the British, however, were at length forced to withdraw, owing to the fact that Metternich was determined to use it for his despotic purposes, and with the Congress of Verona (1822) and the coming of Canning to the Foreign Office the Period of the Congresses, and with it the slender hope of some sort of Confederation of Europe, was at an end. Yet the Concert of Europe extended its life, though in a somewhat emaciated form, it is true, beyond this early period, and rallied from time to time to cope with such problems as the Eastern Question, especially in 1878. But it was too great a wreck to be revivified at the time when its activity was most urgently required, in the days of the breathless diplomatic struggle immediately preceding the outbreak of war in 1914.

Meanwhile, another attempt, again emanating from a Russian Tsar, had been made to secure the triumph of diplomacy over arms. This was by the establishment of the Hague Conferences. In 1899 the envoys of twenty-six states met at The Hague to discuss such questions as the limitation of armaments, the humanising of the laws of war, and the employment of mediation and arbitration by parties to international disputes. It concluded with three conventions which were solemnly ratified by all the greater Powers. The second Hague Conference, attended by the delegates of fifty-four states, met in 1907. It elaborated the legislation (if we may call it that) of the earlier Conference and produced a vast bulk of memoranda and agreements. The Hague Conferences, no doubt, were of use as pioneers, so to speak, of the movement that was to come, but their decisions lacked effectiveness, and amid the clash of arms their laws were silent. The Hague Conferences, in short, had no constitution. Moreover, they were struggling to build a Palace of Peace at just the time when diplomacy was putting its faith in another scheme, called the Balance of Power, which, in fact, since it was founded upon the baneful system of opposing alliances, made war at length inevitable.

The First World War, however, brought a third stage in the development of international projects. Whereas, in the first stage, efforts were confined to a few idealists, and, in the second, to prominent individuals, in this third period, following and owing to the war, the establishment of a real world-organisation became the aim of large numbers of the citizens of every advanced political community. During the second half of the war there was a positive fever to put forward schemes for the constitution of machinery for peace which should be more permanent and effective than any which had gone before. It thus became possible to establish such a machinery as an integral part of the peace.

II. THE LEAGUE OF NATIONS

The Covenant of the League of Nations had twenty-six Articles and was placed at the head of the Treaty of Versailles and the other treaties made between the victorious Allied Powers and Germany and her companions in defeat, so that every state signatory to the Treaty was bound to endorse the League. There were 27 original signatories to the Covenant, which came into force in January, 1920. In 1921, 48 states were members of the League, and from that time to the outbreak of the Second World War in 1939 the number of state members fluctuated with the admission of new ones and the withdrawal of old. Thus, for example, Germany was admitted in 1926, Turkey in 1932, the U.S.S.R. in 1934, and Egypt in 1937; while, on the other hand, Germany and Japan withdrew in 1933, Italy in 1937, Hungary and Russia (on the outbreak of the Russo-Finnish War) in 1939. The United States, in spite of Wilson's advocacy, declined to become a member, repudiating both the Treaty and the Covenant. Yet, despite America's refusal to join, the League, at one time or another, was concerned with the international welfare of fifty states, comprising about 75 per cent of the world's total population and covering about 65 per cent of the land area of the globe.

Article 1 of the Covenant stated the rules of membership. Any fully self-governing state or dominion might be admitted by the Assembly, provided that it gave the prescribed guarantees. Articles 2 to 7 and 14 dealt with the organs of the League, and, as they were all forerunners of those of the United Nations Organisation, it is useful to examine them in some detail. The four main organs were: the Assembly, the Council, the Secretariat, and the Permanent International Court of Justice. These organs corresponded, but only very broadly, to those we have earlier described as the three necessary departments of government: the legislature, the executive, and the judiciary. The Assembly was a sort of international Parliament, though it normally had only one brief session a year. The Council could hardly be compared with a Cabinet, though it had certain executive functions: it was rather a deliberate body, more easily convened than the Assembly. The Secretariat closely resembled the Civil Service of an individual state and was a permanent body of officers. The Permanent Court was as near an approximation to a state judiciary, at least on the side of civil law, as international law, actual or potential, allowed.

The Assembly consisted of not more than three representatives of every member state, though only one could vote on behalf of his state on any issue. It met at least once a year, for about three weeks (or more often as occasion might require). It could debate any matter within the sphere of the League affecting the peace of the world. The Council was made up of five permanent and nine non-permanent members (both numbers varied with the changing membership of the League), representing respectively the Great Powers and the smaller nations, the non-permanent members being elected for three years. The Council was to meet as occasion required, and in practice generally met four times a year. Its powers were similar to those of the Assembly, but actually, because it met more often and was more easily convened, it tended to debate in detail matters afterwards submitted to the Assembly.

The Secretariat was an entirely non-political body of salaried officers permanently employed at the seat of the League at Geneva. The members of the Secretariat, from the Secretary-General downwards, were not representatives of the state from which they came, but servants of the League. The Secretariat was divided into three main branches for purposes of administration: the General Secretariat, which included several Under-Secretaries-General for special missions; the Technical Sections, which dealt with such matters as information, transport and communications; the Administrative Departments, including finance, library and registry. The main functions of the Secretariat were to carry out investigations into matters of common interest to all civilised states, to build up records of a permanent character, and to prepare reports for submission to the Council and the Assembly.

The Permanent International Court of Justice was constituted in accordance with a direction given in Article 14 of the Covenant. Its constitution was laid down in a lengthy protocol to the Covenant, and it finally came into being in 1921. It consisted of a bench of eleven judges, five representing the Latin group of states, three representing the Germanic and Scandinavian group, two the Common Law group (Britain, the British

Dominions, and—if she joined—the United States), and one for Asia. By Article 13 of the Covenant the Court was competent only to determine disputes submitted to it, though it might arbitrate at the request of the parties. The Court had its permanent home, not at the headquarters of the League itself at Geneva, but at The Hague, the traditional seat of the Permanent Court set up by the old Hague Conference.

One other institution established as part of the framework of the League and working side by side with its other organs at Geneva was the International Labour Organisation (I.L.O.). The plan of such an international organisation grew out of the Labour Charter of Rights, which, like the Covenant of the League, had been made a corporate part of the Treaty of Versailles. For the first time in history a conference of envoys of national governments thus recognised the claims of labour throughout the world and the importance of the part it must play in any durable peace. As in the case of the Assembly of the League, the International Labour Conference met annually to frame proposals, which were afterwards submitted for consideration and approval by the states in membership of the League. Remote though it may have seemed from contact with the day-to-day problems of labour and industry within the various states, the I.L.O. did most valuable work in collating and distributing information on the economic side of the international problem. So alive, indeed, did it become that it survived the outbreak of the Second World War, and from 1940 the International Labour Conference met in America. Since the War it has been brought into relation with the United Nations Organisation and has returned to its original home in Geneva.

The great promise of the constitution of the League of Nations, as compared with any other practical plan for the maintenance of the peace of the world since the fall of the Roman Empire, lay in the fact that its organs were permanently established. For its makers realised that peace is not a mere negation, which exists between outbursts of international strife, but a positive attitude which has to be slowly and painstakingly built up among the nations of the world. The constitution of the League provided the machinery; it was for the nations to make it work.

In the first decade of its existence the League of Nations did invaluable work and reached a position of great prestige as an instrument of international conciliation and aid. In 1923 it settled a dispute between Italy and Greece, which otherwise might easily have led to war. In the same year it materially assisted in the financial restoration of Austria and of Hungary whose detachment from the rest of the old "Ramshackle Empire" and from each other the Treaties had enforced. Besides, in 1923 the League supervised the complicated task of settling in Greece refugees from Asia Minor under the terms of the Treaty of Lausanne. In 1925 it composed a frontier quarrel between Greece and Bulgaria. Over the same period also it carried out other obligations under the Treaties, such as the allotment and oversight of mandated territories which had formerly been German colonies, and the organisation and maintenance of international régimes, like that of the Free City of Danzig. Meanwhile, the Secretariat went rapidly forward with its work of collecting and collating information connected with the international aspects of such questions as labour and health, and the drafting of rules for the suppression or regulation of world-wide evils, like the White Slave Traffic and the marketing of pernicious drugs. The League, in short, became a storehouse of facts and a clearing-house of ideas about truly international affairs, and on this side of its work promised to be of the greatest benefit to Europe and the world at large.

The most disputed of the devices suggested for the prevention of war was contained in Article 16. It is so important as to be worth quoting in full:

"Should any member of the League resort to war in disregard of its covenants under Articles 12, 13 or 15, it shall *ipso facto* be deemed to have committed an act of war against all other members of the League which hereby undertake immediately to subject it to the severance of all trade or financial relations, the prohibition of all intercourse between persons residing in their territory and persons residing in the territory of the covenant-breaking State, and the prevention of all financial, commercial or personal inter-course between persons residing in the territory of the Covenant-breaking State and persons residing in the territory of any other State whether a member of the League or not.

"It is for the Council to give an opinion whether or not a breach of the Covenant has taken place. In deliberations on this question in the Council, the votes of members of the League alleged to have resorted to war and of members against whom such action was directed shall not be counted.

"The Council will notify to all members of the League the date which it recommends for the application of the economic pressure under this Article.

"Nevertheless, the Council may, in the case of particular members, postpone the coming into force of any of these measures for a specified period where it is satisfied that such a postponement will facilitate the attainment of the object of the measures referred to in the preceding paragraph, or that it is necessary in order to minimise the loss and inconvenience which will be caused to such members."[1]

The acid test of the League's sincerity of purpose and reality of power was bound to come as soon as it was called upon to protect one of its members against aggressive action by another. It failed abjectly in the two principal tests of this kind that were made upon it. The first was in 1931 when the Japanese seized the Chinese province of Manchuria, both Japan and China being members of the League. China appealed in vain for the help of the League against the aggressor, who escaped with his ill-gotten gains. The second was in 1935, when Mussolini invaded Abyssinia. Not only were both states members of the League, but Italy had actually sponsored Abyssinia's admission. The League responded to Abyssinia's appeal and declared Italy the aggressor, but utterly failed in its attempt to impose economic sanctions under Article 16. The League never recovered from the loss of prestige which it suffered through Italy's unpunished rape of Ethiopia. After it, some attempts were made to reform the Covenant, but the solemn resolutions passed in this connection could have little more than an academic interest in the face of the stark realities of the international situation which then rapidly deteriorated until total war broke out again in 1939.

The reasons for the decline and eclipse of the League and the system of collective security which it had worked so painstakingly to build up are not far to seek. From its foundation it suffered the insuperable handicap of the absence from its membership of the United States, without whose contribution it could never be truly effective. With the defection of the three Great Powers of Japan, Germany and Italy, notwithstanding the entry of Russia meanwhile, the League became a mere

[1] The Text given above is as amended by the Council and Assembly in 1922.

truncation of its original self; in fact, an association of nations standing for peace against an alliance of nations bent on war. The League had no money-raising power and had to live on the contributions of its state members. It disposed of no armed forces, but depended on the will of its members to carry out their solemn undertakings. Its law, in the last analysis, had only moral authority to back it, and as soon as important states were determined and ready to risk flouting that authority, the plan broke down. In other words, the League lacked sovereign power, which remained undiminished in the hands of each state member of it.

III. THE ORGANS OF THE UNITED NATIONS

The United Nations began as a fighting alliance in the Second World War. The term "United Nations" was first officially used in an international agreement, the Joint Declaration by the United Nations, signed at Washington in January, 1942, by 26 nations allied in the war. The signatories to the Washington Declaration agreed to subscribe to the common declaration of purposes and principles contained in the Atlantic Charter which the American President and the British Prime Minister had issued after their meeting at sea in the previous August. The Atlantic Charter contained eight points, and declared that the United States and Britain sought no aggrandisement, desired to see no territorial changes which did not accord with the wishes of the people concerned, respected the rights of all peoples to choose their own form of government, would do their utmost to secure the access on equal terms of all peoples to the trade and raw materials of the world, would aim at securing improved labour standards throughout the world, seek a peace, after the destruction of the Nazi tyranny, which should secure for all nations the hope of living in peace and security and for all men the right to traverse the seas without hindrance, and would do all in their power to achieve at last the abandonment of the use of force and the abolition of aggression as a means of settling international disputes.

The Washington Declaration was followed up at a Conference in Moscow in October, 1943, when representatives of Russia, the United States, Britain, and China signed a convention known as the Moscow Declaration. Article 4 of this Declaration stated that the "four Powers recognise the necessity of establishing at the earliest practical date a general international organisation, based on the principle of the sovereign equality of all peace-loving states, and open to membership by all such states, for the maintenance of international peace and security." About a year later, in November, 1944, the actual framework of the proposed organisation was informally laid down by representatives of the same four Powers at a conference held at Dumbarton Oaks in the United States, where it was agreed that the proposals should be cast in the form of a treaty, to be known as the Charter, and that the organisation should be called the United Nations. The principles enunciated at Dumbarton Oaks were endorsed, with some modifications, at the Stalin-Roosevelt-Churchill meeting at Yalta in the Crimea in February, 1945, and finally formulated, without any radical alteration of the basic design, in a Charter signed by the representatives of fifty nations sitting in conference at San Francisco from April to June in the same year.

The Charter of the United Nations, which was published on 27th June, 1945, is a lengthy document with a Preamble and 111 Articles contained in 19 Chapters. The Preamble is as follows:

We, the people of the United Nations, determined to save succeeding generations from the scourge of war, which twice in our lifetime has brought untold sorrow to mankind, and

to reaffirm faith in fundamental human rights, in the dignity and worth of the human person, in the equal rights of men and women and of nations large and small, and

to establish conditions under which justice and respect for the obligations arising from treaties and other sources of international law can be maintained, and

to promote social progress and better standards of life in larger freedom, and for these ends,

to practise tolerance and live together in peace with one another as good neighbours, and

to unite our strength to maintain international peace and security, and

to secure by the acceptance of principles and the institution of methods, that armed force shall not be used, save in the common interest, and

to employ international machinery for the promotion of the economic and social advancement of all peoples, have resolved to combine our efforts to accomplish these aims.

Accordingly, our respective Governments, through representatives assembled in the City of San Francisco, who have exhibited their full powers found to be in good and due form, have agreed to the present Charter of the United Nations and do hereby establish an international organisation to be known as the United Nations.

Article 1 states the four purposes of the Organisation, which are: to maintain international peace and security through effective collective measures; to develop friendly relations among nations based on respect for the principle of equal rights and self-determination of peoples; to achieve international co-operation in solving international problems of an economic, social, cultural, or humanitarian character; and to be a centre for harmonising the actions of nations in the attainment of these common ends.

Article 2 states that the Organisation is based on the principle of the sovereign equality of all its members and that nothing in the Charter shall authorise the United Nations to intervene in matters which are essentially within the jurisdiction of any state, except where enforcement measures (described in Chapter VII of the Charter) are necessary in the interests of peace. In pursuit of these purposes there are to be established six principal organs: (i) the General Assembly, (ii) the Security Council, (iii) the Economic and Social Council, (iv) the Trusteeship Council, (v) the International Court of Justice, and (vi) the Secretariat.

What this set-up owes to the earlier organisation of the League of Nations is evident. For, as we have seen, the League had an Assembly, a Council, an International Court, and a Secretariat. The organs of the United Nations not found among those of the League are the Economic and Social Council and the Trusteeship Council, though even these are, in a sense, elaborations of special bodies which the League either sponsored or evolved; namely, the International Labour Organisation (though this still exists for special purposes side by side with the new Council whose functions are much broader) and the special Commission on Mandates.

(i) *The General Assembly.* The General Assembly, whose composition and functions are fully stated in Articles 9-22 of the Charter, is similar in powers, though not in composition, to the Assembly of the League. Any member state may send up to five representatives, but only one may vote. On important questions a decision of the General Assembly requires a two-thirds majority of the members present and voting; on less important matters only a simple majority. The Assembly meets annually, though special sessions may be convoked at the request either of the Security Council or of a majority of member states. Like the old Assembly of the League, the General Assembly may discuss any question relating to the maintenance of peace and security brought before it by the Council or any state, whether a member or not. The Assembly may consider any question relating to armaments and the promotion of co-operation for any international purpose. It controls the work of both the Economic and Social Council and the Trusteeship Council, receives annual reports from the Security Council, and approves the budget of the Organisation.

(ii) *The Security Council.* Though the Security Council (Articles 23–54) derives from the Council of the old League, it has much wider scope and larger powers than its forerunner. It consists of eleven members. Five of them—Britain, the United States, the U.S.S.R., France, and China—are permanent. The remaining six are elected by the General Assembly for terms of two years, three retiring every year and being ineligible for immediate re-election. Each state member may have only one representative and only one vote. Any decision of the Security Council requires an affirmative vote of at least seven out of eleven, but on all but procedural matters the seven affirmative votes must include the concurring votes of the five permanent members, though any party to a dispute must not take part in the voting on decisions concerning that dispute. This restrictive clause concerning non-procedural matters means, in effect, that, while a permanent member may not veto discussion by the Security Council of any dispute threatening international peace, the veto applies to all subsequent stages of the discussion: investigation of the dispute, recommendation of enforcement action by the Council, and the actual application of force.

The Charter confers on the Security Council the responsibility to deal with any dispute "likely to endanger the maintenance of international peace and security", and member states undertake to accept and execute the Council's decisions reached in accordance with the Charter. The Security Council may call upon the United Nations to take measures to this end, and special agreements will be entered into among the members of the Organisation indicating the forces which they will place at the disposal of the Council to carry out its intentions.

The essence of the plan may thus be said to be "organised defence and concerted activity," and the measures proposed to secure this aim are what constitute the fundamental differences between the new plan of the United Nations and the old plan of the League of Nations. In this vital work the Security Council is to be assisted by a Military Staffs Committee composed of the chiefs-of-staff of the Great Powers. This body must give technical advice as to the size and nature of the quotas of military, naval and air forces which each member-nation will contribute to the common pool. But the problem for the new world Organisation is not only how it shall ensure the possession of sufficient armed power to enforce its will on recalcitrant nations but also how that power shall be disposed so as to be in a position to operate immediately and effectively wherever danger threatens. To meet this double need the scheme envisages not only a world-wide organisation but within it also associations for regional defence, and, going with this regionalisation, a continuous chain of bases under the common control throughout the world.

(iii) *The Economic and Social Council.* Articles 61–74 deal with the form and functions of the Economic and Social Council. It is elected by the General Assembly and consists of eighteen member states, each with one vote. Six members are elected every year to serve for three years, though in this case retiring members may be re-elected immediately. The decisions of the Council are taken by a simple majority of those present and voting. The Council may meet whenever necessary or on the request of a majority of its members. The functions of the Council are large and complex. It must study and report to the General Assembly on all economic, social, cultural and educational questions, as well as health and related matters connected with the United Nations all over the world. It has the right to call international conferences and to undertake special enquiries asked for by member states, with the approval of the General Assembly.

There are few international questions, outside politics and

arms, with which the Economic and Social Council will not be either directly or indirectly concerned. So true is this that the Charter empowers the Council, with the approval of the Assembly, to make agreements with other international agencies already set up by various conventions for economic and social purposes and closely associated with the activities of the United Nations Organisation. These so-called Specialised Agencies include the World Health Organisation (WHO), the United Nations Educational, Scientific and Cultural Organisation (UNESCO), and the International Labour Organisation (ILO). The object of such agreements is to co-ordinate the work of the various agencies working in this vast post-war field. And, finally, so that the humanitarian scope of the Economic and Social Council may be unrestricted, it may invite representatives of any state member of the United Nations or of any of the Specialised Agencies already mentioned, to participate, without vote, in its deliberations, or, alternatively, appoint representatives to participate in the deliberations of any of those Specialised Agencies.

(iv) *The Trusteeship Council.* The Trusteeship Council (Articles 75–91) consists of five permanent members of the Security Council, those member states administering Trust Territories, and as many member states elected for three-year terms by the General Assembly as may be necessary to ensure that the total number of members of the Council is equally divided between those members of the United Nations which administer Trust Territories and those which do not. Each member state must designate one specially qualified person to represent it on the Council. Each member of the Council has one vote, and decisions will be reached by a simple majority of those present and voting. The Council shall meet as required and must be convened on a request from the majority of its members.

The Trusteeship Council is concerned with non-self-governing territories, and these may be territories held under former League of Nations Mandate, or territories detached from enemy states as a result of the Second World War, or territories voluntarily placed under the system by states responsible for their administration. As we saw earlier, member states responsible for such territories must recognise the interests of the inhabitants as paramount and accept the obligation to promote their well-being to the utmost. The basic objectives of a trusteeship system are to further international peace and security; to promote the political, economic, social and educational advancement of the inhabitants of the Trust Territories and their progressive development towards self-government or independence; to encourage respect for human rights and for fundamental freedoms for all, without distinction as to race, sex, language, or religion; and to ensure equal treatment in social, economic and commercial matters for all members of the United Nations and their nationals. The administering authority of a Trust Territory must submit an annual report to the General Assembly, which, through the Trusteeship Council, may arrange for periodical visits to Trust Territories or for the reception of petitions from such territories.

(v) *The International Court of Justice.* The International Court of Justice (Articles 92–96) is the principal judicial organ of the United Nations. It is to function in accordance with a Statute, which is based on that of the Permanent Court under the League of Nations and forms an integral part of the Charter of the United Nations. But non-member states may become parties to the Statute with the approval of the General Assembly on the recommendation of the Security Council. Each member of the United Nations undertakes to comply with the decision of the Court in any case to which it is a party, and, if it fails to do so, the Security Council may take appropriate measures to enforce the judgment. But nothing in the Charter requires member states to use the Court or precludes them from entrusting their differences to other tribunals already in existence or to be set up in the future. The General Assembly, or the Security Council, or the other organs of the United Nations, or any Specialised Agencies may request the Court to give an advisory opinion on any legal question within the ambit of the activities of these bodies.

(vi) *The Secretariat.* The composition and duties of the Secretariat are laid down in Articles 97–101 of the Charter. The chief administrative officer of the Organisation, as under the League, is the Secretary-General, appointed by the General Assembly on the recommendation of the Security Council. The Secretary-General acts in that capacity at all meetings of the General Assembly, the Security Council, the Economic and

Social Council, and the Trusteeship Council, and must make an annual report to the General Assembly on the work of the whole Organisation. He may bring to the notice of the Security Council any matter which, in his opinion, may threaten the maintenance of peace and security. The Secretary-General and his staff are international officials, responsible to the Organisation, and may not seek or receive instructions from any authority external to it. Each state member undertakes to respect the exclusively international character of the Secretariat. The Secretary-General appoints his staff under the regulations of the General Assembly, the objects of which are to secure the highest standards of efficiency and integrity, and to recruit on as wide a geographical basis as possible.

Such, then, are the organs of the United Nations as constituted by the Charter. Their constitution cannot be changed except by due process of amendment, the conditions of which are laid down in Articles 108 and 109 of the Charter. Amendments to the Charter shall come into force for all members when they have been adopted by a vote of two-thirds of the members of the General Assembly and ratified, in accordance with their respective constitutional processes, by two-thirds of the member-states of the United Nations, including *all* permanent members of the Security Council. For the purpose of reviewing the Charter a General Conference of the United Nations may be held at a date and place to be fixed by a two-thirds vote of the members of the General Assembly and by a vote of any seven members of the Security Council. At such a Conference each member-state shall have one vote. But, so that the Charter may not become too set and out of step with changing circumstances, it is specifically laid down that, if no such General Conference has been held before the tenth annual meeting of the General Assembly following the coming into force of the Charter, the proposal to call such a conference must be placed on the Agenda of that session of the General Assembly, and the conference must be held if so decided by a majority vote of the members of the Assembly and by a vote of seven members of the Security Council.

IV. THE UNITED NATIONS ORGANISATION AT WORK

In spite of the complex international problems by which the world was beset in the diplomatic confusion following the end of the Second World War in 1945, the United Nations Organisation was formed and working within a few months of the close of hostilities. The General Assembly held its first session in London in January and February, 1946, and carried through an enormous amount of preparatory work. It chose the non-permanent members of the Security Council and constituted the Economic and Social Council. It also played its part in the election of the Secretary-General and the International Court. Finally, it reached agreement for appropriate action on many burning post-war questions, such as refugees and war criminals. It also set about the problem of finding a permanent home for the Organisation and finally decided that its seat should be in the United States.

The Security Council also held its first meeting in London in January, 1946, and immediately found itself confronting problems of the first importance arising out of the war. It is natural that in the Council the permanent members should play the decisive role. But on every major issue Britain and America have found themselves strongly opposed by Russia. And, since by the veto any of the permanent members may prevent a decision, this constitutes a constant threat to the existence of the Organisation. But because this veto power exists in the Council and not in the General Assembly, where Russia and her policies are more likely to be outvoted, it is in the Council that the decisive struggle goes on. A brave attempt to circumvent this obstacle was made in 1950 when the Assembly resolved that, "where the Security Council is unable to reach a decision on a matter of peace or security, a special session of the Assembly may be convened and make a recommendation by a two-thirds majority". The weakness here is that, whereas Council resolutions are, in theory at least, binding obligations, those of the Assembly are only recommendations. Nevertheless, they may lead—and, in fact, on more than one occasion have led— to effective international action.

But the truth remains that the United Nations Organisation, or some form of international organisation standing for the same principles, must succeed, or civilisation is doomed. And in one respect at least the Charter of the United Nations marks a considerable advance on the Covenant of the League. Running right through the Charter is an implicit concern for the individual. Indeed, it is explicit in the United Nations Declaration of Human Rights (1948). The Covenant of the League talked of the "High Contracting Parties," while, as we have seen from our quotation from the Preamble, the Charter of the United Nations opens with the words: "We, the Peoples of the United Nations," a patent derivative from the American Constitution, which begins with the words: "We, the people of the United States". This human quality marks the whole of the Preamble, and it is also of the essence of two of the most important organs of the United Nations: the Economic and Social Council and the Trusteeship Council, both of which are fully in being. UNESCO, a Specialised Agency closely associated with the Economic and Social Council, is, in particular, concerned with the welfare of the ordinary citizen, and, through its many ramifications in each state in membership of the United Nations it offers him opportunities to play a part in the work of saving the world from another total war, which could only end in the destruction of all that we mean by Western Civilisation.

In this sense the constitution of the United Nations is much more comparable with the constitutions of national political communities which we have examined than was that of the League. It is true that the United Nations Organisation is based on the principle of the sovereign equality of all its members, and to this extent the sovereignty of each member-state remains intact. But, whereas each member of the League could decide for itself whether it would adopt a recommendation of the Assembly or the Council to put sanctions into force, under the Charter of the United Nations each member undertakes to impose economic sanctions and contribute its agreed armed quota immediately at the demand of the Security Council. As a test of this new machinery of collective security, the United Nations Organisation has since the end of the Second World War succeeded in taking effective action where the League between the wars twice failed to do so. For, whereas the League did nothing to prevent Japan's seizure of Manchuria in 1931 and was unable to rally its members against Italy when she assaulted Abyssinia in 1935, the United Nations—though, admittedly, in the absence of Russia—combined to resist the aggression of the North Koreans against South Korea in 1950. In 1956, again, the United Nations effectively intervened in

Egypt to end the Suez crisis, and led the liberal opinion of the world in its condemnation of the methods used to suppress the Hungarian revolt. Such examples of action surely justify the existence of the United Nations Organisation. Indeed, it is a moral certainty that, if in this Atomic Age the nations do not make this world constitution work, no national constitution can survive.

READING

BOYD: *The United Nations Organisation Handbook* (especially the Appendices for the text of the Covenant of the League of Nations, of the Atlantic Charter, and of the Charter of the United Nations).
BURNS: *Political Ideals*, Ch. xiii.
BUTLER: *Handbook to the League of Nations*, pp. 28–80.
GETTELL: *Readings in Political Science*, Ch. xi.
JENKS: *State and Nation*, pp. 276–288.
LASKI: *Grammar of Politics*, Pt. II, Ch. xi.
SIDGWICK: *Elements of Politics*, Chs. xiv–xviii.
Encyclopaedia Britannica, Articles on "League of Nations," Vol. 31 (11th Edition, Additional Volume) and New Vol. II.

BOOKS FOR FURTHER STUDY

COBBAN: *National Self-Determination*.
ELLIS: *Origin, Structure and Working of the League of Nations*.
FACHIRI: *Permanent Court of International Justice*.
HOLLS: *Peace Conference at The Hague*.
MUIR: *Nationalism and Internationalism*.
ZIMMERN: *Nationality and Government*.

SUBJECTS FOR ESSAYS

1. Recount the history of projects for the more harmonious working of international relations up to the outbreak of war in 1914.
2. Explain the composition and functions of the organs of the League of Nations, as established after the First World War.
3. Account for the failure of the League experiment.
4. Outline the form and functions of the organs of the United Nations.
5. Compare and contrast the circumstances in which the Charter of the United Nations was drawn up with those in which the Covenant of the League of Nations was promulgated, and assess the prospects of greater success for the United Nations than the League enjoyed.
6. How far do you consider that the United Nations Organisation creates machinery for the implementation of the principles set forth in the Atlantic Charter?
7. To what extent is it true that the Charter of the United Nations is a more human document than the Covenant of the League?
8. In what respects are the powers of the Security Council of the United Nations greater than those of the Council of the League?
9. What is the importance of the International Court of Justice and what part can it play in the establishment of permanent peace?
10. "By UNESCO we may learn how to live if by the political organs and the armed power of UNO we can first learn how not to die." Discuss this statement as a text for the cultivation of world citizenship.

CHAPTER XVII

THE OUTLOOK FOR CONSTITUTIONALISM

IMMEDIATELY after the First World War the outlook for political constitutionalism was very bright. Indeed, there was hardly a civilised state in the world which had not adopted a national democratic constitution, in one form or another. But the spirit of optimism which this situation engendered was soon broken by events, for before very long there were reactions against constitutional forms of government in various parts of Europe. Already the success of the revolutionary régime in Russia, which had violently overthrown the Liberal Provisional Government, was assured by its victory over the counter-revolution. Then followed the Fascist outbreak in Italy, the Nazi upheaval in Germany, the triumph of Franco in Spain, and the emergence of quasi-dictatorships in Poland, Rumania, Greece, and other states in Eastern Europe. Nevertheless, political constitutionalism held generally in the western states, though with rather less certainty in France and Belgium, until the German onslaught in the Second World War.

The situation following the Second World War was very different from that following the First. Belgium, Holland and the Scandinavian states rapidly restored the constitutions which had been suspended during the German occupation. France revived in the constitution of the Fourth Republic the main features of the Third. And Italy, in promulgating a Republican Constitution, clearly rejected the Fascist virus from her system. At the same time, Sweden and Switzerland, which had remained neutral in the war, maintained their original constitutions. But the picture in the rest of Europe, from the point of view of political constitutionalism, as in most other respects, was exceedingly dark. The peace made Germany a political as well as an economic desert, dominated by the Occupying Powers. There was, it is true, in the British, American and French Zones, some attempt at a renaissance of democratic forms through the establishment of State Parliaments and of a Federal Republic in Western Germany in 1949, but in the east of Germany and in the rest of Europe under Russian ægis there was little hope for the people freely to choose the forms of government under which they would live.

It is clear, therefore, that national democratic constitutionalism is still on trial, and if it is to survive it must be prepared to adapt itself to changing times and circumstances. Political constitutionalism, as we have seen, is in one sense very old. But as an instrument of democracy it is comparatively new. Even in Britain, its cradle, the democratisation of the ancient Constitution is a development that has occurred within the space of little more than the last eighty years. There is, therefore, no reason to suppose that it has reached the limit of change. So we may usefully examine the ways in which it may overcome the weaknesses from which it undoubtedly suffers and meet the demands that are bound in the future to be made upon it. Among the most obvious weaknesses of modern parliamentary systems is, as we have already indicated, the fact that the central machine has already more work than it can properly cope with. At the same time, as we have earlier suggested, the new demands made upon it are chiefly economic, since a vast extension of the economic activities of the state is envisaged in the programmes of most social reformers. Together with these two points must be considered the fact that the formula of political democracy—namely, that each citizen shall count as one and no more than one—largely fails in the average state to satisfy the mass of the workers in whose interest such a method is presumed to have been devised.

This last point complicates the other two; for while, in the economic interests of the less prosperous part of the community, the central organs of the state must be further loaded with duties, of which they have already more than they can adequately discharge, in a parliament convened under the present system of voting the industrial workers find it difficult to gain a majority, and in desperation may easily be led to resort to wild, unconstitutional courses. And the constitutional state is bound to face this difficulty; for if the industrial workers do not form a majority, they at least constitute a sufficiently forceful minority to cause schism in the state and to paralyse the community if something is not done to meet their demands. Let us see what constitutionalism can do by way of attempting a solution of this complicated problem.

The crucial fact at the back of any such discussion is the sovereignty of the state. Any political society is bound to reserve sovereign powers to itself if it is to be preserved from anarchy; for a community which permitted every individual belonging to it to do exactly as he liked (which is the argument of Anarchists) would not be a society but a chaos. At the same time, it must be remembered that men and women are members of a state not for *its* good but for their own. The state must satisfy the mass of the community whose best interests it is intended to safeguard (it can have no other purpose), and the machinery through which the state functions—that is, its constitution—must be so adjusted as to secure this end. For this reason modern constitutionalism has evolved on the basis of the assumption that sovereignty belongs to the people. This also is the argument of most revolutionists. Indeed, they are revolutionists precisely because they believe that it is impossible for modern state machinery to give effect to the sovereignty of the people. The Fascist doctrine, on the other hand, according to Mussolini, denied the dogma of popular sovereignty which was, he said, disproved by the realities of life. "We proclaim, on the other hand," he added, "simply the dogma of the sovereignty of the state, which is the juridical organisation of the nation and the expression of its historic needs."

In order that the sovereign state may prove acceptable to the mass of citizens in an educated community, it must satisfy them that they ultimately control their political destiny. Sovereignty must be so handled and poised that individual rights are not unwarrantably injured by it. And to secure this enjoyment of rights the organs of the state must be arranged in such a manner as to ensure that the mass of the community shall not only comprehend them but take a lively interest in their constitution and development. In order to achieve this the constitutional state may have to go very much farther than it has already gone, or perhaps undo much that it has already done. Such reforms as a new type of representation in a re-modelled Second Chamber and an extension of direct democratic checks, like the Referendum, the Popular Initiative and the

Recall, would doubtless go far in some cases to secure this living interest, but they hardly touch the threefold problem at which we have hinted earlier, namely, the overcrowding of the legislature, the difficulty of satisfying the economic demands of certain sections of the community, and the inadequacy for the latter purpose of the principle of "one man one vote." Let us consider what else the constitutional state can do in view of this thorny problem of sovereignty.

In the first place, there seems to be no good reason for supposing that sovereignty must necessarily retain the particular form it now possesses in any given state. Let us admit that sovereignty, in an ultimately legal sense, is indivisible. But that is not to deny that it is malleable. As we have shown, in states with flexible constitutions, the legislature is sovereign, and in states with rigid constitutions the constitutional document is sovereign. But there is nothing to prevent a flexible constitution being made rigid by means of the enactment of a constitutional law saying that certain questions shall henceforth not be dealt with by the legislature through its normal procedure. Nor is there any reason why a rigid constitution should not become flexible by the removal of the existing restrictions upon parliamentary action in certain departments. For example, in Britain, with its flexible constitution, if the unrestricted action of Parliament were thought to have become an engine of tyranny, then its effectual sovereignty could be limited. Again, France has a rigid constitution, but if it came to be felt that individual rights were unnecessarily injured by the restrictions at present placed upon the normal action of the Chambers, those restrictions could be constitutionally removed, and the sovereign power placed in the keeping of the French Parliament.

But these are examples of unitary states. We have shown that the sovereignty in a federal state necessarily lies in the constitutional document, or, in other words, that the constitution of a federal state must be rigid. The constitution in a federal state, therefore, could become flexible only by changing the federal state into a unitary one. If Congress in the United States, for example, should become the repository of the sovereign power (and if the Constitution became flexible, such would necessarily be the case), state rights would no longer be safeguarded as they are now, and that lack would involve the virtual destruction of the basis upon which the federal structure is built, and, consequently, the virtual establishment of a unitary state. But there is no inherent reason why this should not be done. If the states belonging to the Union could have originally planned a unitary instead of a federal state (and they certainly could legally have done so) there is no reason why they should not, if they wished, now transform the one into the other.

The very existence of the federal plan, in fact, proves that for practical purposes it is possible to divide sovereignty, so long as there is some ultimate security against the issue of anarchy from the conflict of the co-ordinate holders of it. This practicability of a virtual division of sovereignty suggests a possible line of reform in certain unitary states. If the total area is so large that the only law-making body is distant from the constituents, or if the business of legislating for a thickly populated area leads to the overcrowding of the work of the legislature, it is certain that the constituents will lose interest in the proceedings of their representatives, the legislature will lose touch with those it represents, the representative system will tend to become unreal and discredited, and the way will be open for the trial of other methods of an unconstitutional kind. This is the danger in a heavily-populated area like that of Great Britain. This is, as we have shown, a unitary state. With the advance of social legislation—an inevitable concomitant of democratic progress—the pressure upon the central legislature has become so great that the only business which has a proper chance of being dealt with is that initiated by the Government. What, then, it may be asked, is the use of electing a great number of representatives and paying them a salary from the public funds if their sole real business is to support or reject Government measures?

The way of possible reform here is suggested by the device of federalism. The best examples of federal states have grown out of a number of communities formerly isolated. But there is no reason why a unitary state should not split itself up into a number of smaller bodies politic retaining for its central purposes only those powers fully necessary to the maintenance of the common good. This plan is called Devolution. It was suggested in this country at one time as a way out of the difficulties arising from the Irish Question, with the slogan, "Home Rule all Round." The plan suggested then was that England, Wales, Scotland, and Ireland should become partially self-governing units, while Parliament should continue to sit at Westminster dealing with matters of interest common to them all. The division having been achieved under such a scheme (not necessarily the particular division above mentioned), a constitution could be drawn up after the manner of federal constitutions, whereby either certain powers would be granted to the units and the remainder left to the central Parliament, or the rights of the central authority could be definitely enumerated and the "reserve of powers" be left with the smaller units.

This, then, would be to create a federal state out of a unitary one, the first step in the process being devolution. The effect of such a reform would be, first, to lighten the almost unbearable burden which at present rests upon such a central legislature as that which now exists in Great Britain; secondly, to lessen the danger of bureaucracy by making it possible to keep a closer watch upon the action of the executive; and thirdly—and this is the most important consideration of all—to enliven politics, to open avenues of local legislation not possible now, and to keep up a real and constant contact between the elector and the representative. Such units of self-government, it must be understood, would be by no means mere local governing bodies, but quasi-sovereign bodies, sharing the sovereignty with the central Parliament. This scheme would, of course, involve a rigid constitution, whose amendment could be carried only by some special machinery and whose sanctity would be ultimately safeguarded by some authority such as a supreme judicature.

If it is possible practically to divide political sovereignty in this territorial fashion, the question next arises whether it would not be feasible to share it among authorities political and economic. We have discussed what has so far actually been done in the matter of economic representation in constitutional states, in Chapter XV, and there indicated the difficulty created by the question of this sort of divided sovereignty. The difficulty undoubtedly exists, but we must remember that we are discussing how political constitutionalism may preserve itself against unconstitutional schemes. To do so, it may be forced, at some future time, to try all sorts of experiments which at present seem to lie outside its province or area of action. And the question may have to be seriously debated whether it is possible for the state to be federal in something more than a territorial sense. For the state, after all, is but society politically organised, and society may yet make demands upon political machinery which in its present form it cannot bear. In such a case the machinery must either be remodelled to meet the new demands or be scrapped altogether, in which latter case constitutionalism will be at an end and will yield to the forces that frankly challenge its efficiency, whether Communist or Fascist; for enlightened society will not endure a political machinery which uses the power to coerce in a direction inimical to society itself and against its own preservation and advancement.

Such a federal scheme as that of which we have spoken would regard society not as a federation of territorial units—provinces or states or cantons—but as a federation of all kinds of associations, economic, religious and social, in which men and women do in practice express themselves far more fully than they do through the normal political organisation. We have seen how advisory economic councils were tried in Germany and the Irish Free State, and again under the French Fourth Republic, and how economic and other special interests may be made to play a part in the action of the political machine by means of a reformed Second Chamber which might represent this side of a nation's activities. But the federal ideal, when it gets beyond mere territorial limits, has a much wider scope than this. It implies the establishment of semi-sovereign bodies with definite rights within the sphere of their action, corresponding to such rights at present enjoyed by the federating units in such federations as the United States and the Commonwealth of Australia, the difference being that they would have, not political, but economic or religious or social functions. The state, of course, would remain, as it is bound to remain, to co-ordinate these new parts and maintain order among them. But in this case the state becomes an association of interests which every citizen can appreciate. Sovereignty then begins to assume a new guise; it becomes, instead of a fixed legal idea, a pliant tool for man's welfare. And once this is felt of it, there is hardly any limit to the possibilities of constitutional development, whether national or international.

Much that we have said concerning the possibility of manipulating sovereignty within existing political units applies with equal, or even greater, force to international organisation. In fact, international organisation is the indispensable condition of the continued security of political constitutionalism. There is no ground for supposing that the nation state, in its present form, is the final unit of social organisation in its political aspects. Indeed, it is obvious that the sovereign nation state, as it now exists after five centuries of evolution in Europe, is in some respects decadent. Nor can it be denied that the present political divisions of Europe are in many ways hopelessly irrelevant to modern needs. Manifestly, it is an intolerable anomaly, for example, that a large number of petty states should be able, by the exercise of their sovereignty, to stand in the way of a reasonable economic union for the exploitation of the world's resources to the common benefit. The nation state as a sovereign body may, in fact, turn out to be nothing more than a phase in historical experience.

It would appear, then, that some form of world federalism is the only cure for the international anarchy which has produced two world wars, and, if not checked, will produce a third which will leave our civilisation in ruins. But this does not necessarily imply, as some think, the formation of a vast multi-national state or even of a number of separate multi-national states. For the problem of world unity calls not so much perhaps for the total correlation of areas as for the partial correlation of functions. A true federation, as we have seen, can be successfully made only among states which *desire* union, and it cannot be said that any such desire manifests itself at present among the nations. A constitution which, however earnest in intention and impeccable in form, is not in harmony with the will of the people to whom it applies, becomes, as recent history has clearly proved, a mere scrap of paper, and a federal union, created before its time, would not in itself prevent war: it would merely replace the danger of international war by the equally terrible peril of civil war.

In the development of the situation following the Second World War there is a danger that the world may become divided into spheres of influence each under a Great Power, and that these vast regional groupings may become mutually hostile beyond hope of peaceful settlement. On the other hand, it is conceivable that, in course of time, the members of these regional groups may develop so strong a sense of common interest and purpose as to encourage an urge to political union among them. Indeed, this trend may be already observed in the several post-war international organisations—such as the North Atlantic Treaty Organisation, Western European Union, the Organisation of American States, and the Arab League— which are recognisably within the ambit of " regional arrangements" as sanctioned by the Charter of the United Nations. What, at all events, is certain is that federalism is a highly developed type of political organisation and is not to be achieved either by wishful thinking or by an academic leap in the dark. It can, in fact, only come by such a process of political education as has not yet been attempted. The United Nations Organisation specifically preserves the principle of the sovereign equality of its members, but if it can hold the world in peace long enough, the nations may, through its special organs, forge a permanent instrument of education in world citizenship which is the only sure foundation of a true world unity.

Thus the ultimate objective would be the establishment not of an international but of a supranational authority, to which the nations would sacrifice their external sovereignty. Nation state sovereignty is, at best, an illusive weapon. There is a wide area of political experience and happiness to be enjoyed without it. What the nation state needs, in fact, is not sovereignty, which, externally considered, is the right to behave as it likes towards its neighbours, so much as autonomy, which is the right to control its own purely local affairs. In conclusion, then, we may fairly say that if national democratic constitutionalism is to be preserved we must be ready to admit that democracy can take many shapes and that it may be necessary to experiment greatly in order to discover the ideal form of it, that nationalism has both good and bad aspects, and that it should become possible to sacrifice some of its badness in order to achieve permanent international peace without in the least diminishing its power to benefit mankind through the instrumentality of the limited nation state.

READING

Bryce: *Modern Democracies*, Vol. II, Chs. lxxvii–lxxx.
Dicey: *Law of Constitution*, pp. lxxv–xci.
Finer: *Modern Government*, Vol. II, Ch. xx. *Future of Government*, Ch. vii.
Laski: *Grammar of Politics*, pp. 309–311.
Lowell: *Government of England*, Vol. II, Pt. viii and Chs. lxiii–lxvii.
Maciver: *Modern State*, Chs. xv–xvi.
Marriott: *Mechanism of Modern State*, Vol. II, Ch. xxxviii.
Sidgwick: *Elements of Politics*, Ch. xxxi.
Contemporary Review for February and March, 1928. Two Articles by H. A. L.
   Fisher on "The Adequacy of Parliaments."

BOOKS FOR FURTHER STUDY

Carr: (1) *Nationalism and After*. (2) *The New Society*.
Curry: *The Case for Federal Union*.
Curtis: *World War, its Cause and Cure*.
Dickinson: *Modern Symposium*.
Green: *Principles of Political Obligation*.
Laski: *Reflections on the Revolution of our Time*.
Lippmann: *The Good Society*.
Maciver: *Web of Government*.
Montague: *Limits of Individual Liberty*.
Russell: *Principles of Social Reconstruction*.
Streit: *Union Now*.

SUBJECTS FOR ESSAYS

1. Discuss the statement that sovereignty is indivisible.
2. Examine the device called Devolution as a means of reforming the Constitution of the United Kingdom.
3. How might the modern constitutional state be federalised to its economic advantage?
4. Examine modern democratic development as an illustration of Aristotle's dictum that "man is by nature a political animal."
5. "Liberty and equality are mutually exclusive." Discuss the bearing of this aphorism on the future of the constitutional state.
6. "Man is born free; yet he is everywhere in chains," said Rousseau. If this is true, what can national democratic constitutionalism do to make the chains bearable?
7. "Every creation of a new scheme of government is a precious addition to the political resources of mankind." Discuss this as a motto for political constitutionalists.
8. Aristotle said: "The state exists not merely to make life possible but to make life good." How far do you consider that this dictum holds true for the modern national democratic state?
9. Do you consider that nationalism must necessarily be the basis of any true scheme of world political organisation?
10. Discuss the federal plan as a means of establishing a world-state consistent with national rights.

BOOKS RECOMMENDED

The books named below give fuller particulars of those mentioned at the end of each chapter and are divided in the same way, namely, under the headings *Reading* and *Books for Further Study*. These two lists are followed by a third, headed *Source Books*, in which the reader may find the actual texts, or summaries of the texts, of many of the Constitutions examined in this book. The lists are not intended as a bibliography of this vast subject, but as an aid to the student who may wish to read further. Some of the books named are now out of print but are still generally available in public libraries.

The first list consists of books from which exact readings, appropriate to the subject-matter, are given at the end of each chapter. Their titles clearly indicate their nature, and most of them are sufficiently established as standard books, or even as classics of the subject, as to seem to require no words of explanation. The second list, however, is necessarily much wider and more comprehensive, and here, where it has seemed likely to be helpful, an explanatory note is added to assist the reader readily to gather the purport and significance of a particular title.

In all three lists the date following the name of the publisher is that of publication, but where two dates appear (as with most of the older books) the first is that of publication and the second that of a more recent edition.

I.—READING

BAGEHOT, W. : *The English Constitution* (with an Introduction by the Earl of Balfour). (World's Classics, Oxford, 1928.)

BARKER, E. : *Essays on Government.* (Oxford, 1945.)

BASSETT, R. : *The Essentials of Parliamentary Democracy.* (Macmillan, 1935.)

BOYD, A. : *The United Nations Organisation Handbook.* (Pilot Press, 1946.)

BRYCE, J. : *The American Commonwealth.* 2 Vols. (Macmillan, 1888, 1910.) *Modern Democracies.* 2 Vols. (Macmillan, 1921.) *Studies in History and Jurisprudence.* 2 Vols. (Oxford, 1901.) (The Constitutional Essays have been published by the same publisher in one volume under the title, "Constitutions.")

BUELL, R. L. (Edited) : *Democratic Governments in Europe.* (Nelson, 1926.)

BURNS, C. D. : *Political Ideals.* (Oxford, 1921, 1929.)

DICEY, A. V. : *Law and Opinion in England.* (Macmillan, 1885, 1939.) *The Law of the Constitution.* (Macmillan, 1885, 1939.)

DICKINSON, G. L. : *The Greek View of Life.* (Methuen, 1896, 1941.)

DUNNING, W. A. : *A History of Political Theories.* 4 Vols. Vol. I, *Ancient and Mediæval;* Vol. II, *From Luther to Montesquieu;* Vol. III, *From Rousseau to Spencer;* Vol. IV, *Recent Times.* (Macmillan, 1902–1926.)

FINER, H. : *The Theory and Practice of Modern Government.* 2 Vols. (Methuen, 1932, 1947.) *The Future of Government.* (Methuen, 1946.)

GETTELL, R. G. : *Readings in Political Science.* (Ginn, 1911.)

HAYES, C. J. H. : *A Political and Social History of Modern Europe.* 2 Vols. (Macmillan, 1916, 1932.)

JENKS, E. : *The Government of the British Empire.* (Murray, 1918, 1937.) *The State and the Nation.* (Dent, 1919, 1939.)

JENNINGS, W. I. : *Cabinet Government*. (Cambridge, 1936.) *The Law and the Constitution*. (University of London Press, 1933, 1947.) *Parliament*. (Cambridge, 1939.)

KEITH, A. B. : *The Constitution, Administration and Laws of the Empire*. One of 12 Volumes on *The Empire*, edited by Hugh Gunn. (Collins, 1924.) *Responsible Government in the Dominions*. 2 Vols. (Oxford, 1928.)

LASKI, H. J. : *A Grammar of Politics*. (Allen and Unwin, 1925, 1942.)

LOWELL, A. L. : *The Government of England*. 2 Vols. (Macmillan, 1920.) *Governments and Parties in Continental Europe*. 2 Vols. (Longmans, 1896, 1918.) *Greater European Governments*. (Cambridge University Press, 1925.)

MACIVER, R. M. : *The Modern State*. (Oxford, 1926.)

MAITLAND, F. W. : *The Constitutional History of England*. (Cambridge, 1908.)

MARRIOTT, J. A. R. : *English Political Institutions*. (Oxford, 1925, 1938.) *The Mechanism of the Modern State*. 2 Vols. (Oxford, 1927.)

NEWTON, A. P. : *Federal and Unified Constitutions*. (Longmans, 1923.)

REED, T. H. : *Form and Functions of American Government*. (Government Handbooks. Harrap, 1920.)

SAIT, E. McC. : *Government and Politics of France*. (Government Handbooks. Harrap, 1920.)

SIDGWICK, H. : *The Elements of Politics*. (Macmillan, 1920, 1929.)

STRONG, C. F. : *The Story of the American People*. (Hodder and Stoughton, and University of London Press, 1942, 1950.)

WILLIAMSON, J. A. : *A Short History of British Expansion*. (Macmillan, 1922, 1945.)

WILSON, WOODROW : *The State*. (Harrap, 1919.)

II.—BOOKS FOR FURTHER STUDY

ALLEN, C. K. : *Law and Orders*. (Stevens, 1945.) A criticism of the most recent bureaucratic tendencies of social legislation. See also Hewart (below).

AMERY, L. S. : *Thoughts on the Constitution*. (Oxford, 1947.) A new analysis of the British Constitution at work, highly critical of earlier interpretations.

ANSON, W. R. : *The Law and Custom of the Constitution*. Vol. II, 4th Edition. (Oxford, 1935.) First published in 1892, Volume II of this standard work has been thoroughly revised and brought up to date by A. B. Keith.

BOUTMY, E. : *Studies in Constitutional Law: France, England, United States*. Translated by E. M. Dicey. (Macmillan, 1891.)

BOWMAN, I. : *The New World*. (Harrap, 1921, 1929.) An indispensable guide to historical and political geography.

BROGAN, D. W. : *The American Political System*. (Hamish Hamilton, 1933.) *The Development of Modern France*. (Hamish Hamilton, 1933.) *An Introduction to American Politics*. (Hamish Hamilton, 1954.)

BROOKS, R. C. : *Government and Politics of Switzerland*. (Government Handbooks. Harrap, 1920.)

BRYCE, J. : *The Holy Roman Empire*. (Macmillan, 1864, 1941.)

BUSSELL, F. W. : *Essays on the Constitutional History of the Roman Empire*, A.D. 81–1801. (Longmans, 1910.)

CARR, E. H. : *Nationalism and After*. (Macmillan, 1945.) A brilliant short essay. *The New Society*. (Macmillan, 1951.) B.B.C. Third Programme Talks.

CARRINGTON, C. E. : *The British Overseas*. (Cambridge, 1950.) An account of what the author calls "exploits of a nation of shopkeepers."

COBBAN, A. : *National Self-Determination*. (Oxford, 1945.) A penetrating study of the place of nationalism in modern political organisation.

Books Recommended 357

COLE, G. D. H. : *Guild-Socialism Restated.* (Parsons, 1920.) *Social Theory* (Methuen, 1921.)

CURRY, W. B. : *The Case for Federal Union.* (Penguin Special, 1939.)

CURTIS, L. : *World War: Its Cause and Cure.* (Oxford, 1945.) A powerful plea for federalism.

DANIELS, S. R. : *The Case for Electoral Reform.* (Allen and Unwin, 1938.) A critical study of Proportional Representation in all countries.

DAWSON, R. Mc.G., *The Government of Canada.* (University of Toronto Press, 1947.)

DICKINSON, G. L. : *A Modern Symposium.* (Dent, 1911, 1948.)

DUVERGER, M. : *Political Parties: Their Organisation and Activity in the Modern State* [Translated by B. and R. North]. (Methuen, 1954.)

ELLIS, C. H. : *The Origin, Structure and Working of the League of Nations.* (Allen and Unwin, 1928.)

FACHIRI, A. P. : *The Permanent Court of International Justice.* (Oxford, 1925, 1932.)

FINER, H. : *The Case against P.R.* (Fabian Society, 1924.) *Representative Government and a Parliament of Industry: A Study of the German Federal Council.* (Fabian Society, 1923.) *Governments of Greater European Powers* [Britain, France, Germany, Soviet Russia]. (Methuen, 1956.)

FOWLER, W. W. : *The City State of the Greeks and the Romans.* (Macmillan, 1895, 1913.)

FREEMAN, E. A. : *Comparative Politics.* (Macmillan, 1896.)

FUSTEL DE COULANGES : *The Ancient City.* Translated by W. Small. (Lothrop, Lee and Shepherd, 1901, 1916.)

GLOVER, T. R. : *The Ancient World* (Cambridge, 1935.) An excellent survey of three cultures—Greek, Roman and Jewish—in relation to one another.

GOODNOW, F. J. : *Comparative Administrative Law.* 2 Vols. (Putman, 1893. 1902.)

GREAVES, H. R. G. : *The British Constitution.* (Allen and Unwin, 1938.)

GREEN, T. H.: *The Principles of Political Obligation.* (Longman, 1895.)

HALL, H. D. : *The British Commonwealth of Nations.* (Methuen, 1920.)

HAWGOOD, J. A. : *Modern Constitutions since 1787.* (Macmillan, 1939.)

HAYES, C. J. H. : *Essays on Nationalism.* (Macmillan, 1926.)

HETHERINGTON, H. J. W. and MUIRHEAD, J. H. : *Social Purpose.* (Allen and Unwin, 1918.)

HEWART, LORD (Lord Chief Justice) : *The New Despotism.* (Benn, 1929, 1945.) A study of the dangers of bureaucracy in modern social legislation. See also Allen (above).

HILLER, K. (Edited) : *After Nazism—Democracy?* (Drummond, 1945.) Four essays on the form of government best suited to a regenerated Germany.

HOLLIS, C. : *Can Parliament Survive ?* (Hollis and Carter, 1949.) An enquiry into the prospects of a Parliament of Industry.

HOLLS, F. W. : *The Peace Conference at The Hague.* (Macmillan, 1915.)

HUMPHREYS, J. H. : *Proportional Representation—A Study in Methods of Election.* (Methuen, 1911.) *Practical Aspects of Electoral Reform—A Study of the General Election of 1922.* (King, 1923.)

ILBERT, C.: *Parliament : Its History, Constitution and Practice.* (Home University Library, 1911, 1948.)

JACKSON, J. HAMPDEN : *Finland.* (Allen and Unwin, 1939.)

JENKS, E. : *Law and Politics in the Middle Ages.* (Murray, 1898, 1905.)

KEIR, D. L. : *Constitutional History of Britain.* (Black, 1938, 1948.)

KEITH, A. B. : *The Constitution of England: From Queen Victoria to George VI.* 2 Vols. (Macmillan, 1940.) *Dominion Home Rule in Practice.* (Oxford, 1921.) *The Dominions as Sovereign States.* (Macmillan, 1938.) *The Governments of the British Empire.* (Macmillan, 1935.) *The Sovereignty of the British Dominions.* (Macmillan, 1929.)

KRÜGER, F. K.: *Government and Politics of the German Empire.* (Government Handbooks. Harrap, 1920.)

LASKI, H. J. : *The American Presidency.* [1940] *The American Democracy.* [1949] (Allen and Unwin). *Communism.* (Home University Library, 1927.) An invaluable background book for the study of Soviet Constitutions. *The Foundations of Sovereignty.* (Allen and Unwin, 1921, 1931.) *Parliamentary Government in England.* (Allen and Unwin, 1938.) A commentary on those aspects "most relevant to the pressing problems of our time." *Reflections on the Revolution of our Time.* (Allen and Unwin, 1943.) Throws a flood of light on current constitutional problems. *The Rise of European Liberalism.* (Allen and Unwin, 1936, 1948.) Indispensable for the history of constitutionalism, especially in the nineteenth century.

LEES-SMITH, H. B. : *Second Chambers in Theory and Practice.* (Allen and Unwin, 1923.)

LICHTENBERGER, H. : *The Third Reich.* (Duckworth, 1938.) An authoritative critique by a French scholar. Original documents in Appendix.

LIDDERDALE, D. W. S. : *The Parliament of France.* (Hansard Society, 1951.)

LIPPMANN, W. : *The Good Society.* (Allen and Unwin, 1939.) An American study of the dangers to democracy of a planned society.

LOW, S. : *The Governance of England.* (Fisher Unwin, 1918.)

LOWELL, A. L. : *Essays on Government.* (Houghton, Mifflin, 1880.)

MACIVER, R. M. : *Community.* (Macmillan, 1924.) *The Elements of Social Science.* (Methuen, 1921.) *The Web of Government.* (Macmillan, 1947.)

McKENZIE, R. T. : *British Political Parties.* (Heinemann, 1955.)

MAITLAND, F. W. : *Political Theories of the Middle Ages.* (Translated from the German of Otto Gierke.) (Cambridge, 1900, 1913.)

MARRIOTT, J. A. R. : *Second Chambers.* (Oxford, 1927.)

MELLOR, A. : *India since Partition.* (Turnstile Press, 1951.)

MILL, J. S. : *Representative Government.* (With *Liberty*, edited, with an Introduction, by R. B. McCallum, Basil Blackwell, 1946.)

MONTAGUE, F. C. : *The Limits of Individual Liberty.* (Longmans, 1885.)

MOORE, R. W. : *The Roman Commonwealth.* (Hodder and Stoughton, 1943.) A useful outline of political and social aspects of life in Ancient Rome.

MOORE, W. H. : *The Constitution of the Commonwealth of Australia.* (Maxwell, Melbourne, 1910.)

MUIR, R. : *The Expansion of Europe.* (Constable, 1926, 1939.) *National Self-Government.* (Constable, 1918.) *Nationalism and Internationalism.* (Constable, 1919.)

MURRAY, R. H. : *The History of Political Science from Plato to To-day.* (Heffer, 1926, 1929.) *The Political Consequences of the Reformation.* (Benn, 1926.)

OSTROGORSKI, M. : *Democracy and the Organisation of Political Parties.* 2 Vols. (Translated by F. Clarke.) (Macmillan, 1902.) Old but still valuable.

PICKLES, DOROTHY : *France: The Fourth Republic.* (Methuen, 1955.)

POLLARD, A. F. : *The Evolution of Parliament*. (Longmans, 1926.) *Factors in American History*. (Cambridge, 1925.) *Factors in Modern History*. (Constable, 1907, 1948.)

PORRITT, E. : *The Evolution of the Dominion of Canada*. (Government Handbooks. Harrap, 1920.)

RIDGES, E. W. : *Constitutional Law of England*. (Stevens, 1922, 1937.)

RITCHIE, A. G. : *Natural Rights*. (Allen and Unwin, 1895, 1916.)

ROSE, J. H. : *Nationality as a Factor in Modern History*. (Rivington, 1916.)

RUSSELL, B. : *Principles of Social Reconstruction* (1816, 1920). *Prospects of Industrial Civilisation* (1922, 1926). *Freedom and Organisation:* 1814–1914 (1934). *Roads to Freedom: Socialism, Anarchism and Syndicalism* (1918–1920). (All published by Allen and Unwin.) The student will find these four books of great help in appreciating the social, economic, and ideological factors of constitutional growth.

SABINE, G. H. : *A History of Political Theory*. (Harrap, 1937.) Specially valuable for the philosophical background of modern ideologies.

SALVEMINI, G. : *The Fascist Dictatorship*. (Cape, 1928.)

SEELEY, J. R. : *Introduction to Political Science*. (Macmillan, 1914, 1923.)

SILONE, I : *The School for Dictators*. (Cape, 1939.) A penetrating study of dictatorship in the form of a Socratic dialogue, translated from the Italian.

SLOAN, P. A. : *How the Soviet State is Run*. (Marxist Text Book Series, 1944.) An excellent brief statement of the working of the Soviet political machine.

SMITH, A. L. : *Church and State in the Middle Ages*. (Oxford, 1913.)

STILLMAN, W. J. : *The Union of Italy*. (Cambridge, 1898.)

STREIT, C. K. : *Union Now*. (Cape, 1939.) A demand for a federal union, on the American model, among democratic states.

STRONG, C. F. : *Dynamic Europe*. (Hodder and Stoughton, and University of London Press, 1945.) For the general historical background of modern constitutional politics.

TAYLOR, O. R. : *The Fourth French Republic*. (Oxford, 1951.) The first complete analysis in English.

TEMPERLEY, H. W. V. : *Senates and Upper Chambers*. (Chapman and Hall, 1910.)

THOMSON, D. : *Democracy in France*. (Oxford, 1946.) A comprehensive and well-documented inquiry into the democratic ideals and institutions of the Third Republic.

VILLARI, L. : *Italy*. (Benn, 1929.)

WEBB, S. and B. : *Soviet Communism: A New Civilisation*. 2 Vols. (Longmans, 1935. Issued in one volume, 1945.) *Industrial Democracy*. (Longmans, 1898, 1920.)

WHEARE, K. C. : *Federal Government*. (Oxford, 1946.) A comparative study in the working of federal government, especially in the United States, the British Dominions and Switzerland. A valuable book for students. *Modern Constitutions*. (Home University Library, 1951.) A brief but scholarly essay.

WILLIAMS, J. F. : *The Reform of Political Representation*. (Murray, 1918.)

WOODWARD, E. L. : *French Revolutions*. (Oxford, 1934.) A brilliant study of the various revolutions in France from 1789 to 1871.

ZIMMERN, A. E. : *The Greek Commonwealth*. (Oxford, 1924, 1932.) *Nationality and Government*. (Chatto and Windus, 1918.)

ZINK, H. : *Government and Politics in the United States*. (Macmillan Company, New York, 1951.) A valuable guide.

"REPRESENTATION." The Journal of the Proportional Representation Society. (Published monthly by the Society, 86, Eccleston Square, S.W.1.)

III.—SOURCE BOOKS

DODD, W. F. : *Modern Constitutions.* 2 Vols. (Fisher Unwin, 1909.) Complete texts of all important Constitutions before the First World War.

FINER, H. : *Governments of Greater European Powers* (listed also under II above). Contains an extensive Appendix, which gives the full text of the Constitutions of the French Republic (1946); of the Federal Republic of Germany [Basic Law] (1949); of the German Democratic Republic [East Germany] (1949); and of the U.S.S.R. (1936, as amended to 1950).

MACBAIN, H. L. and ROGERS, L. : *The New Constitutions.* (Doubleday Page, 1922.) Gives the complete text of the Constitution of every European state created or re-organised after the First World War.

NEWTON, A. P. : *Federal and Unified Constitutions.* (Longmans, 1923.) (Already referred to in List I above.) Contains texts of several important Constitutions.

PEASLEE, A. J. : *Constitutions of the Nations.* 3 Vols. (Rumford Press, Concord, New Hampshire, U.S.A., 1950.) Contains the text of the constitutions of existing sovereign states and some useful comparative tables.

WRIGHT, M : *British Colonial Constitutions.* (Oxford, 1951). Contains several texts and a valuable Introduction.

SELECT CONSTITUTIONS OF THE WORLD. (Prepared for Dail Eireann by order of the Irish Provisional Government, 1922, and published by H.M. Stationery Office, 1924.) Contains complete texts of several important Constitutions then existing.

CONSTITUTIONS OF ALL COUNTRIES. Compiled by the Foreign Office and published by H.M. Stationery Office. Vol. I. *The British Empire* (1938). Contains the text—in the more important cases *in extenso*, in others abridged—of the Constitution of every part of the British Commonwealth and Empire beyond the United Kingdom. Vol. II. *Continental European Countries and their Dependencies*, long projected, has not yet appeared.

EUROPA YEAR BOOK FOR 1928. In this issue there is a summary of the Constitution of every important state then existing, prepared by H. Finer.

THE ANNUAL REGISTER OF WORLD EVENTS, especially since 1919. (Published by Longmans.) Each number contains, besides an outline of events of the year, the full text of important and valuable documents of constitutional interest.

CHAMBERS'S ENCYCLOPAEDIA WORLD SURVEY. Annual Supplements to the new edition of the Encyclopaedia (George Newnes, 1950.) Contain, *inter alia*, information about current constitutional changes in various states.

POLITICAL HANDBOOK OF THE WORLD, published annually by Harpers (New York) for the American Council of Foreign Relations. Useful for topical reference.

WHITAKER'S ALMANACK for recent years. Contains helpful facts and figures about government under heading of each state.

INDEX

NOTE.—For the convenience of the reader the sub-headings are arranged in alphabetical order and not in the order in which the subjects appear in the text.

Willoughby, W. W., on differentiation of states, 60

Wilson, Woodrow, American Articles of Confederation, on, 103; Congress in U.S.A., and, 244; democracy, and, 43; Germany, and, 71; League of Nations and, 204, 328; legislation in Britain and U.S.A., on, 105; Peace Programme in 1918 of, 278; President, elected as, 243; Russian Provisional Government, and, 325; state defined by, 4

Woman Suffrage Campaign, Great Britain, in, 169; U.S.A., in, 170

Woolsack, and change of government, 256

Yugoslavia, Bulgaria, and, 124; cabinet in, 231; constitution of, 78, 124–5, 208–9; Council of Nationalities in, 208–9; Federal People's Republic of, 124–5, 167, 313; provinces of, 124; Serbs, Croats, and Slovenes in, 124; suffrage in, 167; voting age in, 168

PRINTED BY WILLIAM CLOWES AND SONS LTD., LONDON AND BECCLES